Applications of Simulation
to Social Sciences

ISBN 1-903398-04-5

Head of publication: Sami Ménascé

HERMES Science Publishing Ltd.
28, Church Road
Stanmore, Middlesex HA7 4XR
United Kingdom

http://www.hermes-science.com
http://www.hermes-journals.com

Printed and distributed by Hermes Science Publications, Paris.

Applications
of Simulation
to Social Sciences

editors

Gérard Ballot

Gérard Weisbuch

The present volume contains the proceedings of the second International Conference on Computer Simulations and the Social Sciences, held in Paris in September 2000 (from the 18th to the 20th).

Organising comittee:

Gérard BALLOT and Gérard WEISBUCH

Scientific comittee:

Esben Sloth ANDERSEN, Aarlborg, Economics
Gérard BALLOT, Paris, Evolutionary Economics
Eric BONABEAU, Paris, Complex systems dynamics
Edmund CHATTOE, Guilford, Sociology
Rosaria CONTE, Roma, Sociology
Jim DORAN, Essex U., Anthropology
Giovanni DOSI, Pisa, Economics
Alexis DROGOUL, Paris, Computer Science
Gunnar ELIASSON, Stockholm, Economics
Nils FERRAND, Clermont Ferrand, Environment
Nigel GILBERT, Guilford, Sociology
Rainer HEGSELMANN, Bayreuth, Philosophy
Wander JAGER, Groningen, Economics
Alan KIRMAN, Marseille, Economics
David LANE, Venezia, Economics
Jacques LESOURNE, Paris, Economics
Scott MOSS, Manchester, Policy Modelling
Bob SAVIT, Ann Arbor, Complex systems dynamics
Lena SANDERS, Paris, Geography
Sorin SOLOMON, Jerusalem, Complex systems dynamics
Dietrich STAUFFER, Koln, Econophysics
Ramzi SULEIMAN, Haifa, Policy Modelling
Pietro TERNA, Torino, Economics
Klaus TROITZSCH, Koblentz, Computer Science and Sociology
Gérard WEISBUCH, Paris, Complex systems dynamics

with the financial support of University of Paris 2 Panthéon-Assas and of the Centre National de la Recherche Scientifique

Table of contents

Introduction

Why Simulation in Social Sciences?

The most widely accepted rationale for computer simulation in Social Sciences is the difficulty of obtaining results with analytical approaches : very few mathematical models are actually soluble and give analytical solutions providing insight and precise predictions. On the other hand, a model that is completely defined can be translated into a computer program the output of which reveals the behaviour of the system under study. The idea is that the computer allows one to obtain a numerical solution to any specified problem.

It is then very tempting to consider a social system as equivalent in terms of computation to some technical system, say e.g. an electronic circuit, whose function and characteristics can be deduced from the individual characteristics of its components. The only difference would be the complexity of individual components: human agents would have more complicated characteristics and individual behaviour than electronic components. But once these individual components have been defined by "experts" (to use the language of Artificial Intelligence), one should simply run the computer simulation. This is often the idea behind multi-agent systems.

This approach to computer simulation is widely illustrated in the present volume and Ascha-Leygonie et al. article, "A spatial microsimulation of population dynamics in Southern France : a model integrating individual decisions and spatial constraints" is a typical example. The individual process and the initial conditions of the system are supposed to be known, the simulation is run over a given period of time and the output of the simulation describes the state of the system at the end of the period.

The "*if ...then*" approach

One other big difference between an electronic system made of off the shelf components and a social system, is that individual characteristics of electronic components are known or easily tested which is *not* the case for the human components of the social system. In every social system, some unknown about individual processes remains : one solution is then to run different simulations with varying hypotheses and to compare simulation results.

In fact, studying several set of parameters already introduces the idea of alternative scenarii and *if... then* reasoning : "For a given set of parameters, the corresponding scenario with related output is observed".

The chapters on geographical systems and on evolutionary economics provide several examples of this approach.

The search for generic properties

The methodology of "genericity" is different: for a number of issues in social sciences, one might recognise our ignorance in terms of which individual process are used by the agents. Furthermore, even if we could work out all possible modes of reasoning, which one will be actually used by the agents to make choices and undertake actions ?

This lack of knowledge brings us to ask the following question : among the global properties of the system, are there any that allow to characterise an equivalence class made of all systems which share the property ?
For instance, suppose that the attractors of the dynamics of a model are uniform (e.g. all agents actually take the same decision among several a priori possible). What is the set of systems exhibiting the uniformity behaviour ?

The above questions stem naturally from the indeterminacy of models : the number of possible models is much larger than the set of distinguishable empirical observations due to the combinatorial explosion of the set of parameters and elementary processes. Because of this over determinacy of models, the idea is to classify empirical observations into stylised facts and relate stylised facts to classes of models.

The search for genericity is one answer to the general issue of model validation addressed by other authors, to be mentioned later.

In some sense we change the perspective from predicting the behaviour of one model, supposedly the "true" model of the social system, to reverse dynamics. What are the models which exhibit some observed stylised facts ? The exhaustive search for the set of models is a formidable task which would make sense if we had enough data to eliminate any model not fitting the available empirical data.

In most cases, this search which has been so successful in the physical sciences seems to be highly unpractical in the social sciences. However, looking for the simplest models exhibiting some empirically observed behaviour can be very rewarding in terms of gaining some insight into the most important phenomena underlying the observed behaviour, even though simplicity is not a criteria for realism in the social sciences.

The papers by Deffuant et al "Mixing beliefs among interacting agents", by Galam "Space Renormalization Group and Totalitarianism : Paradox of Majority Rule Voting", by A. Nowak et al, "Modelling the temporal coordination of behavior and internal states" by Savit et al, "Variable Payoffs in the Minority Game" and that by Solomon, "Generalized Lotka Volterra, power laws, and Levy distributions" illustrate this search for generic properties on the simplest models.

The contributions presented here will not settle the debate between "realistic models" that their authors claim to be based on thorough knowledge of the real social system to be understood and those who search for generic properties. In fact, as one can see in this volume, different approaches may be appropriate for the analysis of different cases. Furthermore the above discussion contrasts two extreme views for the purpose of clarity, and intermediate positions are generally used as for instance in two papers in the Geography and Urbanism section by Vanbergue et al, "Modelling urban phenomena with cellular automata" and by Matteo and Occelli, "Simulating accessibility by Swarm".

Norms and Institutions

One set of issues relevant to the above discussion is that related to the emergence of norms and institutions. Under what conditions and for which kind of actors would some behaviour be observed as discussed in Conte, "Why we need intelligent agents in social simulation", who pleads very eloquently for agents with at least some sophistication, as opposed to the search for generic properties with simple agents.

However, the two other papers in the sociology section are based on simple agents. Such is the case for Mario Paolucci "False reputation in social control" and Francesco C. Billari, "Searching for Mates Using Fast and Frugal Heuristics...". To be honest, one should mention some papers in the sections on economics which argue for some degree of sophistication of the agents.

Part of the section on Politics and History is also devoted to the question of norms and institutions : Albert and Balzer, in "Towards Computational Institutional Analysis : Discrete Simulation of a 3P Model" address the issue of time allocation of activities of production, predation or protection among heterogeneous actors with different abilities for these activities. N. Lepperhoff, in "Dreamscape - Testing the rational choice theory", studies a similar problem in social interactions concerning the survival of cheating behaviour under social pressure. F. Beckenbach in "Multi-agent modeling of resource systems and markets" follows the line started by Epstein and Axtell with Sugarscape. He introduces trade with money as a medium of exchange and shows that the economy can then sustain a higher population, rediscovering Ricardian results. Caldas and Coelho, in "The Interplay of Power on the Horizon", use evolving networks with asymmetric tribute dependence interactions to study group dynamics.

The paper by Bonnefoy et al, "Modelling spatial practices and social representations of space using multi-agent systems", also addresses the issue of institutions in resource exploitation. The paradoxes concerning elections and democracy are discussed in Lepelley et al "Computer simulations of voting systems" and in the paper by Galam already mentioned. Laptev proposes an ambitious model for the cyclic evolution of societies entitled "modelling of some periodic social processes".

Microeconomics and decisions

In microeconomic theory multi-agent models enable us to increase the refinement of the decision processes of agents as compared with analytically solved microeconomic models. Several tracks are represented in this book: decision theory in which agents do not take into account other agents' decisions, and game on social choice theories in which they do. The contribution by Zimmerman et al. " cooperation in an adaptive network" uses game theory to show when cooperation emerges between individualist agents who play a repeated game with their neighbours. Savit, Li and VanDeemen study a particular type of game in their contribution "Variable payoffs in the minority game". In this game, the payoff is influenced by being a member of the minority. They show that cooperation can emerge in a game with payoffs depending on the size of the minority, as it does in the case of fixed payoffs.

Some other contributions study different non game decision processes

Terna in "The "mind no-mind" dilemma in agents behaving in a market" also raises the issue of the importance of the sophistication of the decision process of agents (an issue also raised in the earlier mentioned contribution by Conte), for example through learning, in order to reproduce markets with realistic and complex behaviour. He is able to show that learning leads to a stable market without the need of the unrealistic assumption of an auctioneer (central to microeconomic theory of markets), since it yields more stability. Cognitive processes are also modelled by other authors, such as Janssen and Jager, in "Psychological factors affecting market dynamics : the role of uncertainty and need satisfaction", with agents who can engage in different decision processes based on psychology theory, such as deliberation, social comparison, imitation or repetition. They show that decision processes do matter for market stability in terms of the survival of products. More examples can be found in the book of the importance of decision processes for market outcomes, illustrating the idea, very controversial amongst economists, that procedural rationality yields aggregate results different from those computed on the basis of substantive rationality or optimisation.

Heterogeneity among agents.

Heterogeneity among agents complements and allows one to pursue further the issue of the aggregate effects of decision processes. Simulation here provides the modelling flexibility which allows one to abandon the assumption of the representative agent, characteristic of much analytical work in economics. Heterogeneity may be necessary to reproduce the basic workings of the market as in the financial market model by Iwamura and Takefuji, "artificial market based on agents with fluid attitude towards risks". The authors model the essential distinction between bulls and bears on the basis of a subjective attitude towards risk. Heterogeneity may not be a necessity in many other models, yet matter a lot for the aggregate outcomes.

A very general distinction between different types of behaviour is that between invention and imitation. Invention is sufficient to yield long term growth but imitation can enhance or diminish its effects. Several authors study this question. Carayol in a contribution entitled "Modelling creation vs. diffusion of structured knowledge" models the choice of agents between creating knowledge and acquiring knowledge from neighbours. They show that there exists an optimal rate of disclosure of knowledge, a rate which can be influenced by structural policy. Ballot and Taymaz in their contribution "Competition, training, heterogeneity persistence, and aggregate growth in a multi-agent evolutionary model" also study a market with agents who invest in intangible capital and agents who benefit from the diffusion of this investment. More precisely the investment is here in human capital and the market is the labour market. Some firms train their workers and innovate, while other firms rely on poaching some trained workers to imitate the firms who train and improve their own technology. They show that the coexistence of the two types of firms is possible in the long term, and is even beneficial to aggregate growth, since inefficient trainers are eliminated by poachers. In spite of selection which takes place on the market, either in terms of rules, or in terms of agents, variety may then persist in these models. However, this is not always the case, as Janssen and Jager show, with the possibility of emergence of a dominant behaviour.

Externalities

This raises the question of the features of global dynamics in multi-agent models. Diverse dynamics can be obtained, and may reproduce interesting real phenomena which are not easily generated by analytical models.

Externalities, positive or negative, play an important role in the domination of one type of agent or good. Recent theory starting with Arthur's pathbreaking paper has emphasised the occurrence of dynamic increasing returns which lead to lock-in into a standard such as Windows NT. Dalle and Jullien in the contribution "Windows vs. Linux : some explorations into the economics of free software" study the rivalry between Linux and Windows NT in an attempt to identify those factors which may induce a "delock-in" from the Windows NT standard. Mazzucato in "Firm size, innovation, and market share instability: the role of negative feedback and idiosyncratic events" investigates in particular the opposite case of dynamic decreasing returns which may penalise large firms in the innovation process. Small firms have a higher dynamic efficiency, i.e. innovate more. However the periods of high innovation are characterised by high market share instability. The author is able to reproduce this situation by simulation, but also investigates the role of random shocks into the two types of feedbacks.

Most of the simulation models are stochastic, and this, with path dependency, may lead to different and unpredictable evolutions, even with the same initial conditions… Yet the importance of institutions remains and allows one to derive or rediscover results from economic theory.

Institutions.

The flexibility of simulation tools allow some authors to take into account the institutional features of a market, as well as the more or less complex decision processes mentioned above. They then show that these institutional features are essential to reproduce some stylised facts. Hence they are able to build models which mimic real markets, and open the way to prediction and policy. Rosenthal in his contribution "Simulating transaction networks in housing markets" simulates the specific features of these markets with success.

Financial markets with stylised facts as speculation bubbles and chaos have attracted the attention of different contributors such as Terna in the paper mentioned above, and Bonabeau in his contribution "Business applications of social agent-based simulation".

Terna is able to show that institutional features may be enough to generate such bubbles without the need to model sophisticated decision processes by agents. However Bonabeau insists on the interest of modelling in some details the behaviour of agents, since some details may be important such as the tick size in the NASDAQ simulation.

The realism of a simulation model in terms of institutions and decision processes is further justified by the argument that it is much easier for practitioners to understand such a model than an analytical model, and therefore, it is more suitable for practical use. The opposite approach is illustrated in the paper by Savit et al, since the minority game they discuss was inspired by financial markets.

Validation of models

The issue of validation of the models should of course be taken seriously. Mueller in the contribution "Exploring the dynamics of social policy models : a computer simulation of long-term unemployment" offers a methodology for testing the prediction of a labour market model. Let us recall than the search for generic properties mentioned earlier is another approach to validation.

More work is obviously needed on the topic of calibration and validation.

A brief historical perspective

A very brief history of previous meetings about simulation in social sciences can be found in the First Issue of the Journal of Artificial Societies and Social Simulation.

World-wide interest in the potential of computer simulation for addressing issues in the social sciences has been growing since at least the beginning of the 1990s. In April 1992, people interested in using multi-agent simulations for social science problems met at the first 'Simulating Societies' workshop (see Gilbert and Doran, 1994).

Further workshops followed, first in Siena, Italy (Gilbert and Conte, 1995) and then in Boca Raton, USA in 1995, and in Cortona, Italy in 1997. In 1995, a meeting was held in Schloß Dagstuhl in Germany (Troitzsch et al 1996; see also Hegselmann, Mueller and Troitzsch 1996).

Meanwhile, in the United States, the Santa Fe Institute was developing ideas about complexity and applying them to economics. Much of this work was based on the use of computer modelling. In September 1997, the first international conference, on computer simulation and the social sciences (ICSS&SS) was held at Cortona (Conte, Hegselmann and Terna 1997).

During the three years following the first international conference on Computer Simulations and Social Sciences in 1997 in Cortona, several important developments occurred such as :

> - the publication of a new electronic Journal of Artificial Societies and Social Simulation, http://jasss.soc.surrey.ac.uk/JASSS.html, edited by Nigel Gilbert.

> - A strong emphasis on practical applications as discussed in Eric Bonabeau's invited paper :
> "Business applications of social agent-based simulation".

Acknowledgments.

We would like to thank University of Paris 2 Panthéon-Assas and the Centre National de la Recherche Scientifique for financial support, Arlette Raobe for secretarial help and the members of the scientific committee for their advice including manuscripts refereeing.

Bibliography

http://jasss.soc.surrey.ac.uk/1/1/editorial.html

[AND] ANDERSON P. W., ARROW K. J. and PINES D. (1988). "The Economy as an Evolving Complex System", SFI Studies in the Sciences of Complexity Reading : Addison Wesley Longman

[ART] ARTHUR B, DURLAUF S. and LANE D. (1997). "The Economy as an Evolving Complex System II", SFI Studies in the Sciences of Complexity Reading : Addison Wesley Longman

[CON] CONTE, R., HEGSELMANN R. and TERNA P. Eds. (1997). "Simulating Social Phenomena" Berlin : Springer.

[GIL] GILBERT, N. and CONTE R. , Eds. (1995). "Artificial Societies : the computer simulation of social life", London : UCL Press.

[GIL] GILBERT N. and DORAN J.E., London : UCL Press.

[HEG] HEGSELMANN R., MUELLER U. and TROITZSCH K.G., Eds. (1996). "Modelling and simulation in the social sciences from the philosophy of science point of view", Dordrecht : Kluwer.

[TRO] TROITZSCH K.G., MUELLER U., GILBERT N. and DORAN J.E., Eds. (1996. "Social science microsimulation" Berlin : Springer.

SOCIOLOGY

The necessity of intelligent agents in social simulation

Rosaria Conte

National Research Council, Institute of Psychology,
PSS (Project on Social Simulation)
email: rosaria@pscs2.irmkant.rm.cnr.it - http://ip.rm.cnr.it
University of Siena - Communication Sciences

ABSTRACT: *The social simulation field is here argued to show a history of growing complexity, especially at the agent level. The simulation of the emergence of Macro-social phenomena has required heterogeneous and dynamic agents, at least in the sense of agents moving in a physical and social space. In turn, the simulation of learning and evolutionary algorithms allowed for a two-way account of the Micro-Macro link. In this presentation, a third step is envisaged in this process, and a 3-layer representation is outlined: the Micro, Mental, and Macro layers. This complex representation is shown to be necessary for understanding the functioning of social institutions. The 3-layer model is briefly discussed, and specific cognitive structures, which evolved to cooperate with emerging Macro-social systems and institutions, are analysed. Finally, social intelligence is argued to receive growing attention is several fields and applications of the science of artificial, with which social simulation is interfaced or will soon be.*

1. Simple Models and Intelligent Agents: An Actual Incompatibility?

Social simulation is not a field of the cognitive science, and certainly not a field of psychology. Rather, it may be situated at the intersection between the social sciences and what Simon (1969) called the science of the artificial. So far, computer simulation has been applied to several fields of science and application (for a comprehensive view of the field, see Gilbert and Troitzsch, 1999): to social and welfare policy (see, for example, the microsimulation models in Troitzsch et al., 1996), to economical and financial modelling (Davis, 1987; Beltratti et al., 1996; Albin, 1998), to modelling and optimising organisations (Prietula et al., 1998), etc.. Indeed, the field of social simulation does not necessarily, and for quite some time it did not, have an agent base.

Now, the necessity of agent-based social simulation (ABSS) is widely acknowledged (Conte & Moss, 1999). But while ever more sophisticated techniques and tools are being developed (cf .Suleiman et al., 2000) and demanded (Teran and Edmonds, 2000), the explicit methodological principle to which agent-based social simulation is inspired is rather conservatory from the point of the agent modelling. As stated by Axelrod (1997), one of the pioneers of agent-based simulation, agents must be kept as simple and stupid as possible (KISS principle: Keep It Simple, Stupid). The dumber the agents, the more interpretable the results of simulations.

Here, I would like to question the validity of this principle, under two different perspectives, historical and theoretical, or actually metatheoretical. In substance, I will endeavour to show that
- past developments of social simulation have entailed a process of growing mental complexity of the agent models used;
- this trend is being confirmed by present developments and current interfaces of social simulation, which necessitate ever more intelligent agents.

The remaining of the paper is organised as follows. In the next section, I will illustrate a process of growing complexity in the agent base for social simulation. Next, I will argue that while the hits of the field largely depend upon this process, the missed points depend on its insufficient accomplishment. In the successive section, new developments of the field and the necessity for a more complex view of the Micro-Macro link are discussed . Finally, Axelrod's claim for simplicity in simulation modelling will be reformulated in terms of ideal agents, and the difference between intelligence and rationality will be resumed.

2. Past and Present

In the last three decades, it is possible to envisage a process towards a growing complexity and importance of the agent base for social simulation. The impact of this process on the history of social simulation is largely acknowledged (Halpin, 1998; Troitzsch, 1997). Several important achievements have been obtained thanks to the shift from the homogeneous and static Cellular Automata (for a review, cf. Hegselmann, 1996) to the learning and adaptive agents(Holland, 1995; 1998) currently implemented in artificial societies, through a number of intermediary steps (represented for example by Schelling's (1969; 1971) migration models). Nowadays, agents are expected to be not only flexible and adaptive, but also endowed with a knowledge-base of varying complexity. In particular, agents are increasingly expected to exhibit some sort of *social intelligence* (Edmonds, 1998; Conte, 1999).

Below, I will outline the reasons for a growing complexity in the agent models for social simulation.

2.1. From Classical Social Simulation to Agent-Based Social Simulation (ABSS)

One good question about social simulation is whether this field has always implied an agent base, and if not, when have agents been introduced and why?

It is not easy to answer this question. Is there one simulation model to which the birth of agent-based social simulation can be traced back? Probably not. Or, better, attribution would probably depend on which type of agent one has in mind. Can we say that microsimulation models have an agent base (Troitzsch et al., 1996)? In a sense, we can, since microsimulation models units (households, cities, settlements, etc.) in terms of transitions from one given state to another, and agents can be described very simply as units which operate transitions between states (cf. Shoham and Tennenholz, 1992). Indeed, microsimulation represents a progress from the system dynamic models (cf., again, Troitzsch, 1997), in which the simulation modelled one-object (the world) with a huge number of properties. In microsimulation models, instead, units represent a micro-level of analysis, and their transitions produce a macro-level, or aggregate effect. For example, birth rate is a micro-level (families) phenomenon which has a global effect on the increase or stagnation of the entire population. Analogously, multi-level simulation (Moehring, 1996; Troitzsch, 1996) "consists of simulating interacting populations where the *population attributes depend on aggregated individual attributes and individual attributes depend on the population attributes*" (see Gilbert, 1999; italics are mine). This shows a fundamental objective of social simulation which could not be achieved with system dynamic models: to implement the so-called Micro-Macro link, or the circularity of social phenomena. To do this, it was necessary to distinguish between different levels of analysis and to model their mutual influence. To attain this objective, it was sufficient to describe individual attributes and their dynamics and observe their effects on the population attributes. Therefore, one of the first and most important development of social simulation was to distinguish different levels in the phenomena under study, and observe their interplay.

2.2. Artificial Societies

On a parallel line, developments in the natural sciences (cf. Gilbert & Troitzsch, 1999) have paved the way for a new conceptualisation of agency in social simulation, namely the use of Cellular Automata for social simulation. In this approach, agents are no more units of simulation whose attributes interact with attributes at a higher level. They are interacting units, in the sense that each cell's (or each automaton's, which is the same) states are determined by the states of other cells in a given space. Here, the focus is on the following characteristics:

- state transitions are not established according to pre-existing statistics as is the case with microsimulation (e.g., families increase/decrease every n time units) but according to some *rule* (e.g., stay off if..., otherwise turn on, as in the famous Game of Life);
- state transitions depend not only upon attributes at the higher level as is the case with multi-level simulation (e.g., birth rate may be seen as a combined effect of both units and population attributes), but also upon properties of units at the same level (e.g., a cell is off as long as a given number of cells in its neighbourhood are off, otherwise, it turns on). In this sense cellular automata depend upon and interact with one another. Cellular automata exhibit a new important property: the *interactive* one.
- state transitions depend only upon what *happens within the simulation*.
- attributes at the macro level are not determined from aggregate individual attributes at the lower level as is the case with multi-level models, but from *interaction* among automata.

Why did cellular automata play a deep influence on social simulation? One good reason is the popularity which this type of modelling enjoyed in the natural sciences, from where models and theories are often imported into the social sciences. But a more significant reason probably lies in the possibility which cellular automata offered to implement and observe *artificial societies*. Preceding models were meant to simulate real-life phenomena. Cellular automata allowed to implement the minimal conditions (that is, a number of interacting units) to observe the effects of interaction in a given environment. The main objective of artificial societies was no more to predict the effects of a given phenomenon over time (as in preceding simulation models), but to identify the minimal conditions for the insurgence of ideal-type social phenomena (cooperation, segregation, social impact, or solidarity). The focus is on ideal-type, rather than real-life, phenomena. But in a sense, cellular automata modelling made a step backward with regard to sophisticated social simulation models: whilst a multi-level model aims to make more subtle predictions, and must take into account the complex interrelationships between attributes at different levels, the onset of cellular automata had perhaps lower or more modest ambitions, namely to set the conditions for a higher social level to *emerge* from a lower level. The way-up of the Micro-Macro link is the main or perhaps the unique concern, at least initially, of cellular automata scientists. They were trying to make a methodological/epistemological point: what kind of macro social phenomena can I obtain (account for) from modelling and implementing only the micro social level? And, second, what kind of phenomena can I obtain with the simplest possible model at the individual level?

Cellular automata are homogenous units which interact according to some simple rules. Let us compare them with the agents usually referred to in the agent systems literature (for a recent formulation, see Wooldridge,1999), where an agent, even at the more elementary level, is defined as

- autonomous
- interactive
- proactive

Does a cellular automaton correspond to this definition? Certainly not automata are not proactive, to say the least. But as will be shown below, the field of artificial societies has gradually moved from the rigid cellular automata of its first days to more flexible and complex models, closer to current agent systems. Why was this development necessary?

2.2.1. *From Static and Homogenous Agents to Learning and EvolvingAgents*

Cellular automata modelling allowed a number of crucial scientific issues to be raised and partially answered. In its simplest form, this approach was *characterised* by

- *homogeneous* micro-units
- represented as *cells* in a one- or more-dimensional grid (cf. Hegselmann & Flache,1998).

and was *applied to* model and explore important orders of social phenomena:

- *Propagation of opinion and opinion change.* One of the classical social application were the "majority models", aimed to explore the influence of the majority on the modification of the individual opinion. A major development of these models concerned the simulation (Nowak et al., 1990;Rockloff & Latané, 1996) of the social psychological theory of social impact (Latané, 1981) where social impact is defined as a combined effect of vicinity to and strength of the opinion source.
- *Cooperation.* Cellular automata have been applied to explore the conditions for the emergence of cooperation (Axelord, 1984) from game theoretical (Nowak and Sigmund, 1992; 1993) and social dilemmas (Schulz et al., 1994).
- *Solidarity and help.* One important application concerns the simulation of support networks(cf. Hegselmann and Flache, 1998), where the conditions for the emergence of networks of mutual help among self-interested agents are explored on a cellular automata basis.

The main *outputs* of these applications is to what extent (desirable) global effects can spontaneously emerge from local interactions (cooperation, support network, opinion change). Indeed, the majority models made a step forward into the opposite direction, i.e. to observe the local effects of the most frequent opinion.

However, no higher-level social entity (groups, coalitions, etc.; cf. Axelrod, 1995)could emerge from this approach, mainly because automata are static agents,which do neither evolve nor learn.

The necessity to implement dynamic agents in a concrete, physical sense was one of the main reasons of modification of the cellular automata modelling. In the migration model (Schelling, 1971), agents are no more cells but entities which *move on* the grid. Through this important modification, Schelling was able to study the minimal conditions for social segregation, and demolish the legend that segregation is caused by high social intolerance: even a low rate of intolerance actually produces a dramatic spatial segregation of social groups!

The development of artificial societies(Gilbert & Conte, 1995) where agents and the world are separated (but interacting) *objects* (Epstein & Axtell, 1996) allowed for agents to be seen as heterogeneous and autonomous units, which interact with their social *and* physical environment. Indeed, they modify the state of the world according to rules of varying complexity (even very simple ones). This had some important consequences at the scientific level

- model and implement *proactive* action, that is action executed in order to in store some effect in the world (for example, to get to some food), and not only as an effect of others' states (cf. Conte & Castelfranchi, 1995;Epstein and Axtell, 1996), and consequently,
- model heterogeneous agents, as characterised not only by different interactive strategies(tit-for-tat as opposed to, say, always-defect), but also by different goals and sub-goals, actions, plans, etc.;
- approximate the (weak) notion of agent prevailing in the agent systems literature: artificial societies include autonomous, interactive, proactive agents, and even AI-agents (Doran et al., 1994);
- study the emergence of social entities (of spatial clusters as well as of social structures, cf. Doran et al., 1994) and social action from individual qualitative differences (cf. the DEPNET system in Sichman et al., 1994; Conte & Sichman, 1995; Epstein &Axtell, 1996).

In a few words, in the field of artificial societies it is possible to simulate the emergence of some Macro-social level from interactions and relationships at the Micro-social level. Qualitative differences between agents acting in a common world allow for social relationships and interactions to emerge at different levels of complexity: from trade and exchange to coalitions, groups, social hierarchies, etc..

However, heterogeneous agents do not allow to answer some questions: what is the further effects of emergent social structures? How do agents respond to macro-social structures? Which properties are required for agents to adapt to them? Adaptive agents (Holland, 1992a; 1992b; 1998) and evolutionary algorithms obviously provide a fundamental body of theories and techniques to answer these questions.

Indeed, the evolution of cooperation soon called for the implementation of learning rules (for example, a rule like "win-shift, lose-stay" has been shown (Nowak and Sigmund, 1993) to outperform tit-for-tat in the Prisoners' Dilemma game) and Genetic Algorithms (GA; cf. Axelrod, 1987; 1997). With GA, an interesting *circuit* occurs (see fig. 1): the positive outcomes of cooperation affects agents' reproductive success, and therefore the chance that cooperation stabilises overtime.

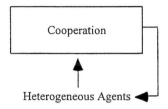

Figure 1. *The evolution of cooperation*

Several simulations adopted various kinds of evolutionary algorithms (including Genetic Algorithms, Evolutionary Strategies, Genetic Programming, and Classifier Systems; for a useful discussion see Chattoe, 1998) to represent social and particularly economic processes, as those used in game theory and applying the so called replicator dynamics[1] (Weibull 1995, Vega-Redondo 1996). Classifier Systems (CS) actually function in a rather similar way to Genetic Algorithms (cf. again Chattoe,1998, and Nissen, 1993), since these systems are based upon a set of production rules, and each rule has associated a strength which reflects its past success (fitness) at generating "appropriate" output and therefore the probability that it will be executed. The reader is turned to Chattoe (1998) for a detailed critique of these models especially from the point of view of the economic theory. Here, however, it is perhaps important to stress one main difficulty of these models from a social point of view. The whole point about evolutionary models in social simulation is to account not only for the evolution of macro social phenomena, but also for the adaptation of agents to the emerging effects (see fig. 1).The main social factor of adaptation hypothesised within evolutionary models is imitation. But it is yet unclear what imitation is and especially which properties it requires at the agent level in order to increase agents' fitness! How do agents know what is to be imitated and what is not? How can agents "*observe* the fitnesses of other individuals" (Chattoe, 1998, ¤5.5-5.6; italics are mine)?

Finally, neural networks were applied to simulations not only of economic processes (Beltratti et al., 1996) and of the emergence of primitive social institutional forms (Cecconi and Parisi,1998).

---

[1]Replicator dynamics model shifts in the proportions of genes or species of differing fitness. In extremely simple terms, a gene or species will increase (decrease) its share in the population if its own fitness is greater (less) than the average fitness and the change will be proportional to the difference between the average and the particular gene/species fitness. All models of this kind face the same difficulty.

What do different evolutionary models have in common? Essentially they try do without intelligent, deliberative agents. The question that I intend to raise here is, how far can one go without intelligent deliberative agents in modelling social processes? Chattoe's (1998) answer to this question is legitimately cautious. As he observes, to extend evolutionary models (like GA, CA and neural networks)to the social environment, one should be able to account for how *cognitive* agents influence their (social) environment with their perceptions and interpretations, modify their actions accordingly, and influence others to do the same. This affects adaptation and learning. Consequently, the "credit assignment for particular modifications to the genotype is particularly hard to implement" (Chattoe, ibi., ¤ 4.8). I think this critical line is essentially correct. Below, I will endeavour to strengthen this argument in the light of a view, which I propose here, of the Micro-Macro link.

But before doing this, it is necessary to look at what the field of ABSS, with either static or dynamic agents, has achieved so far and where it has failed.

3. ABSS: Hits and Misses

This section is focused on the achievements and failures within the field of artificial societies. In particular, the outcomes obtained so far will be evaluated in the light of the social-scientific issue of interest in this presentation, i.e., the understanding and modelling of the Micro-Macro link.

3.1. Hits

The field of artificial societies has achieved important epistemological, theoretical and methodological results, and, although to a lower degree, also results oriented to application.

The epistemological results include,
- a strong interaction with other fields of science, and especially with the science of artificial;
- the possibility to test important approaches, such as decision theory and the evolutionary models;
- operational models of important social concepts, such as social hierarchy(Doran et al., 1994); group, coalition (Axelrod, 1995); social distance and social impact (Nowak et al.,); segregation (Shelling, 1971), etc..

Methodologically, it is still debated(Troitzsch, 1997; but see also the proceedings of the ECSR workshop on the potentials of social simulation for the social sciences[2]) to what extent social simulation with or without agents achieves

---

[2] held at Guildford, Surrey, UK, January 14-15, 1998
(http://jasss.soc.surrey.ac.uk/admin/notices/potential.html)

good predictive results. But it is far less doubted that artificial societies incomparably enhanced the experimental and explanatory power of social theory (cf. Conte & Gilbert, 1995; Epstein & Axtell, 1996)

At the level of application, several important results have been achieved in the study and optimisation of organisations (Carley et al., 1998). Other important applications concern participatory policy-making both in the area of social (Dean, 1997) and environmental policy (cf. Integrated Assessment Modelling; see Moss,1998). In participatory policy-making, agent-based social simulation is now seen as a fundamental instrument to obtain feedback about the acceptability and efficacy of given policies while developing them.

But the most important results are still theoretical, mainly consisting in highlighting and exploring micro-foundations of social processes, as have been described above (the minimal requirements for the emergence of social clusters and cooperation, social order and control, social differentiation and hierarchy, etc.). These results have had important effects at the metatheoretical level: they have allowed a renewed interest in the study of the Micro-Macro problem. In particular, agent-based simulation allowed to observe experimentally the way-up of this link, the emergence of higher-order social structures from local interactions among even static agents (like cellular automata). What is more, the implementation of evolutionary models and learning agents allowed to investigate also the way back from the Macro to the Micro level (see fig. 2)

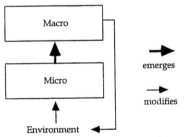

Figure 2. *Micro-Macro circuit through adaptation*

In figure 2, the Micro-Macro link satisfies the minimal condition for the Micro-Macro two-way link: the environment affects interactions at the micro-level, which in turn produce higher-level social structures which modify the environment, and this calls for agents to adapt to a new environment. This picture is not very different from figure 1,which represents the application of evolutionary models to the evolution of cooperation. In both cases, the environment mediates the circuit between Micro and Macro. Social structures emerging from local interactions modify the environment and call for a new process of agents' adaptation. This is what happens with adaptive agents and neural networks (cf. Beltratti et al., 1996; Parisi, 1998) applied to social simulation.

However, is the model of the Micro-Macro link represented in figure 2 good enough? Is there something which is still missing in this picture?

3.2. Misses

Starting from the level of interaction, the following phenomena are poorly understood and modelled as yet,

- *One-shot cooperation.* One-shot cooperation does not seem to emerge among self-interested rational agents.
- *Variety of social action,* in particular the difference between cooperation and exchange. Models of social action fail to distinguish between different forms of socially desirable action.
- *Micro foundations of probabilistic phenomena.* Simulation models do often represent differences in probabilistic terms without investigating the reasons for probabilistic distribution. This is a fundamental aspect of the evolutionary models, but it is also true of more classical models based on static agents (social impact theory, migration models, solidarity models, etc.).The question is then, what are the processes responsible for a given probabilistic distribution?

Why such failures?

One important reason lies in the strong influence of rational action theory and game theory with their own issues and dilemmas. This is responsible for a poor understanding of one-shot cooperation and of the variety of social action. In this approach, agents are not endowed with mental states (i.e., goals, beliefs, etc.) but with subjective preferences, which are taken for granted rather than investigated. By contrast, mental states seem essential to account for one-shot cooperation. Cooperation can emerge among agents with common goals but different actions and resources, provided they are complementary (equally necessary to achieve a common goal). In this sense, it is highly convenient for self-interested agents to cooperate to achieve a common goal (cf. Sichmanet al., 1994).

A fortiori, being unconcerned with the individual reasons for choice, and with the qualitative aspects of agent modelling, game theory fails to capture differences among phenomena which require a qualitative description (as happens with cooperation and exchange; see Conte & Sichman, 1995). Agents' goals and beliefs account for the difference between cooperation and exchange. The symbolic representation of goals allows to define cooperation as something different from exchange, and grounds such a difference on the more fundamental one between complementary actions for *common* goals (which characterises cooperation) and mutual need for *different* goals (which characterises exchange).

Analogously, the dynamics of given phenomena(e.g., beliefs) depends upon a probabilistic distribution of given factors (e.g., how strongly each agent believes something). But this distribution is in turn determined by the underlying mental processes of belief formation and revision coupled with given social processes. Social agents accept beliefs from given others (say, institutional authorities) for given reasons (say, because these are acknowledged as authorities; cf. Conte & Dignum, 2000). This means that a model of these processes helps predict which beliefs will more easily propagate to which agents. Somehow, the same processes affect the strength of rules in CS. In CS, strength is determined by the past success of each rule. However, social processes may affect rules strength. Agents often infer the success of rules from the social status or the competence of those other agents which apply them. Furthermore, agents "import" rules even independent of the inferred success of these rules: they follow others also for conformity, norm compliance, benevolence, etc.. What is still missing is a theory of imitation and social learning which takes into account the interaction between mental and social processes, and the interplay between these processes and the probability that the fittest rules propagate. One such theory must be based upon a model of social *reasoning*, i.e. of agents' reasoning upon their own and others' mental states (cf. Conte, 2000)[3].

To sum up, the fundamental requirement at the level of the agent to account for interaction are
- agents' mental states and processes, their
- qualitative differences, and
- social reasoning capacity.

As for the Micro-Macro link, existing agent-based simulations models account for the emergence of given social structures, and to some extent also of some institutions, not only economic (like the market), but also social, although primitive, institutions (see Cecconi & Parisi, 1998). A growing attention is paid by social scientists and even by system dynamic scientists to the circularity of social systems. Evolutionary models have undoubtedly improved simulation models of the Micro-Macro link. However, the circularity between the two levels of social analysis is usually represented as in figure 1, or at most, as in figure 2. But there is another type of relationship between social structures and agents, which is not mediated by adaptation to a new environment, and which is sometimes referred to as second-level emergence (see fig. 3).

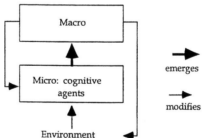

Figure 3. *Micro-Macro circuit through the mind*

Weisbuch and Duchateau-Nguyen for instance observe that "The general view is that (individual) preferences, for instance, can be taken as *external* to the model. In fact, ..., the agents' views can vary according to changes in the environment. In other

---

[3]Unlike the notion employed by connectionist models (Read and Miller, 1998),here social reasoning is meant as the capacity to reason upon, compare, interpret and manipulate one's own and others' mental states.

words, another loop coupling environment and agents' cognitive properties further complicates the coupling loop between economics and the environment" (Weisbuch & Duchateau-Nguyen, 1998; italics are mine). This is an extremely important point which needs further clarification and perhaps elaboration.

First of all, a *third* level of analysis is hypothesised here, the mental one. Mental phenomena are not only affected by the environment as a result of action at the Macro level, but they are also directly affected by this level (see fig. 3). This is sometimes called by social scientists as second-order emergence (Gilbert, 1999) and Meso level (Schillo et al.,2000).

Secondly, when the mental level is acknowledged as a necessary intermediary between the Macro and the Micro levels, this usually that agents' *views* are modified by social institutions (see the passage from Weisbuch and Duchateau-Nguyen quoted above).Social scientists generally speak about agents' (conscious) *beliefs* about social institutions. However, this is a partial account of theMental level. Mental properties and mechanisms cannot be reduced to conscious or unconscious views, beliefs, or world representations. On the contrary, new mental objects and rules emerge in the mind as an effect of the Micro-Macro link, for example norms and their ingredients (obligation, commitment, right, permission, responsibility, etc.), as well as the mental mechanisms through which they work (norm-based reasoning, control, influence, compliance, social emotions, moral sentiments and motivations, guilt feeling, etc.).

Third, the mental level is not a mere consequence of the Micro-Macro link. It is an instrument to make the Macro level work. The Macro level emerges from micro interactions, but it regulates them through the Mental level. From a two-layer circularity, a three-layer circularity emerges. Indeed, the complexity of society necessitates further mental complexity (Castelfranchi, 1997).

To some extent, the emergence of mental complexity can be dealt with the current evolutionary models, and in particular with GA. For example, a current key-word in multi agent-based social simulation (Sichman et al.,1998) is altruism and benevolence. It is possible to show that altruistic behaviour can emerge from adaptation mechanisms (close to the picture displayed in fig. 2). In terms of CS, an altruistic rule may be implemented and to the extent that it proves successful be re-executed. The same line of reasoning may be applied to positive social emotions, and perhaps even to moral sentiments. But these things do not(necessarily) presuppose social institutions, and are subject to genetic distribution. On the contrary, in its most interesting version, the Macro-social level consists of:
- changing social institutions, which are not compatible with spontaneous and time-consuming processes of adaptation, and which are designed to
- rule autonomous agents, whether benevolent or ill-willed.

The difficult problem is not how to design *agents which learn to exhibit what in fact is a socially acceptable behaviour.* The problem is how to design autonomous, even selfish agents which *accept to be ruled by dynamic and complex social institutions,* which accept "prescriptions", fulfil "obligations" and "commitment", respect "rights" etc.; discriminate between a prescriptive and a non-prescriptive command (or between a legitimate and a non-legitimate one), between a desirable and a non-desirable social conduct *ceteris paribus* (that is, when they are equally frequent in a given environment or the latter is even more frequent than the former); monitor others' behaviour to find out what the institution wants; influence others to observe the institutional requests; find out and punish violators, etc.. A related problem is the interrelationships between socially-oriented motivations and emotions and institution-driven representations: for example, adaptive agents may evolve altruistic behaviour, but how can they evolve the motivation to adopt norms, laws, etc.? The latter necessarily requires not only an evolutionary model of altruism, but a model of how altruism interacts with institution-driven representations.

4. The Future: Intelligent-Agent-Based Social Simulation (IABSS)

So far, I endeavoured to show that the field of social simulation necessitates not only to implement learning and evolving agents, which adjust themselves to changes in their environment, including those occurring at the Macro level; but also to model and implement intelligent social agents, which allow the Macro level to function through their representations, reasoning and other mental mechanisms. In particular, what is needed is modelling agents which

- learn from others in a selective and intelligent way (imitation, social facilitation, etc.; cf. Conte & Paolucci, 2000)
- exercise social influence and control
- are endowed with beliefs concerning others, and with cultural and institutional representations of social institutions (norms, hierarchies, etc.)
- and with the capacity to reason/act/decide (and possibly solve conflicts) upon these representations.

To some extent, this necessity is perceived by social simulators. Simulations based on AI-agents with explicit representations of social hierarchies and collective beliefs have been realised (cf. Doran, 1998).Even complex deliberative agents (Castelfranchi et al., 1999), with explicit representations of social norms and the capacity to reason upon them, are being implemented for the purposes of social simulation. But unfortunately these projects, especially the latter, are still at a rather preliminary stage.

Why bother with this more complex view of the Micro-Macro link? This viewis certainly closer to what happens in natural human societies, and perhaps in some non-human societies as well. But reasons of interest abound in several fields. Current interfaces of ABSS with dynamic (learning and evolving) agents abound: from evolutionary models to Artificial Life, from Artificial Culture (Reynolds, 1994), to memetics (cf. Hales, 1998); from Multi-Agent Systems (cf. Sichman et al., 1998; Conte & Moss, 1999, etc.) to synthetic actors and "edutainment" (education and entertainment) (cf. interactive and believable agents), etc..

All of these fields would greatly profit from the development of Intelligent Agent-Based Social Simulation (IABSS),because in each of them the question of the Micro-Macro link will represent a major challenge in the future.

In cultural evolution and memetics, where the importance of the "theory of mind" approach is acknowledged (see Dennett, 1995), a fundamental question is what is the impact of agents on the transmissibility of cultural units(fecundity, longevity, and fertility; cf. Dawkins, 1976). Imitation is certainly not the only, and perhaps not even the main factor, of cultural transmission. Other aspects of social learning should be taken into account, as well as a complex typology of active influence (cf. Cavalli-Sforza and Feldmann, 1985). A difficult issue concerns the complex interrelationships between (a) the agent's representation of the source of given beliefs (whether personal or institutional) and the agent's acceptance and commitment to those beliefs, and (b) between such commitment and transmissibility of beliefs. Undoubtedly, intelligent agent-based simulation would both profit from and prove invaluable for developments of the field in this sense.

In agent-mediated interaction, the utility of artificial societies and social simulation is transparent (cf. again, Conte and Moss, 1999). But certainly the interface between these fields calls for developments in the agent base of simulation models. In agent-mediated interaction, non-trivial problems of social order and regulation necessitate a 3-layer version of the Micro-Macro link. For example, in e-commerce one serious problem is how to reconcile good performance in bargaining with trustworthiness. In fact, bargain is essentially based upon deception (cf. Cecchi et al., in preparation). Atypical solution proposed is to implement complex systems of incentives and sanctions (cf. Dellarocas, 2000), which inevitably lead to model/implement institution-based deciding agents. Another problem is to implement agents which help users to achieve a good understanding of on-line institutions (for example, brokers and other intermediaries, bank systems, etc.). This in turn implies that software agents (a) are endowed with representations of institutions, (b) help users to take decisions based upon this knowledge, (c) possibly interact directly with institutions.

In Multi Agent Systems, a specific concern for social control and monitoring is felt. In evolutionary models, social order is viewed as an emergent effect of adaptive agents, which does not imply active social influence. By contrast, social monitoring and control are seen as tasks assigned to intelligent agents in dynamic multi-agent environments. Kaminka and Tambe (2000) show that a "distributed ... monitoring algorithm results in correct and complete detection of teamwork failures, despite relying on limited, uncertain knowledge, and monitoring only key agents in a team" (:1). But this capacity implies explicit representation of teamwork, conventions, etc. and therefore a deliberative agent architecture.

In social and environmental policy, the impact of participatory policy-making is growing, and consequently the influence of agent-based simulation is strengthening. One important development in this field is Integrated Assessment Modelling, in which socio-economic factors are coupled with cognitive factors in order to check the agents' understanding and response to policies under elaboration.

Achievements in this field are a direct function of developments in the agent base of simulation models, and in particular, of simulated agents which perceive, acknowledge, accept and cooperate with candidate institutional policies.

5. Axelrod's Principle Rephrased: Keep It as Simple as Suitable!

Axelrod's recommendation (to keep simulation models as simple as possible in order to facilitate validation and interpretation of results) is hardly questionable, if it is read as "do not implement more complexity (and therefore more intelligence) than needed". The question is, when is more (mental) complexity needed?

The history of social simulation is a history of growing complexity, especially at the agent level. The simulation of the emergence of Macro-social phenomena has required heterogeneous and dynamic agents, at least in the sense of agents moving in a physical and social space. In turn, the simulation of learning and evolutionary algorithms allowed for a two-way account of the Micro-Macro link. Now, we are facing a third step in this process. A 3-layer representation of the Micro-Mind-Macro link is required to account for the mental functioning of social institutions. According to the 3-layer model, specific cognitive structures evolve which cooperate with emerging Macro-social systems and institutions. The main task of these cognitive structures is to allow agents to accept to be ruled by changing social institutions, independent of built-in motivations, good will, etc.. In order to execute this task, agents need intelligence, namely social intelligence. Social intelligence is no more than *what is strictly needed* to understand this important aspect of (artificial) societies. What is more, this aspect is receiving growing attention is several fields and applications of the science of artificial, with which social simulation is interfaced or will soon be.

A clarification is needed concerning the meaning of (social) intelligence as is meant in this presentation. Conceptually, Axelrod's principle confounds two properties, dumbness and abstraction. Models, and especially simulation models, need to be *abstract enough* to achieve an adequate level of generality, to highlight the fundamentals of the phenomena under study, and to facilitate interpretation. However, they need to be no *less complex* than what is required by the simulation purpose. Obviously, "stupid" agents are abstract enough. But they may be less complex than what is required by some simulation models. On the other hand, abstraction does not coincide with dumbness. For example, rational agents are abstract, ideal-type agents, which are not stupid. Analogously, intelligent agents can be as abstract as rational agents. However, intelligence is other than a concrete and limited version of rationality (as some author seems to believe, cf. Elster, 1985). Here, intelligence is not meant as a mild form of rationality, and intelligent agents are not the less predictable cousins of rational agents: IABSS - RABSS! What is the difference between intelligence, as it is meant here, and rationality?

First, intelligence is a complex phenomenon which includes rationality. Rationality is a requirement of decision-making, whilst intelligence is a complex and integrated set of properties which enter in all aspects of belief-based action, from the perception and representation of the external world, to the activation and modification of internal regulatory mechanisms (including but not reduced to preferences), from problem-slaving and planning, to decision-making and execution.

Secondly, intelligence is a strongly dynamic property, whilst rationality is essentially a static property unconcerned with the agents' motives for choice and their modification of these motives.

Third, intelligence is crucial to model the process, whilst rationality is oriented to the outcomes, of action.

Fourth, a theory of intelligence has explanatory objectives, whilst rationality has prescriptive objectives.

Fifth, intelligence focuses on qualitative phenomena (internal representations) and differences (among agents), whilst rationality takes for granted these, and focuses on the quantitative dimension of phenomena(utility function) and differences (subjective utility).   Consequently, and moreover, what is needed for a 3-layertheory of the Micro-Macro link are intelligent rather than rational agents. Indeed, we need

- a model of the process, rather than a prediction of the effects
- a model of different aspects of the mind, and not only of the decision-making strategies
- a dynamic model of the mind
- a qualitative description of mental objects and operations.

If recent achievements of social simulation called for flexible, adaptive, dynamic agents, current developments of the field seem to require more intelligent ones. The most reasonable lesson to be drawn therefore is, never make models (including agent models) more complex than needed, but, important corollary, but take agents seriously!

References

[ALB 98] ALBIN P.S., *Barriers and Bounds to Rationality : Essays on Economic Complexity and Dynamics in Interactive Systems*, NJ : Princeton University Press, Princeton, 1998.

[AXE 84] AXELROD R., *The Evolution of Cooperation*. Basic Books, New York, 1984

[AXE 97] AXELROD R., In R. Conte, R. Hegselmann and P. Terna (eds) *Simulating Social Phenomena*. Berlin : Springer-Verlag, Lecture Notes in Economics and Mathematical Systems, 1997.

[BEL 96] BELTRATTI A., MARGARITA S, TERNA P., *Neural Networks for Economic and Financial Modelling*. International Thomson Computer Press, London 1996.

[CAR 98] CARLEY K.M., PRIETULA M.J. and LIN Z., Design Versus Cognition: The interaction of agent cognition and organisational design on organisational performance. *Journal of Artificial Societies and Social Simulation* vol. 1, no. 3, 1998.

[CAS 97] CASTELFRANCHI C., *Invited paper at the 4th Simulating Societies Symposium*, Cortona, Siena,20-21 September, 1997.

[CAV 81] CAVALLI SFORZA L.L., FELDMAN M., *Cultural Transmission and Evolution. A Quantitative Approach*. Princeton Univ. Press, Princeton, N.J (1981).

[CEC] CECCHI R., CONTE R., CASTELFRANCHI C., *Fraud, Exchange, and Cooperation*. In B. Schmidt (ed) Springer, in preparation.

[CEC 98] CECCONI F., PARISI D., Individual versus social survival strategies. *Journal of Artificial Societies and Social Simulation* vol. 1, no. 2, 1998.

[CHA 98] CHATTOE E., Just How (Un)realistic are Evolutionary Algorithms as Representations of Social Processes ?', *Journal of Artificial Societies and Social Simulation* vol. 1, no. 3, 1998.

[CON 95] CONTE R., GILBERT N., Introduction. In N. Gilbert and R. Conte (eds) *Artificial Societies : the Computer Simulation of Social Life*. UCL Press: London. 1995.

[CON 95] CONTE R., SICHMAN JS. DEPNET : How to benefit from social dependence *Journal of Mathematical Sociology, 2-3*, 161-177. 1995

[CON 00] CONTE R., DIGNUM F., From Social Monitoring To Normative Influence. MODELLING AGENTS INTERACTIONS, INNATURAL RESOURCES AND ENVIRONMENT MANAGEMENT, *Game theory and agent-based simulation, International workshop 2000*,MARCH, 29, 30, 31. Montpellier INRA ENSAM " La Gaillarde Campus "2, place Viala. 2000.

[CON 99] CONTE R., MOSS S., Special Interest Group on Agent-Based Social Simulation, *Journal of Artificial Societies and Social Simulation* vol. 2, no. 1, 1999.

[CON 99] CONTE R., Social Intelligence Among Autonomous Agents. *Computational and Mathematical Organisation Theory* , 5(3) : 203-228. 1999.

[CON 00] CONTE R., PAOLUCCI M., Intelligent social learning. *Symposium "Starting from society. The Application of Social Analogies to Computational Systems"*, at AISB 2000,Birmingham, 17-20 April 2000.

[DAV 87] DAVIS L., (ed.), *Genetic Algorithms and Simulated Annealing*. Morgan Kaufmann, Los Altos, CA. 1987.

[DAW 76] DAWKINS R., *The Selfish Gene*. Oxford Univ. Press. 1976.

[DEA 97] DEAN A., *Chaos and Intoxication: Complexity and Adaptation in the Structure of Human Nature*. London : Routledge, 1997.

[DEL 00] DELLAROCAS C., Contractual Agent Societies : Negotiated shared context and social control in open multi-agent systems, Proceedings Workshop 10 *"Norms and Institutions"*, Autonomous Agents 2000, Barcelona, Spain, June 4, 2000.

[DEN 95] DENNETT D., *Darwin's Dangerous Idea*. Penguin, 1995.

[DOR 98] DORAN J., Simulating Collective Misbelief, *Journal of Artificial Societies and Social Simulation* vol. 1, no. 1, 1998.

[ECS 98] ECSR workshop on the potentials of social simulation for the social sciences, Guildford, Surrey, UK, December, 1998.

[EDM 98] EDMONDS B., Modelling Socially Intelligent Agents. *Applied Artificial Intelligence*, 12 : 677-699. (An earlier version is available, 1998.

[ELS 85] ELSTER J., *Sour Grapes. Studies in the Subversion of Rationality*, Cambridge : Cambridge University Press, 1985.

[EPS 96] EPSTEIN J.M. , AXTELL R., *Growing Artificial Societies*. Cambridge, MA : The MIT Press, 1996.

[GIL] GILBERT G.N., TROITZSCH K.G., *Simulation for the social scientist*. The Open Press, 1999.

[GIL 99] GILBERT G.N., Multi-level simulation in Lisp-Stat. *Journal of Artificial Societies and Social Simulation* vol. 2, no. 1, 1999.

[GIL 99] GILBERT N., Invited Paper at the *1st Meeting of the ABSS Special Interest Group*, London, Imperial College, April 21-23, 1999.

[GIL 95] GILBERT N., CONTE R., (Eds) *Artificial Societies : the Computer Simulation of Social Life*. UCL Press : London, 1995.

[HAL 98] HALES D., An Open Mind is not an Empty Mind: Experiments in the Meta-Noosphere. *Journal of Artificial Societies and Social Simulation* vol. 1, no. 4, (1998).

[HAL 98] HALPIN B., Simulation in Sociology : A review of the literature. Paper read at the Workshop on *"Potential of the computer simulation for the social sciences"*, Centre for Research in the Social Sciences (CRESS), University of Surrey, 14-15 January, 1998.

[HEG 96] HEGSELMANN R., Cellular automata in the social sciences : Perspectives, restrictions and artefacts. In : R .Hegselmann, U. Mueller and K. G. Troitzsch (eds.) *Modelling and simulation in the social sciences from a philosophy of science point of view*. Kluwer : Dordrecht, pp. 209-234, 1996.

[HEG 98] HEGSELMANN R., FLACHE A., Understanding Complex Social Dynamics : A Plea For Cellular Automata Based Modelling. *Journal of Artificial Societies and Social Simulation* vol. 1, no. 3, 1998.

[HOL 92] HOLLAND J., *Adaptation in Natural and Artificial Systems*. University of Michigan Press, Ann Arbor, MI. (Second edition, first published 1975), 1992a.

[HOL 92] HOLLAND J., Genetic algorithms. *Scientific American*, 267:66-72, 1992b.

[HOL 95] HOLLAND J.H., *Hidden Order : How Adaptation Builds Complexity*. Addison-Wesley, Redwood City, CA, 1995.

[HOL 98] HOLLAND J.H., *Emergence : From Chaos to Order*. Addison-Wesley, Redwood City, CA., 1998.

[KAM 00] KAMINKA G.A., TAMBE M., Robust Agent Teams via Socially-Attentive Monitoring", *Journal of Artificial Intelligent Research,* Volume 12, 105-147, 2000.

[LAT 81] LATANZ B., The psychology of social impact. *American Psychologist*, 36: 343-356, 1981.

[MOE 96] MOEHRING M., Social Science Multi level Simulation with MIMOSE, in K.G. Troitzsch, U. Mueller, G.N. Gilbert and J.E. Doran (eds) *Social Science Microsimulation* Berlin : Springer, 1996.

[MOS 98] MOSS S., Critical Incident Management : An Empirically Derived Computational Model. *Journal of Artificial Societies and Social Simulation* vol. 1, no. 4, 1998.

[NIS 93] NISSEN V., Evolutionary Algorithms in Management Science - An Overview and List of References, *Papers on Economics and Evolution*, Number 9303, edited by the European Study Group for Evolutionary Economics, Max Planck Institute, Evolutionary Economics Unit, Jena, Germany, 1993.

[NOW 92] NOWAK M., SIGMUND K., Tit for tat in heterogeneous populations. *Nature*, 355 : 250-253, 1992.

[NOW 93] NOWAK M., SIGMUND K., A strategy of win-shift, lose-stay that outperforms tit-for-tat in the Prisoners' Dilemma game. *Nature*, 364 : 56-57, 1993.

[NOW 90] NOWAK A, SZAMREZ J., LATANŽ B., From private attitude to public opinion - Dynamic theory of social impact. *Psychological Review* 97 : 362-376. 1990.

[PRI 98] PRIETULA M.J., CARLEY *and groups*. Menlo Park, CA : AAAI Press / The MIT Press, 1998

[REA 98] READ S. J., MILLER L.C., *Connectionist Models of Social Reasoning and Social Behaviour*. Lawrence Erlbaum Associates, Mahwah, NJ, 1998.

[REY 94] REYNOLDS R., Learning to Co-operate using Cultural Algorithms. In N. Gilbert & J. Doran (Eds.) *Simulating Societies : The Computer Simulation of Social Phenomena*. London : UCL Press, 1994.

[ROC 96] ROCKLOFF M.J., LATANZ B., Simulating the social context of human choice. In K. G. Troitzsch U. Mueller, N. Gilbert J. Doran (eds) *Social Science Microsimulation*, Berlin : Springer, 1996.

[SAK 71] SAKODA J.M., The checkerboard model of social interaction. *Journal of Mathematical Sociology*1: 119-132, 1971.

[SCH 69] SCHELLING T., Models of segregation .*American Economic Review* 59 : 488-493, 1969.

[SCH 71] SCHELLING T., Dynamic models of segregation. *Journal of Mathematical Sociology*1: 143-186, 1971.

[SCH 00] SCHILLO M., FISCHER K., KLEIN C.T., The Micro-Macro Link in DAI and Sociology, MABS 2000 (ICMAS-2000), *The Second Workshop on Multi Agent Based Simulation*, 9 July, 2000, at The Boston Park Plaza Hotel, Boston MA, USA

[SCH 94] SCHULZ U., ALBERS W., MUELLER U., (eds.). *Social Dilemmas and Cooperation*. Springer : Berlin, 1994.

[SHO 92a] SHOHAM Y., TENNEHOLTZ M., On the synthesis of useful social laws for artificial agent societies (preliminary report). *Proceedings of the AAAI Conference*, 276-281, 1992a.

[SIC 94] SICHMAN J.S., CONTE R., CASTELFRANCHI C., DEMAZEAU Y., A social reasoning mechanism based on dependence networks In A. G. Cohn (Ed) *Proceedings of the 11th European Conference on Artificial Intelligence*, Baffins Lane, England : John Wiley & Sons, 188-192, 1994.

[SIC 98] SICHMAN J., CONTE R., GILBERT N., (eds). *Multi-agent systems and agent-based simulation*, Berlin, Springer, 1998.

[SIM 69] SIMON H.A., *The sciences of the artificial*. Cambridge, MIT Press, 1969.

[SUL 00] SULEIMAN R., TROITZSCH K., GILBERT N. (eds). *Tools and Techniques for social science simulation*, Berlin : Springer, 2000.

[TER 00] TERAN O. and EDMONDS B., A Technique for the Efficient Determination of Tendencies and Emergence in Social Simulation. *MABS2000 at ICMAS-2000, The Second Workshop on Multi Agent Based Simulation*, 9 July, 2000 , The Boston Park Plaza Hotel, Boston MA, USA.

[TRO 97] TROITZSCH K.G., Social science simulation - Origin, prospects, purposes. In R. Conte, R. Hegselmann, P.Terna (Eds) *Simulating social phenomena*, Heidelberg : Springer, 1997.

[TRO 96] TROITZSCH K.G., MUELLER U., GILBERT G.N., DORAN J.E. (eds). *Social science microsimulation*. Heidelberg, Springer, 1996.

[TRO 96] TROITZSCH K. G., Multilevel simulation, in K.G. Troitzsch, U. Mueller, G.N. Gilbert and J.E. Doran (eds) *Social Science Microsimulation* Berlin : Springer, (1996).

[WEI 98] WEISBUCH G., DUCHATEAU-NGUYEN G., Societies, cultures and fisheries from a modelling perspective. *Journal of Artificial Societies and Social Simulation* vol. 1, no. 2, 1998

[WOO 99] WOOLDRIGE M., Intelligent Agents. InG. Weiss (ed.) *Multiagent systems : A modern approach to distribute artificial intelligence*, 27-78, MIT Press, 1999.

False reputation in social control

Mario Paolucci

IP-CNR, Italian National Research Council
Viale Marx, 15, I-00137 Rome, Italy

paolucci@istat.it

ABSTRACT: *A simulation study is conduced on the spread of reputation in mixed respectful-cheater population. The effects of various mechanism giving raise to false reputation are shown, together with a discussion of foreseen results. The actual results of the simulation are then presented; informational accuracy is found to be an essential condition to maintain an advantage for the norms-followers.*

RÉSUMÉ: *Une étude de simulation est conduite sur la diffusion de la réputation dans une population mélangée de respectueux-tricheur. Les effets du divers mechianism produisant la réputation fausse sont montrés, ainsi qu'une discussion des résultats prévus. Les résultats réels de la simulation sont présentés par la suite; l'exactitude informationnelle s'avère essentiel pour maintenir l'avantage pour le respectueux.*

KEY WORDS: *simulation, norms, information exchange*

"La calunnia è un venticello,/un'auretta assai gentile/
che insensibile, sottile,/leggermente, dolcemente,/
incomincia a sussurrar./ Piano piano, terra terra,/
sotto voce, sibilando,/va scorrendo, va ronzando;/
nelle orecchie della gente, /s'introduce destramente,/
e le teste ed i cervelli,/ fa stordire e fa gonfiar./
(...) Alla fin trabocca e scoppia,/ si propaga, si raddoppia/
e produce un'esplosion/ come un colpo di cannone,/
un tremuoto, un temporale,/ un tumulto generale,/
che fa l'aria rimbombar./ "

(Cesare Sterbini, from *Il Barbiere di Siviglia*, Act I)

1. Introduction

This paper presents the results of a simulation study of the spread of reputation in intra-group social control. This study is part of a research project on the social norms in artificial societies. In particular, the norm under study is a norm of precedence in access to food. Previous studies ([CAS 98], [PAO 99]) brought about the role of a mechanism of reputation and exchange of information about reputation in re-distributing the costs of normative compliance. In fact, in mixed populations, including agents respecting a given norm and agents violating it, the latter (the cheaters) are found better-off than the respectful, unless the latter exchange information about the reputation of cheaters [CAS 98], and punish them. If agents exercize what sociologists call social control and punish norm transgressors, their outcomes will be competitive with those obtained by cheaters. Results were found highly stable (cf. [PAO 97]) in conditions of incomplete but true information.

The present study is aimed to check the effects of incorrect information: what happens if false beliefs propagate among respectful? Is the advantage which they obtain from communication affected by the truth value of their beliefs? These questions arise from the necessity to check the efficiency of social control in more realistic conditions. The ease and speed of the mechanism of propagation are in sharp contrast with its accuracy. How then can it be relied upon? Is it really possible that the success of social norms depends upon such a superficial mechanism as gossip, when calumny and other types of false reputation spread so easily and quickly?

The paper is organized as follows. In the next section, relevant work and theories will be examined, with a special emphasis on social control. In the third section, the previous studies on social control will be described and our hypotheses about the effects of false reputation will be discussed at some length. In the fourth section, the present experiment will be designed and the expected results will be presented. In the fourth section, the findings from simulation experiments with different types of informational errors in the propagation of reputation will be discussed. In the final section, some conclusions will be drawn and the relevance of this experiments will be discussed.

2. Related Work

Social control (cf. [HEC 90]; [HOM 74]; [MAC 95]; [FLA 96]) is usually meant as a distributed, non-institutional sanctioning (such as disapproval) of transgressions. By sanctioning the transgressions of their in-groups, agents cooperate with the norms in force in their group. Social control is then a norm-cooperative process. The question is why agents cooperate with the norms. In exchange theory ([HOM 74]), social control is explained as an exchange of a special type of resource, i.e. social approval. Agents approve of others, in order to obtain their approval. The more the agents which I will approve of, and the more approval I will obtain in return.

The exchange of social approval is a fragile form of cooperation with the norms, because agents will approve of others when they have an interest in doing so. Indeed, the theory accounts for the formation of sub-groups which might interfere with the norms in force at the large group level. This effect has been shown by simulation studies ([MAC 95], [FLA 96]). These studies point out a threshold effect, a critical point in group's density, after which the density negatively interferes with the efficiency of social control. When exchange frequency exceeds the threshold, it may give rise to behavioural regularities which contrast with the norms in force. This phenomenon, of great scientific interest, is the effect of local implicit agreements, which give rise to local conventions. Rather than a theory of social control, the exchange of approval is one possible explanation for the emergence of conventions.

Heckathorn poses the question of social control in rational, game-theoretic terms. In his view, agents not only must decide whether to obey a norm or not, but they will also make a corresponding decision at the higher level. Social control is a second-order cooperation, and therefore it is given the same explanation which is given to first-order cooperation, namely, as a rational decision. Agents will cooperate both at the first and at the second level if it is rational to do so, that is, when the entity of sanction multiplied by its probability is more costly than the convenience of transgression. Heckathorn seems to take for granted that agents perform social control in order to avoid sanctions. If exchange of approval is a weak form of social control, the theory of the second-order cooperation is too strong. Or, better, it is does not provide a convincing account of the individual reasons for agents to perform social control. For example, which sanctions are applied, how are they applied and by whom? Heckathorn does not address these questions explicitly.

3. The Present Work

This study is a continuation of a series of studies ([CAS 98]; [PAO 99]) on the effects of respectful agents exchanging information about the reputation of cheaters in social control. Social control is meant as punishing norm transgressors. Information exchange allows the good guys to know which are the bad guys without directly sustaining the costs of learning information. The previous results will be summarized in the following subsection. The present study intends to clarify and control what we call "reciprocal altruism of beliefs", and explore both the socially desirable effects of this phenomenon (e.g. social control) and the socially undesirable ones (e.g., the diffusion of social prejudice).

3.1. Previous Work

Castelfranchi and associates ([CAS 1998]) carried out a simulation study of two forms of social control. The frame of the experiment is a two-dimensional, discrete, torical world in which the agent seek (scarce) resources scattered on the grid. At the onset of each simulation, an equal value of strength is assigned to agents; this value varies with their moving around, eating, and attacking one another. Physical aggression is directed to acquire food, and consists of the agents' attempts to snatch food from one another's hands.

The norm implemented in both cases was a norm of precedence on food resources. Agents in fact are designed to attack "eaters" to get hold of their food, when no cheaper alternative is feasible (attacks are costly). The norm was meant to reduce the number of attacks, and was implemented in the following way. At the onset of the simulation, food appearing in the vicinity of any given agent will be marked as its own, and the norm prevents agents eating their own food to be attacked. The entire population of agents is divided into two main sets, those which respect the norm (called Respectful) and those who violate the norm (the Cheaters). The latter will observe a simpler and selfish rule: they attack eaters which are not stronger than themselves (since the success of an attack is determined by the physical strength of competitors: the stronger always wins), whether these are owners or not.

In the first form of social control, the respectful keep a record of cheaters (reputation), and retaliate against them in future encounters. Retaliation was meant to affect the final redistribution of costs and benefits: agents identified as cheaters were treated by the respectful as cheaters, and therefore were expected to share (some of) the costs of cheat. However, this form of social control did not produce the expected results, because the respectful acquired information about reputation by their direct experience with cheaters, and therefore only after having been exploited at least once by them.

In the second set of experiment on social control, we have checked the effect of the propagation of reputation through the population: when meeting (i.e., if in adjacent grid cells), respectful agents exchange information about the reputation of others. In this condition (spread of reputation), the respectful obtain far better results than in the previous one. Their outcomes are generally competitive with those obtained by cheaters, and in some circumstances exceed them. In the result from the previous experiment, reported in Table 1, the agents population is composed by two subpopulations of 40 respectful agents and 10 cheaters. Their results are compared on the *Number* of living agents at the end (in the reference conditions, nearly all the agents manage to survive at the end of the 2000 moves), and on the average *Strength* and internal standard deviation (*StdDev*) of the subpopulations. In this case, there is a definite advantage for respectfuls, both in terms of average strength, and in fairness of the distribution.

Apparently, the spread of reputation proves essential for an efficacious social control. However, the results obtained so far refer to an ideal condition: information exchanged is not complete but is necessarily correct. Neither bluff nor errors are allowed. What happens in sub-ideal conditions, in which the constraint upon correct information is relaxed, and errors start to spread? What are the effects of false reputation in social control? This is the focus of the present study.

	Number	Strength	StdDev
Respectful	39,98	5353,36	600,00
Cheaters	9,92	4600,24	2465,84

Table 1. *Previous Experiment*

3.2. *Why Bother With False Reputation*

There are several reasons of interest in these questions. First, it contributes to the plausibility and realism of results, since in real matters often only partial and incorrect information is available. This is even more crucial with information about reputation, which is known to be often wrong. Secondly, it raises the issue of the utility of such information. Taking a rational theory viewpoint, one might doubt about the benefit of incorrect information: in this approach, partial and false information is a limit, an obstacle for rational agents. That false beliefs are not always disadvantageous has already been shown (cf. [DOR 98]). Here, we investigate a special type of beliefs, i.e. social, and more specifically group beliefs, that is beliefs about a given sub-population and shared by another part of the population. We hypothesize that these may be advantageous for the agents holding them provided these achieve them through one another, even at the risk of incorrectness. This type of belief ha a special feature: they do not need to be "accepted" before being transmitted. Agents spread gossip which they do not trust completely. This makes transmission easy and fast.

The easier and faster the transmission, the wider the propagation of beliefs and the number of agents which can profit from them, and the more it is advantageous for them. But the speed and easiness of the mechanism of transmission facilitates errors since agents do not need to control the validity of the information received. Indeed, agents accept information about reputation for prudence; Therefore, they will behave according to the information received even when they do not trust it completely. Consequently, the transmission of beliefs about cheaters leaves room for the spread of false information.

3.3. Expected Results

Information may be incorrect in two senses:

- inclusive error: agents which are believed to be good guys are hidden cheaters. This error may be seen as an ingenuity, an exceeding credulity on the side of respectful.
- exclusive error: some respectful agents are target of a calumny, and believed to be cheaters.

Which results could we expect from these two different errors? In principle, when they fall prey of an exclusive error, respectful agents are expected to punish some members of their own group. The population of respectful should attack a subset of their weaker members, i.e. those which are erroneously believed to be cheaters. These are expected to impoverish to the benefit of the stronger respectful, whether they are believed to be cheaters or not. Results should be closer to those of effective cheaters.

With an inclusive error, a subset of cheaters, i.e. the hidden cheaters, will not be punished even if they are weaker. Consequently, the effects of reputation will be reduced. In this condition, the outcomes of respectful should be lowered. In sum, incorrect information is expected to be advantageous when it reduces the set of respectful and enlarges that of cheaters (exclusive belief), and disadvantageous when it reduces the set of cheaters and enlarges that of respectful (inclusive belief). One could then draw the conclusion that the two errors neutralize themselves.

4. The Design of the Experiment

In the previous studies, agents kept a partial record of their social experience: they registered into their knowledge base only the identity of cheaters. If an agent eating its own food is attacked by a neighbour, this is recorded by the attacked agent as a cheater. Given the design of the simulation, direct experience of a cheater is always correct. Beliefs are then exchanged among respectful, according to a simple mechanism: each will update its own list by incorporating into it the entries comprised in the list of the other.

In the present study, the algorithm was slightly modified so as to allow the respectful to keep a record of both social categories, cheaters and respectful. When an agent is not attacked by a stronger neighbour, this should be record as a respectful. This leaves a large space to incorrect information (since a stronger neighbour might be about to attack someone else), and acts as a bias in favour of the respectful, a strong presumption of innocence. Furthermore, it generates a rather self-centered view of reputation: agents record as respectful those agents which respect the norm to their own benefit.

Information about others' reputation may be acquired or updated thanks to inputs from others. Exchange of information always occurs among respectful. More precisely, agents will accept information only from those which they know to be respectful, and reject it when it comes from cheaters. Besides, agents accept any new piece of information from others: anytime they are informed about the reputation of someone which is not mentioned in either of their lists, they will update their knowledge to converge with that received. When two records are incompatible, they will be cancelled from the lists of both agents. Finally, when one agent receives contradictory information from two or more neighbours, one of them will be chosen randomly.

In order to mitigate the bias in the direct acquisition of information, a variable threshold controls the acceptance of indirectly acquired information (information received by others). This threshold can be set to a high or low value. A low threshold of acceptance will confirm the presumption of acceptance; a high threshold will instead contrast with it.

There are two sources of error,

- direct experience, this concerns only the respectful; agents have a bias to accept as respectful anyone which respect the norm to their own advantage. The obtained list of R is usually longer than initial lists of Cs, and may contain errors (inclusive errors).

- communication: this concerns both respectful and cheaters. A variable noise produces a mutation in the lists which agents communicate to one another. At every tournament of the simulation, a randomly generated number of entries will be modified into their opposite: a C will be "read" as R, and viceversa. To simplify matters, the noise parameter can be set to a high or low value.

The noise is expected to magnify the error and increase the speed of propagation. The threshold is expected to determine the prevailing error: a high threshold is expected to favour exclusive errors, a low threshold is expected to favour inclusive errors.

5. Findings

Our expectations concerned two different but strictly intertwined aspects of the propagation of false reputation in social control: (a) its effects on the respective outcomes of cheaters and honest, and (b) features of its transmissibility ([DAW 76]), i.e. the relative speed and pervasiveness of inclusive vs. exclusive errors.

5.1. Transmissibility of False Reputation

We expected calumny and credulity to spread as an effect of the initial conditions of the simulations. In order to observe the effect of opposite types of errors in the transmission of reputation, we have implemented two mechanisms, a variable noise (which essentially turns a reputation marker (R, for respectful, or C, for cheater) into its opposite, and a variable threshold of acceptance of beliefs about good reputation.

- A low threshold of acceptance was expected to favour the spread of the good reputation (since agents are more easily recorded as R),

- a high threshold of acceptance was expected to obstacle the spread of the good reputation and proportionately to favour the spread of the opposite reputation.

- On the other hand, the noise was expected to equally favour both errors.

Findings confirmed this expectation, and show that the mechanism of propagation is extremely powerful. False reputation spreads easily. The prevailing error (whether inclusive or exclusive) essentially depends upon the threshold of acceptance: if threshold of acceptance of good reputation is low, good reputation will prevail over bad reputation (whether deserved or not). The number of hidden cheaters out-competes the number of calumnied, if any. On the other hand, if the threshold of acceptance is high, the number of calumnied exceeds the number of hidden cheaters, if any (exclusive error). However, when the threshold of acceptance is high and noise is low, errors tend to be eliminated during transmission. In these conditions, propagation is allowed to reduce and eventually eliminate false reputation (accuracy).

	Low Noise	High Noise
Low Threshold	Prevalence of Cheaters, Credulity (inclusive error)	Prevalence of Cheaters, Credulity (inclusive error)
High Threshold	Prevalence of Respectful, no error	Prevalence of Cheaters, Calumny (exclusive error)

Table 2. *Overview of results*

Details of results are shown in the following Tables 3 to 9, accompanied by graphical representation. The tables show again the *Number* of living agents at the end, plus the average *Strength* and internal standard deviation (*StdDev*) of the subpopulations.

	Number	Strength	StdDev
Respectful	39,92	5252,42	605,64
Cheaters	9,94	5053,80	2533,38

Table 3. *Reference Values: high threshold, low noise*

For each setting except the previous one, detailed results are shown for the subpopulations whose diffused reputation is different from their effective behaviour. In the following two tables, *hidden* cheaters are the ones which managed to obtain a respectful reputation, while *open* cheaters are recognized as such from the agents following the norm. Hidden and open cheaters together return the total value for cheaters.

	Number	Strength	StdDev
Respectful	39.93	4912.82	580.70
Cheaters	9.93	6367.68	1710.51
Hidden cheaters	4.67	6966.21	604.59
open cheaters	5.26	5836.28	2692.38

Table 4. *Credulity I. Low threshold, low noise*

	Number	Strength	StdDev
Respectful	39.93	4821.40	613.85
Cheaters	9.98	6672.23	1301.66
Hidden Cheaters	4.60	6913.50	628.39
Open Cheaters	5.39	6466.35	1876.15

Table 5. *Credulity II. Low threshold, high noise*

In the *calumny* setting, detailed values are shown for the respectful agents that are recognized as such, and for the *calumnied* ones. The results for strength are then compared, for all settings, in Figure 1.

	Number	Strength	StdDev
Respectful	39.91	4923.24	917.64
Calumnied R.	10.50	3969.25	1100.72
Recognized R.	29.41	5263.89	852.26
Cheaters	9.99	5818.53	2085.87

Table 6. *Calumny*

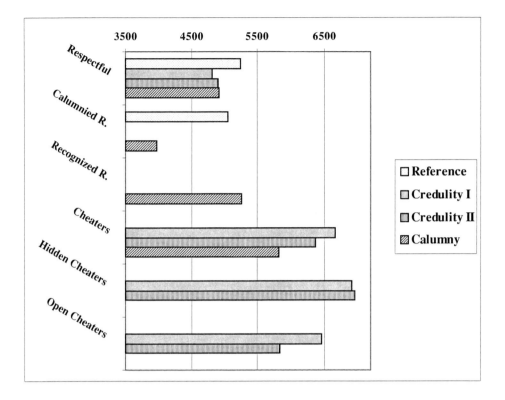

Figure 1. *Strength comparison*

5.2 Effects of False Reputation

The situation which we have called inclusive error, or credulity, was expected to be convenient to cheaters, a subset of which (hidden cheaters) should be treated as honest, and continue to practice their anti-social activity without sustaining the cost of their reputation.

In the opposite case, which we have called exclusive error or calumny, we expected a subset of the honest group (i.e., those which enjoy a good and deserved reputation) to obtain an advantage at the expense of the complementary subset, which instead suffers from an undeserved bad reputation (calumnied). Therefore, the calumny was not expected to make a substantial difference from a no-error situation.

Findings confirmed only in part the expectations. Unlike what was expected, false reputation, whether at the expense of a subset of honest (calumny), or to the benefit of hidden cheaters (credulity), is always convenient for the whole population of cheaters, and disadvantageous for the honest if considered as a whole (cf. Table 3 as compared to Tables 4 to 6). False beliefs about reputation always penalize honesty and norm-obedience, and reinforce cheat.

However, as expected, the two errors show a different effect. In particular, credulity is more convenient for cheaters than calumny (cf. tables 4 and 5 vs. Table 6): cheaters do not have much to gain from calumny. But unlike what was expected, neither the honest and respected guys (those who enjoy a deserved good reputation) do! The interpretation of this unexpected finding points to some sort of self-fulfilling prophecy ([SYN 78]). Consequent to the propagation of false reputation at their expense, the honest guys suffer from frequent and "unexpected" attacks also on the part of those guys which they "believe" to be their fellows (other respectful). Consequently, the calumnied will revise their lists, update the records corresponding to these agents (turning them into Cheaters), and will behave accordingly. Rather than perishing under undeserved attacks, the calumnied will start to retaliate, and behave according to their false reputation, which in our algorithm will determine a sudden improvement of their outcomes.

In sum, whilst informational accuracy is an essential condition for maintaining the advantage of honest over cheaters, false reputation may produce different effects. False good reputation (inclusive error) is mostly convenient for cheaters and mostly inconvenient for the honest. False bad reputation (calumny) is still more convenient for cheaters, but not as inconvenient for the honest as one could expect. In particular, the respected honest will suffer from the retaliations of the calumnied fellows, but these will enjoy the consequences of such retaliations.

6. Concluding Remarks and Discussion

Which lessons can we draw from the results presented above? That false good reputation penalizes the honest citizens is not surprising. Perhaps, it is less obvious that credulity is more detrimental to the honest than it is calumny, however socially unattractive or unfair this effect may appear since gullibility is certainly more acceptable and less reproacheable than calumny. What appears decisively far from our intuition is the fate of the calumnied, which are usually (and probably correctly) perceived as the weakest and unarmed part of the population. This finding deserves some careful consideration.

On one hand, our algorithm is not yet fully apt to deal with such complex and subtle social phenomena as those underlying the transmission of reputation. In the real matters, the calumnied agents which receive unfair attacks do not proceed immediately to revise their social beliefs. They will most probably face a delicate decision-making, whether to update their beliefs about the reputation of their presumed fellows, or else to acquire another important social belief, concerning their own reputation: they learn that they are ill-reputed by others. Consequently, they will have to take another important decision, whether to stick to the norm, or else to accept their undeserved fate and join the crew of cheaters. As we know from experience and from some good social psychological evidence, the latter option is rather frequent: people will not get rid easily of bad reputation (whether deserved or not) once this starts to spread, and this bad reputation will acts as a self-fulfilling prophecy, forcing them into the corresponding behaviour. However, this effect is not as immediate and pervasive as it results from our simulations. Plausibly, to implement the agents' beliefs about their own reputation is necessary to account for the effect of calumny.

A second important lesson which can be drawn from these findings is the efficacy and speed of false reputation. Our simulation model does justice to the intuition that a low degree of noise is insufficient to prevent inaccuracy of beliefs, since false reputation spreads even with low noise. Rather, accuracy is a combined effect of low noise and high threshold of acceptance of information about (good) reputation. In addition, the initial conditions strongly affect the propagation process: if there is an initial bias towards the good reputation, this is bound to spread until all agents are believed to be good guys, and the same is true for the opposite bias. Finally, the two mechanisms which we have implemented give rise to four possible combinations (high threshold high noise, low threshold low noise, high threshold low noise, low threshold and high noise). Of these four conditions, only one produces eventual accuracy. Therefore, in the three remaining conditions, noise produces error, and this was found to penalize the good guys and reinforce cheaters. But then what is the real advantage of the spread of reputation for the honest? How can they trust a mechanism so fragile and often detrimental to them?

One answer could depend upon a comparison between the outcomes which the honest obtain from the propagation of (false) reputation and those which they obtain in absence of this mechanism. This comparison shows that in one case out of four (information accuracy), the honest gain from the spread of reputation. And in one of the three remaining cases (calumny), they gain much more, or lose much less than is the case when no propagation mechanism is activated. Their utility in the case of propagation is therefore higher then it is in absence of such a mechanism. Moreover, the higher the threshold of acceptance of good reputation, the higher the utility of the propagation mechanism for the honest. With a high threshold, either propagation will end up with eliminating errors, and re-establishing information accuracy (which gives a superiority to the honest); or it will end up with a lower difference between the honest and the cheaters than is the case without propagation. Especially with high threshold, propagation is worth the costs of errors!

Acknowledgements

Many ideas in this paper come from discussions with Cristiano Castelfranchi. The preparation of this work would have been impossible were not for the support of Rosaria Conte. The author is glad to have a chance to thank them both.

Bibliography

[CAS 98] CASTELFRANCHI C., CONTE R., PAOLUCCI M., "Normative reputation and the costs of compliance", *Journal of Artificial Societies and Social Simulation,* vol. 1 no. 3, 1998, http://www.soc.surrey.ac.uk/JASSS/1/3/3.html.

[DOR 98] DORAN J., "Simulating Collective Misbelief", *Journal of Artificial Societies and Social Simulation,* vol. 1 no. 1, 1998, http://www.soc.surrey.ac.uk/JASSS/1/1/3.html.

[DAW 76] DAWKINS, R., *The Selfish Gene,* New York, 1976, Oxford University Press.

[FLA 96] FLACHE, A., The double edge of networks: An analysis of the effect of informal networks on co-operation in social dilemmas, Amsterdam, Thesis Publishers, 1996.

[HEC 90] HECKATHORN, D.D., "Collective sanctions and compliance norms: a formal theory of group-mediated social control", *American Sociological Review,* 55, 1990, p. 366-383.

[HOM 74] HOMANS, G.C., *Social Behaviour. Its elementary forms.,* N.Y., Harcourt, 1974.

[MAC 95] MACY, M., FLACHE, A., "Beyond rationality in models of choice", *Annual Review of Sociology,* 21, 1995, p. 73-91.

[PAO 99] PAOLUCCI, M., CONTE, R., "Reproduction of normative agents: A simulation study", *Adaptive Behavior,* forthcoming, 1999

[PAO 97] PAOLUCCI, M., MARSERO, M., CONTE, R., "What's the use of gossip? A sensitivity analysis of the spreading of respectful reputation", presented at the *Schloss Dagstuhl Seminar on Social Science Microsimulation. Tools for Modeling, Parameter Optimization, and Sensitivity Analysis,* 1997.

[SYN 78] SNYDER, M., SWANN, W.B.JR, "Hypothesis testing procsses in social interaction", *Journal of Experimental Social Psychology,* 14, 1978, p. 148-162.

Searching for Mates Using 'Fast and Frugal' Heuristics: a Demographic Perspective

Francesco C. Billari

Max Planck Institute for Demographic Research
Doberaner Str. 114
D-18057 Rostock
Germany
billari@demogr.mpg.de

ABSTRACT*: The paper deals with the search for a mate in human populations, where agents behave according to the bounded rational, 'fast and frugal' heuristics proposed by Todd (1997), which he calls Take the Next Best (TNB). The perspective is that of a demographer, and the main focus is on the macro regularities, in particular, the shape of the frequency distribution of mating time and the proportion of ever-mated, arising from the micro hypotheses. We show – both by simulation and by formal proof – that if agents behave homogeneously according to the same TNB rule the shape of the distribution is monotonically decreasing. Switching then to the hypothesis that individuals act heterogeneously, with different TNB rules, the typical shape of the union formation curve emerges. Finally, we argue that students of demography might gain important hints for their theories by simulation-based approaches and that a population-oriented focus might also be advantageous for studying the mental models for agents.*

KEY WORDS: *Mate search; Marriage curve; Micro-macro demography; Population heterogeneity; Agent-based computational demography*

1. Introduction[1]

This paper deals with the search for a mate in human populations of the contemporary western type. The perspective is that of a demographer, and the main focus is on the aggregate distributional properties arising from plausible search rules for human mating behaviour. That is, we try to marry the literature on mating heuristics with the standard demographic knowledge on marriage and union formation. Simulation is used to evaluate the consequences of hypothesising that individuals are heterogeneous.

An extensive literature on matching has dealt with mating in a game-theoretical framework (see [ROT 90] for a comprehensive account thereof). Another direction of research has been using search models. In that framework, it has been repeatedly been suggested that the search for partners takes too little time for rational actors, and this has consequences for union stability [FRE 96]. Nevertheless, some justifications have been put forth for this hastened behaviour. First, short search times have been noticed in several experiments on search behaviour of different types (see e.g. [SON 98]), and they are mainly explained by the adoption of bounded rational strategies by agents. Second, the psychological models of bounded rationality defined as Probabilistic Mental Models [GIG 96] emphasise that reasoning conducted in a 'fast and frugal' manner – following heuristics plausible for human minds – may give very good results when individuals act according to inferences regarding unknown properties of the world (such as the quality of a prospective union).

Following his 'fast and frugal' intuition, Todd [TOD 97] analyses the class of what he defines as Take the Next Best (TNB from now on) rules as simple heuristics for human mate search. Such rules are psychologically plausible, and they are based on modifications to the optimal solution – the so-called 'secretary', 'beauty contest' or 'dowry' problem. This has fostered a huge body of literature in applied probability since the 1960s, and it continues to be a topic for research into optimal behaviour [FRE 89, FER 89]. Applying these rules to the interviewing process, Seale and Rapoport [SEA 97] – who deal with the issue independently of Todd – define such heuristics as 'cutoff rules' and propose two supplementary families of rules.

TNB rules postulate to test a percentage, or number, of partners in what we can define as a 'learning' period and then to mate the first candidate who in the successive 'mating' period has a score higher than the highest score of the learning period. Todd shows by simulation that using TNB rules can give good results even when agents use shorter search times – in so far as a one-dimensional score for quality of the mate is concerned – with respect to the optimal solution. Similar

---

[1] Disclaimer: the views expressed in this paper are attributable to the author and do not necessarily reflect those of the Max Planck Institute for Demographic Research.

simulations [SEA 97] show that relatively small variations (which are, however, large for their interval) in the length of the learning period achieve a high level of 'effectiveness', i.e. they provide for a high payoff compared to the optimal one. Todd also shows that, when targeting someone other than the best candidate – for instance, a candidate from the best decile – shorter search times perform even better. It is interesting to note that Todd's example is quoted as the first example in Gilbert and Troitzsch [GIL 99] in order to underline the usefulness of simulation in the social sciences.

This paper addresses the issue of evaluating the performance of TNB rules against some of the central features of the demographic tradition. In particular, we deal with the aggregate-level consequences of such algorithms. The distribution of time at mating – where the basic time unit is defined as the length of the evaluation of a candidate – is the main feature we aim to reproduce using TNB rules. Demographers have shown that the bell shape of this distribution is one of the most regular features of human populations, and we investigate the shape of the distributions arising from TNB search algorithms. In addition, we are interested in studying the possibility that mating might not be exhaustive, that is, that not everybody finds a mate by the end of the process. The latter is another omnipresent feature of human populations, a sort of universal law of marriage.

Diekmann [DIE 89] distinguishes three broad categories of formal models explaining the regularity of the shape of the union formation curve. First, latent-state models, such as the one proposed by Coale and McNeil [COA 72], hypothesise that individuals – who are normally supposed to be homogeneous – pass through various stages. Second, one finds diffusion models in the literature, where mating happens by 'contagion' from other people already mated. Third, there are economic models based on search theory, where agents accept offers in heterogeneous ways. TNB rules are connected to the third kind of approach, even if the starting point is based not on rational choice assumptions but on bounded rational agents.

The paper is structured as follows. In Section 2, we briefly define the world we are considering and the TNB class of rules. In the following section, the rule is implemented in a simulated population of non-interacting agents who behave homogeneously as regards the length of the learning period. We show that the distribution is monotonically decreasing and that its shape can be formally proven to be decreasing with time. In Section 4, we introduce the hypothesis that agents are heterogeneous as regards the length of the learning period, and we show – using simulation – that in this case the bell-shaped marriage curve emerges under some conditions on the distribution of heterogeneity. Section 5 contains some final remarks. In particular, we sketch out the idea that bounded rational agents in mate selection are likely to have different degrees of 'fast and frugalness'.

2. Take the Next Best rules: learning by dating, mating by recalling

Let us now define the TNB rules and the world we are taking into account. The definition is slightly modified from the one proposed by Todd [TOD 97], so that we can account for the possibility that agents never mate. The context is as follows: one population of agents works as searcher, and a second population is composed of candidates to be sought.

The population of candidates is theoretically unlimited, and it can be ordered according to a single dimension, which we label 'attractiveness'. Attractiveness is independently and identically distributed according to a discrete uniform random variable, with values between 1 and a. Candidates are sequentially offered to the searching agents. In the paper we shall use $a=100$.

Searching agents follow this rule: examine the first n candidates, and memorise the maximum attractiveness x in the set of these candidates. For simplicity, we call this phase the 'learning period'. Starting from the $n+1$th candidate, choose as a mate the first candidate with attractiveness higher than x. We shall define this as the 'mating period'. If after t number of candidates no candidate has been met who satisfies the attractiveness condition, then no mating occurs. In this paper, we shall assume that a maximum number of $t+n=100$ candidates are encountered before the decision is made not to mate.

For the sake of simplicity, we shall hypothesise that the evaluation of each candidate takes the same amount of time, so that the number of candidates evaluated can be viewed as a time clock for each agent. It is then possible to call, for instance, n as the length of the learning period. The number of candidates totally evaluated before mating is then the time at mating.

The candidates are heterogeneous by definition, but this is of no interest to us. What is interesting is that in our world, we shall hypothesise that the searching agents might be heterogeneous as regards the length of the learning period.

3. Time at mating with homogeneous agents

Let us start by simulating the behaviour of 1,000 homogeneous agents, assuming varying lengths of the learning period. (We use Mathematica® as our platform for simulation and data analysis throughout the paper.) We can study, for instance, the proportion of people who ever enter a union (the so-called 'quantum' of the phenomenon in demography) as a function of n. The results show that the short learning times that have been suggested by Todd [TOD 97] give demographically plausible proportions of people ever entering unions (fig. 1). We then examine the frequency distribution of times at union formation.

The application of TNB rules never results in a bell-shaped frequency distribution at the level of the population of agents. In Fig. 2 we show the distribution that results when agents follow the rule $n=12$ ("take a dozen"). This result does not come about by chance. It can be easily proved formally, given the features of the random processes going on.

We now prove that under any kind of population of homogenous agents acting according to a TNB rule, the shape of the marriage curve is monotonically decreasing through time. For the sake of simplicity, we leave out the issue of the length of the mating period, allowing for an unlimited time for mating (which does not allow, however, for people who never mate). The idea is to examine the joint probability distribution of a bivariate random variable on the maximum attractiveness in the learning period and of the time at marriage. When the individuals are heterogeneous with respect to the length of the learning period, each individual observation is a realisation of this bivariate random variable, and it is thus relatively easy to study the shape of the probability distribution function as regards time at marriage.

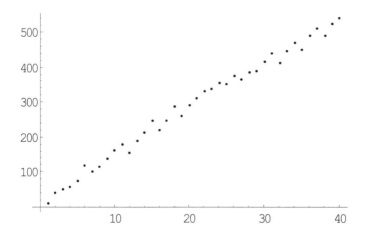

Figure 1. *Number of never-mated agents (out of 1,000) after 100 candidates, by number of candidates evaluated in the learning phase*

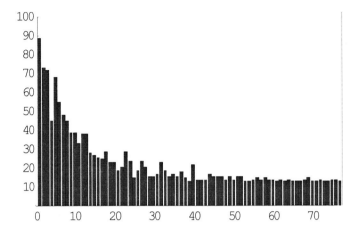

Figure 2. *Frequency distribution of the number of candidates evaluated before mating. The learning time is 12 candidates (i.e., mating can occur as of the 13th candidate). Population of 1,000 agents*

PROPOSITION. If in both the learning phase and the mating phase candidates are offered with a degree of attractiveness given by the realisation of i.i.d. discrete uniform random variables, $X_1, X_2, \ldots, X_n$ with support $[1, a]$ (where a is the maximum possible attractiveness of candidates) and mating takes place according to a TNB rule with a learning phase of n candidates, then the probability of mating decreases with the number of candidates evaluated in the mating phase.

PROOF. It is easy to see that the p.d.f. of the generic X_i in the support points $x=1,2,..,a$ and for $i=1,2,\ldots,n$, is

$$F_{X_i}(x;a) = \Pr\{X_i \leq x\} = a^{-1}x \qquad [1]$$

The reference value for mating is an extreme value statistic: the maximum of the n observed values for attractiveness in the learning case. Let us define this maximum as X. As it may be easily shown (Reiss and Thomas, 1997), the probability distribution function of X is

$$F_X(x;a,n) = \left[F_{X_i}(x;a)\right]^n = a^{-n}x^n \qquad [2]$$

so that, for $x=1,2,..,a$, the probability function of X is:

$$p_X(x;a,n) = \Pr\{X = x\} = a^{-n} \cdot \left[x^n - (x-1)^n\right] \qquad [3]$$

Now, let us define T as a discrete random variable representing the time at marriage. As the learning period is of length n, we can define a random variable representing time at marriage as $T=n+M$, where M is the number of candidates evaluated in the mating period up to the time of mating. As n is fixed and supposed to be a constant, for random properties we can focus on M only (this is the key point where the hypothesis that agents are homogeneous is used). We can factorise the joint probability function of X and M:

$$\Pr\{T = m + n, X = x\} = \Pr\{M = m, X = x\} = \Pr\{M = m | X = x\} \cdot \Pr\{X = x\}$$

When x is known, the probability of mating with the next candidate is constant and equal to

$$a^{-1}(a - x)$$ [4]

Conditional on X, M follows a geometric distribution and the joint distribution of M and X is thus

$$p_{MX}(m, x; a, n) = \Pr\{M = m, X = x\} = \left[a^{-1}x\right]^{m-1} a^{-1}(a - x) \cdot p_X(x; a, n)$$ [5]

which always decreases monotonically as a function of m for $m > 1$.

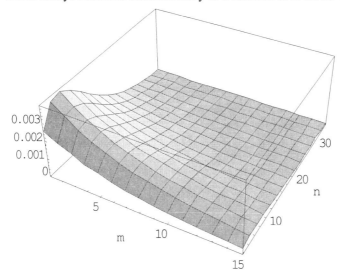

Figure 3. *Values of the probability function with varying m and n (x=85, a=100)*

In Fig. 3 we give a graphical representation of function [5], taking x and a as given. One can see that, for any choice of n, the probability decreases with m. The initial increase in n is due to the relatively high value chosen for x.

What can we learn from studying the case with homogeneous agents? On the one hand, the short search times seem to be able to account, in our framework, for a reasonable proportion of never-mated people. On the other hand, the concern about the use of TNB rules comes from the shape of the frequency distributions of the time at marriage. The shortcoming of the approach we just followed is that agents are homogeneous as far as their heuristic rules are concerned. However, heterogeneity cannot be ignored, because people simply take decisions such as getting married at different speeds and with different degrees of rational reasoning involved. Some individuals may wish to experience long learning periods and others may be prone to taking fast and frugal decisions, falling victim, for example, to 'love at first sight'. In general, it has been shown that in search behaviour some individuals use simple rules, while others follow more complex rules (see e.g. [SEA 97] and [SON 98]). We thus view homogeneity as a problem when it comes to the study of aggregate regularities. This is also evident when one considers the fact that the same TNB rule for each individual produces results that are not empirically plausible even at the qualitative level.

Various different specifications for heterogeneity are imaginable. For instance, individuals might follow different families of rules [SEA 97]. One might also assume that agents are heterogeneous as regards to the time they need to evaluate candidates. Nevertheless, here we shall limit ourselves to the case where the time spent learning varies, so that each agent follows an own TNB rule.

4. Time at mating with TNB rule followers heterogeneous in their learning times

Let us turn now to the case of a population of agents who are heterogeneous as regards the length of the learning period but who share their (TNB) rule-governed mating behaviour.

We model agent heterogeneity according to a discretised beta distribution with expanded domain. Formally, the length of the learning period now becomes a random variable N, the probability function of which is defined as:

$$p_N(n; \alpha, \beta, v) = \int_{(n-1)/v}^{n/v} \frac{(1-\xi)^{\beta-1} \xi^{\alpha-1}}{B(\alpha, \beta)} d\xi, \text{ for } n=1,2,\ldots,v \qquad [6]$$

The average of the distribution is

$$v\alpha(\alpha + \beta)^{-1}$$

and its variance is

$$v\alpha b(\alpha + b)^{-2}(\alpha + \beta + 1).$$

In order to evaluate the impact of different hypotheses on the distribution of mating times and on the proportion of never-mated, we ran simulations on 10,000 individuals, fixing the value of v, the maximum length of the learning period in the population, at 40, $\beta=1$ and letting α vary between 0.2 and 5, with steps of 0.2. So, the average length varies between 6+1/6 and 33+1/3.

In figure 4, we show the number of agents have not mated after 100 candidates (including the ones evaluated in the learning period) as a function of α. As one can see, qualitatively plausible proportions are produced for α less than or equal to about 1.2. The proportion of never-mated grows in a logarithmic fashion, and it reaches about 45% for $\alpha=5$. In fact, at that point its value is fairly similar to the value obtained for the homogeneous distribution with the same average value.

If one wishes to study the timing, one can look at the median number of candidates evaluated before mating as a function of α (fig. 5). This also grows in a logarithmic fashion, with a slightly lower slope.

It is then particularly interesting to look at the overall frequency distribution of mating times. We considered four cases here: $\alpha=0.4$; $\alpha=1$ (which, in fact, produces a discrete uniform distribution); $\alpha=2$; and $\alpha=5$. To make the composition of the population in each of these cases simpler to grasp, we represent the frequency distribution of the length of the learning time (i.e. the realisation of the random variable [6]) in Fig. 6.

The main results for the four examples are reported in Fig. 7. One can see that the distribution decreases monotonically until $\alpha=1$ if one disregards random variability. Then, the traditional bell shape emerges. There are thus some values of α that produce both a plausible proportion of never-mated and a bell-shaped distribution. This happens between $\alpha=1$ (with the uniform distribution of length of the learning period and an average number of 20 candidates) and $\alpha=2$ (with a right-skewed distribution for the learning period and an average number of 26+2/3 candidates).

What we might thus gather from this exercise is that TNB rules can produce qualitatively plausible results on the distribution of time at mating under the hypothesis that agents have learning times of varying lengths.

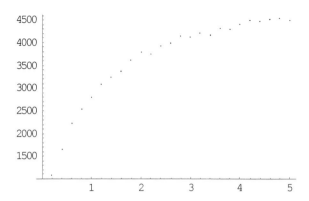

Figure 4. *The number of never mated agents (out of 10,000) after 100 candidates, assuming the values α=3 (ν=40, β=1).*

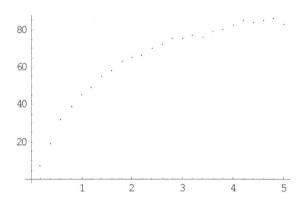

Figure 5. *Median number of candidates evaluated before mating, assuming the values α=3 (ν=40, β=1).*

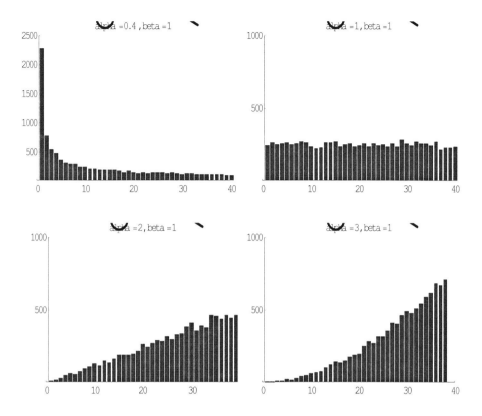

Figure 6. *Frequency distribution of the length of the learning period in the simulated population of 10,000 agents.*

5. Conclusions and discussions

We have seen that peculiar aggregate regularities of the demography of first marriage may be reconstructed starting from 'fast and frugal' search algorithms with heterogeneous agents. This is indeed a starting point.

It seems important to introduce explicitly the interaction between individuals as a topic for future research. Individual search histories are important factors in the search for a mate and they can be used to investigate specific situations. The role of time (or the number of previous partners) also merits further attention: the satisficing level might change (presumably it will decrease) as time goes by. There might be, for instance, social norms stating that 'who marries late marries ill' [HER 72] and they might influence the threshold value for the acceptance of a partner.

It might also be interesting to consider investigating whether search behaviour might be represented by simple heuristics. This is a difficult issue for empirical investigation, of course, and qualitative research might be the only answer.

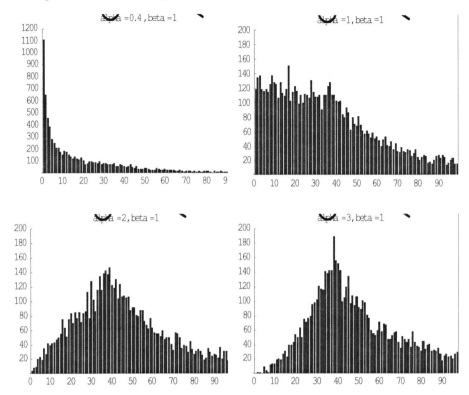

Figure 7. *Frequency distribution of the number of candidates evaluated before mating in a population of 10,000 heterogeneous agents with learning time distributed according to a discretised beta distribution with expanded domain*

In general, we feel that scholars using a demographic approach stand much to gain by studying decision processes in artificial societies – even in very simplified societies such as the one we have built here. This sentiment has been explicitly mentioned in the literature: in the 'artificial societies' community by Epstein and Axtell [EPS 96] and in the demographic community by Burch [BUR 99]. But there is also plenty of room for feedback in the other direction as well. A demographic perspective could provide precious hints about how to evaluate the behavioural hypotheses underlying the 'mental models' used in modelling the behaviour of agents.

Acknowledgements

The author would like to thank Karl Brehmer for language editing.

Bibliographic references

[BUR 99] BURCH T.K., "Computer Modelling of Theory: Explanation for the 21st Century", Discussion Paper no 99-4, Population Studies Centre, University of Western Ontario, London, ON, 1999.

[COA 72] COALE A.J., MCNEIL D.R., "The distribution by age of the frequency of first marriage in a female cohort", *Journal of the American Statistical Association*, 1972, 67, p. 743-749.

[DIE 89] DIEKMANN A., "Diffusion and Survival Models for the Process of Entry into Marriage", *Journal of Mathematical Sociology*, 1989, 14, p. 31-44.

[EPS 96} EPSTEIN J.M., AXTELL R., *Growing Artificial Societies. Social Science from the Bottom Up*, Brookings Institutions Press, Washington, DC, 1996.

[HER 72] HERNES G., "The Process of Entry into First Marriage", *American Sociological Review*, 1972, 37, p. 173-182.

[FER 89] FERGUSON T.S., "Who Solved the Secretary Problem?", *Statistical Science*, 1989, 4, p. 282-296.

[FRE 83] FREEMAN P.R., "The Secretary Problem and its Extensions: A Review", *International Statistical Review*, 1983, 51, p. 189-206.

[FRE 96] FREY B.S, EICHENBERGER R., "Marriage Paradoxes", *Rationality and Society*, 1996, 8, p. 187-206.

[GIG 96] GIGERENZER G., GOLDSTEIN D.G., "Reasoning the Fast and Frugal Way: Models of Bounded Rationality", *Psychological Review*, 1996, 103, p. 650-669.

[GIL 99] GILBERT N., TROITZSCH K.G., *Simulation for the Social Scientist*, Open University Press, Buckingham-Philadelphia, 1999.

[REI 97] REISS R.D., THOMAS M., *Statistical Analysis of Extreme Values*, Birkhäuser, Basel, 1997.

[ROT 90], ROTH A.E., SOTOMAYOR M.A.O., *Two-Sided Matching. A study in Game-Theoretic Modeling and Analysis*, Cambridge University Press, Cambridge, 1990.

[SEA 97] SEALE D.A., RAPOPORT A., "Sequential Decision Making with Relative Ranks: An Experimental Investigation of the "Secretary Problem"", *Organizational Behavior and Human Decision Processes*, 1997, 69, p. 221-236.

[SON 98] SONNEMANS J., "Strategies of search", *Journal of Economic Behavior & Organization*, 1998, 35, p. 309-332.

[TOD 97] TODD P.M., 1997, "Searching for the next best mate", in CONTE R., HEGSELMANN R. AND TERNA P. (eds.), *Simulating Social Phenomena*, Springer-Verlag, Berlin.

Modeling the temporal coordination of behavior and internal states

Andrzej Nowak* — Robin R. Vallacher**
Wojciech Borkowski*

* Warsaw University
** Florida Atlantic University

One of the key phenomena that distinguish couples and social groups from mere collections of individuals is the coordination of individual thoughts, feelings, and actions that occurs in social interaction. The importance of coordination for social relations is reflected in common wisdom, where individuals who are connected by a satisfying social relationship are often termed to "be on the same wavelength" or to "resonate with one another," whereas those in a problematic relationship are said to be "out of synch with each other." Coordination may take many different forms and involve different specific mechanisms. In organizations, for example, the coordination of individual actions is of the primary concern, since the productivity of the group depends to a high degree on the quality of coordination of individual actions. In close relationships, on the other hand, coordination of feelings and thoughts may be more important since it directly affects the degree of satisfaction with the relationship. The lack of synchrony and mutual understanding is a source of dissatisfaction in marriages and other close relationships. Despite the wide variety of phenomena associated with coordination, there is reason to believe that many aspects of coordination are invariant across phenomena.

In the social sciences, as well as in the computer simulation literature, temporal coordination of individual dynamics has received much less attention than coordination of states of individuals. In the social sciences, issues of coordination have often been reframed in terms of social orientations such as orientation to individual vs. group outcome, cooperation vs. competition, or compatibility of values, goals, and plans. In the computer simulation tradition, on the other hand, most research has investigated either the emergence and resultant features of equilibrium states (e.g Hegselman 1996, Nowak Latane & Szamrej 1990), or temporal properties of the dynamics of a global group properties. The issues of temporal coordination of dynamics of individual system's dynamics have received considerable attention in the natural sciences (Kenako, 1991), however, where models of coupled dynamical systems have been employed to study coordination.

In the present paper, we propose a framework for modeling coordination phenomena in social relationships. We argue that coupled non-linear systems may serve as models of temporal coordination of individual dynamics in social groups and social relations. We use the simplest dynamical systems capable of chaotic behavior—logistic equations or coupled maps—to study the temporal aspects of coordination of individual dynamics. We study how coordination changes as a function of changes in the strength of influence between individuals, and in the degree of similarity of their internal states.

The Nature of Coordination

In its most basic form, coordination refers to the synchronization of behavior. This aspect of interpersonal coordination has been investigated in the context of movement coordination (e.g., Beek & Hopkins, 1992; Schmidt, Beek, Treffner, & Turvey, 1991; Turvey, 1990). In this line or research, individuals are simply asked to swing their legs. One of them swings his or her legs in time to a metronome and the other person tries to match those movements. Two form of coordination are of most interest: synchronization in-phase, with people swinging their legs in unison, and synchronization in anti-phase, with people swinging their legs with the same frequency but in the opposite direction. When subjects are instructed to synchronize out-of-phase and the frequency of movement increases, at some tempo they are no longer able to synchronize in this manner and they switch their synchronization mode to in-phase. Hysteresis, which is a sign of non-linear dynamical systems, is also commonly observed (cf. Kelso, 1995). When the tempo decreases again, at some value they are able to reestablish anti-phase coordination, but this tempo is significantly lower than the point at which they originally started to synchronize in-phase.

Coordination of more complex forms of motor behavior may be captured by a method developed by Newtson (1994; Newtson et al., 1987). The basic idea in Newtson's approach is measuring the intensity of behavior in an interval of time. He assigns a single point for each body part that moves during the interval. Moving a hand, for example, would correspond to a single point. Sitting down, meanwhile, would correspond to many points because several body parts change their configuration. It turns out that human motor behavior correspond to *waves*. Initial isolated movements (low scores) gradually combine and build to massive movements corresponding to high scores, which then dissolve back into isolated movements. When two people interact, the behavior of each of them may be represented as a wave. One can thus describe the interaction as a temporal relation between the respective waves representing the movements of each person. When performing a common task (such as carrying a case), the movements of individuals may be synchronized in-phase. When they are engaged in conversation, on the other hand, individuals tend to alternate their speaking turns in a simple anti-phase pattern.

Coordination between individuals extends beyond synchronization of behavior to include the internal states of the respective individuals. Some of these internal states are variable, such as arousal or mood. Others, however, are more enduring properties of the person, such as temperament, personality traits, values, goals, and plans. Synchronization that transcends behavior is characteristic for individuals in close relationships. The coordination of internal states is commonly referred to as sharing values, empathy, perspective-taking, and emotional compatibility. Although everyone would agree on the importance of coordination of internal states in social relations, it is far from obvious how the coordination of internal states is achieved. A person's values, after all, cannot be directly observed in the same was as motor behavior, and signals of emotional states may be quite subtle.

There is linkage between the coordination of internal states and the coordination of overt behavior. When the internal parameters of two people are set at similar values, minimal cues about the other person's behavior are needed to maintain behavioral and mental coordination. It is much easier, after all to coordinate with people with whom we share common values and to coordinate with happy people when we are in a good mood, but with angry people when we are in a mood to fight. There is evidence that people tend to match the expected mood of a future interaction partner, even if this means intentionally changing their current mood from happiness to sadness (Erber, Wegner, & Thierrault, 1996). If, however, the settings of the internal parameters of two people are very different, the maintenance of behavioral coordination is difficult, since the intrinsic dynamics of each system are very different.

The quality of coordination is related to the quality of relationships, such that positive interactions are associated with smooth coordination between participants (Tickle-Degnen & Rosenthal, 1987; McGrath & Kelly, 1986). This essentially means that an individual synchronizes to the rhythms and movements of another person with whom he or she has a positive relationship. On the other hand, it seems likely that synchronization facilitates the development of positive relationships, and that the lack of coordination has disruptive effects on relationships. Berscheid (1983), for example, has observed that the emotional quality of a relationship is often not revealed until severe disruption of coordination occurs.

Modeling the Coordination of Dynamics

The dual nature of coordination, involving both the coordination on the level of behavior and the level of internal states, may be captured within the framework of coupled dynamical systems, as developed within the physical sciences. Historically, coupled oscillators provided the formal model of coordination. Coupled chaotic systems, however, have captured more attention recently, because they can capture a richer variety of synchronization phenomena. The simplest example of synchronizing chaotic dynamical systems is provided by coupled logistic equations, also referred to as coupled logisitic maps. Depending on the value of its control parameter, each equation by itself may display qualitatively different types of behavior, from simple fixed-point attractors to periodic regimes of differing periods to deterministic chaos. It has been shown that when the value of the dynamical variable (x) for one equation depends not only on its previous value but also to some degree on the value of x for the other equation, the two equations tend to synchronize (Kaneko, 1989, 1993; Shinbrot, 1994). This basic property has been used as a prototype for understanding synchronization underlying different collective processes in physics, chemistry, and biology (cf. Shinbrot, 1994).

When used to model synchronization between individuals, the dynamics of each interaction partner is represented by two variables of a logistic equation: a dynamical variable, x, and a control parameter, *lambda*. The time evolution of the dynamical variable, x, corresponds to the dynamics of the person's behavior. In the absence of external influences (e.g., an interaction partner), the next value of x depends on the value of x at the previous moment in time according to the equation and therefore the time evolution of x reflects intrinsic dynamics. The type of intrinsic dynamics depends on the value of the control parameter, *lambda*. Increases in the value of *lambda* (up to the value of 4.0) generally result in increased complexity of the system's time evolution. For values of *lambda* between 0 and approximately 2.95, the system evolves toward a fixed-point attractor. For values between 2.95 and approximately 3.56, the system displays periodic behavior with periods increasing in a period-doubling manner. Above this value, the system behaves chaotically, with increasing complexity. As noted above, *lambda* corresponds to internal mental and emotional states that initiate and regulate behavior.

Because interaction partners obviously influence each other, there is reciprocal influence between the respective dynamics of the partners. The state of each partner depends not only his or her preceding state but also on the preceding state of the other person. As discussed above, each person can influence the other either on the level of behavior (dynamical variable, x) or at the level of internal states (control parameter, *lambda*). By influencing one another on the level of behavior, the partners can achieve momentary coordination, whereas by matching the values of their respective control parameters, the partners achieve similarity with respect to prolonged patterns of behavior (e.g., periodic behavior of a given frequency, chaotic behavior with given complexity and irregularity, etc.). Despite the obvious simplifications, this model can feature some emergent properties of individuals in relationships, where each individual is modeled as a separate system that strives for coordination.

To say that the members of a relationship influence each other means that the behavior of one member impinges on the behavior of the other member. Formally, such influence is introduced by the assumption that the behavior of each partner in the next moment in time depends to a certain degree on the behavior of the other partner at the preceding moment in time. The coupling is done in a simple way, according to the following equation:

$$x_1(t+1) = \frac{r_1 x_1(t)(1-x_1(t)) + \alpha r_2 x_2(t)(1-x_2(t))}{1+\alpha}$$

$$x_2(t+1) = \frac{r_2 x_2(t)(1-x_2(t)) + \alpha r_1 x_1(t)(1-x_1(t))}{1+\alpha}$$

To the value of the dynamical variable representing one's own behavior (x_1), one adds a fraction, denoted by *alpha*, of the value of the dynamical variable representing the behavior of the partner (x_2). The size of this fraction (*alpha*) corresponds to the strength of coupling and reflects the closeness or mutual interdependency of the relationship. When the fraction is 0, there is no coupling on the behavior level, whereas a value of 1.0 corresponds to the situation where one's own behavior is determined equally by one's preceding behavior and the preceding behavior of the partner. Intermediate values of *alpha* correspond to intermediate values of coupling.

When the control parameters of coupled systems have the same value, the dependence between their respective dynamical variables will cause the maps to coordinate fully, so that the values of x_1 and x_2 become identical (e.g., Kaneko, 1984). Our first simulation investigated how the coordination of dynamical variables (corresponding to behavior of individuals) depends on the similarity of control parameters (corresponding to internal states) and the strength of coupling (corresponding to the strength of influence between individuals).

The control parameter for one map (corresponding to one partner) was held constant at a value of 3.6, which corresponds to low levels of chaotic behavior. We systematically varied the value of the control parameter for the other partner between values of 3.6 and 4.0, which corresponds to the highest value of the chaotic regime. The value of the control parameter for the second map is represented on the vertical axis on the graph below. We should note that since the value of the control map for the first map is fixed, the vertical axis in effect corresponds to the difference between the control parameters of the respective maps. We also systematically varied the strength of the coupling between the maps, between values of 0 and .3. The horizontal axis corresponds to this variable. Each point on the graph thus corresponds to a unique combination of the difference in control parameters and strength of coupling. We used 900 divisions along the vertical axis and 1,024 divisions along the horizontal axis, so the graph portrays the results of 921,600 simulations. Each simulation, in turn, consisted of 800 steps.

Mean difference in relationships L1:3.67 L2:3.67+0.33 Alpha:0+0.36 x1,x2:RAND(0..1)

Figure 1a. *Mean difference between values of dynamical variables coming from two coupled chaotic systems (coupled logistic equations). X axis corresponds to the strength of coupling varying from 0 to .36. Y axis corresponds to the difference between the control parameters of the two respective systems. The darker is the color, the smaller is the difference*

For each simulation, we started from a random value of the dynamical variables for each person, drawn from a uniform distribution that varied from 0 to 1. We let the two coupled systems run for 300 steps, so that each system had a chance to come close to its attractor and both systems had a chance to synchronize. For the next 500 simulation steps, we recorded the values of the dynamical variables for each system and computed the difference between them. The color of each point on this graph corresponds to the value of the mean difference, with white representing maximal difference, black representing no difference, and levels of gray representing intermediate differences.

The main result is pretty straightforward and corresponds to intuitions expressed in the previous section. The larger the difference between the respective control parameters, the stronger the coupling required to maintain full synchrony. When two people have substantially different moods, temperaments, and so forth, their intrinsic dynamics would cause them to drift toward different patterns of behavior, so strong mutual influence is necessary to maintain synchrony. Therefore, for low levels of coupling (*alpha* < .15), the black region of the graph, which corresponds to full synchrony (i.e., a difference close to 0), ends abruptly, indicating a sudden change in synchronization. For relatively strong mutual influence, as reflected in high values of coupling (around .), full synchronization in-phase is possible even for systems characterized by very different values of their respective control parameters. The strength of the coupling, in other words, can compensate for the lack of similarity in internal states between the relationship partners.

This suggests that if two people are highly dissimilar in their settings of internal parameters, they may nonetheless achieve a fair degree of coordination by directly influencing one another's behavior. In this case, however, there is a strong potential for instability in the relationship. As soon as the behavioral influence is broken, the dynamics of the two people will immediately diverge. If there is a high degree of similarity in the setting of control parameters, however, synchronization will be preserved for some time. Moreover, even if the behaviors do not synchronize in time, the overall form of their respective dynamics will remain similar, so that re-coordination with respect to behavior at a later time will be relatively easy.

Closer inspection of Figure 1a .reveals that the relationship between the difference in control parameters and the strength of coupling becomes much more complex at low values of coupling. This region is characterized by the appearance of the light triangular shape. For small differences in control parameters (at the bottom of the light triangle), the two maps can either synchronize or fail to do so, depending on the initial values of the respective dynamical variables (x). This region is therefore characterized by a mixture of light points (indicating low and even negative correlation in behavior) and dark points (indicating high positive correlation in behavior). In the light triangle, the two maps synchronize in periodic behavior of different periods, with the value of one dynamical variable negatively related to the value of the other. It is interesting that in this region, coupling between maps performs the function of the control of chaos, a phenomenon defined by Ott, Grebogi, and York (1990). Each map separately would evolve chaotically for those values of control parameters. By virtue of their coupling, however, the evolution of each becomes quite regular, such that it adopts only a limited number of states arranged in an orderly manner. In this region, then, the behavior of a dyad is qualitatively different than the behavior of each person. This demonstrates how entering a relationship may perform stabilizing functions for one or both of the partners. This form of coordination may occur even for vast differences between control parameters. Figure 1b shows systems that evolve on periodic orbits. Black regions correspond to non-periodic evolution, and lighter points to systems that evolve periodically. The lighter the color of the point, the smaller the period.

Period of relationships L1:3.67 L2:3.67+0.33 Alpha:0+0.36 x1,x2:RAND(0..1)   ■

Figure 1b. *Periodic structures in coupled logistic equations. The bright points corresponds to short periods. As a result of coordination two chaotic systems can evolve on periodic orbits*

For very small values of coupling (to the left of the light triangle), each map generally evolves independently of the other. For somewhat larger values of coupling (on the periphery of the light triangle), the two systems can achieve complex modes of coordination, such that they seem to function as a single higher order system. Finally, for medium values of coupling and large discrepancies in control parameters (far to the right of the light triangle), the coordination of behavior consists mainly of the individuals establishing the range for each other's behavior. One cannot have a high value of x when the other has a low value of x.

In the series of graphs below (Fig. 2), different types of coordination of behavior obtained in the simulations are portrayed. These types in general correspond to the types of coordination described above. Each picture portrays the coordination between two maps with two control parameters and coupled at a specific level. Each picture is a scatter-plot of the values of the respective dynamical variables from two coupled maps, and shows the value of both maps at 10,000 consecutive simulation steps. The horizontal axis corresponds to the values of x for one person and the vertical axis corresponds to the values of *x* for the other person.

The straight line displayed in Picture A indicates perfect correlation between the two people, reflecting complete synchronization of their behavior. Picture B shows a high correlation, such that one system serves to limit the values of the other system in a linear manner. The scatter-plot of points in Picture C indicates a lack of correlation in the behavior of the two systems. Picture D provides an example of a nonlinear pattern emerging from some complex mode of coordination between maps.

X1[0] ver X2[0]. lambda1=3.67 lambda2=3.68355 alpha=0.34596 x1[0]=0.691959 x2[0]=0.900486

Figure 2a.

X1[0] ver X2[0]. lambda1=3.67 lambda2=3.92238 alpha=0.32184 x1[0]=0.971817 x2[0]=0.760799

Figure 2b.

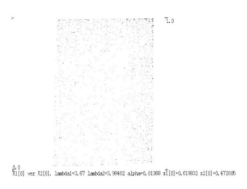

X1[0] ver X2[0]. lambda1=3.67 lambda2=3.98402 alpha=0.01368 x1[0]=0.619832 x2[0]=0.472905

Figure 2c.

X1[0] ver X2[0]. lambda1=3.67 lambda2=3.91976 alpha=0.15768 x1[0]=0.675184 x2[0]=0.498025

Figure 2d.

It is interesting that for relatively high values of coupling, the predominant mode of coordination is synchrony and what varies is primarily the strength of the synchrony. For low values of coupling, however, different modes of coordination are possible. In addition to synchrony, systems may display asynchrony, independence, stabilization, and other complex forms of coordination. In general, for weak couplings there seem to be a richer repertoire of modes of coordination available.

Modeling the direct coordination of control parameters could, in principle, be relatively straightforward. All one needs to assume is that on each simulation step, the values of each person's control parameter drifts somewhat in the direction of the value of the partner's control parameter. The rate of this drift and the size of the initial discrepancy between the values of the respective control parameters determine how quickly the control parameters begin to match. As we noted above, however, direct observation of internal states of interaction partner may be difficult, or even impossible in some cases. Control parameters, however, may be coordinated on the basis of observation of partner's behavior. Zochowski and Liebowitch (1997) have demonstrated this form of coordination for coupled maps. In this form of coupling, each individual attempts to modify the value of his or her own control parameter to match the overall pattern of behavior of the other person. The exact value of the control parameter is invisible to the interaction partner. Each person, however, remembers the set of most recent behaviors (i.e., the most recent values of *x*) of both oneself and the partner. If the pattern of observed behaviors of the partner is more complex than the pattern of one's own behavior, the individual slightly increases the value of his or her own control parameter, *alpha*. If the partner's behavior is less complex than one's own behavior, on the other hand, the person decreases slightly the value of his or her own control parameter, *alpha*. This suggests that if we can follow the dynamics of the person with only minimal behavioral cues from the other person, it is a sign that the values of our control parameters correspond to the values of the other person.

In the graph below (Fig. 3), we show how the coordination between two maps develops over time as they progressively match one another's control parameters in the manner described above. This simulation was run for relatively weak coupling (*alpha*=.2). The x-axis corresponds to time in simulation steps, and the y-axis portrays the value of the difference between the control parameters of the two respective maps. Over time, the two maps perfectly synchronize their behavior, as the difference between their respective control parameters decreases. Note that the evolution of the difference in control parameters covaries with the difference in dynamical variables.

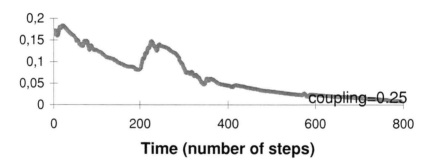

Diference between control parameters for two synchronizing maps

Time (number of steps)

Figure 3.

Other simulations have shown that for a stronger value of coupling (*alpha*=.7) coordination in behavior develops almost immediately, but the control parameters fail to synchronize, even after 1,000 simulation steps. This is because strong coupling causes full synchronization of behavior even for maps with quite different control parameters. Once the behavior is in full synchrony, the two maps do not have a clue that there control parameters are different. This, of course, would become immediately apparent if the coupling was removed—the dynamics of the two respective maps would immediately diverge. This suggests that attempting behavioral synchronization with weak levels of influence and control over one another's behavior will facilitate matching of one another's internal states. Using too strong an influence to obtain coordination of behavior, on the other hand, may effectively hinder coordination at a deeper level.

The above considerations suggest that there is an optimal level of influence and control over behavior in close relationships. Too weak an influence may lead to a lack of coordination, whereas too strong an influence may prevent the development of the relationship into one that is based on mutual understanding and empathy. The observation that high values of coupling restrict the range of possible modes of coordination suggests that intricate types of coordination are difficult when people strongly control one another's behavior. Too strong a coupling may therefore result in a relationship that is experienced as highly predictable and therefore boring. By the same token, relationships may have very rich dynamics and switch between different modes of coordination when the influence between the partners is not very strong. In a newly formed relationship, for example, the dynamics and coordination phenomena may be very surprising for both partners. On balance, the most desirable degree of coupling is one that allows for effective coordination, but keeps direct influence at a relatively low level.

Modeling Bi-directional Causality

Since similarity provides a basis for forming relationships, it enhances the opportunity for influence. And since influence occurs mostly among people located close to each other in social space (Nowak, Szamrej, & Latane, 1990), attraction is likely to increase the degree of similarity among relationship partners. This bi-directional effect can take on the function of a positive feedback loop, such that similarity promotes greater attraction and greater attraction serves to decrease distance in social space. This bi-directional causality provides the basic mechanism for the dynamic model of similarity-attraction described below. This model integrates two seemingly conflicting findings about the predictors of interpersonal attraction. Newcomb (1961) showed that propinquity was the best predictor of attraction. This perspective resonates well with findings of Bossard (1932), who found that 50% of married couples lived within one block of one another prior to their marriage. Propinquity provides for exposure, which in turn paves the way for influence. Influence, meanwhile, provides the means by which similarity between people is increased.

Bi-directionality can be captured in terms of the synchronization of maps, as developed by Zochowski & Liebowitch (1997). As noted earlier, individuals can adjust their own control parameters to match the behavior or others with whom they have a relationship. To model the bi-directional nature of similarity and attraction within this general framework, we assume that each individual changes his or her control parameters in an attempt to match the dynamics of behavior of the relationship partner. The strength of this tendency is proportional to the strength of the relationship. Second, individuals tend to strengthen those relationships involving partners with similar dynamics, indicative of similarity in control parameters, and tend to weaken those relationships that involve partners with different dynamics, indicative of dissimilarity in control parameters.

To build a simulation model, we start with a set of individuals, each of whom is represented as a logistic map. In the beginning, the value of control parameter, *lambda*, and of the behavior, x, are set at random values. Each individual is located in a random cell of a 2-dimensional grid which represents social space. The notion of social space captures elements of both physical propinquity, providing for exposure to other individuals (Hall, 1966; Hilliard & Penn, 1992), and psychological closeness, providing for strength of the relationship (cf. Lewin, 1936). The strength of influence between persons A and B corresponds to their proximity in this grid.

There are two kinds of dynamics in this simulation. The first kind is related to the coordination of dynamics. All individuals, as described in the equation from the previous section, attempt to couple their behavior with that of others. Formally, the individuals are portrayed as coupled maps, and the strength between the x values of any two coupled maps is inversely proportional to the square of the distance between them. Each individual is therefore most strongly coupled with those who are nearby in social space. Each individual also attempts to achieve a match with others at the level of control parameters. This is done by comparing the dynamics of own and partner behaviors in the manner described in the previous section. The tendency for this type of coordination also decreases as the square of the distance between individuals.

The second type of dynamics consists in adjusting the strength of the relationship on the basis of similarity in dynamics. This is achieved by allowing individuals to relocate in the social space—that is, move in the simulation matrix. In each simulation step, every individual is provided with an opportunity to adjust his or her relationships with others. This adjustment is represented as the change of position (i.e, movement) in the social space, and is generated by a simply optimizing algorithm. Each individual computes a stress function for the position they currently occupy and all the neighboring positions (i.e., 8 grids--four to the side and the four corners). The value of stress is increased by dissimilar others and decreased by similar others. The rule for relocation is similar to that proposed by Gardner (1988). The relative impact of each partner decreases with the square of the distance. As a result, individuals tend to move toward similar individuals and away from individuals who display different dynamics. The value of stress is the sum of dissimilarity of dynamics with a given person divided by the square of the distance from that person.

Figure 5 shows the typical course of a simulation. The circles represent individuals, with the size of the circle corresponding to the value of the control parameter, *lambda*, and the color of the circle corresponding to the current value of the behavior, x. Figure 4a shows the beginning of the simulation, 4b shows the state of the system after 50 simulation steps, and 4c shows a near-equilibrium stage reached after 400 steps. To track the fate of individuals over time, each circle is represented by a number. Note two main results. Initially, there is no coordination with respect to either behavior or control parameters. Over time, however, strong coordination develops with respect to control parameters. Individuals with similar *lambdas* tend to migrate toward each other and synchronize their respective behaviors and control parameters. Over time, strong coordination develops for close individuals but not for individuals who are located far away from each other. This happens, first of all, because individuals located nearby tend to influence each other, which leads to synchronization and increased similarity in dynamics. Second, individuals with similar dynamics tend to migrate toward each other and thus set the stage for further influence.

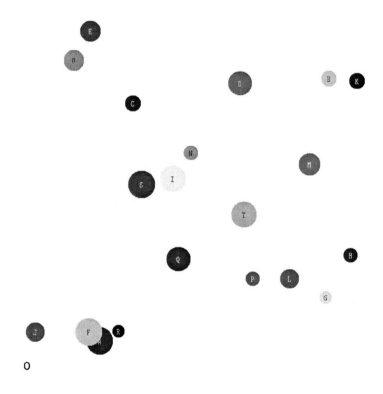

Figure 4a.

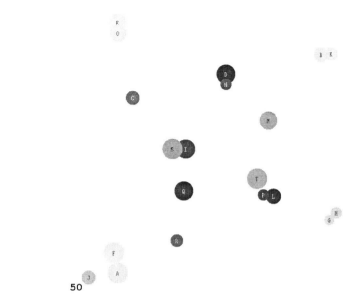

Figure 4b.

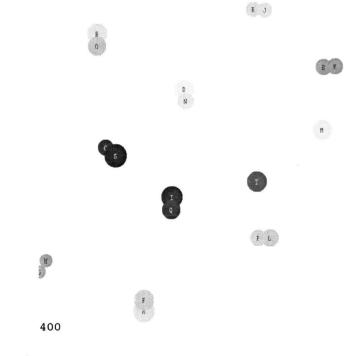

Figure 4c.

Note that the final configuration consists almost entirely of dyads. There is nothing in the design of the simulation to directly prevent the formation of larger groups. Larger groups do in fact form at intermediate steps, but they tend to be unstable and break up. We should note that at other settings of simulation parameters (e.g., strength of attraction, rate of change in *lambdas*, etc.), larger groups may form and remain stable. At yet other settings, rich dynamics may be observed when larger groups achieve temporary coordination. In such situations, however, some individuals may fail to coordinate and this lack of coordination may reflect on other individuals and thereby break up the groups of which they are a part. These individuals then migrate to other groups and repeat the pattern of group dissolution and regrouping. In general, we feel that this formalism provides a very rich metaphor for studying the evolution of groups as well as close relationships. It remains for subsequent work to identify the conditions responsible for different scenarios in this approach.

To show the bi-directional nature of this relationship, we ran four more sets of simulations, each consisting of 50 simulations. The first set was intended to establish a baseline against which the three others could be compared. The fourth set of simulations correspond to the basic model in which individuals both migrate in social space and change their respective control parameters. Each of the two middle sets investigated one causal direction of the similarity-attraction relationship. In the second set of simulations, individuals were allowed to change their control parameters but they could not move in social space, whereas in the third set, individuals were allowed to change their position but could not change their control parameters.

For each set of simulations, we compared results for nearby individuals and those located further apart. This allowed us to see how individuals in close proximity coordinate in comparison to individuals who are at different locations. The first graph (Fig. 5a) portrays the mean differences in the values of *lambda* for pairs of individuals. Note that coordination of internal states (control parameters) is enhanced both by changing position and changing control parameters. The maximum benefit, however, is observed when individuals have the opportunity to change both their location and their internal state. This is the only condition in which some global coordination develops, such that individuals located far apart match their control parameters to a certain degree. This is the effect of past adjustments to many group members. This would suggest that the process of mixing with different individuals in social space tends to enhance coordination at the level of the whole group.

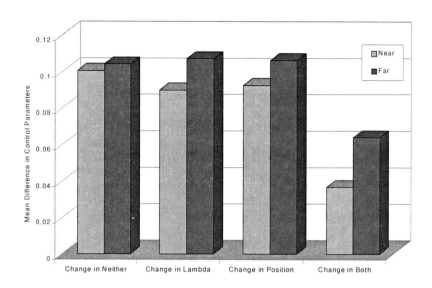

Figure 5a. *Mean difference in control parameters for coordinating logistic equations located close to each other, and far away, in four experimental conditions*

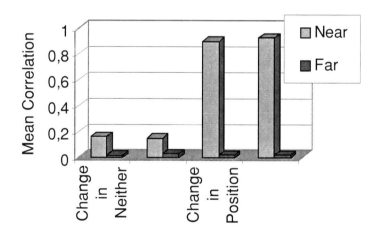

Figure 5b. *Mean correlation of values of dynamical variables for coordinating logistic equations located close to each other, and far away, in four experimental conditions*

The second graph (Fig. 5b) portrays coordination on the level of behavior. The height of the bars represents the magnitude of the mean correlation coefficient between the dynamical variables for pairs of individuals rather than the difference in value between the variables. In contrast to previous graphs, then, high bars reflect strong coordination. The difference measure allows one to portray the momentary level of coordination at each step. It is thus a good measure for portraying the time evolution of coordination. The correlation measure, which is based on 50 consecutive simulation steps, is more reliable but cannot be computed for less than 50 steps and is relatively insensitive to momentary changes in coordination. The highest coordination occurred in the bi-directional condition. Coordination at close to this level was also obtained when individuals could change their positions in social space. Changes in control parameters alone did not provide for increased coordination in behavior. We should note this particular result reflects the relatively distant locations of individuals in the social space, such that individuals are rarely located in sufficient proximity to promote the level of coupling characteristic of close relationships. Recall that when coupling is sufficient, convergence in *lambdas* does indeed lead to the development of coordination in behavior.

Conclusions

This model provides a perspective for viewing the stability and change in individual patterns of relationships. The fact that people are shaped by their relationship partners underlies the tendency to maintain a sustained pattern in forming relationships. The settings of one's internal states bears the marks of previous attempts at coordination. On the other hand, people choose partners on the basis of similarity with respect to their characteristic patterns of thoughts, feelings, and behavior. In consequence, people may look for relationship partners whose dynamics are similar to that of their previous partners. Prolonged exposure to individuals with different characteristics may destabilize such patterns. When subjected to prolonged influence from such people, individuals may come to adjust their own internal states and thereby increase similarity to them, creating the potential for increased attraction and the development of a close relationship.

We stress that this work is in its beginning stages and thus one must exercise caution when generalizing the results to human relationships. Some parallels, however, are quite striking. The fact that strong influence can compensate for differences in intrinsic dynamics, for example, resonates well with intuitions regarding control in close relationships. Clearly, before fully accepting these results as applicable to human intimate relationships, one needs to perform empirical tests with actual relationships. Computer simulations may help to generate the hypotheses to be tested, and they can highlight those phenomena (e.g., modes of coordination and transitions between them) that are worthy of special attention.

Some of the coordination phenomena occurring in real social relations may be specific for humans and be due to social and cultural norms, social motives and orientations of interacting individuals, or even to biological properties of human organisms. Some other phenomena, however, may by generic to different types of coordinating systems. Computer simulations may help us to discover the generic types of phenomena, but empirical research with human subjects is needed to decide which findings may be extended to interacting individuals.

References

Beek, P. J. & Hopkins, B. (1992). Four requirements for a dynamical systems approach to the development of social coordination. *Human Movement Science, 11*, 425-442.

Berscheid, E. (1983). Emotion. In H. H. Kelley et al. (Eds.), *Close relationships* (pp. 110-168). New York: W. H. Freeman.

Byrne, D., Clore, G. L., & Smeaton, G. (1986). The attraction hypothesis: Do similar attitudes affect anything? *Journal of Personality and Social Psychology, 51*, 1167-1170.

Erber, R., Wegner, D. M., & Thierrault, N. (1996). On being cool and collected: Mood regulation in anticipation of social interaction. *Journal of Personality and Social Psychology, 70*, 757-766.

Gardner, E. (1988). The space of interactions in neural network models. *Journal of Physics A, 21*, 257-270.

Hall, E. T. (1966). *The hidden dimension*. New York: Doubleday.

Hilliard & Penn, 1992 *The Social Logic of Space. London:*

Kaneko, K. (1984). Like structures and spatiotemporal intermittency of coupled logistic lattice: Toward a field theory of chaos. *Progress in Theoretical Physics, 72*, 480.

Kaneko, K. (1989). Chaotic but regular Posi-Nega Switch among coded attractors by clustersize variation. *Physical Review Letters, 63*, 219-223.

Kaneko, K. (Ed.) (1993). *Theory and applications of coupled map lattices*. Singapore: World Scientific.

Kelso, J. A. S. (1995). *Dynamic patterns: The self-organization of brain and behavior*. Cambridge, MA: The MIT Press.

Lewin, K. (1936). *Principles of topological psychology*. New York: McGraw-Hill.

McGrath, J. E. & Kelly, J. R. (1986). *Time and human interaction: Toward a social psychology of time*. NY: Guilford Press.

Newcomb, T. M. (1961). *The acquaintance process*. New York: Holt, Rinehart, & Winston.

Newtson, D. (1994). The perception and coupling of behavior waves. In R. R. Vallacher & A. Nowak (Eds.), *Dynamical systems in social psychology* (pp. 139-167). San Diego: Academic Press.

Newtson, D., Hairfield, J., Bloomingdale, J., & Cutino, S. (1987). The structure of action and interaction. *Social Cognition, 5*, 48-82.

Nowak, A., Szamrej, J., & Latané, B. (1990). From private attitude to public opinion: A dynamic theory of social impact. *Psychological Review, 97*, 362-376.

Ott, E., Grebogi, C., & York, J. A. (1990). Controlling chaos. *Physics Review Letter, 64*, 1196-1199.

Schmidt, R. C., Beek, P. J., Treffner, P. J., & Turvey, M. T. (1991). Dynamical substructure of coordinated rhythmic movements. *Journal of Experimental Psychology: Human Perception and Performance, 17*, 635-651.

Shinbrot, T. (1994). Synchronization of coupled maps and stable windows. *Physics Review E, 50*, 3230-3233.

Tickle-Degnen, L. & Rosenthal, R. (1987). Group rapport and nonverbal behavior. *Review of Personality and Social Psychology, 9*, 113-136.

Turvey, M. T. (1990). Coordination. *American Psychologist, 4*, 938-953.

Zochowski, M. & Liebovitch, L. (1997). Synchronization of trajectory as a way to control the dynamics of the coupled system. *Physics Review E, 56*, 3701.

Mixing beliefs among interacting agents

Guillaume Deffuant*, David Neau**, Frederic Amblard* and Gérard Weisbuch**

Laboratoire d'Ingénierie pour les Systèmes Complexes (LISC)
Cemagref - Grpt de Clermont-Ferrand
24 Av. des Landais - BP50085
F-63172 Aubière Cedex (FRANCE)
**Laboratoire de Physique Statistique[1]*
de l'Ecole Normale Supérieure,
24 rue Lhomond, F 75231 Paris Cedex 5, France.
email:weisbuch@physique.ens.fr

ABSTRACT. *We present a model of opinion dynamics in which agents adjust continuous opinions as a result of random binary encounters whenever their difference in opinion is below a given threshold. High thresholds yield convergence of opinions towards an average opinion, whereas low thresholds result in several opinion clusters: members of the same cluster share the same opinion but are no longer influenced by members of other clusters.*

1. Laboratoire associé au CNRS (URA 1306), à l'ENS et aux Universités Paris 6 et Paris 7

1. Introduction

Many models about opinion dynamics [FOL 74], [ART 94], [ORL 95], [LAT 97], [GAL 97], [WEI 99], are based on binary opinions which social actors update as a result of social influence. One issue of interest concerns the importance of the binary assumption: what would happen if opinion were a continuous variable such as the worthiness of a choice (a utility in economics), or some belief about the adjustment of a control parameter? In some European countries, the Right/Left political choices were often considered as continuous and were represented for instance by the geometrical position of the seat of a deputy in the Chamber.

Binary opinion dynamics under imitation processes have been well studied, and we expect that in most cases the attractor of the dynamics will display uniformity of opinions, either 0 or 1, when interactions occur across the whole population. This is the "herd" behaviour often described by economists [FOL 74], [ART 94], [ORL 95]. Clusters of opposite opinions appear when the dynamics occur on a social network with exchanges restricted to connected agents. Clustering is reinforced when agent diversity, such as a disparity in influence, is introduced, [LAT 97], [GAL 97], [WEI 99].

The a priori guess for continuous opinions is also homogenisation, but tending towards average initial opinion [LAS 89]. The purpose of this paper is to present results concerning continuous opinion dynamics subject to the constraint that convergent opinion adjustments only proceed when opinion difference is below a given threshold. We will give results concerning homogeneous mixing across the whole population and mixing across a social network. Preliminary results about binary vectors of opinions will also be presented.

2. Complete Mixing

2.1. *The basic model*

Let us consider a population of N agents i with continuous opinions x_i. At each time step any two randomly chosen agents meet. They re-adjust their opinion when their difference of opinion is smaller in magnitude than a threshold d. Suppose that the two agents have opinion x and x' and that $|x - x'| < d$; opinions are then adjusted according to:

$$x = x + \mu \cdot (x' - x)$$
$$x' = x' + \mu \cdot (x - x')$$

where μ is the convergence parameter whose values during the simulations may range from 0 to 0.5.

The rationale for the threshold condition is that agents only interact when their opinion are already close enough; otherwise they do not even bother to discuss. The reason for such behaviour might be for instance lack of understanding, conflicts of interest, or social pressure. Although there is no reason to suppose that openness to discussion, here represented by threshold d, is constant across population or even symmetric on the occasion of a binary encounter, we will nontheless take it as a constant simulation parameter in the present paper. (We conjecture that the results we get would remain similar provided that the distribution of d accross the whole population is sharp rather than uniform).

The evolution of opinions may be mathematically predicted in the limiting case of small values of d [NEA 00]. Density variations $\delta \rho(x)$ of opinions x obey the following dynamics:

$$\delta \rho(x) = \frac{d^3}{2} \cdot \mu \cdot (\mu - 1) \cdot \frac{\partial^2(\rho^2)}{\partial x^2}$$

This implies that starting from an initial distribution of opinions in the population, any local higher opinion density is amplified. Peaks of opinions increase and valleys are depleted until very narrow peaks remains among a desert of intermediate opinions.

2.2. Results

Figures 1 and 2, obtained by computer simulations, display the time evolution of opinions among a population of $N = 1000$ agents for two values of the threshold d. Initial opinions were randomly generated across a uniform distribution on [0,1]. At each time step a random pair is chosen and agents re-adjust their opinion according to equations 1 and 2 if their opinions are closer than d. Convergence of opinions is observed, but consensus is only achieved for the larger value of d.

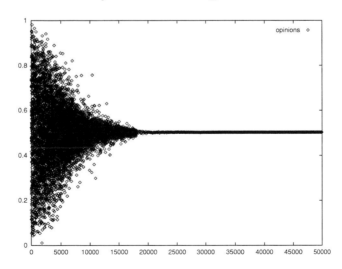

Figure 1. *Time chart of opinions ($d = 0.5$ $\mu = 0.5$ $N = 2000$). One time unit corresponds to sampling 1000 pairs of agents.*

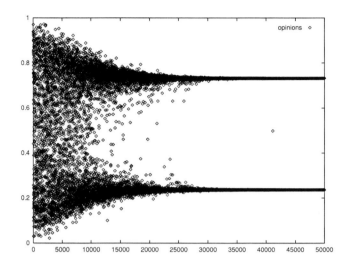

Figure 2. *Time chart of opinions (d = 0.2   μ = 0.5   N = 1000). One time unit corresponds to sampling 1000 pairs of agents.*

Another way to monitor agents' opinion dynamics is to plot final opinions as a function of initial opinions. Figure 3 shows how final opinions "reflect" initial opinions for $\mu = 0.5$. One may observe that some agents with initial opinions roughly equidistant from final peaks of opinions may end up in either peak: basins of attractions in the space of opinions overlap close to the clusters boundaries. The overlap observed when $\mu = 0.5$ is strongly reduced when $\mu = 0.05$ (not represented here): agents then have more time to make up their mind as opinions are changing 10 times more slowly and their final opinions are those of the nearest peak.

A large number of simulations was carried out and we found that the qualitative dynamics depend most strongly on the threshold d. μ and N only influence the convergence time and the width of the distribution of final opinions (when a large number of different random samples are made). d controls the number of peaks of the final distribution of opinions as shown in figure 4. The maximum number of peaks, p_{max}, decreases as a function of d. A rough evaluation of p_{max}, based on a minimal distance of $2d$ between peaks (all other intermediate opinions being attracted by one of the peaks), plus a minimal distance of d of extreme peaks from 0 and 1 edges, gives $p_{max} = \frac{1}{2d}$, in accordance with the observations of figure 4.

The finite size of the population allows for slight variations of the number of peaks for intermediate values of d, as a result of random samplings. These size effects were confirmed when studying larger and smaller population sizes. In the intermediate regions one also observes small populations of "wings" (corresponding to a few percent of the population) in the vicinity of the extreme opinions 0 and 1 (the term wings refers to asymmetric peaks with a vertical bound of either 0 or 1).

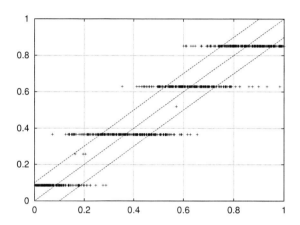

Figure 3. *Diagram of final opinions vs initial opinions (*$\mu = 0.5$, $d = 0.1$*)*

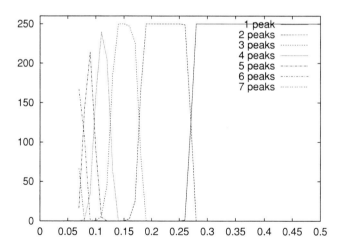

Figure 4. *Statistics of the number of peaks of opinions as a function of d on the x axis for 250 samples (*$\mu = 0.5$, $N = 1000$*). Wings are excluded from the statistics.*

3. Social Networks

The literature on social influence and social choice also considers the case when interactions occur along social connections between agents [FOL 74] rather than randomly across the whole population. Apart from the similarity condition, we now add to our model a condition on proximity, i.e. agents only interact if they are directly connected through a pre-existing social relation. Although one might certainly consider the possibility that opinions on certain unsignificant subjects could be influenced by complete strangers, we expect important decisions to be influenced by advice taken either from professionals (doctors, for instance) or from socially connected persons (e.g. through family, business, or clubs). Facing the difficulty of inventing a credible instance of a social network as in the literature on social binary choice [WEI 99], we here adopted the standard simplification and carried out our simulations on square lattices: square lattices are simple, allow easy visualisation of opinion configurations and contain many short loops, a property that they share with real social networks.

We then started from a 2 dimensional network of connected agents on a square grid. Any agent can only interact with his four connected neighbours (N, S, E and W). We used the same initial random sampling of opinions from 0 to 1 and the same basic interaction process between agents as in the previous sections. At each time step a pair is randomly selected among *connected agents* and opinions are updated according to equations 1 and 2 provided of course that their distance is less than d.

The results are not very different from those observed with non-local opinion mixing as described in the previous section, at least for the larger values of d ($d > 0.3$, all results displayed in this section are equilibrium results at large times). As seen in figure 5, the lattice is filled with a large majority of agents who have reached consensus around $x = 0.5$ while a few isolated agents have "extremists" opinions closer to 0 or 1. The importance of extremists is the most noticeable difference with the full mixing case described in the previous section.

Interesting differences are noticeable for the smaller values of $d < 0.3$ as observed in figure 6. When several values are possible for clusters of converging opinions, consensus can only be reached on connected clusters of agents.

For connectivity 4 on a square lattice, only one cluster can percolate [STA 94] across the lattice. All agents of the percolating cluster share the same opinion. Otherwise, non percolating clusters have homogeneous opinions inside the cluster and these opinions correspond to groups of non-connected clusters with similar but not exactly equal opinions as observed on the histogram (figure 7) and on the pattern of opinions on the lattice (figure 6). The differences of opinions between groups of clusters relates to d, but the actual values inside a group of clusters fluctuate from cluster to cluster because homogenisation occurred independently among the different clusters: the resulting opinion depends on fluctuations of initial opinions and histories from one cluster to the other. The same increase in fluctuations compared to the full mixing case is observed from sample to sample with the same parameter values.

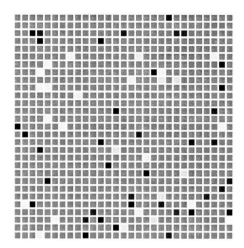

Figure 5. *Display of final opinions of agents connected on a square lattice of size 29x29 (d = 0.3   μ = 0.3 after 100 000 iterations). Opinions between 0 and 1 are coded by gray level. Note the percolation of the large cluster of homogeneous opinion and the presence of isolated "extremists".*

Figure 6. *Display of final opinions of agents connected on a square lattice of size 29x29 (d = 0.15   μ = 0.3 after 100 000 iterations). One still observes a large percolating cluster of homogeneous opinion as well as the presence of smaller non-percolating clusters with similar but not identical opinions.*

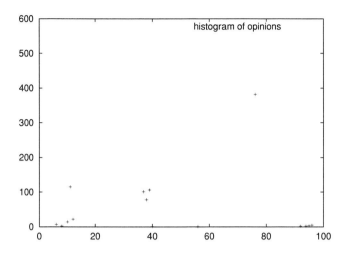

Figure 7. *Histogram of final opinions corresponding to the pattern observed in figure 6 . The 101 bins numbered from 0 to 100 correspond to a hundred times the final opinions which vary between 0 and 1.0. Note the high narrow peak at 76 which corresponds to the percolating cluster and the smaller and wider peaks which correspond to non-percolating clusters.*

The qualitative results obtained with 2D lattices should be observed with any connectivity, either periodic, random, or small world since they are related with the percolation phenomenon [STA 94].

4. Vector opinions

4.1. *The model*

Another subject for investigation is vectors of opinions. Usually people have opinions on different subjects, which can be represented by vectors of opinions. In accordance with our previous hypotheses, we suppose that one agent interacts concerning different subjects with another agent according to some distance with the other agent's vector of opinions. In order to simplify the model, we revert to binary opinions. An agent is characterised by a vector of m binary opinions about the complete set of m subjects, shared by all agents. We use the notion of Hamming distance between binary opinion vectors (the Hamming distance between two binary opinion vectors is the number of different bits between the two vectors). Here, we only treat the case of complete mixing; any pair of agents might interact and adjust opinions according to how many opinions they share. The adjustment process occurs when agents agree on at least $m - d$ subjects (i. e. they disagree on $d - 1$ or fewer subjects). The rules for adjustment are as follows: all equal opinions are conserved; when opinions on a subject differ, one agent (randomly selected from the pair) is convinced by the other agent with probability μ. Obviously this model has connections with population genetics in the presence of sexual recombination when reproduction only occurs if genome distance is smaller than a given threshold. Such a dynamics results in the emergence of species (see [HIG 91]).

We are again interested in the clustering of opinion vectors. In fact clusters of opinions here play the same role as biological species in evolution. A first guess is that vector opinions dynamics might be intermediate between the binary opinion case and continuous opinions.

4.2. Results

We observed once again that μ and N only modify convergence times towards equilibrium; the most influencial factors are threshold d and m the number of subjects under discussion. Most simulations were done for $m = 13$. For $N = 1000$, convergence times are of the order of 10 million pair iterations. For $m = 13$:

– When $d > 7$, the radius of the hypercube, convergence towards a single opinion occurs (the radius of the hypercube is half its diameter which is equal to 13, the maximum distance in the hypercube).

– Between $d = 7$ and $d = 4$ a similar convergence is observed for more than 99.5 per cent of the agents with the exception of a few clustered or isolated opinions distant from the main peak by roughly 7.

– For $d = 3$, one observes from 2 to 7 significant peaks (with a population larger than 1 per cent) plus some isolated opinions.

– For $d = 2$ a large number (around 500) of small clusters is observed (The number of opinions is still smaller than the maximum number of opinions within a distance of 2).

The same kind of results are obtained with larger values of m: two regimes, uniformity of opinions for larger d values and extreme diversity for smaller d values, are separated by one d_c value for which a small number of clusters is observed (e.g for $m = 21$, $d_c = 5$. d_c seems to scale in proportion with m).

Since there is no a priori reference opinion as in the previous cases of continuous opinions, information about the distribution of opinions is obtained from the histogram of distances among couples of opinions represented in figure 8. The results of the two next figures were obtained by averaging over 200 samples.

After all agents have been involved in 1000 possible exchanges of opinions on average, most pairs of opinions are different. One important result is that polarisation of opinions (opposite vectors of opinions) is not observed. The clustering process rather results in orthogonalisation of opinions with an average distance around 6: opinion vectors have no correlation, positive or negative, whatsoever. Similar results were observed concerning distances of binary strategies in the minority game [MAR 97].

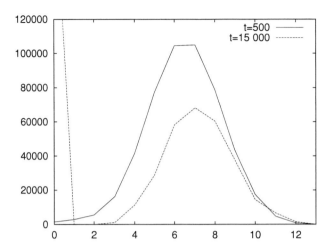

Figure 8. *Histogram of distances in vector opinions for N = 1000 agents and thus 500 000 pairs of agents. (d = 3,   μ = 1). Times are given in 1000 iterations units.*

We were also interested in the populations of the different clusters. Figure 9 represents these populations at equilibrium (iteration time was 12 000 000) in a log-log plot according to their rank-order of size. No scaling law is obvious from these plots, but we observe the strong qualitative difference in decay rates for various thresholds d.

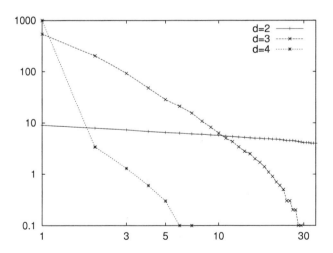

Figure 9. *Log-log plot of average populations of clusters of opinions arranged by decreasing order. for N = 1000 agents (μ = 1).*

5. Conclusions

We thus observe than when opinion exchange is limited by similarity of opinions among agents, the dynamics yield isolated clusters among initially randomly distributed opinions. In the end, exchange only occurs inside clusters as a the result of the exchange dynamics; initially all agents were communicating either directly or indirectly through several directly connected agents. The concertation process as described here is sufficient to ensure clustering even in the absence of difference in private interests or in experience about the external world.

We have studied three very basic models and observed the same clustering behaviour, at least for some parameter regimes, which make us believe that the observed clustering is robust and should be observed in more complicated models, not to mention political life! Many variations and extensions can be proposed, including further opinion selection according to experience with some external world ("social reinforcement learning"). An interesting extension would be a kind of historical perspective in which subjects (or problems) would appear one after the other: position and discussions concerning an entirely new problem would then be conditioned by the clustering resulting from previous problems.

Acknowledgments:

We thank Jean Pierre Nadal and John Padgett and the members of the IMAGES FAIR project, Edmund Chattoe, Nils Ferrand and Nigel Gilbert for helpful discussions. This study has been carried out with financial support from the Commission of the European Communities, Agriculture and Fisheries (FAIR) Specific RTD program, CT96-2092, "Improving Agri-Environmental Policies : A Simulation Approach to the Role of the Cognitive Properties of Farmers and Institutions". It does not necessarily reflect its views and in no way anticipates the Commission's future policy in this area.

References

Arthur, B. W. (1994) "Increasing Returns and Path Dependence in the Economy", (University of Michigan Press).

Föllmer H. (1974) "Random Economies with Many Interacting Agents", Journal of Mathematical Economics, 1/1, 51-62.

Galam S. (1997) "Rational group decision making: A random field Ising model at T=0", Physica A, 238, 66-80.

Higgs P.G. and Derrida, B. (1991) "Stochastic models for species formation in evolving populations", J. Phys. A: Math. Gen., 24, 985-991.

Laslier, J.F. (1989) "Diffusion d'information et évaluations séquentielles" Economie appliquée.

Latané, B. and Nowak, A. (1997) "Self- Organizing Social Systems: Necessary and Sufficient Conditions for the Emergence of Clustering, Consolidation and Continuing Diversity", in Barnett, G. A. and Boster, F. J. (eds.) Progress in Communication Sciences.

Neau, D (2000), "Révisions des croyances dans un système d'agents en interaction", rapport d'option de l'école polytechnique, available at http://www.lps.fr/ weisbuch/rapneau.ps.

Orléan A. (1995), "Bayesian Interactions and Collective Dynamics of Opinions: Herd Behavior and Mimetic Contagion", *Journal of Economic Behavior and Organization*, 28, 257-274.

Stauffer D. and Aharony A., (1994) "Introduction to Percolation Theory", Taylor and Francis, London.

Weisbuch G. and Boudjema G. (1999), "Dynamical aspects in the Adoption of Agri-Environmental Measures", Adv. Complex Systems, 2, 11-36.

Modeling of Social Processes Based on T.Parsons Ideas

Alexander A. Laptev

Chair of Mathematical Modeling,
Omsk State University,
55A, Mira pr.,
644077 Omsk,
Russia

laptev@univer.omsk.su

ABSTRACT: *The goal of our work is to attempt and describe social processes in a mathematical language and to build a system of differential equations describing global evolution of the society. We build a model of social process with a periodic (cyclic) stable solution.*

KEY WORDS: *social process, society, mathematical modeling, differential equation.*

1. Introduction

This paper outlines the construction of a model of the society. This problem has arisen from the idea to describe global processes in the society.

In the past, methods of prognosis compilation came from humanities, and so were based on either a narrow set of phenomena and facts or a concrete theory which could not process data in the precise manner of mathematics. We detect many alternate causes for events, which have occurred, and therefore we can't always directly point out the immediate cause of given event. An important distinction of the mathematical data processing is that the result is obtained in the course of long and formal computations, which lack independent meaning. Usually this result is unpredictable (with the exception of trivial cases) and consequently it is objective.

A subjective bias may appear at the prior stage of construction of a mathematical model, but the mathematical analysis of the model is impartial and objective. One advantage of mathematical models is the possibility of computer production of experiments, i.e. the possibility to compute various situations under different parameters. This is helpful in the search for optimal solutions.

The society is viewed as a certain structure, composed of bio-, ethno- and sociospheres. We develop a model describing the behavior and interaction of the social structures.

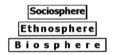

At the geobiological level (biosphere), the human society is a subsystem of the ecological system which exists at the expense of solar energy and participates in the exchange of the biomass with other subsystems of this level. At the same time, the entire terrestrial society can be composed of local regional subsocieties which differ from each other by the type of consumed food (biomass) and both rate of population growth or population deathrate and the industrial pollution level. A better term for this society is *population*. A mathematical model of this level was described in [KRA 82].

At the second level (ethnosphere), the society is a collective of individuals which an ability for common unconscious actions and who are characterized by the identical unconscious reciprocal reactions to an external action, i.e. by a definite stereotype of behavior generated by the landscape (regional) conditions of the domicile. Such a society is called *ethnos*. This level was described in L.Gumilev's theory of ethnogenesis [GUM 93]. According to Gumilev's definition, ethnos is a stable naturally existing community of people which oppose themselves to other analogous communities (this opposition is defined by their subconscious "friend-or-foe" feeling) and which differ in peculiar stereotype of behavior.

A mathematical model of ethnos is described by the system of differential equations proposed by A.Guts [GUT 97]. A computer simulation was conducted based on base these equations to verify conclusions which had been made within the frame of the given mathematical model and to compare them with L.Gumilev's statements of about the course of ethnogenesis.

At the third level (sociosphere) we deal with society in the commonly prevailing sense of the word. In the construction of our model of society, we rely on the ideas of T.Parsons, an American sociologist, on the cyclic evolution of society.

Obviously, there exist superior levels, e.g. *psychosphere* [GUT 98].

2. Theory of cycles

There is a number of models and concepts of social development in the socio-political sciences which if fact could be reduced to two fundamental paradigms: the theory of linear onward progress and the theory of closed cycle of local existence of social systems. In the real social process these paradigms practically do not exist in the "pure form" but they overlap on each other. Therefore, new models, which are synthesis of linearity and cyclic recurrence, emerge as a result.

Theory of cycles is an interpretation of world history. It was established at the turn of XIX century in Europe in works of N.Danilevsky [DAN 91], K.Leontiev and others. In XX century, the idea of cyclic development of local civilization was developed by O.Spengler [SPE 91], A.Toynbee [TOI 91], K.Jaspers and others. In their opinion, each society passes through certain stages of development, growing, fracture and decomposition.

L.N.Gumilev's ethnosocial theory is quite original. After researching life cycles of forty ethnos, he derived the curve of ethnogenesis (1200-1500 years) based on his own passionarity theory.

Russian economists are considered to be founders of cyclic dynamics theory of society. Based on a large collection of statistical data and mathematical modeling of socioeconomic processes, N.D.Kondratyev concluded in the 1930s that, every 50 years, cycles of economic conjuncture replace each other. Each such cycle is in turn an element of "century" civilization cycle, changing every 200-300 years. N.D.Kondratyev thought that this regularity allows better forecasts of trends in the development of economy and appearances of crises.

At the present time, a new approach is being formed, which considers *wavelike* nature of evolution of social systems. This approach presumes both the definite direction of change and the existence of waves succeeding each other, which correspond to various states of social systems. The wavelike nature of evolution of natural and social systems is more complicated then the purely linear onward or the purely cyclic types of progress.

The wavelike and cyclic approach have a common feature if the cycle is viewed not like a closed circle of historic development but as *evolution cycles,* in which the system passes states similar to, but not necessarily identical with, prior periods. A cycle is viewed as a spiral-like or wavelike motion. This is a repetition of similar, but not identical phases in onward motion. Researchers select several types of cycles, ranging from short-term cycles covering a few years, to thousand-years-long cycles. Modern authors make a note of existence of "century" 108-year-long cycles (two "long" waves of N.Kondratyev can be inserted into in each cycle) which in turn insert into a 300-year-old era.

3. Constructing Model

Theory of cycles is connected with structure. We see the structure of society as three spheres: socioenthal community, ethnosphere and biosphere. We consider sociosphere theory by T.Parsons, who stressed four subsystems. Development of this problem was begun by A.K.Guts. Refer to http://www.univer.omsk.su/MEP/.

We are constructing the model using a system of differential equations, which describe the following subsystems of the social system: societal community (normative order), system of maintenance of institutional ethnic (cultural) samples, political system and economic system.

We use numerous sociological sources to come up with equations. After the construction is completed, we analyze the system analytically (applying known bifurcation theorems), and model it on the computer. We also try to take into account periodicity of the historical process. For this, we apply theorems and show that the system has a periodic solution.

Societal community (normative order), system of maintenance of institutional ethnic (cultural) samples, Political and Economic systems are described by functions $D(t)$, $K(t)$, $P(t)$ and $E(t)$ respectively. Their growth reflects a strengthening of integrating public forces and their decrease reflects a weakening.

In the course of construction, several systems were obtained (different factors and different definitions of control parameter were taken into account), but nearly in all solutions the cyclicity condition was absent. As a control parameter (it is needed for the study of cyclicity), we take the "Passionarity" level, a subsystem of ethnos, since the social system is controlled (within the framework of our theory) by ethnic factors only.

According to the definition of L.Gumilev, *passionarity level* is the passionarity accorded to one member of a society. *Passionarity* as energy is the excess of biochemical energy of living matter (people) which suppresses the instinct of self-preservation and which provides the ability to a determined ultraeffort. *Passionarity* as a behavioral characteristic is the effect of excess of biochemical energy of living matter (people) generating the ability for a self-sacrifice for the sake of an often illusory goal. The qualitative characteristic of passionarity level is a certain averaged estimation of a representative of the ethnos.

For example, the dynamics of economy is described by the following differential equation:

$$dE/dt = E_E - E_G - E_K.$$

1) Here $E_E = k_{EE} \cdot (e^{\delta \cdot P - \delta 1} - 1) \cdot E$ measures the efforts of people to develop economy. $k_{EE} \cdot (e^{\delta \cdot P - \delta 1} - 1)$ is the influence of passionarity to develop economy (see graph).

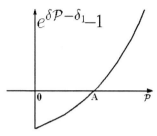

The bigger passionarity (**P**) is, the more effective these measures are. Under a small passionarity level (**P<A**), a weakening take place in economy

$(k_{EE} \cdot (e^{\delta \cdot P - \delta 1} - 1) < 0)$.

A developed economic system (**E>0**) can afford to contribute to growth, where as a weakened economy (**E<0**) selfdeteriorates (**E_E<0**).

2) Here $E_G = k_{EG} \cdot (e^{-\eta \cdot G + \eta 1} - 1) \cdot G$ measures restrictions on economy imposed by politics. ("Economic system aims to move away ... from political system." [PAR 95, p.118]).

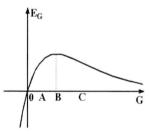

Political system is weak when **0<G<A** and exerts little influence on economy (under **G<0** a weakened political system dedicates certain resource to economic system with the hope to improve its situation at the expense of economy). A developing political system (**A<G<C**) demands economic expenditure for its support. A more developed political system (**G>C**) already needs less economic replenishment and to deprive absorb of large economic resources discontinues (see graph).

3) Here $E_K = k_{EK} \cdot (P - P_2)(K + D) \cdot E$ measures restrictions on the economy imposed by the tradition and normative order under its high level, high "social" activity (**K+D**), and high passionarity level (**P>P_2**). In the beginning stage of evolution (**P<P_2**), E_K is a certain impulse (support) of economic development.

There k_{EE}, k_{EG}, k_{EK}, δ, δ_1, η, η_1 and P_2 are some positive factors.

In a similar way we constructed the full system:

$$\begin{cases} \frac{dG}{dt} = k_{GG}(e^{\delta P - \delta_1} - 1)G + k_{GE}\ e^{-\mu E + \mu_1} \cdot E + k_{GK}(P - P_1)(K + D)G \\[2mm] \frac{dE}{dt} = k_{EE}(e^{\delta P - \delta_1} - 1)E - k_{EG}\ e^{-\eta G + \eta_1} \cdot G - k_{EK}(P - P_2)(K + D)E \\[2mm] \frac{dK}{dt} = k_{KG} \cdot (G^2 + E^2) - k_{KK}\ e^{-\gamma K + \gamma_1} \cdot K \cdot P - k_{KD} \cdot D^2 \\[2mm] \frac{dD}{dt} = k_{DG} \cdot G^2 - k_{DD}\ e^{-\omega D + \omega_1} \cdot D \cdot P - k_{DK} \cdot K^2 \end{cases}$$

4. Analysing Model

The constructed and analyzed system agrees well with the theory offered by sociologists. The obtained solution is periodic, and the behavior of the described systems conforms to the theory. The solution of system has a bifurcation point (Andronov-Hopf theorem [MAR 83; TER 89]); that is, at certain parameter values, the stable equilibrium develops into a stable cycle (a cycle appears from the stable equilibrium). For the numerical analysis, we borrow the parameter **P** from the model of ethnogenesis [GUT 97].

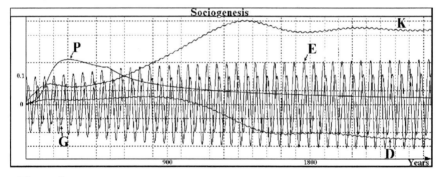

Figure 1.

We have constructed a mathematical model of sociogenesis and conducted its computer simulation. To ensure validity of the proposed mathematical model, it would be useful to analyze the character of the obtained curves **K(t), D(t), E(t), P(t)**. But what can we compare them with? In the case of ethnogenesis, A.K.Guts compared them to "experimental curves". In this case, however, there are no such curves. In their place, useful information on cyclic developments of the economic and political systems had been collected.

As it can be seen from obtained solution of differential equations (Fig.1), after some time, the social system comes to a balance. It is not static, but in a constant movement. After achieving a certain level, the curves oscillate periodically near this level with a constant amplitude. The phase portrait of solution is shown in Fig. 2. In left part of the graph, a cycle in development of political (**G**) and economic (**E**) systems clearly stands out.

Characteristic growth of the curve of the "societal community" (before stabilizing) is explained by the fact that initially, norms and values are only being planted in the consciousness of the people; but afterwards, once the absolute values and norms of the society have been established, they are difficult to change. The fall in the level of the "system of maintenance of institutional ethnic samples" is a result of weakening of the society's collective consciousness in the process of liberation of individual consciousnesses of members of the society. Economic system and political system varies near the initial level.

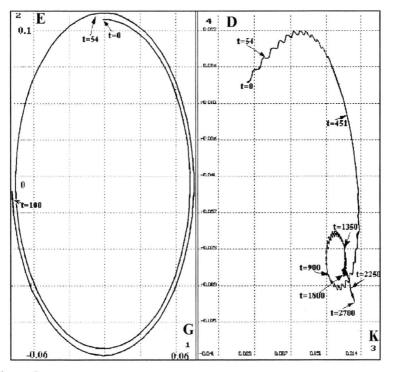

Figure 2.

Therefore, the simplest model of the social process with a periodic solution was obtained as a result of construction. Thus, the given approach at the current level of study has a right to existence.

5. Conclusion

As a result, applying the constructed model, it is possible to predict social processes. At the current stage, we model global social processes (lasting more than 100 years), and the model is mostly of academic interest only. However, we expect further developments of the model (better approximations, expansions, additions) will bring it to an appropriate level, so that it becomes useable for practical purposes.

6. References

[DAN 91] DANYLEVSKY N. *Russia and Europe* - M.: Kniga, 1991. (Russian)

[GUM 93] GUMILEV L.N. *Ethnogenesis and Biosphere of Earth*, Moscow, 1993. (Russian)

[GUT 97] GUTS A.K. *Global Ethnosociology*, Omsk, Omsk University, 1997. (Russian)

[GUT 98] GUTS A.K. M*odeling of sociopsychical processes* // Mathematical structure and modeling. 1998. N1 (Omsk State University) - P.48-53 (Russian)

[KON 93] KONDRATYEV N.D. *Selected works.* - M.: 1993. (Russian)

[KRA 82] KRAPIVIN V., SVIREZHEV YU., TARKO A. *Mathematical modeling of global processes in biosphere.* - M., 1982. (Russian)

[LAP 96] GUTS A.K., LAPTEV A.A. *Birth of cycles in the development of political and economic systems as a consequence of weakenings of power.* // Cycles of nature and society. - Stavropol, 1996. (Russian)

[LAP 99] LAPTEV A.A. *Mathematical modeling of social processes* // Mathematical structure and modeling. 1999. N3 (Omsk State University) - P.109-124 (Russian)

[MAR 83] MARSDEN J.E., MACCRACKEN M. *The bifurcation of cycle birth and its applications.* - M.: 1983. (Russian) (Translation of The Hopf bifurcation and its applications.)

[PAR 95] PARSONS T. *The concept of society: the components and their interrelations.* // Thesis. - T.1, N.2, 1995. - P.94-122. (Russian)

[SPE 91] SPENGLER O. *The Decline of the West.* - M.: 1991. (Russian)

[TER 89] TEREKHIN M.T. *The bifurcation of systems of differential equations.* - M., 1989.(Russian)

[TOI 91] TOINBEE A. *A Study of history.* - M.: Progress, 1991. (Russian)

GEOGRAPHY AND URBANISM

A spatial microsimulation of population dynamics in Southern France: a model integrating individual decisions and spatial constraints

C.Aschan-Leygonie* — H.Mathian* — L.Sanders*
K.Mäkilä**

*UMR-Géographie-cités (P.A.R.I.S)., CNRS-Universités Paris I et Paris 7-ENS
13, rue du four
F-75006 Paris
aschan, mathian, lena.sanders@parisgeo.cnrs.fr

**University of Umeå
Department of Social and Economic Geography
SE-901 87 Umeå
kalle@geoserv.geo.umu.se

ABSTRACT: *The aim is to model the spatial distribution of the population dynamics in Southern France. First the philosophical differences between a micro-level approach and a meso-level approach are presented and their respective advantages are briefly compared from a general point of view. Then the model is presented. It is a microsimulation model but it has some rules defined at the aggregate level of the communes. Change occur through events as birth, death and migration, that depend on probabilities that are linked to different individuals characteristics as sex, age etc. Four scenarios of development are tested and some future improvements are proposed.*

RESUME: *L'objectif est de modéliser la distribution spatiale de la dynamique de population dans les départements du Gard et de l'Hérault. Après une discussion préliminaire sur les questions d'échelle de la modélisation, un modèle de microsimulation intégrant à la fois des règles définies au niveau des individus et des agrégats spatiaux est présenté. Le moteur du changement est déterminé par des événements tels que les naissances, les décès, les migrations dont les probabilités sont tabulées par rapport à des caractéristiques individuelles (sexe, âge,...). Quatre scénarios d'évolution sont testés, et enfin des prolongements sont proposés.*

KEY-WORDS: *dynamic modelling – microsimulation – settlement system – spatial analysis*

MOTS-CLES: *modélisation dynamique - microsimulation - système de peuplement - analyse spatiale.*

1. Introduction

This presentation focuses on the application of a microsimulation model to the dynamics of the population in a region in Southern France. The purpose is both theoretical and methodological. From a theoretical point of view the aim is to discuss at what level to formalise a model of population dynamics. From a thematic point of view, the question is to get a better understanding of the spatial redistribution of the population in a region with a population increase and to test the effects in the future of different scenarios on this redistribution.

The region of Languedoc-Roussillon belongs to the more attractive in France if one considers the importance of in-migration [BRU 94]. The main purpose here is not to propose an estimation of the population in the coming years, but to focus on *where* the new inhabitants will settle and how the existing population is likely to redistribute through space in coming decades. The main purpose is then to simulate the spatial redistribution of the population *between* the communes[1] in the region according to different scenarios of regional development. The results of the model are given at a meso-level, but the core of the modelling could be defined either at the level of the individuals, or at the level of the communes. In the first case one focuses on the determinants of individuals preferences and choices [CLA 87], [CLA 96], [HOL 2000] in the second on the factors that define the communes' attractivity, that is the result of a collective behaviour [ALL 97]. Each level makes sense and the choice of one approach or the other depends mostly on the philosophical perspective of the modeller [SAN 99].

2. Basic principles of the MICDYN model

In the microsimulation approach, the hypothesis is that the diversity and the interdependency of individual decisions are of such an importance that they must be taken into account in order to simulate the change at an upper aggregate level. It is therefore necessary to reproduce the individual biographies and to simulate the series of events that might lead to spatial changes. The determinant variables are age, sex, family composition, education and activity, and the changes are modelled through ageing, transition probabilities, and logical rules. The passage to the meso-level is then done by simple counting. A complete description of a microsimulation model can be found in [VEN 99]. In the case of a spatial aggregated approach one defines the mechanisms of change directly at the level of the communes. The decision process of the individuals is then ignored and replaced by simplifying hypotheses as inter-individual homogeneity at the commune level and the independence of the individuals' decisions [HAA 89], [PUM 89], [SAN 92]. The idea is that there are regularities at the level of the communes' dynamics that refer to the *relative position* and to the *relative attractivity* of the communes in a spatial

---

[1] French communes are small, around 12 km² in average, therefor they allow the observation of the spatial dynamics on a very fine level.

system of interactions [PUM 98]. Determinant variables are the social and demographic profile of each commune, the different types of amenities that are present and its spatial properties (accessibility, position in a network, property of the neighbourhood, distance to structuring poles etc.).

Of course there is a strong interdependency between these two levels of functioning. The results of a set of individual decisions can modify existing spatial patterns and structures within the region, and in return the spatial structures play an important role in the individual behaviours. In this experiment we are both interested in observing structures on the macro-geographical level emerging from individual behaviours and in identifying the meso-level rules which act as constraints on the individual's choices.

2.1. *The individuals behaviour: based on an event logic*[2]

The model, called MICDYN, has been built up starting from a core which has been elaborated in order to model the dynamics of the Swedish population [VEN 99]. This core is essentially based on demographic events and the principal parameters refer to probabilities of birth, death, migration according to the characteristics of the individuals. This core has then been progressively adapted and completed in order to fit the French context. Two kinds of objects are handled in the model. On the one hand individuals with their personal attributes, their location and the location of their workplace. On the other hand the communes whose attributes are stocks (population, housing, workplaces) and the characteristics of neighbourhoods of different ranges (figure 1). At each time-step the stocks are actualised at the level of the communes, summarising all changes at the individuals' level.

Each individual has a certain probability to face events as birth, death, getting married, losing job, etc. but the probability is much higher in some situations. Some of these events induce a migration and contribute to the changes in the spatial pattern of the regional population. Indeed, the tendency to move varies according to the stage in the life cycle of the potential migrants. The individual mobility increases highly between the age of 18 and 30, and is naturally due to migration linked to employment seeking or to the choice of studying at the university or in colleges. Table 1 gives an individual's potentials of moving according to its *attributes*, and table 2 summarises which *events* might result in a decision to migrate in the model.

It should be noted that an intention to move does not necessarily result in a migration, as it depends on the opportunities offered to the concerned person or family. Indeed, in a microsimulation model there are processes at three levels. The first level concerns the intentions to do something, the second level concerns the search procedures and the corresponding opportunities, that makes possible

---

[2] The model that is presented has been developed in the framework of ARCHAEOMEDES II, directed by Sander van der Leeuw. It is an European project that has been subsided by the DG12. The model has been developed through a collaboration with Einar Holm and Urban Lindgren from the University of Umeå and Denis Gautier from INRA.

something which is wanted. Finally there are the actual changes that only constitute a fraction of the initial intentions.

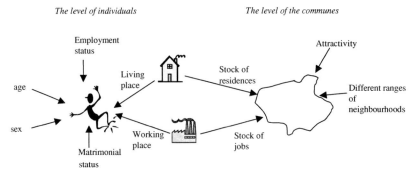

Figure1. *The elements (objects and attributes) of the MICDYN model*

Combination of attributes causing changes			Associated random events	Potential change of residence
Attributes	**Value**	**Other attribute involved**		
Age	15-31 years	Housing situation	Leave their parents	High
		-	Start high education	High
		Employment status	Get a job	High
		Matrimonial status	Get a partner	High
			Death	Low
Sex	female	Age	Give birth	Low
Matrimonial status	Single	Age	Get a partner	High
	Married	-	Separation	High
	Married	-	Widower/hood	Low
Employment status	Unemployed	Age	Get a job	High
	Employed	-	Lose the job	Low
	Employed	Age	Retirement	Low

Table 1. *A simplified representation of an individuals' potential of moving according to its personal attributes*

Very schematically, the model functions as following: the destination of the individuals that decide to move is determined by housing vacancies in the communes and job vacancies in the hinterland of the communes. To start with potential movers look for a new place of residence and if one is found - there must in general be a job vacancy in the right occupation within an acceptable commuting distance. The search is limited to a "spatial context". This context always includes the nearest neighbours, the nearest of the two metropoles in the area (Nîmes or Montpellier) and a set of "local labour market towns". These are restricted by means of a maximum distance, usually somewhat larger than the maximum acceptable commuting distance. We have assimilated this distance to 40 kilometres, as the radius of 40 km corresponds to the distance from work, within which 90 % of the active population in the Languedoc-Roussillon region live. It should be pointed out that there is also a small probability for individuals to move, even though the change of residence will lead to unemployment. This is justified by the existence of non labour market related migration. For a specific individual the model defines a sample of possible destinations. The communes are ranked according to the number of appropriate jobs: the more jobs the higher attraction. In this general framework, the relative proximity between the places thus plays a central role.

Causes of moving	Type of event	Need to find a job	Need to find a dwelling
Household change	Leaving parents	Yes or No	Yes
	Finding a partner	Yes or No	No
	Separation	No	Yes
	Death of partner	No	Yes or No
Labour market related changes	Immigrant	Yes or No	Yes
	Unemployed	Yes	Yes or No
	Leaving school	Yes	Yes
No specific reason		Yes	Yes

Table 2. *Different events leading to the decision to move in the MICDYN model*

According to the different contexts of the migration (as defined in table 1), it is possible to define various categories of people, that follow the general procedure after having taken the decision to try to migrate.

-*A first category* are those who have no job and no dwelling in the region. Indeed the system is open and immigrants will arrive from outside the region. They will have to be generated and given suitable attributes and combined into families.

-*A second category* are those that have no job, but that have a dwelling. In this group we find both *young people living with their parents* (students having finished their studies) and *unemployed*. To this category adds also 5 % of the active population that yearly loose their jobs in the model. These people will try to find a job every year in the surroundings of their residential commune. If they do not succeed, they will try to move in order to find a job somewhere else, and the same research procedure is run all over once a new dwelling has been found.

-*A third group* is formed by those who have a job and a dwelling, but who want to move anyway. People having found a *partner*, *young people living with their parents and that have a job* and finally the group that we might qualify as *"free" people* without particular constraints, i.e. the part of the population that wants to move for no economical or demographic reason (quality of life, family rapprochement...). The pensioners belong to this last subgroup.

In each time step of the microsimulation, i.e. every year, all the individuals are successively examined. According to its situation in terms of age, sex, matrimonial status, and employment status, the occurrence or not of an event will be determined by random, using the associated parameters.

2.2. Introduction of some meso-level rules in the model

The calibration of the model is rather qualitative, based both on comparisons of the estimated values with the first results of the census of 1999, and using intuition for previsions at 2020. Simulations using only previously described classical rules of the microsimulation lead to an overpopulation in the centres of the bigger cities and in remote rural areas as well as an underestimation of the growth of the periurban areas. So in a second step two major meso-level rules have been introduced.

The first concerns the process of periurbanisation and the spatial diffusion of urban growth. The trend is particularly heavy in this region. In order to cope with this phenomena in the model, we have introduced a spatial rule that implements a diffusion of the population around urban communes that have reached a maximum threshold of population density. The diffusion concerns a limited set of communes near the central commune. Both the limit for the search of those communes and the density threshold are given as input parameters. Eventually the border communes also get crowded (there is one more parameter giving the threshold for the population density, usually a little lower than the threshold for the centre). When this second threshold has been passed, the search for potential growth communes will go further away from the central commune for the next year and so on. In future versions of this model it will be possible to refine the direction of the growth on the basis of information on land use, transport network and local housing policy rules in the concerned communes.

The second meso-level rule concerns the growth rates of workplaces. The evolution of the dwelling stocks is determined in most scenarios through mechanisms of adequacy between supply and demand and theoretically the same kind of endogenous mechanism should work for the workplaces. A small feedback has effectively been introduced from population to jobs. The communes that have a significant population growth get proportional increase in jobs (corresponding to some elementary local service needed everywhere). But this mechanism of induction is not sufficient and the evolution of the workplaces is completed through a simple growth rate, applied at the level of the commune according to its size, smaller and even negative in some scenarios for smaller communes, higher for the more populated.

3. More or less sustainable futures: projections for 2020

3.1. An attractive region with spatial reorganisation

The region that we have chosen as a geographical setting for the microsimulation model is composed of the two eastern departments of the region of Languedoc-Roussillon (figure 2[3]). Their evolutions are highly linked through a long history of

---

[3] We thank Eugénie Dumas for the page-settings of the maps.

**Figure 2 - The region of application : departments of
Hérault and Gard**

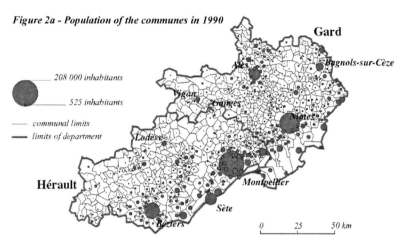

Figure 2a - Population of the communes in 1990

Gard

Bagnols-sur-Cèze

208 000 inhabitants

525 inhabitants

—— communal limits

—— limits of department

Alès

Vigan

Ganges

Nîmes

Lodève

Hérault

Montpellier

Sète

Béziers

0   25   50 km

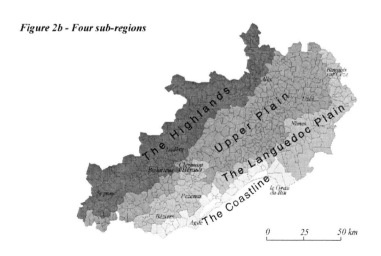

Figure 2b - Four sub-regions

The Highlands

Upper Plain

The Languedoc Plain

The Coastline

0   25   50 km

competition between their two chiefs-towns: Nîmes (Gard) and Montpellier (Hérault), with respectively about 130 000 and 200000 inhabitants. Montpellier represents today the major driving force in the regional population dynamics. The population growth is particularly spectacular around the two main urban poles, and along the coast. The issues of this spreading out of the urban areas, are the resulting land use conflicts, on the one hand, with the main agricultural production that is the winegrowing and, on the other hand, with the tourism activities that are concentrated mainly on the coastline, as today this region is one of the foremost tourist areas in France. The weight of the different land uses, such as urbanisation, tourism and agriculture, and their pressure on the regional territory are different according to the type of biophysical environments. Therefor, it was important to distinguish four sub-regions in the model (figure 2b), according to natural characteristics that mark the population evolution, the capacity of resistance of the agriculture and the potentiality of tourism development. Many questions arise concerning the future evolution of the spatial organisation within the region. In what way will the urbanisation continue and spread ? Which communes are likely to be the most affected ? To attempt to answer this kind of questions, different scenarios of regional development have been run.

3.2. The potential future spatial organisation as illustrated by 4 scenarios

In the basic scenario the parameters values reproduce as much as possible the same tendency as the one observed during the last ten years. In order to use the model in a comparative perspective, alternative scenarios have been developed. They deviate from the basic scenario and are highly differentiated from each other. Three of them are presented in this paper.

Some model parameters	Fixed values
Demographic	
Adjustment factor for fertility rates	1.1
Adjustment factor for mortality rates	0.9
Migration	
Proportion of immigrants that are female	0.47
Probability to try migration without labour market reasons	0.04
Probability to try a long distance random move when all others failed	0.55
Probability to migrate within the two departments	0.25
Employment	
Probability to find a job after having lost one	0.49
Probability to lose a job	0.03
Level of the commune	
Proportion of new born that are girls	0.49
Proportion of adults actively searching for a partner	0.35
Proportion of unemployed amongst those not working	0.31
...	...

Table 3. *A selection of model parameters that are common to all scenarios*

Table 3 gives a selection of the parameters that are maintained through all the simulations presented here. The selection has been chosen in order to illustrate the diversity of the different fields taken into consideration in the model. The parameters are determined on the individual or the communal level.

At this stage of the modelling we have used the alternative scenarios for testing the effects of some exogenous changes. First we have varied the immigration level, as to observe the impacts of a greater number of immigrants on the spatial organisation of the population within the two departments. Secondly, the distribution of the growth rate of the workplaces has been modified. Indirectly these variations have generated a territorial redistribution of the growth of the dwelling stock, as it is automatically adjusted within the model according to the adequate level between supply and demand. The variation of the increase of the stock of working places is interesting in the sense that it is one major driving force of the mobility of the population and influences therefor directly the distribution of the population and the socio-professional profiles in the communes.

3.2.1.*The basic scenario*

In the *basic scenario* (scenario 1) that is simply the prolongation of the recent demographic and mobility trends in the region, all parameters have been given their current values. The number of yearly immigrants corresponds to the observed values in the recent past and the different growth rates for working places are naturally simplified, but close to reality (table 4).

The model presents several types of outputs that are essential tools in order to evaluate the impacts of the parameter variations, both upon the statistical distributions and upon the spatial distributions. Firstly, the most obvious output are maps that visually summarise very well the results of the model:
- the distribution of the population at the end of each simulation (figure 3a);
- the change of population between the beginning and the end of the simulation (figure 3b).

The results of the simulation of this basic scenario are quite predictable as it simply prolongs the recent tendencies. Thus as the figures 2a and 3a show, there are no structural changes between 1990 and 2020, the only visible change is the general population increase. Indeed, the relative positions of the different communes have been kept during the whole period. There is however a reinforcement of the local tendencies, such as a relatively important growth and diffusion of the population around the urban centre of Montpellier and other larger towns such as Bézier, as well as a certain abandonment in the communes that were already declining between 1982 and 1990.

**Figure 3 - Population in the communes of Hérault and Gard in 1990
and estimated by four different scenarios**

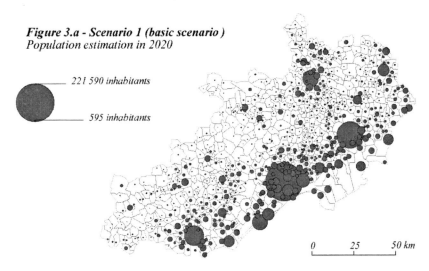

Figure 3.a - Scenario 1 (basic scenario)
Population estimation in 2020

221 590 inhabitants

595 inhabitants

0   25   50 km

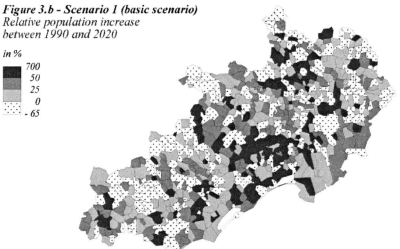

Figure 3.b - Scenario 1 (basic scenario)
Relative population increase
between 1990 and 2020

in %

700
50
25
0
- 65

Another type of outputs illustrate the statistical distribution of attributes more generally summarised at the level of the commune. The population dynamics can be represented by the evolution of the quantities of population of different spatial or social categories. These representations reveal the fundamental spatial or social processes, that is homogenisation or differentiation. The mere description of the general tendency towards a decrease or an increase of the spatial and the social differences is an important step in the analysis (figure 4).

Another territorial division used in the model outputs is the sub-regions as described above (figure 2), in which Nîmes and Montpellier have been isolated. Figure 5 illustrates the territorial differenciations associated to the average commuting distance for the population within each geographical division. These model outputs are particularly interesting as they allow to focus on the importance of the interactions within the region. The scenario 1 shows, for example, that the average commuting distance for the population living in the Montpellier area is stable during the whole period of simulation. It is thus possible to assume that there is a strong autonomy within this area with rather strong and short distance interactions, compared to for example the mountainous area where the average distance of the commuters is sensibly growing. Clearly, at the end of the simulation the commuting active population living in this area often work outside the mountainous region. The very high increase of the average commuting distance in the mountainous region, as well as on the coast-line, expresses an increase of the urban attraction areas.

Figure 4. *Basic scenario : Evolution of the socio-economic categories in Hérault and Gard between 1990 and 2040*

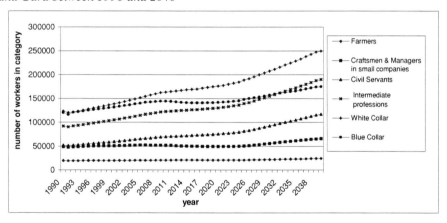

Figure 5. *Basic scenario : Evolution of the average commuting distance per sub-area*

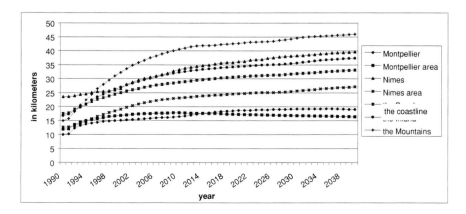

3.2.2. *The alternative scenarios*

We have chosen to test three alternative scenarios, that have been run from 1990 to 2020. They are based on a future settlement system that is more open to the outside as the yearly immigration is twice as high as in the basic scenario (table 4). Such an hypothesis is slightly exaggerated but this choice has been done in order to amplify the consequences of the parameter changes.

	Scenario 1 (basic)	Scenario 2	Scenario 3	Scenario 4
Emigration ratio (%)	0.5	0.5	0.4	0.1
Immigrant level (inh.)	20 000	40 000	40 000	40 000

Average growth rate for work places per commune and per year							
Scenario 1		Scenario 2		Scenario 3		Scenario 4	
Size classes (inhab.)	Growth rates (%)	Size classes (inhab.)	Growth rates (%)	Size classes (inhab.)	Growth rates (%)	Size classes (inhab.)	Growth rates (%)
Less than 1 000	-0.3	Less than 5 000	0.02	Less than 80 000	0.001	Less than 2 000	12
1 000- 150 000	1.6	5 000- 150 000	0.5	80 000- 150 000	12	2 000- 150 000	0.002
More than 150 000	2.5	More than 150 000	6	More than 150 000	0.001	More than 150 000	0.001

Table 4. *Changes in the parameters in the different scenarios*

In the *second scenario* we have affected a very strong growth to workplaces within the urban centre of Montpellier. It corresponds to an hypothesis of economic dynamics concentrated to the city centre. Between 1982 and 1990 the observed annual average growth of jobs in this commune was 2.5%. What might happen if we increase this growth rate in a significant manner and simultaneously double the immigration in the two departments? This scenario will exaggerate the role of Montpellier as an employment pole in the region and its attraction on the migrants will significantly grow.

The *third scenario* creates an important amount of new jobs in Nîmes, contributing thus to the reinforcement of this second regional pole. After a long period of marginal situation and decline in relative terms, this city appears to renew its population and economical dynamics. What effect could be expected if the growth rate of workplaces is much higher than during the last census?

The *fourth scenario* is quite different as literally all the job increase has been allocated to the small rural communes. It corresponds to an hypothesis of attitude changes of the economic actors and expresses a tendency of loss of concentration of the economical activities.

Naturally the choices of parameter values in those scenarios generate a strong population growth in the two departments. However, according to the different scenarios this growth is variable as we can see in the figure 6. It is interesting to note that it is not the growth of Montpellier that generates the most important population increase, but the fourth scenario, that is based on a growth of the smallest rural communes (less than 2 000 inhabitants). The rural location of the new activities give a larger range of choices for the potential immigrants.

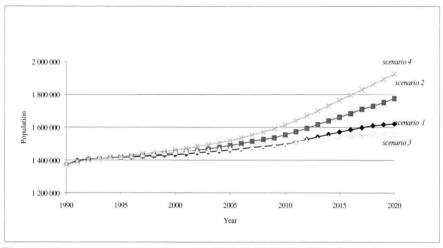

Figure 6. *Population increase between 1990 and 2020 in Hérault and Gard according to four scenarios*

As shown in the maps representing the population distribution at the end of the three alternative scenarios (figures 7a,b,c), the changes in the workplaces within the region certainly have an influence on the respective rhythms of growth and spatial extension of the urban units, as well as on the « urbanisation » within the rural areas. The outputs of the second scenario show a remarkable growth in the surroundings of Montpellier, especially towards the south-west along the coastline. The urban diffusion is such that Montpellier shows a tendency to merge with Sète, a smaller urban centre 30 kilometres South-West. There is also a strong urban diffusion towards the North (figures 7a and 8a). This concentrated growth should be compared to a more even distribution of the population growth between the largest urban poles in the two departments that is the result of the scenario 1 (figure 3b).

In the third scenario, the growth of the Nîmes area is sensibly amplified. There is a notable difference in the spatial distribution of the relative population increase in this scenario compared to the second one (figure 8b). Clearly, the growth of Nîmes does not inhibit the growth of smaller communes in the mountainous areas. This evolution may be explained by the relatively low diversification of the economical activities around Nîmes. A large part of the immigrated population seems to have been forced to move somewhere else as the labour market is too specialised around Nîmes.

The fourth scenario shows a totally different image of the distribution of the population in the region and of its relative growth (figure 8c). The general spatial structure is maintained, but there is a certain tendency to a geographical homogenisation in terms of population (figure 7c). Indeed, the smaller communes have grown in a significant manner and the larger communes have stagnated or even declined as it is the case for Montpellier, Nîmes and Béziers for example. However, in the surroundings of these urban centres the population has increased (figure 7c).

4. Future developments

The purpose of this modelling has been to study the evolutionary dynamics of settlement systems at a microscopic level of observation. The ambition was to obtain emerging spatial regularities from the individual behaviour, but the application of the model has shown that some meso_level rules are necessary in order to take into account the constraints the the spatial dimensions involve. The model has been able to reproduce correctly the decision to move as well as the approximate area of choice of living. But it fails in the choice of the commune itself. At that local level differences in attractivity between the communes and their surroundings plays a fundamental role. In an aggregated model such attractivities are classically defined according to general accessibility, amenities of different kinds, beauty of the site etc. In order to maintain the spirit of the microsimulation, such attractivities should be defined from the point of view of the individuals. For example, the presence of a school is attractive to families with younger children, whereas medical linked amenities are more attractive to retired people etc. The individual sensitivity to accessibility also varies. Therefor, the introduction of an indicator of attractivity defined at the aggregate level of the commune, but as a function of the individuals' perception, would improve the model.

Figure 7 - Population estimation in 2020

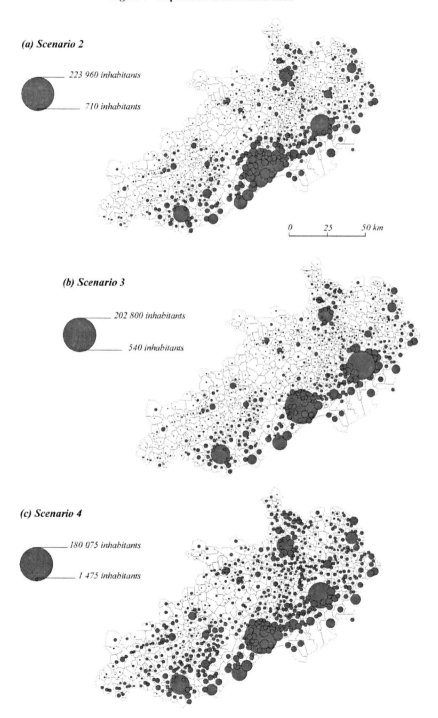

(a) Scenario 2

223 960 inhabitants

710 inhabitants

0   25   50 km

(b) Scenario 3

202 800 inhabitants

540 inhabitants

(c) Scenario 4

180 075 inhabitants

1 475 inhabitants

Figure 8 - Relative population increase between 1990 and 2020

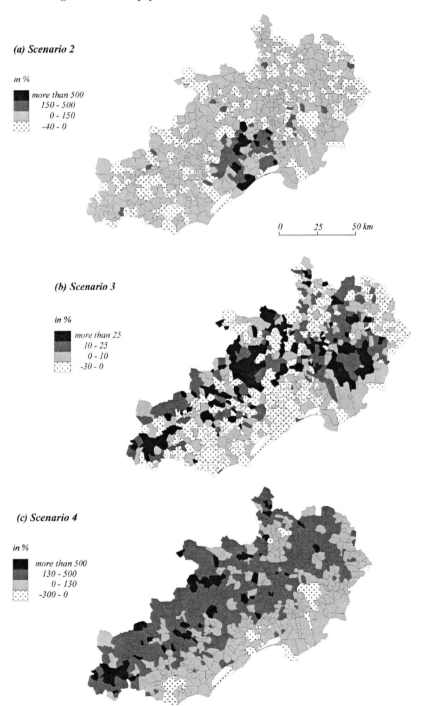

Bibliography

[ALL 97] ALLEN P., *Cities and regions as self-organizing systems; models of complexity*, Gordon and Breach Science Publishers, 1997,275p.

[BRU 94] BRUNET R., 1994. Le Languedoc dans l'ensemble méditerranéen. *C.R. Acad. Agric. Fr.*, 80, **9**, 111-122

[CLA 87] CLARKE M., HOLM E., Microsimulations methods in spatial analysis and planning, *Geografiska Annaler*, 69B, n°2, 1987,p145-164.

[CLA 96] CLARKE G. (ed.), *Microsimulation in policy model and planning*, London, Pion, 1996.

[HAA 89] HAAG G., *Dynamic Decision Theory: Applications to urban and regional topics*, Kluwer Academic Publishers, 1989, 256p.

[HOL 99] HOLM E., LINDGREN U., MÄKILÄ, ASCHAN-LEYGONIE C., BAUDET-Michel S., MATHIAN H., SANDERS L., GAUTIER, Micro-simulation of the population dynamics in a region with a strong urban growth, in A multiscalar investigation into the dynamics of land abandonment in Southern France, vol5, t1, 1999 (contract ENV4-CT95-0159, DGX11 of the European Commission)

[HOL 2000] HOLM E., LINDGREN U, MALMBERG G., *Dynamic microsimulation, in Spatial Models and GIS; New Potential and New Models*, FOTHERINGHAM S. and WEGENER M. (eds), Gisdata 7, Taylor and Francis, p143-165

[PUM 89] PUMAIN D., SANDERS L., SAINT-JULIEN Th., *Villes et auto-organisation*, Paris, Economica, 191p.

[PUM 98] PUMAIN D., Urban Research and Complexity, in C. BERTUGLIA, G. BIANCHI, A. MELA (eds.), *The city and its science*, Springer, Physical Verlag, Heidelberg, 1998, p323-361.

[SAN 92] SANDERS L., *Système de villes et synergétique*, Paris, Anthropos, 274 p.

[SAN 99] SANDERS L., 1999, Modelling within a self-organising or a .microsimulation framework: opposite or complementary approaches? CYBERGEO, No. 90.

[VEN 99] VENCATASAWMY C., HOLM E., REPHANN T., ESKO J., SWAN N., ÖHMAN M., ASTRÖM M., ALFREDSSON E., HOLME K., SIIKAVAARA J., 1999, Building a spatial microsimulation model, http://www.smc.kiruna.se

Modelling urban phenomena with cellular automata

Diane Vanbergue* — Jean-Pierre Treuil* — Alexis Drogoul**

*Laboratoire d'Informatique Appliquée, IRD
32 rue Henri Varagnat, 93143 Bondy Cedex, France
{vanberg,treuil}@bondy.ird.fr

**Laboratoire d'Informatique de Paris 6
4 place Jussieu, 75252 Paris Cedex 05, France
Alexis.Drogoul@lip6.fr

ABSTRACT: Multi-agents systems are frequently used to study complex phenomena and offer tools that interest urban specialists. The aim of this article is to present an example of an approach on the phenomenon of intra-urban migration in Bogota. Our model is based on one of the simplest form of multi-agent systems, kind of cellular automata, where migrants are seen as population flow. It allows us to build an artificial city, based on real census, and also to represent the behaviour of the population, determined by its representation of the different districts. This paper presents the formalism of the model and some results.

RÉSUMÉ : Les systèmes multi-agents sont fréquemment utilisés pour étudier des phénomènes complexes et offrent des outils qui intéressent les spécialistes de l'urbain. Le but de cet article est de présenter un exemple d'une approche du phénomène de la migration intra-urbaine à Bogota. Notre modèle est basé sur l'une des formes les plus simples des modèles multi-agents, une sorte d'automate cellulaire. Il nous permet de construire une ville artificielle, basée sur des recensements réels et aussi de représenter le comportement de la population, déterminé par leur représentation des différents quartiers. Ce papier présente le formalisme du modèle et des résultats.

KEY WORDS: multi-agent simulation, cellular automata, urban modelling

MOTS CLÉS: simulation multi-agent, automate cellulaire, modélisation urbaine

1. Introduction

Cities and metropolises are open, complex, far from equilibrium, and thus self-organising systems [POR 94]. They are open in two ways: firstly, because everyone can enter or leave the city (immigration and emigration), and secondly because cities grow up or decline with time (territory expansion). They are complex because their structure depends on many parameters that induce interactions and retroactions, and they are therefore difficult to grasp and analyse. The definition of equilibrium is a real scientific question ([DER96][PUM89]): if we consider that no change is observed at equilibrium, cities are far from equilibrium because there is constant mobility (daily and residential) between districts and with the outside. Lastly, they are self-organising because there is a production coming from simple yet numerous interactions of spatial organisations able to maintain themselves in time [SAN98].

Classical models have problems with such complex systems because of their numerous levels, interactions, qualitative parameters, and dynamics. Thus, multi-agent systems are frequently used to study complex phenomena because they offer an alternative solution: entities are directly represented as agents; thus, a phenomenon is the result of the behaviours of the entities and their interactions. These entities can be spatial ([BUR93]) or individuals (see, for example, Bousquet [BOU99] which compares "spatial approach" and "actors approach").

Geographers, demographers and cartographers are interested by this means of analysis. By modelling urban phenomena, they want to study the effects of urban policies on the structure of the city, its forms of urbanisation and the residential practices used by the inhabitants and the segregation. We think that multi-agents systems can help to understand the relationships between these different forms of mobility, the spatial organisation and the social distribution.

The aim of this article is to present an example of this approach applied to the town of Bogota (Colombia). Our model is based on a kind of cellular automata, which are a simple form of multi-agents systems and which study the dynamics of the sociospatial distribution. We decided to work on Bogota because of our scientific collaboration with urban specialists who work on urban processes and who own data and expertise on Bogota. The case of Bogota is particularly interesting because of the importance of mobility (emerging country) and the size of the city (5.5 millions of inhabitants).

Our objective was to build an "artificial city", a laboratory where urban specialists (especially our partners) could test their hypotheses about the behaviour of the households and observe the influence on structure and distribution of the town. This approach of experimentation is an innovation in social sciences and can help specialists in formulating their hypothesis and thus, in understanding and analysing complex phenomena; of course, this work needs an expertise on the city studied. Therefore, working on real data was necessary for a fair comparison with reality; we used the Bogota's census of 1993.

We will start with a quick review of the use of cellular automata in urban simulation (Part 2); then, we will present the model, our hypothesis and the transformation rules (Part 3). And finally, after the presentation of different elements of the interface, we will present some results (Part 4).

2. Cellular automata and urban simulation

Cellular automata have been used quite often for modelling geographic, and in particular urban phenomena. They can give a spatial representation in which each cell represents a zone, which state depends of the neighbouring cells' states.

For example, Kirtland [KIR94] studies the urban growth of San Francisco Bay with cellular automata. In his model, cells represent zones obtained with GIS[1] and their states are defined by geographical variables (socio-economic are random ones). The cells evolve according to simple transition rules (a cell becomes urban if its neighbours are urban, if it is near a road, etc.). Phipps and Langlois give another example of the simulation of a real town (Ottawa). In SimUrb, cells still represent zones but their focus is to explain socio-economic structure. Therefore, they use "human" variables like population, housing and employment and they observe the interactions and feedback between themselves [PHI97]. Colonna [COL98] uses adaptive cellular automata, with genetic algorithms that learn rules. The state of a cell is defined by its density, its occupation (residential, industrial, etc). His model has been used to simulate Roma. But these models study the evolution of the city (extent, global structure) itself and do not focus on dynamics of the population (spatial repartition of each category, segregation, etc.) Regarding intra-urban migrations, that is our subject, City-1 [POR94] uses two layers: the first consisting of cellular automata where cells represent houses, and determine their with respect to the neighbouring cells and the second made of multi-agents systems where agents are families that move. This model studies intra-urban migrations but it is rather a "game", where the user is called "player", and not a realistic model, because of its little size (at most 1600 families).

The cellular automata we chose to use can be seen as a simple form of multi-agent systems, where cells are fixed agents. As seen before, this spatial vision is a classic in realistic geographical modelling. Cellular automata can also process a lot of data, (there are 1.5 millions households in Bogota). We consider that intra-urban migration is an exchange of flows of population between the different districts, thus cellular automata allow observation of the behaviour of the population, satisfying the desiderata of the specialists.

---

[1] *Geographical Information System*

3. Hypothesis

Working on real data means choosing variables and parameters that are significant in the migration process, significant in the specialists' mind, usable, and which exist in the census (for the variables).

3.1. *Geographical units*

In the cellular automata, we could have used a classical grid (cells with homogenous geometric properties) but we have chosen to define cells as sectors similar to the ones used in the census: there are 618 of them in Bogota. This choice is usual in urban modelling ([KIR94], [COL98]) and useful because of the geographic and demographic homogeneity of the sectors is well represented in the cells. The population of the sector defines the state of the cell.

3.2. *Decision units*

We do not consider the migration of individuals but that of the household (a household is constituted by individuals who live in the same place and share food charges). They are characterised by their social class, their age[2] and their status (leaseholder or owner). Households with the same characteristics constitute a group; there are 40 groups (5 social categories x 4 age categories x 2 status categories).

The state of a cell is then defined by a vector constituted by the size of each group in the sector.

3.3. *Decision process*

Most of the characteristics of the housing depend on the characteristics of the district. Thus, we first chose to focus on the choice of the district by the households. We consider that the characteristics of a district are given by the characteristics of the population living in this district and then, inhabitants are more concerned by their neighbourhood than by the equipment of the district.

A cell exchanges flows of population with its influence area (cells sharing a frontier with it), that involves that migrants do not go far from their original district and that inhabitants have a limited representation of Bogota: they only have information about the "influence area" of their district.

---

[2] *the one of the head of the family*

To answer to the question "why do people migrate?", we suppose that they have a rational behaviour:

- Each household has a system of preferences.
- Each household can estimate its satisfaction in a sector with this system.
- A household migrates when it thinks it would find something better elsewhere (if its satisfaction elsewhere is better than in its own sector).

In the model, households have preferences for some groups of population. Their satisfaction depends on the population's distribution in the sector. We can consider three steps in the behaviour of households. First, if a household evaluates that it is not satisfied, it will have a desire to migrate to other sectors of its influence area. Second, if it has a desire to migrate and if it thinks that it can be more satisfied in another sector, it will make the decision to migrate. Third, if it makes the decision to migrate, it will migrate with a given probability.

3.4. *Formalisation*

3.4.1. *Preferences*

A household's satisfaction depends on the distribution of the population in the sector and its preference system. Preferences are coefficients of appreciation for categories of people.

For example, if a household prefers to live with households of its group (with the same characteristics), its satisfaction will be at its maximum when only people of its group inhabit its sector. It will otherwise try to migrate to the sector where the proportion of its group is the most important.

We note $\bullet_{GG'}$ the preference of the group G for the group G'. These preferences are in the interval [-1; +1]; +1 representing attraction, 0 indifference and −1 reject. The user fixes these parameters (by default $\bullet_{GG}$=1 and $\bullet_{GG'}$=0 for G•G': people want to be with people like them but do not reject others).

3.4.2. *Threshold of satisfaction*

The threshold of satisfaction can be defined as a minimum limit. If a household evaluates that its satisfaction is below it, it is not satisfied and it will have a desire to migrate.

We note Ψ this threshold. The user fixes this parameter (by default Ψ =100%: households will have a desire to migrate as soon as they are not totally satisfied).

3.4.3. *Propensities*

The propensities can be defined as a probability with which a household, that has taken the decision to migrate, actually migrates.

For example, if a group of households has a propensity equal to 0,8 and if these households have made the decision to migrate, only 80% of them migrate.

We note P_G the propensity of the group G. The user fixes these parameters (by default $P_G=1$: if a household makes the decision to migrate, it will migrate).

3.4.4. *The behaviour of the households*

A household evaluates its satisfaction in the sector s with respect to the preferences of its group to others $\bullet_{GG'}$, the distribution of the different groups in s $n_G(s)/n(s)$ and the evaluation in the sectors of the influence area of s $V(s)$.

The satisfaction function $\bullet_G$ of the group G for the sector s, depending on its influence area is:

$$\Omega_G(s) = \frac{E_G(s) + \sum_{v \in V(s)} E_G(v)}{1 + |V|}$$

where $E_G(s)$ is the evaluation function of the group G only for the sector s

$$E_G(s) = \sum_G \Pi_{GG'} \frac{n_G(s)}{n(s)}$$

If households are not satisfied in their sector (their satisfaction is under the threshold satisfaction), they have a desire to migrate in the sectors of their influence area where they think they can be more satisfied.

$$V_G^*(s) = \begin{cases} \left\{ v \in V(s) \middle| \Omega_G(v) > \Omega_G(s) \right\} & \text{if } \Omega_G(s) < \Psi \\ \varnothing & \text{else} \end{cases}$$

3.4.5. *Transition rules*

We note N(s) the vector that represents the state of the sector s with 40 components. A component is the number of each group in this sector $n_G^t(s)$.

For each group G and each sector s, we need a transition function.

$$n_G^{t+1}(s) = n_G^t(s) - \sum_{v \in V(s)} f_G(s, v)$$

where $f_G(s,v)$ represents the migratory flow between the sector s and the sector v (which is in the influence area of s).

This migratory flow is the difference between emigrants and immigrants.

$$f_G(s,v) = m_G(s,v) - m_G(v,s) = -f_G(v,s)$$

$m_G(s,v)$ is the number of migrants from s to v. It depends of the propensity of migration $P_{G'}$, the size of the population in the sector $n_G^t(s)$ and the evaluation $\bullet_G$.

$$m_G(s,v) = \begin{cases} \left| P_G * n_G^t(s) * \dfrac{\Omega_G(v) - \Omega_G(s)}{\sum\limits_{v \in V_G^*(s)}(\Omega_G(v) - \Omega_G(s))} \right. & if \;\; v \in V_G^*(s) \\[20pt] 0 \;\; else \end{cases}$$

The flow of population will be all the greater that the gain of satisfaction will be important.

The transition function has to respect some properties:
Conservation of the total population:

$$\sum_s n_G^t(s) = \sum_s n_G^{t+1}(s) \; \text{because} \; f(s,v) = -f(v,s)$$

No-negative population:

$$n_G^t(s) \geq 0 \; \text{because} \; \sum_{v \in V(s)} m_G(s,v) \leq n_G(s)$$

4. The simulator

4.1. Interface

We tried to construct a tool for urban specialists with a simple and easy to use interface that would allow them to test their hypotheses without any help.

There are three main parts in our interface:

- The map window, that represents Bogota. It allows observation of the distribution and the evolution of the groups (by density, number, percentage, or majority).
- The parameters windows, that allow easy settings of the parameters of the model (preferences, propensities, and satisfaction threshold).
- The indicators windows that allow to study the evolution of the global indicators (for example, proportion of migrants w.r.t. the time).

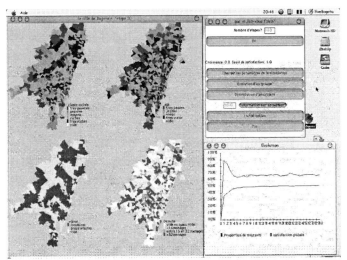

Figure 1. *Interface of the simulator*

For a sharper analysis, specialists can obtain information (graphics or data) on a particular cell about its different variables. Lastly, our program outputs data files that can be used in other softwares like statistic ones (Excel, Stata, SAS, etc.), or cartographic ones (ArcView, Savane).

4.2. Simulation examples

The model we present does not give valid results if we consider that validation is the exact reproduction of reality: the maps we obtain as results do not represent the actual structure of Bogota. However, this model was mostly made in the aim of testing some hypotheses on how parameters influence urban mobility.

4.2.1. Basic examples

We can notice:
- If all the propensities are equal to 0, there is no movement and satisfaction is constant. The households make the decision to migrate but they do not migrate (their probability to move is 0).
- If all the preferences are equal to 0, the households are not satisfied but they don't find a better sector elsewhere (each cell is evaluated to 0). They have a desire to migrate but they don't make the decision.
- If all the preferences are equal to 1, the households are satisfied everywhere (each cell is evaluated to 1, the maximum). They don't have a desire to migrate.

Our first example is very simple: all the propensities to move are equal to 1 and all the preferences are equal to 1, except for "very rich" people that only like other very rich people (their preferences to other categories are equal to 0).

It is trivial that only "very rich" people will move but we can also observe that at first they are few in cells, and disseminated in the whole city. After 30 migration steps they are concentrated in a few cells.

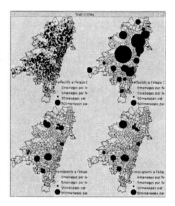

Figure 2. *Very rich people repartition. Up left: Bogota step 0; Up right: Bogota step 30. Bottom left: immigrants between step 29 and 30. Bottom right: emigrants between step 29 and 30. All these results show the effects of the main parameters on our model. We will now present some scenarios to show how the model works*

4.2.2. Scenarios

We have built 4 scenarios under rather extreme hypotheses. More realistic hypotheses are now tested by our partners.

4.2.2.1. Hypotheses

On propensities
- Mobility propensities: households always migrate when they have made the decision to do so (all the propensities are equal to 1).
- Lower category propensities: lower categories (young, poor, leaseholder) are more mobile than upper ones (old, rich, owner).

On preferences
- Homophil preferences: households want to be with households like them.
- Aspiration preferences: households want to be with upper categories and reject lower categories (the preference matrix is not symmetrical). Lower categories (young, poor, leaseholder) want to live with upper ones (old, rich, owner) but upper categories reject them.

4.2.2.2. Results

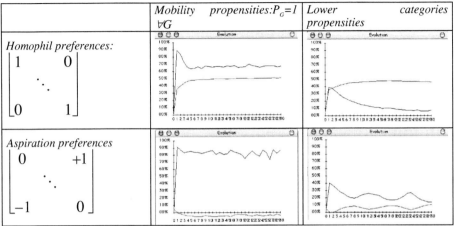

Figure 3. *The evolution of the number of migrants (in black) and the evolution of satisfaction (in red)*

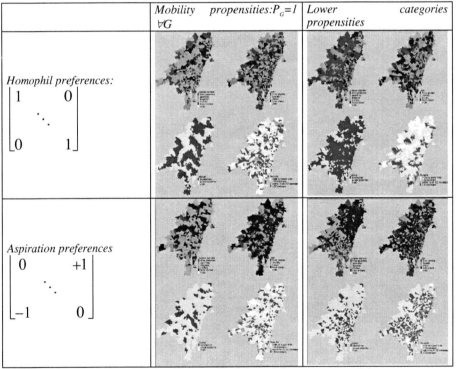

Figure 4. *Bogota's structure after 30 steps. Up left: social structure; up right: age structure; bottom left: status structure; bottom right: density*

4.2.2.3. Analysis

We can notice that a high mobility is not a factor of satisfaction: in the case of homophile preferences, the global satisfaction is the same in both cases of mobility, and in the case of aspiration preferences, the global satisfaction is better in the case of lower categories mobility than in the one of high mobility. We can understand that because, when there is high mobility, everybody moves during each step: when households reach a district, people whom they would like to live with have already moved to another district, so they are not satisfied in their new housing.

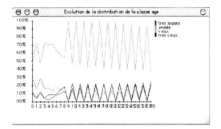

Figure 5. *The high mobility creates a permanent instability*

Figure 6. *A low mobility allows stability in the sectors*

We can see with this example that growth in the cells can be very important (the number is multiplied by 9) That means the density equals 750 households per hectare, that is a very high density.

That is, of course, because, in our model, the density of a cell is not limited as it can be in reality.

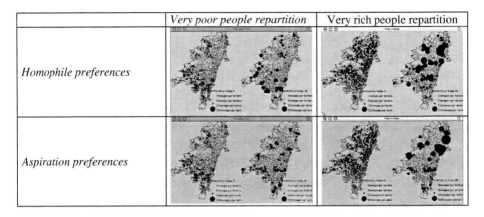

Figure 8. *The repartition of the categorise between step 0 and 30 under homophile and aspiration preferences. (Initial data are the same for both cases)*

The preferences influence the class repartition. In the homophile case, people of the same category concentrate in the same cells and live away from the other categories. In the aspiration case, the same category still concentrates in the same cells but a cell can be a place of concentration of different categories: there is concentration but no segregation.

We can also notice that in the homophile case, the concentration of the categories in particular cells is more stable than in the aspiration case. The aspiration induces concentrations of people to move between different cells, due to the attraction and reject of the other categories.

These extreme hypotheses lead of course to easily predictable phenomena, like concentration and segregation. But we can also observe some behaviour that we did not predict: a high mobility could be thought of as a factor of satisfaction, but actually, it leads to a worse situation than lower mobility.

5. Conclusion and perspectives

Our aim in this article was to show an approach of intra-urban migration modelling, based on a multi-agent system. Cellular automata, that can be considered in our model as a simple form of multi-agent systems, were first chosen because of their place in traditional geographical modelling and because of their capacity to process a lot of real data (each cell is a census sector, defined by a high-dimensional vector). Thus we consider the intra-urban migration as an exchange of flows of population between the different districts.

We have supposed that migration is the result of a search for satisfaction. This satisfaction is based on preferences, here towards some categories of population. This simple behaviour leads by itself to the apparition of complex phenomena.

Another aim was to make our simulator easily usable by the urban specialists we are working with. We thus created a comprehensive interface that allows them to easily gain various maps, global and local indicators, global and local processes.

Urban specialists can test their hypotheses in this "artificial Bogota". We have shown that some of them lead to particular results: we retrieve some classical results (segregation, concentration) but also some non-trivial ones (influence of mobility).

Our partners are now analysing these results and testing sharper hypotheses on Bogota. We are also building in parallel the data files for applying the model on Strasbourg (France). This is a great interest to us and to our colleagues since migration behaviours in industrialised countries are different from those in emerging countries.

We are however interested by more complex approaches, which are not based on cellular automata anymore but on more elaborate multi-agent systems (with a cellular grid [BEN98]): one with a small protocol of collective discussion, which pays attention to the problem of the limited capacity of the cell, and a more cognitive one, based on biographic reports, and not only on the results of census.

6. Acknowledgements

We wish to express our thankfulness to Françoise Dureau, Christiane Weber and Bernard Lortic, our urban specialists who have taken the time to explain us the different processes and phenomena that occur in cities. This work was supported by the Programme on Geographical Information System (CNRS).

7. Bibliography

[BEN98] BENENSON I., 1998, Multi-agents Simulations of residential dynamics in the City, Computer Environnment and Urban Systems, 22, 25-42

[BOU99] BOUSQUET F.,GAUTIER D., 1999, Comparaison de deux approches de modélisation des dynamiques spatiales par Simulation Multi-Agents : les approches « spatiale » et « acteurs », Cybergeo 89

[BUR93] BURA S., GUÉRIN-PACE F., MATHIAN H., PUMAIN D., SANDERS L., 1993, Cities can be agents too: a model for the evolution of settlements systems, in Gilbert N., Artificial Societies, 86-102

[COL98] COLONNA A., DI STEPHANO V., LOMBARDO S., PAPINI L., RABINO A., 1998, Learning cellular automata: modelling urban modelling, Proceedings of the 3rd International conference on GeoComputation, Universuty of Bristol, 17-19 September 1998

[DER96] DERYCKE P.H., HURIOT J.M., PUMAIN D., 1996, Penser la ville, Théorie et modèles, Anthropos 96, ch2&3

[KIR94] KIRTLAND D., GAYOS .L., CLARKE K., DECOLA L., ACEVEDO W., and BELL C., 1994, An Analysis of Human Induced Land Transformations in the San Francisco Bay/Sacramento Area, World RessourcesReview, 6,n°2, 206-217

[PHI97] PHIPPS M.,LANGLOIS A, 1997, Automates cellulaires, applications à la simulation urbaine, Hermes

[POR94] PORTUGALI J, BENENSON I ,1995, Artifical planning experience by means of a heuristic cell-space model/ simulating international migration in the urban process, Environnment and Planning A,, 27, 1647-1665

[PUM89] PUMAIN D., SANDERS L., SAINT-JULIEN T., 1989, Villes et autoorganisation, Economica

[SAN98] SANDERS L., 1998, Les décisions individuelles dans les domaines dynamiques, Colloque Geopoint 1998 (to be published)

Simulating accessibility by SWARM

La simulation de l'accessibilité avec SWARM

Matteo Bellomo[*] — **Sylvie Occelli**[**]

* Via Roma 16,
13030 Caresanablot (VC), Italy
10148 Turin, Italy
matteobellomo@email.com
**IRES - Istituto di Ricerche Economico Sociali del Piemonte,
Via Nizza 18,
10125 Turin, Italy
occelli@ires.piemonte.it

ABSTRACT. *Extending our conventional notion of accessibility is a major topic of interest in the geographical and planning literature. This paper explores one of these possibilities. It describes individuals' action spaces and their associated accessibility by means of computer simulation. A multi-agent model is developed with the aim of providing a deeper understanding of daily life activities in a spatial setting. The SWARM software platform is used as a means to investigate the action spaces of individuals and their management strategies.*

RÉSUMÉ. *L'extension de la notion d'accessibilité est un sujet d'intérêt en géographe et planification. Cet article explore une de ces possibilités. Il décrit les 'espaces d'action' des individus et leur relative accessibilité par la simulation. On développe un modèle multi-agents qui permet décrire le déroulement des activités quotidiennes dans un milieu urbain.. La base informatique SWARM est utilisée pour décrire les espaces d'actions des individus e leurs stratégies de comportement.*

KEY WORDS: *accessibility, action space, social simulation, multi-agent approach, SWARM*

MOTS-CLÉS: *accessibilité, espace d'action, approche multi-agents, simulation sociale, SWARM.*

1. Introduction

Accessibility is a well established concept in the geographical and planning literature. Recently, there has been renewed interest in accessibility and the need to revise current notions has become evident. A number of reasons motivate this upsurge in interest and are extensively dealt with elsewhere [BER 95, 97, COU ed. 96, HAN 95, OCC 98, 99].

Here we explore one of these possibilities. This is based on two main notions related to the accessibility issue [OCC 00]: a) a concept of 'activity space' originally developed in the field of time-geography; and b) a notion of 'urban performance management'.

In this study, we describe individuals' action spaces by means of computer simulation. A multi-agent model is developed with the aim of providing a deeper understanding of daily life activities in a spatial setting. This is an application of a relatively novel field in social science and geography in which simulation allows new ways of thinking about socio-economic and urban processes [COU 98, GIL 99]. The *Swarm* software platform for the simulation of complex adaptive systems is used as a novel means for investigating the action spaces of individuals and their management strategies.

The paper is organised as follows. In section 2, we recall the notion of action space referred to in the multi-agent model for Simulating ACcessibility (SimAC). Section 3 outlines the general architecture of the SimAC model. Section 4 presents some preliminary results of the simulation experiments and in section 5 we make some concluding remarks.

2. Implementing the notion of accessibility

Accessibility is an hybrid entity which shares features (i.e. provides a junction) with two fundamental components of any spatial system, the spatio-temporal pattern of activities, and spatio-temporal pattern of interdependencies [OCC 98].

In our approach, two main levels of definition of accessibility are considered: a) an individual level, which considers the action-space within which an individual currently lives; and b) a systemic level, which reflects the functional and spatial organisation of activities (mix of opportunities, travel times, transport services, opening times of services, etc.) observed at an aggregate level (i.e. as provided by the various transport and service agencies).

We emphasise the co-existence of a multiplicity of representations of accessibility, which can vary as a result of the process of learning undertaken by individuals and evolution of the urban system as a whole (i.e. the changes in the socio-economic, functional and temporal components of urban environments, as well as in the human settlement).

The action space of an individual is the functional, spatial and temporal space available to him/her as a result of his/her participation in activities, in relation to personal and environmental constraints and opportunities created by other individuals as well as by social and economic institutions.

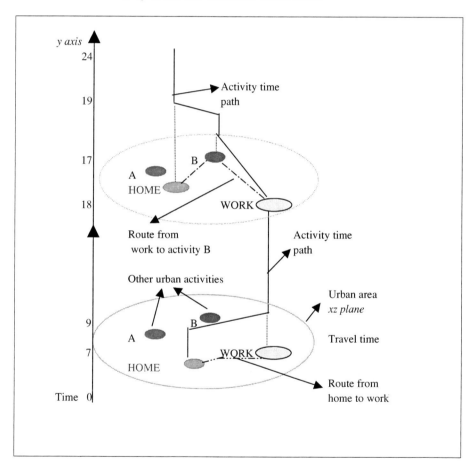

Figure 1. *A spatio-temporal scheme of the action space of an individual*

Since the pioneering work of Hagerstrand [HAG 75], the concept stimulated a long established tradition in time-geography literature and is now attracting new interest [HUI 98, NEW98]. It builds upon the idea that every action and event in an individual's life has to be referred to both temporal and spatial dimensions. These define a two dimensional framework which allows to describe the 'path' followed by an individual as he/she moves through time and space, see Fig.1. In the early formulations, these paths revealed 'prisms' which made it possible to account for the locations to be reached within a given time frame.

3. Modelling accessibility through simulation: building the SimAC model

While having its roots in artificial intelligence and cognitive science, simulation by means of synthetic agents is attracting increasing interest in many domains, ranging from military and commercial, to entertainment, education and scientific computing. In geography and planning the field is also rapidly developing within the related approach of cellular automata [CEC 96, PAP 97, BAT 99, SEM 99].

The potential of using multi-agent approach to deal with the notion of accessibility previously described is straightforward and can be summarised as follows:

— first, this approach allows us to approximate the basic features of an individual's action space better, i.e. their changing profile resulting from the adaptation of individuals' spatial behaviour to a varying environment;

— second, it makes it possible to explore the kind of collective behaviour likely to emerge from the interactions among autonomous and heterogeneous individuals and between these latter and the urban environment;

— finally it involves making explicit the kind of representations an individual has of his or her 'action space', i.e. the set of hypotheses we, as analysts, make in developing our descriptions (models) of accessibility.

In our approach, an 'agent' is a synthetic representation of a person or a collective actor who lives and acts in a urban system, such as a city, a neighbourhood or an area. This presupposes that:

— the agent does not act in a vacuum, but is socially and spatially embedded. Therefore the agent inherits 'knowledge' of his or her action space in the urban environment as a result of the 'prior information' available at a system level (i.e. the kind of knowledge which is encoded in the cultural and social structure of a city);

— the agent is intelligent and also possesses some human-like emotions and attitudes. As such, he or she can learn, acquire new knowledge and change his or her (spatial) behaviour accordingly.

We can further suppose that the interacting agents create a (artificial) world together with the urban environment. In particular, three interacting 'species' of agents populate this world, see Fig. 2.:

— INHABITANTS: these agents closely approximate the spatial behaviour of individuals as typically observed in the study individual behaviour in a geographical context. These agents, therefore, possess 'an action space' and are able to modify it as they move within the urban environment (Fig.1). *Inhabitants* are able to derive a measure of their accessibility as an evaluation of the performance of their action space;

— LOCALITIES: these agents embody a few 'components' of the urban environment belonging to the action spaces of *inhabitants*. They describe certain 'reactions' of 'places'(i.e. service provisions, car parking availability, opening times, traffic restrictions, etc.) which are visited by *inhabitants* as they move within their action space. Compared with the *inhabitants, localities* are spatially 'fixed' and embody a collective type behaviour, which is mostly relevant at a system level. *Localities* are able to observe some aggregate features resulting form the interactions of *inhabitants* as these take part to urban activities. They do not compute a measure of accessibility as *inhabitants* do. Instead they can assess their own performance resulting from the spatial behaviour of inhabitants (i.e. consumers' revenues, congestion, etc.) and observe what occurs in other localities as well. These performance measures, along with the effects produced by the contacts with other agents (the *whispers*), can be used for establishing/updating the set of 'reactions' localities would produce;

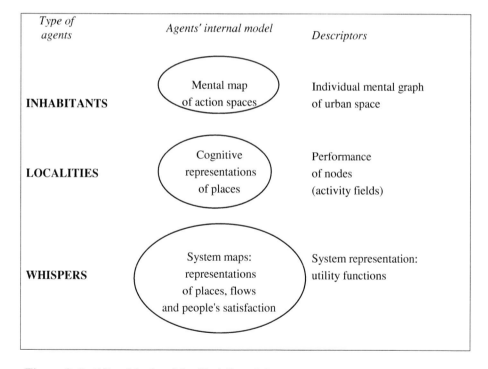

Type of agents	Agents' internal model	Descriptors
INHABITANTS	Mental map of action spaces	Individual mental graph of urban space
LOCALITIES	Cognitive representations of places	Performance of nodes (activity fields)
WHISPERS	System maps: representations of places, flows and people's satisfaction	System representation: utility functions

Figure 2. *Building blocks of the SimAC model*

— WHISPERS: in contrast with the preceding types, these agents do not embody any physical entity. On the contrary, they represent some general intangible entity which mimics the 'information' available in the urban system also for policy purpose. *Whispers* act by making available a set of 'signals' which are provided to both *inhabitants* and *localities*. These signals can take various forms, such as media information, norms, rules, and advertising. They can also be relevant for a variety of 'policy actions', i.e. the introduction of measures of traffic restriction, transportation services and new information technologies. *Whispers* do not have any spatial fixed location, but are able to observe certain outcome of both the interactions among inhabitants (i.e. their individual action spaces) and reactions of *localities*. In the process they can update and/or modify the content of the signals to be made available. Underlying the w*hisper* entity is a notion of 'genotypic information' which, to some extent, would imprint the 'representations' of the various agents.

Three distinctive features characterise the SimAC model.

First, the functioning of each type of agent is 'deliberative' in the sense that it is based on 'the agent's internal models' of the urban environment [SLO 99]. As a result, several representations of accessibility are produced by the ' internal model' of each type of agents. As 'these representations' guide the agents' behaviour, changes in representations can influence it, although the final effects will depend on agents' overall resilience.

Second, the relationships between agents (i.e. the external structure of the model architecture), consist of two main types:

— physical (or functional) relationships resulting from the participation of individuals to the various activities and movements in the urban environment;

— non-physical (i.e. informational) relationships, associated with the connections existing or likely to be established between the various representations of accessibility. The latter, in particular, can be conceived as belonging to a multi-layered structure, only partially ordered in a hierarchical way.

Third, urban environment is not simply a 'space' which contains the interacting agent, but plays an active role. Various descriptions of the urban environment coexist:

— the first is a '*system description*' which reflects the outcome of the agents' behaviour. This can be conceived as a '*pulsing graph*' in which the edges represent a kind of 'generalised distance' between places (i.e. a measure of the effectiveness to reach a place) and the nodes the 'status' of places where urban activities (*localities*) are sited. The edges and nodes of the 'pulsing graph' are dynamically updated at the end of a given schedule of events;

— the second consists of the various representations (maps) derived from the agents' internal models. These all refer to the *pulsing graph* but consider different specifications of it according to the various types of agents. For *inhabitants* the representation is the *mental map (cognitive graph)* of their action space. (i.e. a kind of 'topological sub-graph' of the 'pulsing graph'). For *localities* the map consists of the *cognitive set of nodes.* Associated with the nodes are the fields generated by the demand of the located urban activities. For *whispers* the representation of the urban environment is a set of *weighted utility functions* which account for an assessment of the 'pulsing graph' and situations (i.e. levels of satisfaction) of the agents;

— the last description is external to the agent and consists of the 'grid' supporting the movements of agents (and the pulsing graph). The grid is a useful discrete approximation of both a continuous and a relational geographical space.

4. Implementing the SimAC model by SWARM

4.1. *General outline*

The logical structure of the SimAC model finds a straightforward counterpart in the basic components of SWARM programming software, see Fig.3.

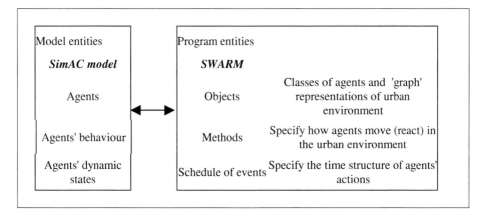

Figure 3. *Main correspondences between SimAC and Swarm*

SWARM belongs to the most recent family of simulation toolkits which is being developed for modelling complex adaptive systems. It uses an object oriented language and is based on a set of classes of libraries. The latter perform various tasks, some of which can be used outside SWARM, while others are domain-specific [MIN 96].

All agents are implemented as a class; other classes are developed to simplify source code structure and give us more flexibility for managing the model. Inhabitants can interact with environment and through environment with localities and other inhabitants, see Fig. 4.

Inhabitants' mental map of space is included in a specific object called 'Mental graph'; it is an inhabitant internal object and implements inhabitant decisional process. As it is a specific object, it can be easily modified in further version of SimAC.

There are four classes of agents

— *Environment*. This is a two-dimensional grid object (*class Grid2d* is used for this purpose) that stores in every cell some information, like inhabitant positions. The grid is not isotropic as some cells can be unavailable (i.e. cannot be crossed) or can have a different carrying capacity. Roads are described as a sequence of cells. Every crossroads is called a 'node'. The grid object is linked with two graphic objects: the first one displays the inhabitant position, the second one the inhabitant density associated with a specific cell.

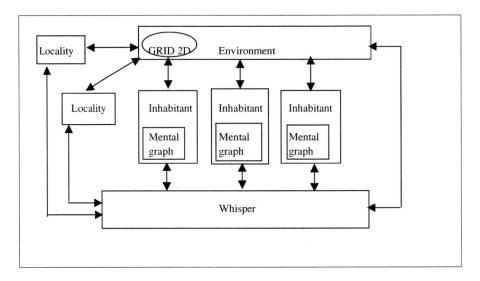

Figure 4. *The SimaAC model as implemented in Swarm version 1*

— *Inhabitants*. They have a certain (limited) number of features: they know where their home and job are located on the two dimensional grid and are able to find their way from home to work and the other way round (they can compute a 'minimum path' from a node to another one, using a Dijkstra algorithm). Inhabitants have a mental representation of the environment (the mental graph) that is created and updated using their individual experience in moving on the grid. This is based on their travel time and quality such as a measure of traffic congestion. All inhabitants have their own mental representation, so every inhabitant is different from the other ones.

— *Localities*. They occupy certain nodes on the grids, have both residences and jobs and are visited by inhabitants every day. All localities know the number of their employees, how many inhabitants are moving toward them in a given time span how many employees have already arrived at a given time and how congested are the roads around them.

— *Whispers*. This particular agent has knowledge of home-to-work flows, traffic jam, locality situation, inhabitant positions and satisfaction. In this version, there is only one kind of whisper, who acts as a kind of 'external manager of the grid', i.e. he computes a number of statistics about flows and travel times and can modify the grid exogenously.

The functioning of the model consists of three main phases.

— *Initialisation*

The program creates and initialises objects (i.e. agents, networks, graphical display). Swarm library manages by itself computer memory. The following operations are performed:

    – localities are assigned to certain 'nodes' on the grid and given a carrying capacity (i.e. maximum number of inhabitants which can visit them)

    – inhabitants are assigned to localities where they live and work.

    – arches (a sequence of cells) connecting the nodes on the grid are given initial time values (nodes not connected or with low connectivity are given very high values).

— *Simulation*

The time span of a simulation is one day. This is measured by the Swarm internal clock, in terms of elementary time steps. Their total number can vary in each day as they depend on the overall time spent by inhabitants for travelling to work and back.

At the beginning of each day, inhabitants determine their home-to-work minimum path, following the sequence of arches having the lowest travel times. Then, following that path, they move on the grid, updating the time of each arc as they pass it. To carry out this task, the following formula is used:

$$w\,(t) = a * s(f, t) + c * g(t)] \hspace{4cm} [1]$$

where,

$s(f, t)$ is the number of time steps necessary to pass an arc, given the flow on it; a is a weight representing the importance of travel time for each inhabitant;

$g(t)$ is a function of congestion (number of inhabitants on each arc), and c is a parameter weighting its importance.

For each agent, therefore, two travel times exist: an observed time (s) and a perceived time (w). The updated perceived travel times (w) are then used by inhabitants for computing a 'new minimum path' in the following day. Minimum path is also calculated by inhabitants on their way back to home. As a result, the matrix of travel times is not symmetrical.

Localities monitor only the arrivals of employees as they approach their job location. In particular they are able to determine: a) the total number of approaching inhabitants at a certain (time) distance from them f(j); b)a measure of saturation of the available resources in the locality expressed as:

$$L\,(j) = f\,(j)/\,C\,(j) \hspace{4cm} [2]$$

where C (j) is the carrying capacity of each locality.

— Indicators of accessibility

These are computed by whispers as a result of the dynamics of both inhabitants and localities during the reference simulation period (a day). On the basis of the simulation results a number of accessibility indicators can be derived. In these experiments, the following conventional indicators are calculated:

– average travel times (s and w) for localities (obtained as a mean of inhabitants' values)

– average time of access among nodes of the grid, d (i, j), with d (i, j) = Σ_n w (i, ,j)] / N (i,j), and N the number of inhabitants passing the arc (i,j)

– accessibility potentials A in a residential locality i expressed as:

$$A(i) = \Sigma_j \, F(i,j)*[1/L \, (j)]* \exp [-b*s \, (i, j)] \qquad [3]$$

where *F(i,j)* are the inhabitants living in residential node i and working in locality j; *b* is the impedance parameter associated with travel time.

4.2. *Some simulation results*

In these experiments, the grid has 64 nodes. There are 300 inhabitants who are randomly distributed on the grid and 6 job localities. The latter can also be residential nodes. Each arch is 5 cells long and its initial time value is 5. The values of the c and b parameters are both 0.10.

We compare here some results of two simulations differing only in the sensitivity to travel time, (parameter *a* in equation 1). In the first simulation, SIM1, half of the inhabitants are weakly sensitive to their travel time (a=0.5), whereas the other half is fully sensitive (a=1). In the second, SIM2, all the inhabitants are equally sensitive (a=1). All the results refer to the 30th simulated day.

The resulting average perceived and observed travel times for the 6 localities are shown in Fig.5

As could be expected, a lower value of the travel sensitivity parameter affects significantly travel times to and from the localities. It mainly influences the perceived travel times (w), which are lower in SIM1 than in SIM2, while its impact on the observed travel times (s) is weaker. The outcome, however, varies among localities. This variability is also reflected in the accessibility values of localities, see Fig.6. Although the absolute values of accessibility increases appreciatively for all localities SIM1, their relative growth is higher for certain of them (i.e. for localities 33 and 55).

Finally, in Fig.7 the average home-to work travel time for each residential node is shown. The effects of the change in the importance of travel time (the weight a) are clearly evident. The figure can be interpreted as a 'statistical' description of the 'pulsing' graph', previously mentioned.

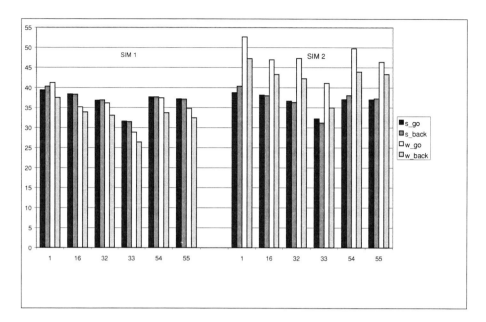

Figure 5. *Travel times s and w for the six localities in SIM1 and SIM2*

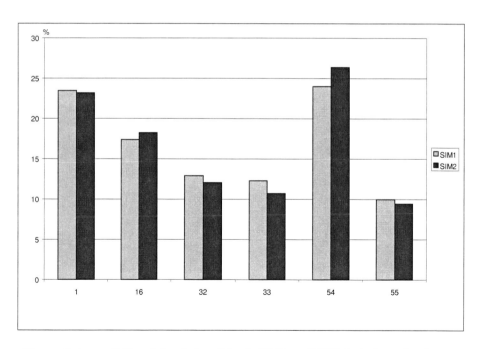

Figure 6. *Accessibility of the six localities in SIM1 and SIM2 (relative values)*

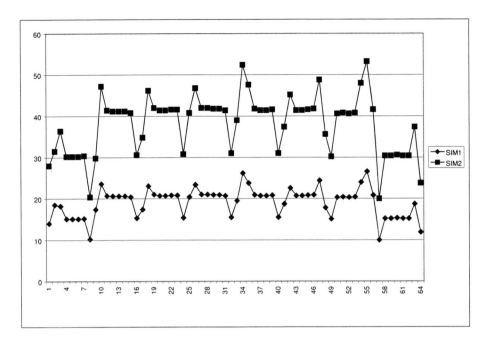

Figure 7. *Total average travel time (w) for each residential node in SIM1 and SIM2*

5. Concluding remarks

Although preliminary, this application of the SimAC model makes it evident that a number of both theoretical and operational questions will have to be dealt with in future work on simulating accessibility.

The first relates to the cognitive process underlying the (spatial) behaviour of agents in the urban environment, i.e. the refinement of the agents' knowledge about accessibility and communication of this knowledge among the various types of agents. These aspects are also attracting an increasing interest in a field of geographical analysis, i.e. cognitive geography and behavioural geography [EGE 98].

The second question stems from the 'emerging property' of accessibility as determined by the interaction of individuals' action spaces. This feature, in fact, has to be connected with other conventional definitions (measures) of accessibility, i.e. accessibility as a 'positive externality' and 'collective resource', in which it is already implicitly overshadowed from a conceptual point of view. In this respect, some possible advancement can be suggested from the adoption of what has been called a 'constructivist' approach [PID 96, BRU 98].

A final question refers to the graphical interface made available by SWARM. Improvements in the visualisation (and realism) of the agents' movement in an urban environment can probably be achieved by an integration of a SWARM simulation toolkit with GIS technology .

References

[BAT 99] Batty M., Xie Y., Sun Z., " Modeling urban dynamics through GIS-based cellular automata ", *Computers, Environment and Urban Systems, 23*, 1999, p. 205-233, Pergamon, New York.

[BER 95] Bertuglia C.S., Occelli S.," Transportation, Communications and Patterns of Location ", in Bertuglia C.S., Fischer M.M. and G. Preto (Eds.), *Technological Change, Economic Development and Space*, Springer, Berlin, 1995, p. 92-117.

[BER 97] Bertuglia C.S., Occelli S., " The Impact of the New Communications Technologies on Economic-Spatial Systems. An Agenda for Future Research ", Paper presented at the International Seminar 'The Impact of the New Communications Technologies on Economic-Spatial Systems', September 12-13, 1997, Pisa.

[BRU 98] Bruce E., " *Capturing Social Embeddedness: a Constructivist Approach* ", CPM Report 98-34, CPM, MMU, 1998, Manchester.

[CEC 96] Cecchini A., " Approaching Generalised Urban Automata with Help on Line (AUGH) ", in Besussi E. and Cecchini A. (Eds)., *Artificial Worlds and Urban Studies*, DEST, 1, Venezia, 1996, p. 231-248.

[COU 96] Couclelis H. (Ed.), " Spatial Technologies, Geographic Information, and the City ", Technical Report, 96-10, NCGIA, 1996 Santa Barbara, CA.

[COU 98] Couclelis H.," Geocomputation in Context ", in Longley P., Brooks S. M., McDonnell R., MacMillan B. (Eds.), *Geocomputation: A Primer*, John Wiley, New York, 1998, p. 17-29.

[EGE 98] Egenhofer M. J., Golledge R.G. (Eds.), " *Spatial and Temporal Reasoning in Geographic Information* Context ", Oxford University Press, New York, 1998.

[FOR 98] Forer P., " Geometric Approaches to the Nexus of Time, Space and Microprocesses: Implementing a Practical Model for Socio-Spatial Systems ", in Egenhofer M. J., Golledge R.G. (Eds.), *Spatial and Temporal Reasoning in Geographic Information Systems*, Oxford University Press, New York, 1998, p. 171-190.

[GIL 99] Gilbert N. , Troitzsch K. G., " *Simulation for the Social Scientist* ", Open University Press, Philadelphia, 1999.

[HAG 75] Hagerstrand T., " Space Time and Human Condition ", in Karlqvist A., Lundqvist L., Snickars F. (Eds.), *Dynamic Allocation of Urban Space*, Saxon House, Lexington, 1975, p.3-12.

[HAN 95] Hanson S. (ed.), " *The Geography of Urban Transportation* ", Guilford, New York, 1995.

[HUI 98] Huisman O., Forer P., " Computational Agents and Urban Life Spaces. A Preliminary Realisation of the Time-Geography of Student Lifestyles ", *Proceedings of the 3rd International Geocomputation Conference*, 17-19 September, Bristol, 1998.

[KIT 97] Kitamura R. , Mokhtarian P. , Laidet L., " A Micro-analysis of Land-use Travel in Five Neighborhoods in the San Francisco Bay Area ", *Transportation*, vol. 24, n° 2, 1997, p. 125-158, Kluwer, Dordrecht.

[KWA 98] Kwan M-P., " Space-Time and Integral Measures of Individual Accessibility: A Comparative Analysis Using a Point-Based Framework ", *Geographical Analysis*, vol. 30, n° 3, 1998, p.191-216. Ohio State University Press, Columbus.

[MIL 99] Miller H., " Measuring Space-time Accessibility Benefits Within Transportation Networks: Basic Theory and Computational Procedures ", *Geographical Analysis,* vol. 31, n° 2, 1999, p.187-212, Ohio State University Press, Columbus.

[MIN 96] Minar N., Burkhart R., Langton C., Askenazi M., " The Swarm Simulation System: a toolkit for building multi-agent simulations ", 1996, http://www.santafe. edu/projects/swarm/swarm.

[NEW 98] NEWSOME T.H., WALCOTT W.A., SMITH P.D., " Urban Activity Spaces: Illustrations and Application of a Conceptual Model for Integrating the Time and Space Dimensions ", *Transportation ,* vol.25, n° 4, p. 357-377, Kluwer, Dordrecht.

[OCC 98] Occelli S., " *Revisiting the Concept of Accessibility: Some Comments and Research Questions* ", Paper presented at the International Meeting on Accessibility in the Information Age, Asilomar, Pacific Grove, November 18-21, 1998.

[OCC 99] Occelli S.," Accessibility and Time Use in a Post-Fordist Urban System. Some Notes for a Research Agenda ", in Metz J. and Ehling M. (Eds.), *Time Use – Research, Data and Policy*, Research Institute on Professions, Department of Economics and Social Sciences, University of Lunenburg, vol. 10, NOMOS, Baden-Baden, 1999, p. 517-534.

[OCC 00] Occelli S., Bellomo M., " SimAC: Simulating Accessibility ", Paper presented at the 6th RSAI World Congress, Lugano, May 16-20, 2000.

[PAP 97] Papini L, Rabino G.A., " An Evolutionary Urban Cellular Automata: the Model and some first Simulations ", in Conte R., Hegselmann R, Terna P. (Eds.), *Simulating Social Phe*nomena, Springer, Berlin, 1997, p. 327-334.

[PID 96] Pidd .M., " *Tools for Thinking. Modelling in Management Science* ", Wiley, New York, 1996.

[SEM 99] Semboloni F., "A Discrete Coupled Map Lattice Approach to the Simulation of Land-Use and Transportation: Case Study of Abidjan", Proceedings of 6th Conference of CUPUM, September 8-10, Venice, 1999, Angeli, Milan

[SLO 99] SLOMAN A., LOGAN B., " Building Cognitively Rich Agents Using the Sim_agent Toolkit ", *Communications,* vol.42, n° 3, 1999, p. 71-77, ACM, New York.

[TUR 97] Turner T, Niemeier D., " Travel to Work and Household Responsibility: New Evidence ", *Transportation,* vol.24, n° 4, 1997, p. 397-419, Kluwer, Dordrecht.

[WAN 96] Wang J. A., " Timing Utility of Daily Activities and its Impact on Travel ", *Transportation Research A ,*vol. 30, n° 3, 1996, p. 189-206, Pergamon, New York.

[WIL 98] Wilson A. G., " Activity Pattern Analysis by Means of Sequence-Alignment Methods ", *Environment and Planning A*, vol.30, p.1017-1038, Pion, London.

Modelling spatial practices and social representations of space using multi-agent systems

Jean-Luc Bonnefoy* — Christophe Le Page**

Juliette Rouchier** — François Bousquet**

* UFR de géographieUniversité de Provence
29, rue R. Schuman, 13 628 Aix-en-Provence
Jean-Luc.Bonnefoy@aixup.univ-mrs.fr

** Cirad Tera Ere
Campus de Baillarguet, BP 5035, 34032 Montpellier Cedex
Lepage@cirad.fr; Rouchier@cirad.fr; Bousquet@cirad.fr

ABSTRACT: This paper demonstrates that multi-agent systems have the capacity to model a region in all its complexity. An example is developed to show that these tools are not only capable of spatializing and distributing the behaviour of individuals, but above all, that they allow individuals to integrate different perceptions of space as well as the constraints imposed on them by a community. A dialectic is established between individuals, spaces and society, which is used to simulate a region using clearly defined social representations and spatial practices, which are suitable for testing our geographical theories and hypotheses.

RÉSUMÉ : Il s'agit de mettre en évidence la capacité des systèmes multi-agents à modéliser un territoire en sa complexité. Un exemple est développé pour démontrer que ces outils sont non seulement susceptibles de spatialiser et de distribuer le comportement des individus mais qu'ils autorisent surtout l'intégration de perceptions différenciées de l'espace par les individus et de contraintes qui leurs sont exercées par une collectivité. Une dialectique s'instaure entre individus, espaces et société, qui contribue à la simulation d'un territoire par le biais de pratiques spatiales et de représentations sociales clairement définies, propres à tester nos théories et hypothèses géographiques.

KEY WORDS: modelling, multi-agent systems, geographical space, social representations, sustainable development

MOTS CLÉS: modélisation, systèmes multi-agents, espace géographique, représentation sociale, développement soutenable.

1. Background

This paper relates to research that has been undertaken by the authors specifically on the modelling of spatial or social dynamics. It presents the methodological approach that is common to their research. F. Bousquet and C. Le Page are interested in the modelling of interactions between natural and social dynamics using multi-agent systems (MAS) in the context of research on renewable resource management[1]. J. Rouchier specialises in the relationships of exchanges between individuals in a society and, particularly, on the role of trust in the context of renewable resource management. J.L. Bonnefoy is interested in networks of individuals' spatial practices which constitute a region or are influenced by a region. The authors hope that this paper will encourage a fresh approach to the concept of region because the development of research on the subject tends to follow a social theory that sometimes neglects spatial constraints and sources and vice versa.

Multi-agent systems are used because they have "the potential to model individuals, their behaviour and interactions directly and offer radically new solutions to modelling" [Ferber, 1995]. We consider that these properties could be beneficial to geography. In fact, "multi-agent modelling is based on the capacity of current software programmes to give individuals a degree of autonomy". The individuals or agents can represent people, animals, trees, etc., or, more broadly, a town, village, herd or forest. An agent is an "entity capable of acting on itself or its environment, which reacts to its changes and has a partial representation of its environment" . By evolving in a modelled space—in the form of a regular grid in which resources are spread out, indeed a more complex reconstruction of an observed reality—each agent builds up its own representation of space and by acting, the agent transforms the space for others. Interactions are central to this type of modelling.

This kind of approach is in itself a theoretical and methodological response—ie a theory is really played out—to dealing with complex phenomena and it has an important contribution to make to environmental issues. For the geographer, it is another way of putting a behavioural approach in a spatial context at the level of individuals. This is achieved by defining the agents and the rules that govern their interaction, and not by applying heavily parametrized formulas that represent dynamic systems and which take more account of inflows and outflows than the behavioural aspects of interactions . Lastly, it is an effective way for researchers to construct experiments, in other words to play out their theories, spatial models or hypotheses and to simulate and compare what happens in a multi-agent universe with an observed "reality".

2. Multi-agent systems and geographical space

A novel geographical approach using MAS involved modelling the dynamics of the evolution of a system of towns [Bura, 1993], particularly the hierarchies in terms of

---

[1] The application used here benefited from advances made with the software Common Pool Resources for Multi-Agent Systems (CORMAS) developed at CIRAD.

the urban functions and the population. The towns observed expansion, which fitted with the theories on urban hierarchy and activities became more specialized because of supply and demand mechanisms. However, the agents' (towns') intrinsic immobility meant that the model did not use the multi-agents' capacities to the full in terms of spatial interaction.

Some research has been conducted on the application of MAS to problems of spatialized resource management. For example, Schmitz [Schmitz, 1997] studied different ways of organizing agents for managing a resource distributed in space. In addition to research in the field of ecology and ethology, where scientists seek to understand the mechanisms for finding food [Folse, 1989 ; Roese, 1991; Drogoul, 1993; Krebs, 1996; Pepper, 1999], studies have also been conducted on societies of social agents that manage common resources [Epstein and Axtell, 1996; Kohler and E., 1996].

These models do not incorporate the different levels on which space can be considered. When resources are put into a spatial context, this is usually a question of simple geographical coordinates in a continuous space or elementary cells in a defined space. The representation of natural spatialized processes or agents' representations of space presupposes that spatial entities are modelled on several different levels which can be manipulated by the agents.

F. Bousquet and D. Gautier [Bousquet, 1999] have demonstrated two ways of approaching the integration of space in MAS using the example of a process of agricultural expansion: farmers cultivate land around their village, whose population is growing; animals roam freely which degrades the forest savannah at varying rates. The first approach is a classic-type integration where space is the support for the resources used by herds (forest) and farmers (fertile areas). The agents have rules that govern their spatial behaviour. They modify their environment and perceive all the modifications that occur within their field of perception objectively. In the second model, the spatial entities such as the forest, fields and savannah are established *a priori*. In this way, the authors present the spatial structure of the multi-agent universe. These spatial units have the characteristics of agents but the herds and farmers are only apparent in the rules that govern how the entities function. It is as if the forest makes way for the savannah, the fertile areas may way for fields, etc. The authors consider that these two approaches mark the beginning of research on the integration of space in MAS.

When the two models are considered from a geographical viewpoint, there are several points to note. In the first model, space is central to the interactions between agents and the model takes account of the individual movements of the farmer and herd agents, their interactions as well as the spatial occurrences that are linked to the relative position of resources and their transformation. However, some aspects are lacking when it comes to converting the model of this support space into a model of a region. Firstly, the level of interaction between space and society is zero because, in the machine, space is merely the support for the forest, savannah, etc., and individuals only act on these elements if they happen to meet. Secondly, over time the agents' individual action produces a space where spatial entities like the forest, fields, savanna and the village community are simply the result of a visual construction assembled by the observer (the simulator). There are no models of other types of contingencies, namely, the relative importance of social issues on behaviour and of collective and individual representations of space. For example, the collective representation of the forest which forms during the simulation cannot be reintroduced in the simulation. Only the observer-simulator's perception can be introduced empirically when the results of the simulation are interpreted, which is a different point of view again.

In the second model, which is the opposite of the above approach, the agents are spatial entities which presupposes their existence *a priori*. The observer-simulator models a geographical construction which requires a thorough understanding of how to balance the degree of spatial generalization and the semantic level of these entities and their rules of exchange. Although modelling exchanges between spatial entities may seem unnatural, it is possible that the behaviour of individuals could give rise to spatial structures that can be identified by the agents during or after the simulation, which is not the case here. In particular, exchanges are totally objective, everything occurs as if an unexpected power was regulating the relationships between entities, overriding individual action. In addition, there is no longer any real spatialization apart from the position of objects in the multi-agent space and the dynamics can only be managed quantitatively. Lastly, in this particular example, it is highly likely that the results will only confirm the original spatial hypotheses [Bonnefoy, 1998]. Nonetheless, this approach can produce results of interest for resource management or the development of an area. To achieve this, the scale of the study must be appropriate to the definition set by the construction of the spatial entities. In this sense, it is advisable to work on a smaller scale and to involve several village units and differentiated topographic configurations, in other words to provide the complexity required for the chosen spatial scale.

One of the benefits of MAS is their capacity to reveal how different stakeholders use space and their perception of it and, if the case should arise, the characterization of types of space, their differentiation and organization, which is every geographer's preoccupation. We envisage a model that associates individual spatial practices and the group's appreciation of space. Here, the region is no longer a spatialized sub-unit of the MAS, on the contrary, the MAS becomes the modelled region. This method is not just a question of integrating space into multi-agent systems, it is the arrangement of theoretical concepts of geographical space. It involves the construction of a dialectic between a space produced by the society and a space that restricts individuals, using individual and collective representations. This calls for what Distributed Artificial Intelligence experts refer to more generally as learning. In addition, the existing interaction between space and society must be integrated, ie the dynamic constraint that the space—which is produced by society—imposes on the society. Our example uses spatial representations to model the interactions between the path taken by shepherds who graze their flocks in the undergrowth and a forestry resource, with the aid of spatial representations. The grazing is actively controlled, to a greater or lesser extent, by the individual or collective representations which are built up during the simulation, integrating the successive states of the forestry resource between savannah deterioration and re-growth. In the model of interactions, the representations act as mediator between the agents and the common resource [Bousquet, Barreteau et al., 1999]. Here, however, the representations are individual or collective constructions that come from spatial practices during the simulation instead of being common references established *a priori* as in the case of religious practices, for example [Lansing, 1994]. Thus, in the model, we consider three elements that interact dynamically: individuals' spatial practices, individual representations of space and collective spatial representation. These three elements interact as time goes by in the machine and the individual practices and representations simultaneously ensue from the collective representation and influence it.

3. Description of the model of the forest's social representations

The aim of the model is to determine whether multi-agent systems have a valuable contribution to make to the understanding of a geographical space and, more generally, to investigate the dynamics between individual and collective representations and how they are manifested. Above all, the model is useful as an illustration. We can draw up a work hypothesis and ask whether the combination of individual and collective spatial representations in a multi-agent "forest" system is sufficient for simulating the management of the forest resource. In other words, how much emphasis should there be in the model on the shepherd agent's "awareness" of the need to manage his environment and on the restrictions that the community imposes on individual spatial practices if a system for using the forestry resource—ranging from simple predation to sustainable management—is to be established?

The model is as follows: each shepherd agent takes his flock to graze in a forest that is divided into groves. This leads to a degradation of the savannah forest. At the same time, the forest regrows naturally according to a probability that gives priority to regeneration at the edges of the forest. Through their spatial practices, the shepherd agents memorize the areas where they have been and form their representations: the state of the whole forest is then judged on the basis of these partial perceptions. The shepherd agents proceed by extrapolation to form their global representation of the forest. The more forest spaces they come across, the more their representation is of an abundant forest and vice versa. Periodically, these different individual representations (referred to as individual thresholds in the model) "meet" in the village and a collective representation is put together. Here, this construction is symbolized by an average evaluation which sets a collective threshold limiting the future grazing. In theory, the groves that are smaller than the collective threshold will not be grazed. However, several strategies are open to the shepherd agent. His individual practices can conform to the group's orders, in which case his strategy is called "collective". He can ignore the collective rules and graze his flock systematically, a strategy which is called "personal". Lastly, he can go against the collective rules by modifying his practices, and so strike a middle course between his habitual practices and the collective threshold. This strategy is called "arrangement". In the model, the shepherds' strategies are established at the start of the simulation and are permanent. The elements: village, shepherd, forest and land are identified by variables and processes which give them their autonomy in the programme (Figure 1)[2].

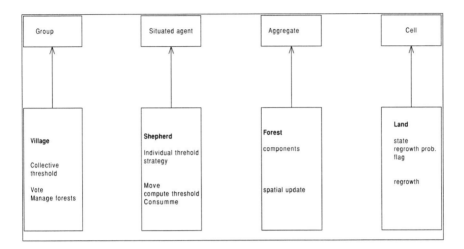

Figure 1. *The model's components. Inheritance from Cormas classes*

In a multi-agent system, space can be represented by a grid made up of cells—that represent a particular use or resource—onto which the agents move as a function of a time step that regulates the artificial world. In our case, the shepherd agents and their flocks move at random but, as far as possible, they stay in the forest once they have reached it. The forest is a set of cells that may or may not be adjacent (Figure 2).

---

[2] Figures 1, 3 and 4 have been set up using Unified Modelling Language which makes it is possible to overcome the constraints relating to the multi-agent systems' programming environment.

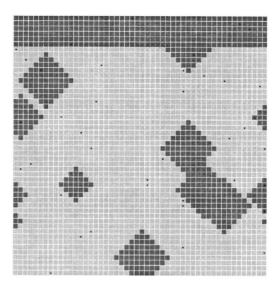

Figure 2. *Initial state. The forest is in dark grey (686 cells are arranged into 11 groves), the savannah is pale grey. The shepherds and their flocks are represented by a dot. This multi-agent universe is a closed grid of 50 x 50 squares, each one has eight adjoining squares*

Each grove (group of forest cells, or one isolated forest cell) is identified cyclically by the community and, depending on its size (the number of squares it contains) and the set collective threshold, an indicator (flag) indicates the village agent's decision concerning its use. The shepherd agent who then wants to go into the grove may or may not graze his animals. The following diagram shows the agents' general behaviour and perception which depends on their surroundings (in or outside the forest) and their strategy (Figure 3). It will be detailed during the course of the simulations.

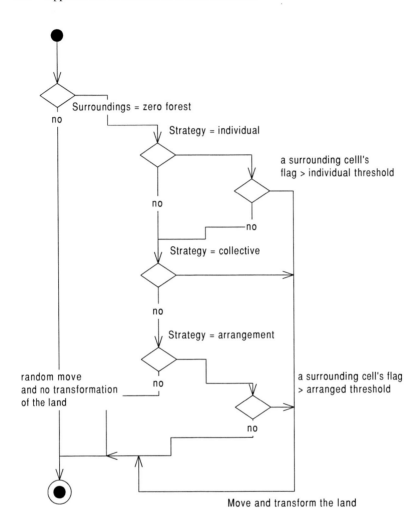

Figure 3. *Behaviour and perception of the shepherd agent. The section in the dotted box is a variation of the "personal" strategy*

The model's rhythm is set according to the rationale described above which is illustrated in Figure 4. Here, we can see the series of different sequences mentioned above: the shepherd agents' behaviour and perception; forest regrowth which depends on a random draw; the calculation of the size of new groves. The last stages have a longer periodicity: the calculation of the individual threshold based on the routes undertaken; the calculation of the collective threshold and the differences between the collective and individual thresholds; updating the flags that ban grazing which the shepherd agents will cross depending on their strategy. Then, the cycle begins again.

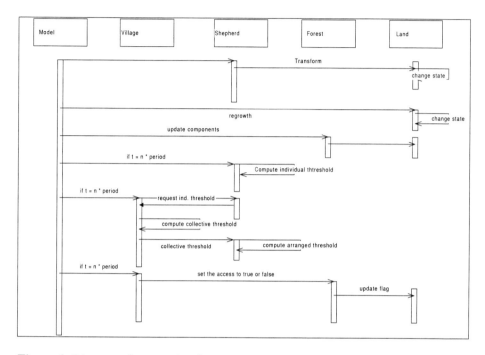

Figure 4. *Diagram of sequencing for one time step*

4. Several simulations

We plan successive simulations where the play of individual and collective representations will increase. In each simulation, 40 shepherd agents move through the space at random. Two simulations involve the "personal" strategy. This "method of modelling interactions is similar to what economists refer to as externalities" (Bousquet *et al.*, to be published). In fact, the shepherd agents' practice influences the practice of others even when there is no direct contact between them. In the first scenario, the representations are nonexistent and the shepherd grazes his flock as soon as he comes across the resource. In each simulation, the forest disappears after 120 to 250 time steps. This scenario illustrates the tragedy of the commons where collective goods are exploited to the point of exhaustion because profits are individualized and costs are shared [Hardin, 1968]. Later research that integrates awareness of the resource and social interactions, in particular (for example, [Bousquet, Duthoit et al., 1996]), has demonstrated the shortcomings of this hypothesis. In addition, the major criticism of this theory concerns the fact that common resources are not necessarily freely available. Societies organize rules to regulate access, and this is one of the objects of our simulations.

A second scenario includes individual representations of the forest that come within the "personal" strategy and take no account of the group. It is the shepherd's own past perception of the forest—his learning—that conditions where he grazes his flock. If the forest is degraded, the shepherd does not memorize many wooded spaces on his route and his new individual threshold goes up[3] which means he will not be able to graze small groves (Figure 3). In this scenario, we could consider that the shepherd agent becomes "aware" of the finite nature of the resource being modelled. The shepherd agent anticipates in accordance with his perception of the immediate surroundings. The individual threshold is comparable to an indicator that is inverse to the flock size. In "reality", the limitation that the shepherd imposes on himself can be interpreted as him giving up a number of animals to adjust flock size to the forest's new carrying capacity. The results of the simulations show that a model with the capacity to integrate the individual representation and individual management of a resource-flock combination, provides an alternative to the tragedy of the commons (table 1).

Of the initial forest, 25% is maintained in 20 groves (Figure 5 and Table 1). The average number of squares covered by the shepherd agent is low (26 squares). Given the considerable standard deviation, these figures show the huge disparity between individual spatial (coming across a large grove, etc.) or economic opportunities (absence of competition with other shepherd agents). The average individual threshold is very high which suggests that flocks are small.

Strategy	Forested cells	Number of groves	Average grazing	Mean threshold
Individual	150	20	26	8
Collective	230	61	32	5
Mixed	233	63	32	6

Table 1. *Results of simulations with the different strategies*

---

[3] In fact, the "route memory" cumulates the number of squares of forest perceived in a period of 10 time steps in order to make up the individual threshold that results from the balance period – route memory (with a period equal to 10). In this way, the individual maximum threshold is 10.

Individual strategy	Collective strategy	Mixed strategy
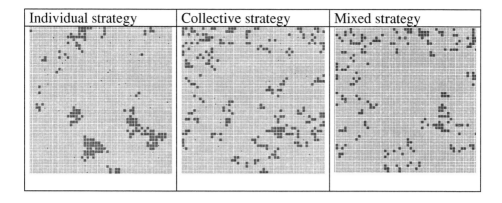		

Figure 5. *State of the forest after 300 time steps*

Our next simulations introduce the restrictions imposed by the group. The first strategy is "collective". An average of the individual thresholds (in other words the individual perceptions of the state of the forest) is calculated every 10 time steps once they have been updated, and groves that are smaller than this threshold are excluded from grazing which is indicated by "hanging flags" to denote a ban. The result of the simulations shows that much more of the forest is maintained than in the previous example (35% of initial forest) but it is fragmented into small groves (Figure 5 and Table 1).

This is only the spatial translation of the method used by the group (and by the simulator) to impose a restriction on the shepherd agents because the ban relates to a minimum size. If a restriction of this type imposed by the group bears little relation to a real situation (protected forest spaces are often large and there are few of them), it seems to be socially effective here: the flocks graze more and the deviations are smaller. There is an apparent normalization carried out by the group which reduces the inequalities between the shepherd agents. In addition, the average threshold indicates that flock size is greater. It could be that the fragmentation of the forest into small groves means that there are more spatial opportunities available to each shepherd agent for reaching forest areas. The inadequacy of this spatial explanation becomes clear later on.

The dynamics and the regulations are activated by the agents' or the group's incomplete knowledge of the forest environment. The collective threshold can be compared to the events in this multi-agent universe in order to determine the difference because the "average" individual "learning" is a quantitative (ie nonspatial) interpretation of the size of the forest. When the value of the collective threshold is five at the end of the simulation, this presupposes that the average shepherd agent estimates that half of the space is wooded. Yet, only 10% of the space is forested. The same applies to the previous model in which the shepherd agents perceived that 20% of land was wooded when in fact the figure was only 7%.

It is true that in our model, one forest square can be counted several times in the reference period. But this very biased representation is obviously part of the regulation. Deviation is caused by numerous factors. The first, which is very important, is the use of an average to represent the behaviour of a group! Another factor is that the orders for management apply to the next 10 time steps while grazing continues, the forest grows back and the orders are also out of sync (in time) because they reflect the memory of the routes undertaken during the preceding 10 time steps. The natural increase in grove size can invalidate the grazing ban. Groves that are only just bigger than those subject to a ban can be totally deforested before the next collective decision is taken because it is the village agent and not the shepherd agent that has the power to impose a ban. This raises an interesting question about whether or not an individual should be given responsibility in the context of sustainable management. This option was simulated in the model so that its impact on forest cover could be assessed: the shepherd agent can exercise self control by comparing the collective threshold with the size of the grove that he wants his animals to graze. The effect is immediate because the inertia due to the decision-making intervals disappears. However, the results from a limited number of simulations were not that different from the above strategy. In fact, it does not answer the frightening question as to what becomes of collective responsibility when there is a "transfer" to individual reason.

The "arrangement" strategy, based on the "collective" strategy, appears like a dispensation adopted by the shepherd agent. By meeting halfway, he allows his flock to graze the groves that are of the size set collectively plus half the difference between that and his own threshold of perception (cf. Figure 3). This violation of the group's orders could be considered as a necessary delay because it gives the agent time to reduce the size of his flock (individual threshold) which would occur anyway since the forest in his immediate environment will continue to diminish. Simulations of this type produce results very similar to the "collective" strategy

We observed that the number of forested squares fluctuated considerably from one simulation to another. The figures explicitly translate the oscillations between "personal" and "collective" strategies. It is also interesting to note that when an individual adaptation of the collective rule is modelled, there is more deviation between agents in relation to the accumulation of grazed spaces. This adaptation leads to slightly more forest fragmentation and slightly smaller flocks (collective threshold is 6 instead of 5). These results have a small contribution to make to the hypothesis of relationships proposed above concerning the fragmentation of the forest into small groves, the grazing opportunity and the difference in grazing between agents with a "collective" strategy. In the light of the last results, it appears that respecting the collective rules reduces the initial deviation in time, i.e. the deviation linked to the relative position—advantageous or otherwise—of each one (in relation to the forest and the other shepherd agents).

5. Conclusion

This model, which is a very simple construction, can be used to simulate a wide range of situations and a great deal of interaction because of the dynamic established between the space and the individual and collective representations. In fact, the individual representations only reflect the learning process that each shepherd agent goes through to find the forest spaces. It does not reflect the "objective reality" of this multi-agent universe because the agent has only evolved in a very small part of the available space and his personal and past experience are no indication of the actual state of the forest. From these individual perceptions, a collective representation emerges which provides a common rule and means that each shepherd has access to the other shepherds' representations. This incomplete knowledge means that there is a disparity between the reality and the perception of the multi-agent universe, which helps enrich the dynamics and regulate the resource. Thus, if the "personal" strategy refers to the concept of externality, we could say that the "collective" strategy refers to the theory of conventions, the "collectivization" of representations within the agents' society which acts here as a stimulus to the triptych of individual, space and society. In terms of modelling, there is a mediator and a catalyst between the three poles which are driven by the disparity between the events that occur in the multi-agent universe. Modelling the play of spatial representations developed by the agents during the course of their action is interesting in the framework of MAS and as an approach to geographical space and even sustainable resource management. Multi-agent modelling can include experts' representations as well as their decisions, which means it is possible to understand their implications for a resource and how they are linked in a social context. The research presented here illustrates the theoretical issues being discussed in the field of MAS on accounting for social constraints and individual autonomy [Gilbert, 1995] in a dynamic environment. Collectively, the agents decide on the restrictions that they impose on themselves for using an environment, they adapt individually to these social restrictions and, thus, transform their common environment, then strengthen or change the social rules depending on their degree of satisfaction.

Bibliography

[Bonnefoy, J.-L., 1998] Bonnefoy, J.-L. (1998). Circularité entre modèles spatiaux et décision spatiales. Géopoint, Avignon.[Bousquet, F., D. Gauthier, 1999]

Bousquet, F., D. Gauthier. (1999). "Comparaison de deux approches de modélisation des dynamiques spatiales par simulation multi-agents : les approches spatiales et acteurs." *Revue Européenne de géographie Cybergeo.*

[Bousquet, F., O. Barreteau, et al., 1999] Bousquet, F., O. Barreteau, et al. (1999). An environmental modelling approach. The use of multi-agents simulations. *Advances in Environmental and Ecological Modelling.* F. Blasco and A. Weill. Paris, Elsevier: 113-122.

[Bousquet, F., Y. Duthoit, et al., 1996] Bousquet, F., Y. Duthoit, et al. (1996). Tragedy of the commons, game theory and spatial simulation of complex systems. Ecology, Society, economy. In pursuit of sustainable development, St Quentin en Yvelines (France).

[Bura, S., Guérin-Pace F., Mathian H., Pumain D., Sanders L., 1993] Bura, S., Guérin-Pace F., Mathian H., Pumain D., Sanders L. (1993). Multi-agent systems and the dynamics of a settlement system. Artificial societies, Siena, UCL Press.

[Drogoul, A., 1993] Drogoul, A. De la simulation multi-agent à la résolution collective de problèmes. Une étude de l'émergence de structures d'organisation dans les systèmes multi-agent. Paris, Paris VI,1993. .

[Epstein, J. and R. Axtell, 1996] Epstein, J. and R. Axtell (1996). *Growing Artificial Societies. Social Science from the Bottom Up*, Brookins Institution Press/ The MIT Press.

[Ferber, J., 1995] Ferber, J. (1995). *Les Systèmes Multi-Agents. Vers une intelligence collective*. Paris, InterEditions.

[Folse, L., Packard J., Grant W., 1989] Folse, L., Packard J., Grant W. (1989). "AI modelling of animal movements in a heterogenous habitat." *Ecological modelling* **46**: 57-72.

[Gilbert, N., 1995] Gilbert, N. (1995). Emergence in social simulation. *Artificial societies. The computer simulation of social life*. R. c. a. N. Gilbert, UCL Press: 144-156.

[Hardin, G., 1968] Hardin, G. (1968). "The tragedy of the commons." *Science* **162**: 1243-1248.

[Kohler, T. A. and C. E., 1996] Kohler, T. A. and C. E. (1996). Swarm based modelling of prehistoric sttlement systems in southwestern North America. Archaeological applications of GIS, UISPP XIIIth Congress, Forli, Italy.

[Krebs, F., Bossel, H., 1996] Krebs, F., Bossel, H. (1996). "Emergent value orientation in self-organization of an animat." *Ecological modelling* **96**: 143-164.

[Lansing, J. S., Kremer J.N., 1994] Lansing, J. S., Kremer J.N. (1994). Emergent properties of Balinese water temple networks: coadaptaion on a rugged fitness landscape. Artificial life III, Santa Fe, Addison-Wesley.

[Pepper, J., Smuts, B., 1999] Pepper, J., Smuts, B. (1999). The evolution of cooperation in an ecological context : an agent based-model. *Dynamics of human and primate societies : agent based-modelling of social and spatial processes*. T. K. a. G. G. s. F. I. f. s. i. t. s. o. complexity. New York, Oxford University Press.

[Roese, H., Ken L. Risenhoover,L. Joseph Folse, 1991] Roese, H., Ken L. Risenhoover,L. Joseph Folse. (1991). "Habitat heterogenity and foraging efficiency: an indiviudual-based model." *Ecological modelling* **57**: 133-143.

[Schmitz, O. J., Ginger Booth, 1997] Schmitz, O. J., Ginger Booth. (1997). "Modelling food web complexity : the consequences of individual-based, spatially explicit behavioural ecology on trophic interactions." *Evolutionary Ecology* **11**: 379-398.

POLITICS AND HISTORY

Democratic Voting in Hierarchical Structures or How to Build a Dictatorship

Serge Galam

Laboratoire des Milieux Désordonnés et Hétérogènes[1],
Tour 13 - Case 86, 4 place Jussieu,
75252 Paris Cedex 05, France

ABSTRACT. *The dynamics of voting in hierarchical structures is modelled using the very efficient tool of the real space renormalization group borrowed from the Physics of collective phenomena. Each hierarchical level elects the one just above from local cells using a majority rule voting. The process is restricted to a two party competition. For each party two critical thresholds are found in the overall support. Below the first one, the associated party is automatically self-eliminated. Above the second one the presidency is guaranteed. In between the results are probabilistic. Depending on the voting rules, these thresholds may differ drastically from one party to the other. Higher thesholds to full power may be simultaneously at 23% for the ruling party while at 77% for the competing one making the system a dictatorship. Our model could shed new light on the collapse of the eastern european communist regime of the last century.*

1. Voting and fluctuating spins

The renormalization group (r. g.) was developed to tackle the difficult problem of singling out long range correlations in fluctuating degrees of freedom from short range ones [1]. Its real space version is simpler to use though less controlled. than the original Fourier space version However, here we are using the real space scheme since it is more adapted to our problem, namely, the dynamics of voting within a hierachical structure [2].

While in physics, the r. g. is a formal tool used to integrate out short ranged fluctuations in the study of phase transitions,, here we use it to build up a real system for which each iteration of the renormalization group transformation corresponds to a real hierarchical level. On this basis it is worth stressing that we are applying statistical physics to political science, in particular the r. g. will be used, not as a qualitative metaphor but rather as a guide to build quantitative models to study the effect of majority rule voting on the democratic representation of groups within hierarchical organizations. This work belongs to the whole new branch of applications of statistical physics outside the field of physics [3]. Among other applications we can cite work on traffic flow [4] and a very recent work using the theory of so-called spin glasses to describe the fragmentation of former Yugoslavia [5].

The model used is built as follows. Starting from the bottom of the hierarchy each level is elected from the one below by cells which use a majority rule voting. At the top level is one elected person, the president. Majority rule voting produces, by definition, a critical threshold to full power. In principle the rule allocates 100% of the power to the group which gets more than 50% in the support in the simplest case of two competing groups.

However, intsead of one unique threshold of 50%, we will now show how two different critical thresholds can be obtained for each party. Below the first one, the associated party is automatically self-eliminated. Above the second threshold, by contrast, the presidency is attained. In between, the results are probabilistic. Moreover these thresholds may differ drastically from one party to the other, depending on some slight and natural local biases in the voting rules. For instance, the higher threshold to full power may be simultaneously at 23% for the ruling party while at to 77% for the competing one making the system a dictatorship. Such a situation will be exemplified below.

The following of the paper is organized as follows. In Section 2 we present the voting model for the competition between two parties A and B in case of cells of size 3. In this case the situation is symmetric with respect to both A and B with a unique and common threshold at 50%. The model is extented in Section 3 to include 4-person groups. Then, in the event of a tie 2A-2B, a bias is introduced in favor of the ruling party, by the election of a ruling party member. Such a "reasonable" bias is found to shift the value of the critical threshold to power from 50% to 77% for the opposition. Simultaneously it reduces the threshold to 23% for the ruling party. The system has turned to a democratic dictatorship. Increased voting group sizes are analyzed in Section 4. Given an initial A support the critical number of levels necessary to the A self-elimination is calculated analytically in Section 5. In parallel, given a fixed number of levels, two thresholds are derived for each party. Below the first one, the associated party self-eliminates absolutely at the top level. Above the second one, it gets the presidency at no doubt. In between, the presidency winner is probabilistic. Results of a numerical simulation are presented in Section 6. To conclude, the collapse of eastern european communist parties in the last century, is discussed briefly in last Section

2. The simple fair case

We start with the simplest unbiased case. People are aggregated randomly in groups of 3 at the bottom of the hierarchy. Such aggregates may be formed according to home or work place location. Each group then elects a representative using a local majority rule. Two political groups A and B are competing with overall support p_0 and $1 - p_0$, respectively. Groups voting either 3 A or 2 A elect an A and otherwise a B. The probability of having an A elected from the bottom level is then,

$$p_1 \equiv P_3(p_0) = p_0^3 + 3p_0^2(1 - p_0), \qquad [1]$$

where $P_3(p_n)$ denotes the voting function. We denote the rank of elected people by level-1.

Within level-1, new cells are formed randomly to elect higher representatives to constitute level-2. The process can be repeated again and again. At each vote a new additional hierarchical level is added, until the last presidential level is reached. At the last level is the president. The probability to have an A elected at level (n+1) from level-n is written as,

$$p_{n+1} \equiv P_3(p_n) = p_n^3 + 3p_n^2(1 - p_n), \qquad [2]$$

where p_n is the proportion of A elected persons at level-n.

The voting function $P_3(p_n)$ has 3 fixed points p^*, i. e., points which satisfy the Equation $P_3(p^*) = p^*$. They are $p_l = 0$, $p_{c,3} = \frac{1}{2}$ and $p_L = 1$. The first fixed point corresponds to no election of A. The last fixed point $p_L = 1$ means only A are elected. Both p_l and p_L are stable fixed points. At a given distance from them, voting reduces that distance. In between the fixed point $p_{c,3}$ is unstable. At contrast, voting increases the distance from it. It determines the threshold of the democratic voting flow towards either full power ($p_L = 1$) or to total elimination ($p_l = 0$). Starting from $p_0 < \frac{1}{2}$ leads democratically to $p_l = 0$ while $p_0 > \frac{1}{2}$ drives to $p_L = 1$. Any initial support lower than 50% leads to $p_l = 0$ provided a sufficient number of voting levels is performed.

Indeed, the fundamental question is to determine the number of levels required to ensure the presidency to the party which has an initial support larger than 50%. To be practical in the real world, this level number must be small enough since most organisations have only a few number of levels (less than 10).

For instance, starting from $p_0 = 0.45$ we successively obtain $p_1 = 0.42$, $p_2 = 0.39$, $p_3 = 0.34$, $p_4 = 0.26$, $p_5 = 0.17$, $p_6 = 0.08$ followed by $p_7 = 0.02$ and $p_8 = 0.00$. Eight levels self-eliminates 45% of the population.

The overall process thus preserves the democratic character of majority rule voting. It is worth to note the situation is fully symmetric with respect to both A and B parties. They have the same and unique threshold at 50%.

3. The ruling inertia

Taking over power is a rather difficult task, even if a large fraction of the population supports it. It appears to require more than 50% of the support. Most often the ruling group benefits from a kind of power inertia, making the situation asymmetric for the competing groups. This ruling inertia is sometimes monitored by giving, for instance, one additional vote to the commitee president, or similarly by adding some designated non-elected members to a voting group.

To change a presidency requires a clear cut majoritary will. When the "for" and the "against" are more or less balanced, nothing is changed. To exemplify this asymmetry, consider 4-size cells. Assuming the B are the ruling party, the A will need either 4 or 3 A in a given cell to elect an A. Otherwise a B is elected since in the event of a tie (2A-2B), the vote goes for B. The probability to get an A elected at level $n + 1$ becomes,

$$p_{n+1} \equiv P_4(p_n) = p_n^4 + 4p_n^3(1 - p_n) , \qquad [3]$$

where p_n is as before the proportion of elected A persons at level-n. In contrast the probability for a B to be elected is,

$$1 - P_4(p_n) = p_n^4 + 4p_n^3(1 - p_n) + 2p_n^2(1 - p_n)^2 , \qquad [4]$$

where last term embodies the bias in favor of B. Eq. (3) still has the stable fixed points 0 and 1. However the unstable one is now drastically shifted to,

$$p_{c,4} = \frac{1 + \sqrt{13}}{6} , \qquad [5]$$

for the A. The resulting A threshold to power becomes 77%. Simultaneously the B threshold to remain in power is only 23% drastically altering the situation. To take over the A needs acquire more than 77% of initial bottom support, while to stick to power the B need to obtain merely 23%.

In addition to the asymmetry, the bias causes full democratic self-elimination to occur within even a smaller number of levels than in above 3-size cell case. Here, starting from $p_0 = 0.45$ we have $p_1 = 0.24$, $p_2 = 0.05$ and $p_3 = 0.00$. Three levels are now enough to make the A to disappear, wheras previously this requires 8 levels.

To grasp how drastic this effect is, let us start from $p_0 = 0.70$. Significantly greater than 50%. Repeated voting gives respectively $p_1 = 0.66$, $p_2 = 0.57$, $p_3 = 0.42$, $p_4 = 0.20$, $p_5 = 0.03$, and $p_6 = 0.00$. Six voting levels are sufficient for democratic self-elimination of 70% of a population. To obtain power the A must posses more than 77% of the support, a number which is out of reach in most two party situations. Majority rule voting has become a procedure to a totalitarian system.

Figs. (1, 2, 3, 4) show some snapshots of a numerical simulation [5]. A and B parties are shown as white and black squares, respectively. The bias is in favor of the blacks (B). The shown hierarchy has 8 levels. Designated percentages are for the

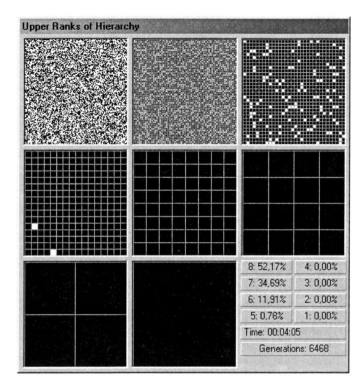

Figure 1. *A 8 level hierarchy for even groups of 4 persons. The two A and B parties are represented respectively in white and black with the bias in favor of the black squares, i. e., a tie 2-2 votes for a black square. Written percentages are for the white representation at each level. The "Time" and "Generations" indicators should be discarded. The initial white support is* 52.17%.

white representation at each level. The "Time" and "Generations" indicators should be ignored.

Figure 1 shows a case with 52.17% initial A (white) support. After 3 levels no more white squares appear.

Figure 2 shows a case with 68.62% initial A (white) support, far more than 50%. After 4 levels no more white squares are found.

Figure 3 shows a case with a huge 76.07% initial A (white) support. Now 6 levels are needed to get a black square (B) elected. The initial B support (black) is only of 23.03%.

Figure 4 shows a case with 77.05% initial A (white) support. Finally the A (white) get the presidency.

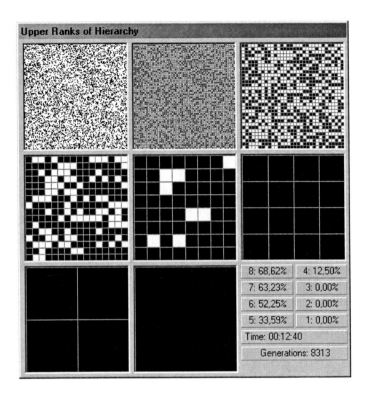

Figure 2. *The same as Figure one with an initial white support of* 68.62%.

4. Going larger in cell sizes

We now study the effect of increasing cell sizes. For a r-size cell the voting function $p_{n+1} = P_r(p_n)$ writes,

$$P_r(p_n) = \sum_{l=m}^{l=r} \frac{r!}{l!(r-l)!} p_n^l (1+p_n)^{r-l}, \qquad [6]$$

where $m = \frac{r+1}{2}$ for odd r and $m = \frac{r}{2} + 1$ for even r which thus accounts for the bias in favor of the ruling B.

The two stable fixed points $p_l = 0$ and $p_L = 1$ are unchanged. They are size independent. For odd sizes, the unstable fixed point also remains unchanged at $p_{c,r} = \frac{1}{2}$. However, for even sizes, the asymmetry between the threshold values for respectively rulers and non rulers weakens with increasing sizes. For the A threshold it is 77% for size 4 and it decreases asymptotically towards $p_{c,r} = \frac{1}{2}$ for r→ ∞. But it stays always larger than $\frac{1}{2}$, making yet the barrier hard to pass for the challenging party (a few percent difference in a two party fight is indeed considered large, at least in democratic countries). In parallel, increasing group sizes accelerates the flow towards the stable fixed points by reducing the number of necessary voting levels.

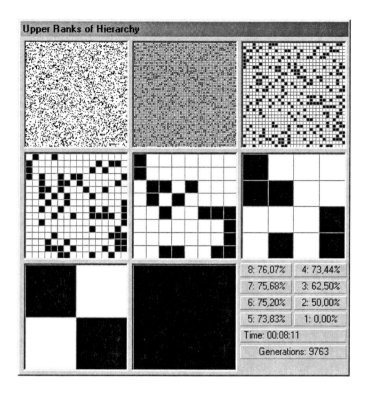

Figure 3. *The same as Figure one with an initial white support of* 76.07%.

5. The scheme, in practise

Given an initial support p_0, we want to calculate analytically p_n, the value for A support after n voting levels. Accordingly, we expand the voting function $p_n = P_r(p_{n-1})$ around the unstable fixed point $p_{c,r}$,

$$p_n \approx p_{c,r} + (p_{n-1} - p_{c,r})\lambda_r , \qquad [7]$$

where $\lambda_r \equiv \frac{dP_r(p_n)}{dp_n}\big|_{p_{c,r}}$ with $P_r(p_{c,r}) = p_{c,r}$. Rewriting last equation as,

$$p_n - p_{c,r} \approx (p_{n-1} - p_{c,r})\lambda_r , \qquad [8]$$

we can iterate the process to,

$$p_n - p_{c,r} \approx (p_0 - p_{c,r})\lambda_r^n , \qquad [9]$$

from which we get,

$$p_n \approx p_{c,r} + (p_0 - p_{c,r})\lambda_r^n . \qquad [10]$$

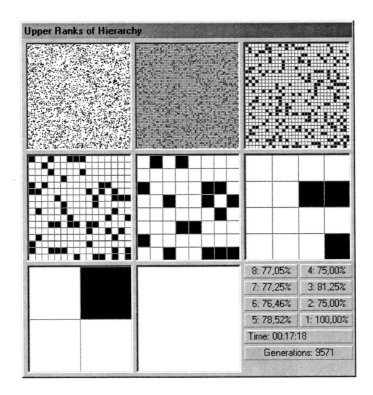

Figure 4. *The same as Figure one with an initial white support of* 77.05%.

¿From Eq. (10) two different critical numbers of levels n_c^l and n_c^L are obtained for respectively $p_{n_c^l} = 0$ and $p_{n_c^L} = 1$. Inserting $p_n = p_{n_c^l} = 0$ into Eq. (10) gives,

$$n_c^l \approx \frac{1}{\ln \lambda_r} \ln \frac{p_{c,r}}{p_{c,r} - p_0} \, , \qquad [11]$$

which is defined only for $p_0 < p_{c,r}$, showing that only below $p_{c,r}$ can the proportion of a party decrease to zero. On the other hand, setting $p_n = p_{n_c^L} = 1$ in the same Eq. (10) yields,

$$n_c^L \approx \frac{1}{\ln \lambda_r} \ln \frac{p_{c,r} - 1}{p_{c,r} - p_0} \, , \qquad [12]$$

which is now defined only for $p_0 > p_{c,r}$ since $p_{c,r} < 1$, showing now that only above $p_{c,r}$ can the support increase to one.

Above expansions are in principle valid only in the vicinity of $p_{c,r}$. Nevertheless, rounding to 1 while taking the integer part of Eqs. (11) and (12) gives good estimates even up to the two stable fixed point 0 and 1.

6. How to use the scheme

Once organisations are created, they are, most of the time, rarely modified. Therefore within a given organisation the number of hierarchical levels is a fixed quantity. On this basis, to make practical the above operative scheme, we need to turn the question of "How many levels are needed to eliminate a party?" into "Given n levels, what is the minimum overall support to unequivocally obtain full power?". Or alternatively, in the case of the ruling party,

"Given n levels what is the critical overall support of the competing party below which it will always self-eliminate totally?".

To implement this practical question, we revisit Eq. (10), rewriting it as,

$$p_0 = p_{c,r} + (p_n - p_{c,r})\lambda_r^{-n} . \tag{13}$$

Two critical thresholds are now obtained. The first one is the disappearence threshold $p_{l,r}^n$ which gives the value of support under which the A definitely disappear at the top of the hierarchy. It is given by Eq. (13) with $p_n = 0$,

$$p_{l,r}^n = p_{c,r}(1 - \lambda_r^{-n}) . \tag{14}$$

In parallel $p_n = 1$ gives the second threshold $p_{L,r}^n$ above which the A obtain complete power. From Eq.(13),

$$p_{L,r}^n = p_{l,r}^n + \lambda_r^{-n} . \tag{15}$$

There now exists a new regime $p_{l,r}^n < p_0 < p_{L,r}^n$. in which A will neither disappear totally nor, without a doubt, grap full power. It is a coexistence region where some democracy still prevails since results of an election are now only probabilistic. Neither party is sure of winning, making overthrowing a leadership a reality.

¿From Eq.(15), this democratic region shrinks as a power law λ_r^{-n} of the number n of hierarchical levels. A small number of levels elevates the threshold to power but simultaneously lowers the threshold to non existence.

The above formulas are only estimates since corrections in the vicinity of the stable fixed points have been neglected. However they yield the right quantitative behavior with $p_{l,r}^n$ fitting to $n + 1$ and $p_{L,r}^n$ to $n + 2$. More accurate formulas may be obtained from Reference (Galam 1990).

To illustrate the case $r = 4$ for which $\lambda = 1.64$ and $p_{c,4} = \frac{1+\sqrt{13}}{6}$, let us consider 3, 4, 5, 6 and 7 level organizations. Then, $p_{l,r}^n$ is equal to respectively 0.59, 0.66, 0.70, 0.73 and 0.74. In parallel, $p_{L,r}^n$ equals 0.82, 0.80, 0.79, 0.78 and 0.78. These series drastically emphasize the totalitarian character of the voting process.

7. Conclusion

A major trend of repeating democratic voting has been singled out, using very simple cases. In particular, an election outcome within hierarchical structures could be predicted from the knowledge of respective initial supports. Critical thresholds were found to be instrumental in the dynamics of majority rule voting. Moreover, these thresholds were found not to be always symmetric with respect to rulers and opponents. Dictatorships were obtained for instance with critical thresholds of 0.77% for the opposition and 0.23% for the rulers.

Extension to a larger number of competing groups presents no a priori difficulty. The situation just becomes much more complex but the above mentioned dictatorship aspects are reinforced.

The present voting model could shed some new light on the general collapse of eastern european communist parties in the last century . Our voting hierarchy resembles at least in theory the communist organization known as democratic centralism. Instead of being the outcome of a sudden and opportunistic attitude change of communist members, it could have instead, result from of very long and massive internal movement which was self-eliminated from top hierarchies during many years.. Only, once the will to change reached the critical threshold, did it show up, making the collapse total and irreversible. Obviously, such an explanation does not oppose, on the contrary, additional constraints and mechanisms. It only emphazises a possible trend within the mechanics of communist organizations..

At this stage, it is of importance to stress that modelling social and political phenomena is not aimed to state an eventual truth. It only aims at singling out some basic features at work within a large class of complex systems.

8. References

S.M. de Oliveira, P.M.C. de Oliveira, and D. Stauffer. *Non-Traditional Applications of Computational Statistical Physics: Sex, Money, War, and Computers.* Springer (2000)

R. Florian and S. Galam, *Optimizing Conflicts in the Formation of Strategic Alliances* Eur. Phys. J. in Press (2000)

Sh-k Ma, *Modern Theory of Critical Phenomena*, The Benjamin Inc.: Reading MA (1976)

S. Galam, *Majority rule, hierarchical structure and democratic totalitarianism*, J. Math. Psychology **30**, 426 (1986); *Social paradoxes of majority rule voting and renormalization group*, J. Stat. Phys. **61**, 943-951 (1990)

S. Galam and S. Wonczak, to be published

Computer simulations of voting systems

Dominique Lepelley*, Ahmed Louichi* and Fabrice Valognes**

*GEMMA-CREME
Faculté de sciences économiques et de gestion
Université de Caen, 14032 Caen Cedex, France
lepelley@econ.unicaen.fr
adli@econ.unicaen.fr

**Université Notre Dame de Namur, Belgique
fabrice.valognes@fundp.ac.be

ABSTRACT. *All voting procedures are susceptible to give rise, if not to paradoxes, at least to violations of some democratic principles. In this paper, we evaluate and compare the propensity of various voting rules –belonging to the class of scoring rules– to satisfy two versions of the majority principle. We consider the asymptotic case where the numbers of voters tends to infinity and, for each rule, we study with the help of Monte Carlo methods how this propensity varies as a function of the number of candidates.*

RÉSUMÉ. *Toutes les procédures de vote sont susceptibles de conduire à des résultats sinon paradoxaux, du moins contraires à ce que suggèrent certains principes dé7îtocratiques. Nous nous proposons dans cet article d'évaluer et de comparer la propension de différentes règles de vote –appartenant toutes à la classe des règles positionnelles– à satisfaire deux versions du principe majoritaire. Nous considérons le cas asymptotique où le nombre de votants tend vers l'infini et, pour chaque règle, nous analysons à l'aide de méthodes de Monte Carlo l'évaluation de cette propension en fonction du nombre de candidats.*

KEY WORDS. *Voting, Condorcet Efficiency, Majority Principle, Scoring Rules, Simulations*

MOTS-CLÉS. *Vote, Efficacité de Condorcet, Principe Majoritaire, Règles Positionnelles, Simulations*

1. Introduction

Modern social choice theory, born with the seminal works of Black (1958) and Arrow (1963), has provided a new perspective for the study of voting and elections. Over the last decades, it has produced a number of results on the properties of voting procedures *qua* methods of individual preference aggregation. Many of these results are of a negative nature (impossibility theorems) and lead to the following conclusion: all voting systems violate reasonable democratic criteria and can give rise to paradoxical situations (Nurmi, 1999; Galam, 1990, 1999). Along (and connected) with these results, another stream of research atempts to evaluate the significance of these negative conclusions from a practical point of view. These contributions try to give estimates of how often a given problematic situation arises when a given voting system is being used.

Recent examples of this kind of investigation are Gehrlein (1997), Merlin, Tataru and Valognes (2000), Lepelley and Valognes (1999) *inter alii*, who provide analytical solutions or exact probability calculations. Typically, most of these studies focus on three-alternative elections, due to considerable combinatorial complexity when the number of alternatives is greater than three. As a consequence, very little is known concerning what happens when more than three alternatives are in contention. The purpose of the present study is to (partially) fill this gap by using Monte Carlo simulations instead of analytical computations. Such a study is of particular interest when one tries to rank some voting rules according to a given criterion; the question is: Does the hierarchy we obtain for three alternatives remain the same when more than three alternatives are considered? Specifically, we shall compare in this paper the propensity of various simple voting rules to satisfy some well known criteria derived from the majority principle.

By contrast with previous studies using Monte Carlo simulations, which only consider the case with a finite (and limited) number of voters (see, *e.g.*, Fishburn and Gehrlein, 1982, and Vandercruyssen,1999), we shall focus in this paper on the infinite case. Specific algorithms are developed for that purpose. These algorithms and the probabilistic assumptions upon which our computations are based are presented in Section 3 and Section 4 is devoted to our results. The general framework of our study is briefly outlined in Section 2.

2. Voting systems and Condorcet criteria

We consider in this paper simple (one-stage) voting systems for local or national elections in which one candidate is to be elected by a large group of voters from three or more candidates. Let $A = \{a, b, c...\}$ be the finite set of candidates, with m the number of candidates. The number of voters will be denoted by N. The opinion of a voter i over A is described by a preference ordering P_i. We assume that P_i is a linear order, that is, each voter is able to rank candidates from most preferred to least preferred with no ties. In addition, we suppose that each individual votes in accordance with his preference ordering. A *preference profile*, or simply a *profile*, is a list $(P_1, P_2, ..., P_N)$ of N linear orders and describes the opinion of the electorate. A *voting system* or *voting rule* is a mapping that associates to each possible profile an element of A, the winner of the election. All the voting rules we examine here belong to the important class of *scoring rules*. A scoring rule is a method of point scoring where points are given according to ranks of candidates in individual preference orders and the alternative collecting the highest score over all voters is elected. A scoring rule is defined *via* a scoring vector $(w_1, w_2, ..., w_m)$ where w_j denotes the number of points given to a candidate each time he is ranked in j^{th} position in one individual ordering. We shall assume that $w_j \geq w_{j+1}$ and $w_1 > w_m$, *i.e.*, the better the position of a candidate is, the higher is the number of points a voter gives to him, and we shall normalize the scoring vector in such a way that $w_1 = 1$ and $w_m = 0$. Therefore, the well-known *Borda rule*, that assigns $m - j$ points when a candidate is ranked in j^{th} position in an individual order, will be defined by the score vector $(1, \frac{m-2}{m-1}, ..., \frac{m-j}{m-1}, ..., 0)$. Another well-known and widely used scoring rule is the *plurality rule*, defined by the the the vector $(1, 0, 0, ..., 0)$; in practice, this rule is implemented by asking each voter to indicate the candidate he or she prefers and the candidate with the largest vote total wins the election. Thus, the plurality rule only considers the first positions in individual rankings. By contrast, the *antiplurality rule* only considers the last positions and is defined by the following scoring vector: $(1, 1, ..., 1, 0)$. Plurality and antiplurality are members of a sub-class of scoring rules, namely the *constant scoring rules*: these rules ask each voter to vote for exactly k candidates, and the winner is the candidate which receives the most votes. For $k = 1$, we obtain the plurality rule and $k = m - 1$ is the antiplurality rule.

As is well-known in voting theory, the main drawback of scoring rules is their failure to satisfy some important desiderata derived from the majority principle, as stated by Condorcet (1785). A candidate a is said to be the *Condorcet winner* if, for each other candidate b, more voters prefer a to b than prefer b to a. Thus, the Condorcet winner would beat every other candidate in majority pairwise comparisons. Clearly, there are profiles where no candidate is the the Condorcet winner and, in fact, the famous Condorcet's paradox exemplifies such a profile. But when such a candidate exists, it seems quite reasonable to choose him as the winner of the election: it is what we call here the first Condorcet criterion. Condorcet himself was the first to state that every scoring rule violates this criterion, *i.e.* does not necessarily choose the Condorcet winner when one exists. Let us now define the notion of a *Condorcet loser*: in an election, a candidate is called the Condorcet loser if that candidate would be beaten by every other candidates in majority pairwise comparisons. Of course, when such a candidate exists, he should not be selected by the voting rule: this is the second Condorcet criterion. Unfortunately, we know from Fishburn and Gehrlein (1976) that every scoring rule but the Borda rule can give rise to the election of the Condorcet loser, thus violating the second Condorcet criterion.

Undoubtedly, these failures of the scoring rules can be regarded as serious obstacles to their use in political elections. At the same time, we are aware of the fact that these difficulties do not arise in every context of social choice. Rather, they are restricted to special types of preference profiles. But are these profiles common? It is not possible to answer this question by analyzing past elections since most voting systems used in practice do not require the voters to reveal their entire preference order. Another way of answering the question is to resort to probability models and computer simulations: it is the strategy we shall adopt in the subsequent sections.

3. Probability models and simulation design

In order to evaluate how frequently a given voting rule violates a normative criterion, we have to use *a priori* assumptions and probability models to describe how voters are distributed over the set of possible preference orderings. We shall number all linear orders on A from 1 to $M = m!$. Thus with three candidates and $M = 6$, we will have:

$$1: \ a \succ b \succ c$$
$$2: \ a \succ c \succ b$$
$$3: \ b \succ a \succ c$$
$$4: \ b \succ c \succ a$$
$$5: \ c \succ a \succ b$$
$$6: \ c \succ b \succ a$$

A *voting situation*, or simply a *situation*, is a vector $(n_1, n_2, ..., n_M)$ that specifies the number of voters who are assigned to each preference order, with $\sum_i n_i = N$.

Two simple probabilistic procedures for generating voting situations have been used in the literature. The first one simply assumes that each voting situation is chosen with equal probability. Since the number of voting situations is given by $\binom{N + M + 1}{N}$, the probability to get a given situation is:

$$P(n_1, n_2, ..., n_M) = \frac{N!(M-1)!}{(N+M-1)!} \tag{1}$$

This model is referred to as the impartial anonymous culture (IAC) condition.

Another widely used probability model is the impartial culture (IC) condition, which takes into account the identities of the voters. With this model, the probability of a voting situation is given by:

$$P(n_1, n_2, ..., n_M) = \frac{N!}{n_1! n_2! ... n_M!} (M)^{-N} \tag{2}$$

The reader will recognize the multinomial model, in which each of the N voters is independently assigned the i-th of the M linear orders with probability $1/M$. Clearly, this model can be given an alternative interpretation *via* the notion of preference profiles: the IC condition postulates that each profile is chosen with equal probability. The reader is referred to Berg and Lepelley (1994) for a more general discussion of these models (see also Feix and Rouet, 1999, who connect IAC and IC conditions to well-known distributions used in physics).

Suppose that we want to compute the probability of an event E, say the occurrence of a Condorcet winner. In three-candidate elections, a is the Condorcet winner if and only if:

$$n_1 + n_2 + n_5 > N/2 \qquad (a \text{ beats } b),$$

$$n_1 + n_2 + n_3 > N/2 \qquad (a \text{ beats } c).$$

Denote by D the set of situations that meet these conditions. Then, it is easily seen (given the symmetry between the candidates in the two models we use) that the desired probability in the three-candidate case is given as:

$$Pr(E) = 3 \sum_{(n_1,\ldots,n_6) \in D} P(n_1, \ldots, n_6) \qquad (3)$$

with $P(n_1, \ldots, n_6)$ defined by either equation (1) or equation (2).

Now, let $p_i = n_i/N$ denote the proportion of voters with the associated preference order and assume that N, the number of voters, tends to infinity. Then the density of the vector $(p_1, \ldots, p_M)$ is given by a Dirichlet distribution when we start from (1) and by a multivariate normal distribution when we start from (2) (see, for example, Johnson and Kotz, 1972); in both cases, the desired probabilities are obtained by evaluating a multiple integral and, in our exemple, the domain of integration is that part of the simplex S, such that $\sum_i p_i < 1$, in which the following inequalities are satisfied[1]:

$$p_1 + p_2 + p_5 > 1/2 \quad \text{and} \quad p_1 + p_2 + p_3 > 1/2. \qquad (4)$$

Such integrals can be solved analytically in some simple cases, but as soon as we consider more than three candidates, these integrals become untractable and we have to resort to Monte carlo techniques.

In the context of Monte-Carlo methods (see *e.g.* Hammesly and Handscomb, 1964), relative frequencies n_i/N are considered as realizations of a uniform random variable on $[0,1[$. In order to generate a vector $(p_1, p_2, \ldots, p_M)$ according to the model IAC, we use the technique of the "broken stick"[2]. For m candidates, we generate $m! - 1 = M - 1$ uniform numbers on $[0,1[$ that we rank in an ascendant order, $x_1 < x_2 \cdots < x_M$; then we define the p_i's in the following way: $p_1 = x_1$; $p_2 = x_2 - x_1, \cdots, p_M = 1 - x_{M-1}$.

Under the IC model, which focuses on the point $(1/M, \cdots, 1/M)$ of the simplex S, the inequalities (4) defining a domain in S can be written as:

$$\sum (1/M + \alpha_i) > 1/2 \qquad (5)$$

where the α_i are normal perturbations, $\alpha_i \sim N(0,1)$. Thus, one can write the p_i's as follows:

$$p_i = 1/M + \alpha_i \qquad (6)$$

Using a control variate, that is a mechanism to reduce the variability, we obtain:

$$p_i = 1/M + \varepsilon(\alpha_i - \bar{\alpha}) \qquad (7)$$

---

[1] Observe that, under IAC, every point in S is given the same weight whereas the IC model focuses on the point $(1/M,\ldots,1/M)$.

[2] Another way for generating the p_i's according to IAC is to resort to the Poisson distribution (see Feix and Rouet, 1999).

where $\bar{\alpha} = 1/M \sum_{i=0}^{M-1} \alpha_i$ and ε is an arbitrary constant that we take equal to $1/M$, with $E(\alpha_i - \bar{\alpha}) = 0$, but $Var(1/M - \alpha_i) < Var(1/M + \varepsilon(\alpha_i - \bar{\alpha}))$. The p_i's obtained following this method are then normalized with the result that their sum equals one.

Once a vector $(p_1, ..., p_M)$ is obtained, we check whether all the inequalities that define the event under consideration are satisfied or not. The procedure is repeated a large number of times and the estimate we are looking for is deduced from the fraction of times the inequalities are satisfied. In order to illustrate with more details our approach, we provide in appendix two algorithms. The first one (appendix 1) shows how we have generated and managed the list of all possible linear orders on m candidates. The second algorithm (appendix 2) deals with the estimation of the probability that a scoring rule selects the Condorcet winner, given there is one, under the IAC model.[3]

4. Results

The results we have obtained are shown in Tables 1, 2 and 3. The number of elections we have simulated depends on the number m of candidates in the following way: $1\,000\,000$ simulations for $m = 3, 4, 5, 6$ and $100\,000$ simulations for $m = 7, 8$. The accuracy of our estimates goes from (about) ± 0.0001 for $m = 3$ to ± 0.0015 for $m = 8$.

The data in the tables suggest two preliminary and general observations. First, under the IC model, there exists a symmetry between the performance of the plurality rule on one hand and the antiplurality rule on the other hand : the estimates we obtain are approximately the same for these two rules. This symmetry (which does not hold under IAC) was already observed by Gehrlein (1997). Second, the results shown in Tables 1 and 2 indicate that IC and IAC models tend to coincide when the number of candidates increases and this is in accordance with what could be expected (see Berg and Lepelley 1994, or Feix and Rouet, 1999). For small values of m, the likelihood of violating the Condorcet criteria appears to be slightly smaller with IAC than with IC. Once again, this is not very surprising for the IC model is based upon an assumption of complete independence between the voters, whereas IAC introduces some degree of homogeneity in voters' preferences (the more homogeneous is an electorate, the less likely is the occurrence of a paradox).

The figures in Table 1 give for three scoring rules what is called their *Condorcet efficiency* in the literature, that is to say the conditional probability of electing the Condorcet winner given that such a candidate exists. For the three rules under consideration, it turns out that their Condorcet efficiency decreases when the number of candidates increases. However, the efficiency of the Borda rule diminishes much more slowly than the efficiency of the two other rules and remains at a relatively high level: for eight candidates, the probability of selecting the Condorcet winner under the Borda rule is more than twice what is obtained with the plurality and antiplurality rules. Concerning these two rules, it is worth noting that the superiority of plurality on antiplurality, that we can observe in three-candidate elections under the IAC assumption, tends to disappear when the number of candidates increases.

---

[3]The other algorithms we have used are based upon the same logic as the one shown in appendix 2. These algorithms are available from the authors upon request.

Table 1. *Probability of electing the Condorcet winner given there is one*
under the plurality, antiplurality and Borda rules
(m candidates, large electorate)

m	Plurality		Antiplurality		Borda	
	IC	IAC	IC	IAC	IC	IAC
3	.7574	.8816	.7571	.6298	.9010	.9108
4	.6416	.7429	.6415	.5517	.8702	.8706
5	.5570	.6139	.5602	.5090	.8552	.8541
6	.4858	.5198	.4946	.4730	.8450	.8471
7	.4663	.4524	.4450	.4386	.8438	.8457
8	.4123	.4088	.4378	.4101	.8362	.8428

Table 2 displays the conditional probabilities of electing the Condorcet loser, given there is one, for the plurality and antiplurality rules (recall that the Borda rule never chooses the Condorcet loser). The figures we obtain are small but not completely negligible: in an assembly of 100 members where each member is elected in three-candidate contests by using the plurality rule, one can expect to find 3 Condorcet losers! Indeed, the probabilities decrease with the number of candidates, but this decrease is rather slow and the risk of electing a Condorcet loser remains (for both rules) about 1% when eight candidates are in contention.

Table 2. *Probability of electing the Condorcet loser, given there is one*
under the plurality and antiplurality rules
(m candidates, large electorate)

m	Plurality		Antiplurality	
	IC	IAC	IC	IAC
3	.0374	.0296	.0377	.0311
4	.0250	.0226	.0251	.0238
5	.0189	.0184	.0190	.0187
6	.0160	.0145	.0155	.0157
7	.0136	.0128	.0133	.0128
8	.0114	.0127	.0113	.0127

The possibility of the choice of a Condocet loser certainly is one of the most puzzling features of the plurality and antiplurality rules. A way to eliminate this risk is to use the Borda rule. But this rule asks the voters to rank the candidates and it can be argued that it is a too strong requirement in mass elections as soon as the number of candidates is not very small. By contrast, the constant scoring rules only require to give a list of k (non ranked) candidates and are easier to implement. We have computed the probability of electing the Condorcet loser under various constant scoring rules for 3, 4, 5, 6 and 7 candidates. The results are shown in Table 3. It turns out from this table that an adequate choice of the k value is susceptible to considerably reduce the risk of selecting the Condorcet loser: for six candidates, this risk is lower than $1/1000$ when asking the voters to vote for exactly three candidates, whereas using the plurality rule ($k = 1$) or the antiplurality rule ($k = 5$) leads to a risk greater than $1/100$. More generally, our results suggest that the probability of electing the Condorcet loser under a constant scoring rule is minimal for $k = m/2$ when the number m of candidates is even and for $k = (m-1)/2$ or $k = (m+1)/2$ when m is odd.

Table 3. *Probability of electing the Condorcet loser given there is one*
under constant scoring rules k
(IAC condition, m candidates, large electorate)

m	$k = 1$	$k = 2$	$k = 3$	$k = 4$	$k = 5$	$k = 6$
3	.0296	.0311				
4	.0226	.0048	.0238			
5	.0184	.0030	.0031	.0187		
6	.0145	.0024	.0009	.0024	.0157	
7	.0128	.0023	.0004	.0004	.0021	.0128

References

ARROW K.J., *Social choice and individual value*, New York, John Wiley, 1963.

BERG S., LEPELLEY D., "Probability models in voting theory", *Statistica Neerlandica*, vol. 48 no. 2, 1994, p. 133-146.

BLACK D., *The theory of committees and elections*, London and New York, Cambridge University Press, 1958.

CONDORCET M.J.A., *Essai sur l'applicaltion de l'analyse à la probabilité des décisions rendues à la pluralité des voix*, Paris, 1785.

FEIX M., ROUET J.L., "L'espace des phases électoral et les statistiques quantiques. Application à la simulation numérique", 1999, mimeo.

FISHBURN P.C., GEHRLEIN W.V., "Borda's rule, positional voting and Condorcet's simple majority principle", *Public Choice*, vol. 28, 1976, p. 79-88.

FISHBURN P.C., GEHRLEIN W.V., "Majority efficiencies for simple voting procedures: summary and interpretation", *Theory and Decision*, vol. 14, 1982, p. 141-153.

GALAM S., "Social paradoxes of majority rule voting and renormalization group", *Journal of Statistical Physics*, vol. 61, 1990, p. 943-951.

GALAM S., "Le vote majoritaire est-il totalitaire?", *Pour la Science*, Hors série, juillet 1999, p. 90-94.

GEHRLEIN W.V. "Condorcet's paradox and the Condorcet efficiency of voting rules", *Mathematica Japonica*, vol. 40, 1997, p. 173-199.

HAMMESLY J.M., HANDSCOMB D.C., *Monte Carlo methods*, London, Methuen and Company, 1964.

JOHNSON N.L., KOTZ S., *Distributions in statistics: Continuous multivariate distributions*, New York, Wiley, 1972.

LEPELLEY D. and VALOGNES F., "On the Kim and Roush voting procedure", *Group Decision and Negotiation*, vol. 8, 1999, p. 109-123.

MERLIN V., TATARU M., VALOGNES F., "On the probability that all decision rules select the same winner", *Journal of Mathematical Economics*, vol. 33 no. 2, 2000, p. 183-207.

NURMI H., *Voting paradoxes and how to deal with them*, Berlin Heidelberg New York, Springer-Verlag, 1999.

VANDERCRUYSSEN D., "Analysis of voting procedures in one-seat elections: Condorcet efficiency and Borda efficiency", Discussion paper DPS 99.11, Katholieke Universiteit Leuven, 1999.

Appendix 1: GENERATING THE PREFERENCE LISTS

GENLISTE ALGORITHM

We want to calculate and enumerate all bijective relations (or permutations of the symmetrical group) of a set $E = \{0,1,2,. .., k - 1 \}$ of k elements (candidates). The number of possible cases is k!. This enumeration can be obtained by various algorithms (for example H.Trotter)[4]; we will choose a simple algorithm avoiding to stock in memory a big matrix[5] containing all the permutations. One can then simply obtain any list (permutation) by generating it from its classification number in the matrix.

$\boxed{1.}$ **Initialisation:**

Let L_0 and $L_i \in N^k$ be 2 line vectors of integers, where k designates the number of candidates.

Let NumListe and Index be two integer numbers designating respectively the number of the list and the Index of each element in the considered list. By convention, one chooses to index from zero.

Thus, for k candidates, NumListe varies from 0 to k!-1, and Index varies from 0 to k - 1.

Let D, Q and R be 3 integers.

For NumListe=0, the starting list is $(L_0(0), L_0(1), ..., L_0(k-1)\} = \{0, 1, 2, ..., k-1)$.

Index = 0, n=k

Determination of the list L_i, i=NumListe.

$\boxed{2.}$ **Calculation of $L_i(0)$:**

    D =(n - 1)!

    Q = NumListe $\div$ D, where '$\div$' designates the Euclidean divsion.

    R $\equiv$ NumListe MOD D, i.e, R is congrue to NumListe MODULO D [6].

The first element of the list is $L_i(Index) = L_0(Q)$.

$\boxed{3.}$ **Generic step:**

— Updating the basic list

We delete $L_0(Q)$ in the list and shift to the left, i.e:

    $L_0(Q+1) := L_0(Q), L_0(Q+2) := L_0(Q+1)..., L_0(n-2) := L_0(n-1).$

— Updating the level:

n:= n -1

Index: = Index + 1

NumListe: = R

$\boxed{4.}$ **Determination of L (k - 1):**

We repeat $\boxed{2.}$ and $\boxed{3.}$ until Index = k - 1. At this stage, we obtain $L_i(Index) = L_i(k-1) = L_0(0)$.

---

[4]"PERM "algorithm $n°$ 115 Comm. of ACM (1962)

[5]This matrix is in the order of $k! \times k$ bytes where k is the number of options, thus, for 8 options this matrixe will occupy $8! \times 8 \times 4 = 1290240$ bytes!

[6]R is the remainder of the Euclidean division of NumListe by D.

Example:

k=3, n=3.

Index	0	1	2
0	0	1	2
1	0	2	1
2	1	0	2
3	1	2	0
4	2	0	1
5	2	1	0

NumListe

Suppose that one wishes to generate the list number 3, therefore NumListe=3, Index=0, D=2! =2, Q=3÷2=1, R=1. $L_3(Index) = L_3(0) = L_0(Q)$, gold Q=1, and in the basic list $L_0 = (0, 1, 2)$ the Index 1 corresponds to 1, consequently $L_3(0) = 1$.

We update the basic list by deleting 1, we obtain the list $L_0 = (0, 2)$. Now, Index=1, NumListe=R=1, k=2-1=1. Return to step $\boxed{2.}$: D=1! =1, (Q=1 ÷ D) =1, R=0, $L_0(1) = 2$ in the previously updated list. The new list is now $L_3 = (1, 2)$ and the updated basic list is $L_0 = (0)$. We update the level: Index=2, k=0, NumListe=2, we can see that index=k-1, therefore we stop because the updated basic list does not contain more than one element. This element will be the last in the list, and we finally obtain $L_3 = (1, 2, 0)$ which corresponds to the list $n°3$ in the table.

Appendix 2: CONDORCET EFFICIENCY OF SCORING RULES (IAC MODEL)
ALGORITHM ALG4 (k candidates and infinite number of voters)

We want to calculate the probability of electing the Condorcet winner under a scoring rule Ψ, given that a Condorcet winner exists.

1. Initialisation of the frequency and weights:
$f_n = 0$ with $f_n \in N$
Let $W = [w_i]$ define the weights with $w_i \in \mathcal{R}$, $i = 0, 1, 2, \cdots, k - 1$, this vector characterizes the rule Ψ.

2. Initialisation of the so-called Dogdson matrix, the Score vector and indicators of numbers of victories:
- $D_{(k X k)} = [d_{ij}] = [0]$(Dogdson matrix).
- $Score = [s_i] = [0]$with $s_i \in \mathcal{R}$.
- N1,N2 $\in N$; N1=N2=0.

3.
A uniform vector of dimension $k! - 1$ is generated: $X = [x_i]$, $x_i \sim \mathcal{U}[0, 1[$

4.
X is sorted in ascending order.

5.
The vector of probabilities $P = [p_i]$ of dimension k! is formed in the following way:

$$
\begin{aligned}
p_0 &= x_0 \\
p_1 &= x_1 - x_0 \\
&\vdots \\
p_i &= x_i - x_{i-1} \\
&\vdots \\
p_{k!-1} &= 1 - x_{k!-2}
\end{aligned}
$$

with $p_i = (x_i - x_{i-2}) - p_{i-1}$ and $\sum_{i=0}^{k!-1} p_i = 1$

6. Generation of preference list:
See the GenList algorithm.

The list L_m, $m = 0, 1, \cdots, k! - 1$ is generated. The vector L_m of dimension k is indexed by a vector $I_n = (0, 1, 2, \cdots, (k-1))$ such that: $I_n(L_m(i)) = i \ \forall \ i = 0, 1, \cdots, k - 1$.

7. Calculation of the Dogdson matrix and the Score vector:

$$D_{(kXk)} = \begin{pmatrix} d_{0,0} & d_{0,1} & d_{0,2} & \cdots & d_{0,k-1} \\ d_{1,0} & \ddots & d_{1,2} & \cdots & d_{1,k-1} \\ \vdots & \vdots & \ddots & \vdots & \vdots \\ d_{k-1,0} & d_{k-1,1} & \cdots & \cdots & d_{k-1,k-1} \end{pmatrix}$$

$$s_k = (s_0, s_1, \cdots, s_{k-1})$$

The $d_{i,j}$ and the s_i are such that:

$\forall\ i = 0, 1, 2, \cdots, k-1;\ \forall\ j = 0, 1, 2, \cdots, k-1$:

If $I_n(L_m(i)) < I_n(L_m(j))$ for i $\neq$ j then:

$$d_{i,j} := d_{i,j} + p_m$$

$$s_i := s_i + p_m.w_i$$

$\boxed{8.}$ Repeat $\boxed{6.}$, $\boxed{7.}$ k! times for $m = 0, 1, 2, \cdots, k! - 1$. The Dogdson matrix and the vector of scores are completely filled up.

$\boxed{9.}$ Test of Ψ-winner / Condorcet winner:

Choose a candidate, i=0 for example (or candidate a), and test simultaneously if:

$-$ a is the Condorcet winner by the analysis of the Dogdson matrix.

Compare $d_{0,i}$ and $d_{i,0}$ for all $i = 1, 2, \cdots, k-1$.

If $d_{o,i} > d_{i,0}\ \forall\ i = 1, 2, \cdots, k-1$, then the number of victories N_1 is increased by 1, i.e, $N_1 := N_1 + 1$.

$-$ a is the $\Psi - winner$ by verifying if he has the greatest score.

Compare s_0 with s_i, $\forall\ i = 1, 2, \cdots, k-1$:

If $s_0 > s_i$, increase N_2 by 1, i.e, $N_2 := N_2 + 1$.

Test: if $N_1 = N_2 = k - 1$ then increase the frequency f_n by 1, i.e, $f_n := f_n + 1$.

At this point, we have completely simulated an election.

$\boxed{10.}$ Calculation of the probability of a winner following the two procedures:

steps $\boxed{2.}$, $\boxed{3.}$, $\boxed{4.}$, $\boxed{5.}$, $\boxed{6.}$, $\boxed{7.}$, $\boxed{8.}$, $\boxed{9.}$ constitute an election or a replication. These steps are repeated N times (N being here the number of replications).

Calculation of probabilities:

Define the two following events:

$E_1 = $ A is Condorcet winner, with $\hat{P}_1 = Prob[E_1] = N_1/N$.

$E_2 = $ A is $\Psi - winner$, with $\hat{P}_2 = Prob[E_2] = N_2/N$.

The joint probability estimation $\hat{P}_{12}$ is:

$$\hat{P}_{12} = Prob[E_1 and E_2] = E(P_{12}) = f_n/N.$$

A measure of the precision of the estimation is given by the standard-deviation of $\hat{P}$:

$$\hat{\sigma}_{\hat{P}} = \left[\hat{P}(1 - \hat{P})/N\right]^{1/2}$$

The probability that a is the Condorcet winner given that he is also the $\Psi - winner$ is given by:

$$\hat{P}_{1/2} = Prob[E_1/E_2] = \hat{P}_{12}/\hat{P}_2$$

with

$$\hat{\sigma}_{\hat{P}_{1/2}} = \left[\hat{P}_{1/2}(1 - \hat{P}_{1/2})/N\right]^{1/2}$$

similarly, the probability that a is the $\Psi - winner$ given that he is also the Condorcet winner is given by:

$$\hat{P}_{2/1} = Prob[E_2/E_1] = \hat{P}_{12}/\hat{P}_1$$

with

$$\hat{\sigma}_{\hat{P}_{2/1}} = \left[\hat{P}_{2/1}(1 - \hat{P}_{2/1})/N\right]^{1/2}$$

Thus, to obtain a precision of $\alpha\%$ one has to undertake $N \simeq \hat{P}(1 - \hat{P})/\alpha^2$ replications. Example: for a precision of 0.001 and a probability $\hat{P} = 0.93$ we have to realize about 65100 replications. It is obvious that this precision increases as a function of N, i.e, $\lim_{N \to \infty} \hat{\sigma}_{\hat{P}} = 0$.

Towards Computational Institutional Analysis: Discrete Simulation of a 3P Model [1]

Alain Albert* - Wolfgang Balzer*

* Address of Author 1
Département des sciences administratives
Université du Québec á Hull
Case postale 1250, succursale B
Hull (Québec) Canada J8X 3X7
Alain_Albert@uqah.uquebec.ca

* Address of Author 2
Institut für Philosophie, Logik und Wissenschaftstheorie
Universität München
Ludwigstr.31
D-80539 München (Germany)
balzer@lrz.uni-muenchen.de

ABSTRACT: *A 3P model (production, predation, protection) which can be game theoretically solved for two actors is generalized to n actors and studied by means of discrete simulation. The simulations confirm robust incentives for actors to produce and predate in an institution free environment, whereas protection activity is not significantly related to the ability for protection. The model is criticized for its neglect of predators predating on each other, and for its inability to reproduce real-life proportions of producers and predators and the times these spend on the three activities.*

RÉSUMÉ: *Un modèle 3P (production, prédation, protection) qui peut être résolu analytiquement dans le cas de deux agents est généralisé à n agents et étudié au moyen d'un modèle de simulation discret. Les simulations confirment les incitations des agents non soumis à des règles institutionnelles à produire et à se livrer à des activités prédatrices mais n'indiquent aucun lien significatif entre les activités de protection et la capacité protectrice des individus. L'absence de prise en considération, dans le modèle original, des activités de prédation entre prédateurs et son incapacité à engendrer des proportions réalistes de producteurs et de prédateurs ainsi qu'à produire une allocation crédible de leur temps entre les trois activités sont les principales critiques faites à ce modèle.*

KEY WORDS: *simulation, discrete simulation, 3p model, economics, game theory*

MOTS-CLÉS: *simulation, simulation discrète, modèle 3P, microéconomie, théorie des jeux.*

---

[1] See http://www.lrz-muenchen.de/: W.Balzer/BALZER.html for an extended version.

1. Introduction

In the last decade, social scientists have shown growing interest in the formal analysis of social institutions.[2] Economists, sociologists, political scientists and philosophers of science have contributed to this formal and mathematical modelling of institutions (their emergence, dynamic properties and stability).

At the same time computer simulations of social phenomena shifted from 'traditional' numerical simulations based on mathematical equations to agent-based, discrete event simulations. This new computational approach to modelling and simulating social phenomena has given birth to several new fields of research such as computational organization theory [PRC 94], [PCG 98], computational sociology [BAI 94], computational anthropology [DOR 95], [DEA 98], computational social psychology [NOW 98] and last but not least , computational economics [TES 98].

The aim of this paper is to contribute to this new research agenda by adding computational institutional analysis or briefly CIA[3] to the list of computational social fields. As we envision it, CIA combines the formal modelling of social institutions with new methods of doing agent-based computational social science.

We take up and generalize an economic, game theoretical two actor model studied in [HOU 95] and investigate its potential for the understanding of institutions by means of simulation. As game theoretic analysis becomes very difficult, if not practically impossible, for numbers of actors greater than two, simulation offers itself as the natural tool to be used.

The two actor model deals with the optimal allocation of actors' times on the three kinds of activities: production, predation, and protection, this is why we speak of a 3P model. Each actor has a given, total amount of time which she can split among the three activities, and her utility function depends on how she *and the other* actor split their time among the three activities (see (8) below), i.e. on the amounts (proportions) of time both actors spend on each of the three activities. By varying these amounts each actor seeks to maximize his utility function. As the utilities also depend on the times devoted by the respective *other* actor this leads to strategic interdependence. Roughly, actor i's utility is composed of three parts, namely of a) what i produces, plus b) what i robs from the other agent j, minus c) what i cannot protect and j takes away from him. Each of these parts in the first place depends on the amount of

---

[2]The formal approach based on deductive reasoning is sometimes opposed to the descriptive approach of the 'old' institutionalist school of the Commons variety [COM 34]. However, such an opposition between a theoretically driven 'new' institutionalism and an 'anti-theoretic' old institutionalism does not seem adequate; see [HOD 98] who stresses the early institutionalists' concern for theoretical issues.

[3]This field of research has something in common with its more famous counterpart. Computational Institutional Analysis is at the *center* of economic analysis, it is (artificial) *intelligence* based and, finally, it is *agent* based. Needless to say, we do not pursue the same objectives.

time i devotes to the respective activity, and on i's *abilities* for these activities which are given in the form of positive coefficients. Strategic interdependence comes in in b) and c). What i can rob from j in b) depends on how much time j spends on protecting himself, and what can be robbed from i in c) depends on how much time i spends on protecting herself.

2. The Basic Hobbesian 3P Model

Since Bush's pioneering work [BUS 76] there have been numerous articles and books[4] devoted to the modelling of conflictual anarchy of the hobbesian variety.[5] In the hobbesian world, there are no property rights or social norms to regulate agent interactions. In order to survive in such a world, individual agents undertake three basic types of activities: they produce, they use force to steal (predate) and they protect themselves against the predatory activities of others. People have different abilities for doing so. Depending on their relative abilities they produce, steal and protect themselves by equating the marginal returns of these three basic activities. The results of an actor's marginal calculus depend on the behavior of the other agents with whom she interacts.

Adopting the two-persons generalization of [HOU 95] of Bush's original model, consider two persons i, j. Let P_{i1}, P_{i2}, P_{i3} be the production, predation and protection functions of individual i (those of j are obtained by interchanging i and j). P_{ip} specifies the utility which person i derives from production ($p{=}1$), predation ($p{=}2$) and protection ($p{=}3$). There is only one good which is produced, and taken away by predators.

(1) Production: $P_{i1} = f_1(a_{i1}, t_{i1})$
(2) Predation: $P_{i2} = f_2(a_{i2}, t_{i2}, P_{j1}, P_{j3}), i \neq j$
(3) Protection: $P_{i3} = f_3(a_{i3}, t_{i3})$,

where the $a_{ip} > 0$ are individual parameters for, respectively, the productive ($p{=}1$), predatory ($p{=}2$) and protective ($p{=}3$) capacities of individual i, called *abilitiy coefficients* in the following, and t_{ip} denotes the time devoted by individual i to activity number p. Whereas the production and protection functions (1 and 3) depend only on i's own parameters and variables, the predation function (2) includes arguments pertaining to actor j. The more j produces the more i can steal from him, but the more j protects himself the more costly is it

---

[4] A critical review of these models is found in ([ALB 99].

[5] We are reluctant to use the term 'anarchy' in connection with conflictual models opposing bandits (predators) to peasants (producers) because this tends to confirm the widespread prejudice that anarchy *implies* fighting or a hobbesian state of nature. Originally, anarchy only means absence of domination. Though predation, robbery and exploitation are compatible with the absence of domination, they are by no means *implied* by such absence, as Hobbes made us believe. See [FLA 85] for a counter example. The hobbesian state of nature in which everyone fights everyone is only one among many other conceptual - including less frightening - alternatives. See also the comments of [DOW 97] on Hirshleifer's model [HIR 95] of conflictual anarchy.

to steal from him.

The ability coefficients may be used to distinguish between different types of actors - at least approximately. Actor i ia called a *producer* iff his ability coefficient for production is greater than his two other coefficients, and analogosly for *predator* and *protector*. For example, an actor with coefficients $(0.8, 0.1, 0.1)$ is very good (0.8) in producing, and equally bad (0.1) in predation and protection, and so is called a *producer*. In using lists of ability coefficients we agree on the fixed order: (production, predation, protection).[6]

Each individual k has an overall utility function U_k it seeks to maximize. A simple form for U_i suggested by [HOU 95] is this:

(4) $U_i = U_i(t_{i1}, t_{i2}, t_{i3}, t_{j1}, t_{j2}, t_{j3}) = P_{i1} + P_{i2} - P_{j2}, j \neq i$

Thus U_i is equal to what i gets out of producing (captured by P_{i1}) plus what she gets out of stealing from j (captured by P_{i2}) minus what j gets out of predating on i (captured by P_{j2}).

In [HOU 95] the functions f_1, f_2 and f_3 are generally specified as follows. For $k = i, j$,

(7) $f_{k1}(a_{k1}, t_{k1}) = a_{k1}t_{k1}$ and $f_{k3}(a_{k3}, t_{k3}) = a_{k3}t_{k3}$
$f_{i2}(a_{i2}, t_{i2}, P_{j1}, P_{j3}) = a_{i2}(t_{i2})^{\alpha_i} P_{j1}(1 - P_{j3})$, and
$f_{j2}(a_{j2}, t_{j2}, P_{i1}, P_{i3}) = a_{j2}(t_{j2})^{\alpha_j} P_{i1}(1 - P_{i3})$.

The exponents α_i, α_j are used to cover varying marignal returns from predating. For the 'standard' value -1/2, the 'factor' predation time yields decreasing returns.

Using (7) we obtain the following general expressions for U_i and U_j.

(8) $U_i(t_{i1}, t_{i2}, t_{i3}, t_{j1}, t_{j2}, t_{j3}) = a_{i1}t_{i1} + a_{i2}(t_{i2})^{\alpha_i}a_{j1}t_{j1}(1 - a_{j3}t_{j3}) -$
$$a_{j2}(t_{j2})^{\alpha_j}a_{i1}t_{i1}(1 - a_{i3}t_{i3}),$$
$U_j(t_{j1}, t_{j2}, t_{j3}, t_{i1}, t_{i2}, t_{i3}) = a_{j1}t_{j1} + a_{j2}(t_{j2})^{\alpha_j}a_{i1}t_{i1}(1 - a_{i3}t_{i3}) -$
$$a_{i2}(t_{i2})^{\alpha_i}a_{j1}t_{j1}(1 - a_{j3}t_{j3}).$$

Each actor k seeks to maximize his utility subject to the constraint that $t_{k1} + t_{k2} + t_{k3} \leq T$ where T is the total amount of time available in the period considered which, for reasons of simplicity, is set equal to 1 for both actors. In other words, each actor k tries to find an optimal allocation of times (t_{k1}, t_{k2}, t_{k3}).[7] Clearly, both actors are strategically interdependent since in (8) i's utility depends on the times chosen by j and conversely. The resulting game can be analytically solved for two actors [HOU 95].

---

[6]Below, predators and protectors will be thrown together. Alternatively, the actor types can also be characterized in terms of the proportions of time they spend on the three activities. In general, the two definitions do not coincide.

[7]Note that the numbers t_{kr} here do not denote *points* of time, but lengths of time *intervals*.

3. The General Model

We generalize this model to the case of n actors as follows, retaining the assumption of one single good that is produced by everyone. Each of the n actors i $(i = 1, ..., n)$ has a utility function U_i depending on the $3n$ times which all actors spend on the three activities. For each i, the times i spends on production, predation and protection, respectively, are denoted by t_i^1, t_i^2 and t_i^3. Thus i's distribution of time on the three activities is given by $\vec{t_i} = (t_i^1, t_i^2, t_i^3)$, $(t_i^1 + t_i^2 + t_i^3 = 1)$, and i's utility function may be written as $U_i = U_i(\vec{t_1}, ..., \vec{t_n})$. We assume that i's utility function has the following form

(9) $U_i(\vec{t_1}, ..., \vec{t_n}) = a_{i1}t_{i1}$
$$+ a_{i2}(t_{i2}/(n-1))^{\alpha_i} \Sigma_{j,j \neq i}(a_{j1}t_{j1}(1 - a_{j3}t_{j3}))$$
$$- min(1, (\Sigma_{j,j \neq i} a_{j2}(t_{j2}/(n-1))^{\alpha_j})) a_{i1}t_{i1}(1 - a_{i3}t_{i3})$$

where $0 < \alpha_i < 1$, $0 \leq a_{i1}, a_{i2}, a_{i3}$ and $a_{i1} + a_{i2} + a_{i3} = 1$ for $i = 1, ..., n$. The ability coefficient a_{ip} expresses the 'ability' or 'efficiency' with which actor i performs activity number p (p=1,2,3 for production, predation, protection), and t_{ip} is the time i spends on activity p. The three components of U_i in (9) may be interpreted as follows.

The second part of U_i may be best understood if we rewrite it as $(n - 1)[a_{i2}(t_{i2}/(n-1))^{\alpha_i}(1/(n-1))\Sigma_{j,j \neq i}a_{j1}t_{j1}(1 - a_{j3}t_{j3})]$. $a_{i2}(t_{i2}/(n-1))^{\alpha_i}$ is the 'weight' of i's activity of predating when i predates one of the n other actors, on the assumption that i splits his 'predation time' equally on all other actors. The average, 'non-protected' production of some actor thus predated by i is $(1/(n-1))\Sigma_{j,j \neq i}a_{j1}t_{j1}(1-a_{j3}t_{j3})$. So $a_{i2}(t_{i2}/(n-1))^{\alpha_i}(1/(n-1))\Sigma_{j,j \neq i}a_{j1}t_{j1}(1-a_{j3}t_{j3})$ is i's utility from predating one 'average' fellow actor. In order to obtain i's total utility this expression has to be taken $n - 1$ times.

In the third part, $(t_{j2}/(n-1))^{\alpha_j}$ gives the 'weight' of that part which j can take away from i's non-protected product $a_{i1}t_{i1}(1 - a_{i3}t_{i3})$ on the assumption that j spends her 'predation time' t_{j2} equally on all other actors. Thus the third part refers to the sum of all parts which are taken away from i's non-protected product by all the other actors. Since in the case of more than two actors the sum of all 'weights' may be greater than 1 we have to take the minimum of this sum and 1 in order to prevent a change of sign in the third component.

An analytic treatment of these general equations is very difficult, if not practically impossible.

4. The Simulation

We use a discrete event simulation shell called SMASS (Sequential Multi-Agent System for Social Simulation) written in SWI-PROLOG [BAL 00], [WIE 93]. This shell executes simulation runs over a fixed number N of simulation periods such that in each simulation period, each actor is called up for action exactly once.

In order to turn the static analytic model into a dynamical process we proceed as follows. The model's total time interval (whose length was set equal to 1) which is captured in one simulation run, is represented by the number N of all simulation periods over which the simulation is run. A simulation period therefore may be imagined as covering a 'part' of length $1/N$ of the total period 1 of the analytical model.[8] Assuming that each actor in each simulation period acts just once we can count the numbers m_1, m_2, m_3 of simulation periods in which he produces, predates, or engages in protection, so $N = m_1 + m_2 + m_3$. We take these numbers m_1, m_2, m_3 to represent the periods of time t_1, t_2, t_3 an actor spends on the three activities in the solution of the analytical model.

In order to formulate a basic rule of behavior as a substitute for the maximization assumptions of the analytic model, in the course of the simulation a 'history' is built up recording in each simulation period T the numbers of simulation periods every single actor spent on each of the three activities up to the present simulation period T. Thus if actor i is called up in simulation period T her history $\vec{h}_{i,T}$ will consist of three numbers $\vec{h}_{i,T} = (h_{i1,T}, h_{i2,T}, h_{i3,T})$ such that $h_{i1,T} + h_{i2,T} + h_{i3,T} = T$ and each $h_{ip,T}$ is the number of simulation periods in which i performed activity number $p(p = 1, 2, 3)$. Such a history gives the distribution of the times i spent on the three activities.[9]

Instead of the utilities $U_i(\vec{t}_1, ..., \vec{t}_n)$ derived from the 'final' proportions of times we now may consider utilities derived from the relative proportions of times spent up to a given simulation period T, i.e. utilities depending on the actors' histories up to T

$$U_i(T) = U_i(\vec{h}_{1,T}, ..., \vec{h}_{n,T}), \text{ where } \vec{h}_{i,T} = (h^1_{i,T}, h^2_{i,T}, h^3_{i,T})$$

We apply the following rule of behavior. An actor i in simulation period T calculates the marginal utilities for each of the three activities, and chooses that activity which yields highest marginal utility. The marginal utilities are those which actor i would derive from spending one more simulation period on production, predation or protection, given that up to simulation period T he spent the times $(h^1_{i,T}, h^2_{i,T}, h^3_{i,T})$ on these activities. i's marginal utility for *production* in simulation period T is thus defined by

$$(10)\ U_i(\vec{h}_{1,T}, ..., (h^1_{i,T} + 1, h^2_{i,T}, h^3_{i,T}), ..., \vec{h}_{n,T}) - U_i(\vec{h}_{1,T}, ..., \vec{h}_{n,T}).$$

The marginal utilities for predation and protection are obtained in the same

---

[8]Now we have two different notions of a period. There is the overall period of the analytic model, and there are the N periods in one simulation run. In order to avoid confusion, the latter will be called simulation periods.

[9]In the present study the histories are used as mere technical devices. The possibility of using them to introduce assumptions on learning or discounting, as proposed by one referee, clearly shows the potential of the simulation version of the model, but also increases its distance from the original mathematical model.

way by adding in (10) one simulation period to $h_{i,T}^2$ and $h_{i,T}^3$, respectively.[10]

In (10) the other actors' histories enter in the calculation of i's marginal utilities; these are taken as they are found at the time of execution in simulation period T.[11]

In the analytical model a solution or state of equilibrium is a list of time distributions $(\vec{t_1}, ..., \vec{t_n})$ (a 'state') satisfying a condition of maximality. In the simulation such a state corresponds to the actors' *final* histories $(\vec{h_{1,N}}, ..., \vec{h_{n,N}})$ where N denotes the total number of simulation periods for which the simulation is run. While the simulation is running, the histories $\vec{h_{i,T}}$ steadily change when T grows from 1 to N. However, we can say that the system in state $(\vec{h_{1,T}}, ..., \vec{h_{n,T}})$ has become *stable* if the fractions $h_{ip,T'}/T'$ do not change significantly for all T' such that $T \leq T'$. For instance, when the final distribution of i's time is $(0.5, 0.5, 0)$ - i.e. i spent half of her time on producing and half of it on predating - then for $N = 100, \vec{h_{i,N}} = (50/100, 50/100, 0)$. When the system has become stable, say in simulation period 70, then $\vec{h_{i,70}} = (35/70, 35/70, 0)$ and these fractions will show only insignificant deviations for $T > 70$. As the system operates with integers, they cannot remain strictly identical because, say, for $N = 100$, in each simulation period one of the history's components will be increased by $1/100$.

The states which are stable in this sense we take as the analogues of analytic solutions. Their stability indicates that the actors' utility functions have local maxima near the corresponding distributions of times which constitute the arguments of the utility functions. As the only random element in the system is the order in which the actors are activated in each simulation period, it seems that random fluctuations will not make the system leaving these local maxima (though we did not investigate this in detail). Anyway, running the system with a greater number of simulation periods will decrease the probability that the local maximum is left, because the increments in calculating the marginal utilities become smaller. All simulations were run for 100 simulation periods, and a stable state was reached when deviations were allowed up to $\epsilon = 0.02$. The stable state in most cases was reached between simulation periods number 60 and 80.

5. Simulation Results

We performed a number of simulations in order to explore the space of possibilities given by variations in the parameters: numbers of actors, ability coefficients, exponents, and initial distributions of predators and producers in the population. This is a huge space and it does not seem a good idea to try to explore it fully systematically. We varied several items in more systematic fashion, but

---

[10] As simulation periods are represented by integers, the natural unit here is 1.

[11] This means asynchronous updating.

only so within relatively narrow boundaries. Each simulation was repeated ten times with the same initial data. The results reported here are the mean values over these repetitions, deviations from these means were usually in the order of 0.01 or less.

In a first series of simulations[12] we used ability coefficients that are lognormally distributed in the population. As these coefficients consist of three components whose interdependency is difficult to judge empirically we used a mix of two different random processes to create them. We first created lognormally distributed numbers b_i - one for each actor i - within the interval $[0, 1]$. We then split the 'rest' $1 - b_i (\geq 0)$ randomly into two parts $b_i = a_i + c_i$, and used (a_i, b_i, c_i) as coefficients of actor i.

For the following, we define 'producers' i those actors whose ability for producing, a_2^i, is strictly greater than that for predating, a_2^i, and all other actors 'predators'. The population then splits up into x% of producers and (1-x)% of predators. With varying numbers of actors, x varied in the interval $[40, 60]$.

The means of the ability coefficients and the time profiles did vary with variations of the number of actors, but this effect is mainly due to the fact that for a different number of actors, the ability coefficients are newly created in the random way described earlier. Table 1 summarizes some results.

Table 1

number of actors	10	50	100
percentage of producers	50	42	43
	.	.	.
mean producer:	.	.	.
ability coeffs	(.36,.10,.53)	(.51,.14,.33)	(.46,.13,.40)
time profiles	(.55,.17,.27)	(.23,.57,.18)	(.18,.64,.17)
variances of time	(.007,.041,.021)	(.035,.174,.052)	(.038,.180,.060)
	.	.	.
mean predator:	.	.	.
ability coeffs	(.18,.58,.22)	(.16,.59,.23)	(.14,.60,.25)
time profiles	(.13,.86,0)	(.01,.98,0)	(.01,.98,0)
variances of time	(.009,.009,0)	(0,0,0)	(0,0,0)
	.	.	.

Remarkably, in populations of more than 40 actors, a 'mean producer' spends more time on predating than on producing. This means that several single producers, i.e. actors who are more able to produce than to predate, nevertheless

---

[12] As a warming up exercise we simulated the Houba-Weikard 2-actor model with the coefficients $[2, 0, 1]$ for the producer and $[1, 1, 0]$ for the predator. This yields the expected Nash equilibrium at $(0, 0.3968, 0.2063)$ - the remaining times being uniquely determined by the time constraint - for the predator, which in this case also can easily be computed by hand.

spend more time on predation, which, for them, is the inferior activity. This result is *prima facie* at odds with the assumption of rationality underlying the model. However, we can interpret it as showing that the incentive for predation which is incorporated in the form of the utility function is much stronger than that for production so that it surpasses the *prima facie* incentive given in terms of the ability coefficients.

By contrast, the 'mean predators' do not spend much time on producing eventhough they have a non-negligible coefficient for production. This confirms the previous interpretation. Moreover, the 'mean predators' do hardly spend any time on protection, which in many simulation means that no single predator does so. This outcome conflicts with the intuition - external to the model - that predators also should predate on their 'fellow' predators. Given the high percentage of predators in the population (often more than 50%), one would want to see a substantial amount of time spent by predators on protecting themselves against each other. However, this incentive is not expressed in the model. The third, negative part of the utility function in (9) depends multiplicatively on the actor's own product $(a_{i1}t_{i1})$ which is negligible for predators. According to (9) a predator spending no time on production has nothing to protect. In reality, even in the basic case in which all products - whether produced or robbed - are consumed in the same period, there is the possibility of one predator taking away from another one the good which the latter just robbed from a third person.

Figure 1

time spent on predating

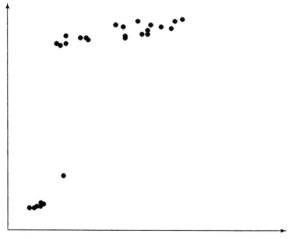

ability coefficients for predation

Looking at how each single time component t_r (e.g. the time spent on predation, $r=2$) depends on a single ability coefficient a_s (e.g. the coefficient for production, $s=1$), we arrange the coefficients that are present in the population in an increasing order so that for the set $\{i_1, ..., i_n\}$ of actors we obtain a series $a_s(i_1) < ... < a_s(i_n)$. When we plot the corresponding time $t_s(i_j)$ against each such coefficient $a_s(i_j)$ the dependence (in a population of 30 actors) can be graphically depicted as in figure 1.

Distinguishing increase (+) from decrease (-), and degrees of the strengths of the connections (1 = strong and regular, 2 = weak and regular, 3 = irregular) all the dependencies are summarized in table 2.

Table 2

	increasing coefficient for		
.	production	predation	protection
time spent on	.	.	.
production	+,2	-,1	+,3
predation	-,2	+,1	-,3
protection	+,3	-,1	+,3

These connections do not change when they are restricted to the two subpopulations of producers and predators.

The absence of a regular increase of protection time with an increase of protection ability (even in the subpopulation of producers) we find unsatisfactory. As producers' product increases over time (in the simulation), and as there are many predators, producers should have a strong incentive for protection which is also in accordance with the form of the utility function (9).

In these simulations on might suspect that the results depend on the initial creation of lognormally distributed ability coefficients. In order to control for this we conducted a second series in which we focused on one ability coefficient. When this was fixed, the percentages of producers, predators and protectors (defined in terms of abilities), as well as all the other coefficients were varied randomly. The random creation of the 'other' parameters was repeated 20 and 50 times. Doing the simulation for different values of the focused ability coefficient, like 0.2, 0.25, 0.3, ..., 1, and plotting the times spent on one activity against the focused coefficient, we obtained qualitatively the same results as in the first series. Figure 2 shows some dependencies for the series 0.2, 0.25, 0.3, ..., 1 of coefficients number s on the x-axis and times number r on the y-axis.

In a third series, we investigated the sensitivity of the model in dependence of the absolute numerical values of the ability coefficients. Instead of normalized ability coefficients (adding up to 1) we used larger numbers, and studied the system's behavior for different, fixed sets of coefficients and proportions of producers and predators. We started with normalized coefficients, multiplied them by 10, 20, 30 and gauged the (1-...) expressions in (9) to the absolute values, e.g. when using coefficients adding up to 10, the '1' was replaced by '10'. In a population of 20 actors we ran all combinations of coefficients (0.8,0,0.2), (0.4,0.4,0.2), (0.1,0.1,0.8) for producers, (0,1,0), (0,0.7,0.3), (0.3, 0.4, 0.3) for predators and percentages 100, 80, 60, 40, 20 of producers in the population.

There was no significant variation of predators' times in dependence on the absolute sizes of ability coefficients, and variation for producers was relatively small, never exceeding 30%. We may say that the model is moderately robust with respect to the absolute sizes of ability coefficients.

Figure 2

time spent on production

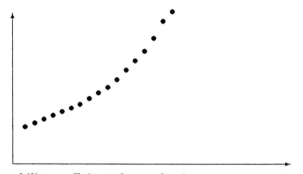

ability coefficients for production

We also varied the exponents α_i attached to predation times in equation (9). In the earlier simulations these exponents had been uniformly set equal to $1/2$. In a fourth series the exponents $1/2$ were replaced by smaller and larger values (0.2, 0.4, 0.8, 1), but still each actor's utility function was calculated with the same exponents. Running the simulation in the setting of series 3 above we found that the times of predators are hardly affected by changes of the exponents. The main effect observed for producers was that when their percentage in the population decreases below a threshold, they split their times nearly equally on production and predation. The only effect of varying exponents is that this threshold decreases with growing exponent, but also with decreasing predating ability of the predators.

In a final series we tried to reproduce 'reasonable' empirical time distributions as found in existing populations. For example, in a slaveholder society [KNI 77], a first guess for time distributions would be (1,0,0) for slaves (which form, say 40 percent of the population), and (0,0.6,0.4) for non-slaves (making up 60 percent of the population). That is, slaves spend all their time on production, while non-slaves split their time on 60% of predation and 40% of protection. We started a search program which tried to find ability coefficients for which the time distributions resulting in a simulation with such coefficients fitted with the times and percentages fixed beforehand.

This resulted in complete failure. For none of three 'reasonable', initial time distributions and percentages the program found coefficients such that the simulation results would fit with the given times and percentages. Even if we admit that the search algorithm used is perhaps very inefficient this indicates that the model in its present form is not sufficiently flexible.[13]

6. Conclusion

First simulations with a multi-agent model in which actors optimize the time distributions for production, predation and protection yield insight in the rational, non-institutionalized incentives for engaging in each of these activities. We found that predation is 'robust' in the sense that actors who are best at predating in most cases spend almost all their time on predation. This points to a natural incentive which theoretically could back Hobbes' state of nature. A second positive result is that production time also increases with an increase of the ability to produce, though the degree of increase varies with other parameters, in particular with the coefficients for the other abilities and the percentage of producers in the population. This also indicates a natural incentive, and the variability of increase opens the way for studying the systematic effects of other, 'external' parameters on the incentive to produce.

Negatively, we found that protection time in most cases does not monotonically increase with protection ability. A first interpretation is that the ability for protection is dominated by the other two abilities, and thus not really an independent variable. This interpretation is also supported by the intuitive observation that the abilities for predation and protection in a pre-historic environment are closely related to similar kinds of bodily skills and strengths.

We were not able with the present model to produce 'real life' time distributions and percentages of producers and predators. This may have two reasons. First, the model's basic equation (9) may be too rigid or too restricted. In future research we will use variations of the model with different exponents and different overall forms of (9) to find 'solutions' which reproduce given, plausible time distributions and percentages. In particular, the absence of predation among predators in (9) has to be removed.

A second reason for failure may be the neglect of institutional features. Broadly speaking, institutions seem to produce and to stabilize certain patterns of time distributions and percentages which do not naturally occur in an institution-free state. We hypothesize that the present model allows to incorporate some such institutional features, which we hope to find and to include in the picture.

---

[13]Of course, this does not mean that this kind of fitting is the only kind of validation procedure for the model.

7. References

[ALB 99] ALBERT A., "Les modèles économiques d'anarchie: une revue de la littérature", manuscript.

[BAI 94] BAINBRIDGE R. et al., Artificial Social Intelligence, Annual Review of Sociology 20, 401-36.

[BAL 00] BALZER, "SMASS: A Sequential Multi-Agent System for Social Simulation", in R.Suleiman, K.-G.Troitzsch, N.Gilbert (eds.), *Tools and Techniques for Social Sciences Simulation*, Heidelberg: Physica Verlag, to appear.

[BUS 76] BUSH W.C., "The Hobbesian Djungle or Orderly Anarchy", in *Essays on Unorthodox Economic Strategies*, A.T.Denazu and R.J.Mackay (eds.), Blacksburg VA: University Publications, 27-37.

[COM 34] COMMONS J.R., *Institutional Economics: Its Place in Political Economy*, New York: Macmillan.

[DEA 98] DEAN J.S. et al., "Understanding Anasazi Culture Change through Agent Based Modelling", http://www.santafe.edu/sfi/publications/working papers/98-10-094.pdf

[DOR 95] DORAN J. "Simulating Prehistoric Societies: Why ? and How?", *Aplicationes Informaticas in Arqueologia: Teorias e Sistemas* 2, Bilbao, 40-55.

[DOW 97] DOWD K., Anarchy, "Warfare and Social Order: Comment of Hirshleifer", *Journal of Political Economy*, 105, 648-51.

[FLA 85] FLAP H., *Conflict, loyaliteit en geweld*, Dissertation, University of Utrecht (Netherlands), english translation: Conflict, Loyalty and Violence: The Effects of Social Networks on Behaviour, Frankfurt/Main: Peter Lang, 1988.

[HIR 95] HIRSHLEIFER J., "Anarchy and its Breakdown", *Journal of Political Economy* 103, 26-52.

[HOD 98] HODGSON G.M., "The Approach of Institutional Economics", *Journal of Economic Literature* 36, 166-92.

[HOU 95] HOUBA H., WEIKARD H., "Interaction in Anarchy and the Social Contract: A Game-theoretic Perspective", Working Paper # TI 95-186, Tinbergen Institute.

[KNI 77] KNIGHT F.W., "The Social Structure of Cuban Slave Society in the Nintheen Century", in V.Rubin & A.Tuden (eds.), *Comparative Perspectives on Slavery in New World Plantation Societies*, Annals of the New York

Academy of Sciences, Vol.292, New York, 297-306.

[NOW 98] NOWAK A., VALLACHER R., "Toward Computational Social Psychology: Cellular Automata and Neural Network Models of Interpersonal Dynamics", in, *Connectionist Models of Social Reasoning and Social Behavior*, S.J.Read & I.C.Miller (eds.), Mahmaw NJ: Lawrence Erlbaum Publishers, 277-311.

[PRC 94] PRIETULA M., CARLEY K., "Computational Organization Theory: Autonomous Agents and Emergent Behavior", *Journal of Organizational Computing* 4, 41-83.

[PCG 98] PRIETULA M., CARLEY K., GASSER L. (eds.), 1998: "Simulating Organizations: Computational Models of Institutions and Groups", Cambridge MA: MIT Press.

[TES 98] TESFATSION L., "Agent-Based Computational Economics: A Brief Guide to the Literature", http://www.econ.iastate.edu/tesfatsi/ace.htm

[WIE 93] WIELEMAKER J., SWI-Prolog 1.8, Reference Manual, University of Amsterdam, Dept. of Social Science Informatics.

Dreamscape
Testing the Rational Choice Theory[1]

Niels Lepperhoff

Programme Group Systems Analysis and Technology Evaluation (STE)
(Forschungszentrum Jülich GmbH, 52425 Jülich, Germany)
n.lepperhoff@fz-juelich.de

ABSTRACT. *This work is an example for the use of computer simulation for testing theory completeness. The multi-agent model Dreamscape is a transformation of the Rational Choice Theory into a computer program. In this work the general applicability of the Rational Choice Theory is tested. The research question is: Does social order emerge out of the "state of nature"? In particular: Do social norms evolve? In a computer-based analysis for non-violent agents it is shown, that conjunct, proscriptive norms are able to emerge – apart from their legitimacy. On the contrary, in a violent population social order does not emerge.*

KEY WORDS: *Social Simulation, Sociological Theory, Rational Choice, Multi-agent Systems*

---

[1] This work was done during my diploma thesis at the University of Dortmund.

1. Introduction

In the last years the Rational-Choice-Theory has often been criticised [e.g. EGG 97; KEL 95; LÜD 96; MIL 94; SCR 92]. Different aspects of the theory have been mentioned, but the criticism stopped on the analytic level. With a computer simulation I will test the Rational-Choice-Theory for completeness.

The advocates of the Rational-Choice-Theory say that the theory is able to explain the emergence of social order. Social order is understood as an unintended result of many interactions from individuals [ESS 91, p. 45; KUN 97, p. 8]. Since the Rational-Choice-Theory is not adapted to certain situations, periods or societies, it should be able to be applied to each human population under all conceivable conditions. I will test the strength of this claim – in particular the emergence of social order out of the "state of nature" [HOB 76] – with an agent-based computer simulation. Social order is a complex phenomenon. Therefore I focus on two parts: the emergence of norms and the effect of deadly violence. Observing the emergence of phenomena is easily done with computer simulation [e.g. EPS 96].

Axelrod [AXE 97, pp. 23] identifies three different types of use of computer simulation: Forecast, testing and discovery. The chances and risks of forecasting are controversially discussed in literature. The controversy is skipped here because the purpose of the investigation is not the forecast, but the examination. In this article simulation experiments are treated as thought experiments:

"Simulation is a way of doing thought experiments. While the assumptions may be simple, the consequences may not be obvious. The large-scale effects of locally interacting agents are called ‚emergent properties‘ of the system. Emergent properties are often surprising because it can be hard to anticipate the full consequences of even simple forms of interactions." [AXE 97, pp. 24]

For analysing the Rational-Choice-Theory some intermediate steps are necessary. First the multi-agent model Dreamscape is constructed along the theory. Second the sociological terms are transferred to the model. Dreamscape is implemented object-oriented, i.e. the actions of each individual agent are simulated. The macro structures developing from the behaviour of the agents can be directly observed [see EPS 96, pp. 1]. The results of the simulation are transferred back to the sociological terms.

In the following paragraph the Rational-Choice-Theory is described briefly. The description of the model Dreamscape follows. Some simulation results are presented and discussed in the last paragraph.

2. Summary of the Rational-Choice-Theory

The Rational-Choice-Theory is both an analysis method, which explain the emergence and the modification of macro phenomena by the exclusive view of actions on the micro level, and a theory about the selection of action by individuals. I focus on the version of Hartmut Esser [ESS 91, 96].

Under the assumption that social structures are only results of actions of different individuals, an indirect connection between two macro phenomena A and B can be postulated. According to Coleman [COL 91] macro phenomenon A determines the situation of the individual. An individual in the Rational Choice Theory is called actor. The actor tries to recognize the situation in one of several learned situation descriptions, from which he then takes the relevant goals, possible actions, and subjectively assumed probability of success. The subjective utilities of different goals are additive. Now the individual now selects the action with the highest subjective utility for the detected situation. According to Coleman [COL 91] the new macro phenomenon B is the result of the actions of many actors.

Out of two basic goals, called *needs*, every other goal is deducted. The needs are "production from social appreciation and the protection of the physical well-being" [ESS 96, p. 7 translated by the author]. These two needs cannot directly be satisfied, but with social, i.e. institutionally, defined *intermediate goods*, which are weighted by the actor.

The intermediate goods can be divided into *primary* and *secondary intermediate goods*. Primary intermediate goods "define the 'preferences' of humans and their dominant goals" [ESS 96, p. 7 translated by the author] and are the highest, recognised or required social goals, e.g. cash or honour. They are produced by secondary (indirect) intermediate goods, e.g. work or performance.

The paradigm of the Rational Choice Theory says, that on the macro-level, each phenomenon is only a result of the interaction of individuals on the micro-level – there is no central control. Multi-agent models refer to this paradigm, too. Esser says that selecting an action proceeds in three steps. First, the agent recognizes its situation, then it evaluates different options for action, and finally it selects the action with the highest utility. To describe selecting an action Esser uses the theory of "Subjective Expected Utility" (SEU) [ESS 91; for an overview see also OPP 83, pp. 41].

Selecting an action means maximizing the expected profit of a potential action A_i according to weight U_j of a goal j. An agent tries to reach m goals at the same time. The subjectively expected utility of action A_i, SEU (A_i), depends on the sum of the product of the goalweights U_j of each goal j and the likelihood of success p_{ij}, see formula 1. An agent will execute the action A_i with the highest utility SEU (A_i) [ESS 91, pp. 53].

$$[1] \quad SEU(A_i) = \sum_{j=1}^{m} p_{ij} \bullet U_j$$

3. The model Dreamscape

Dreamscape is a multi-agent system, a technique from the distributed artificial intelligence. In a multi-agent system the behaviour of several agents is simulated over a period of time. These interact with their environment, i.e. they change their environment and their internal states [GIL 99]. At first glance a multi-agent system implemented on a spatial lattice field, like Dreamscape, appears to be similar to a cellular automata. This impression is wrong. A cellular automata produces the model dynamics with the cells. In Dreamscape the agents who are different from the cells essentially produce the model dynamics, in comparison with the game chess (figures as agents).

An actor – the individual in the Rational-Choice-Theory – is transferred directly into the computer model as a complete unit. An agent is thereby the model of an actor. The different notion of actor and agent allows a clear separation of the Rational-Choice-Theory and the computer model.

Here I would like to point out that Dreamscape is not a simulation of a prisoners' dilemma. Only in a small section – trading – a strongly extended prisoners' dilemma is used, in which observation, communication and rejecting of trading offers are possible.

Dreamscape is described roughly in the following sections. Further details and a formal definition are given in [LEP 99].

3.1. *Goals and action alternatives*

The topic is the emergence of social order. Therefore the simulation starts in a state without any order ("state of nature"). The agents have only innate abilities and needs, because educated needs and abilities are a product of society. The fact that humans are always embedded in social systems after their birth makes an indisputable distinction between innated and educated abilities and needs more difficult. Therefore here I concentrate on two fundamental needs, which innate character is indisputable:

– Need for sleep

– Need for food [see HAL 73, pp. 41]

Thus two primary intermediate goods were defined. From these two primary intermediate goods the indirect intermediate goods are derived, which represent the action alternatives occurring in the model Dreamscape.

By including sexual reproduction the model would be more realistic. However, some questions remain open. The biological reproduction is well understood. Still no generally accepted theory exists, how the sex influences the behaviour of individuals. Hall [HAL 73, p. 43] stated that the observed behaviour of women and men is dependent on the culture. The situation without any culture should be examined. Thus sexual reproduction is skipped in this model.

Each agent has a finite life. If an agent reaches its maximum age, two offsprings will be generated, so the population is able to grow and more adapted characteristics spread in the population. The mechanism of evolution is preserved.

The intermediate good *need for food* can be satisfied in four ways: by gathering the food from cells, by honest trading, by cheating or by "robbery". Trading introduces interactions in the model. Robbery represents deadly violence. If an agent is stronger than another, it can kill this and takes over its food supplies. The meaning of cheating depends on the situation. If an agent cheats, without being cheated from its interaction partner before, then its partner feels this fraud as injustice. If an agent cheats after being cheated by its interaction partner then retaliation occurs. With these two meanings of cheating the circle of cheating and contra-cheating is avoided, co-operation is possible [see AXE 84]. These two meanings of cheating make an additional assumption necessary: Individuals can feel independently from cultural coinage injustice and the desire for retaliation. The acceptance of the injustice feeling appears plausible, since the agent delivers food, without a return, i.e. its primary intermediate property need for food is unfulfilled. The *need for retaliation* is regarded as the third primary intermediate good, which can be achieved either by cheating or by robbery. Satisfying the primary intermediate good need for retaliation increases both the physical well-being and the social appreciation.

Social appreciation can be modelled only indirectly, because the simulation starts in a state without any order. It is modelled as knowledge of behaviours, and expressed by the fourth primary intermediate good *acknowledgement*. By observing and memorizing its neighbours[2] an agent archives this good. Furthermore agents exchange their knowledge of other agent's behaviour (observations, experiences and reports) by talking. Publicity is produced. Some actions can fulfil several goals. Table 1 shows an outline.

	Food	Sleep	Need for Retaliation	Acknowledge
Trading	X			X
Cheating	X		X	X
Talking				X
Collecting	X			
Robbing	X		X	
Sleeping		X		
Being lazy		X		

Table 1. *Representation which goal can by achieved by which action alternative, marked by X*

---

[2] Each agent in the visible area of an agent is its neighbour.

3.2. *The environment*

The environment is represented by a torus-shaped lattice with 30 x 30 cells. The design of the environment is similar to Epstein's and Axtell's [EPS 96] world "Sugerscape". In Dreamscape as well as in Sugarscape only one agent can stand on a cell. Each cell produces two types of food, which are consumed by the agents: Water and berries (Sugarscape: Sugar and spices). A cell regenerates – similar to Sugarscape – of each type of food one unit per turn, as long as the corresponding carrying capacity of the cell is not exceeded. For each type of food and for each cell the carrying capacity is different. At the beginning of the simulation the carrying capacity is chosen by random from a uniform distribution. In contrast to Sugerscape, there is no topology in the distribution of the carrying capacity.

The time is modelled discretely by time steps, called *turns*. At each turn every agent acts once in a random order.

3.3. *The Agent*

The definition of an agent is complex. It can be divided into three parts: the state, the bio constants and the character.

The *state* reflects the time-depended internal condition. Important state variables are the supplies of water and berries and the combat strength, which determines the success in robbery. The strength of an agent depends on the total amount of the water and berry units in its supply. Memories exist as experiences (interactions with an agent), observations and narrations.

The *bio constants* reflect the physical conditions of the agents, which are equal for all agents. The bio constants remain constant during the "life" of an agent. An important bio constant is the consumption of berries and water per turn. If an agent has no more supply of water or berries, it dies.

The non-standard characteristics of the agents are modelled by the *character*, they do not change during the "lifetime" of agent. However it is modified by the memory. The Rational-Choice-Theory describes only the selection of an action not the development of ones character. Dreamscape is a model for analysing the Rational-Choice-Theory. Therefore influences from other theories are not welcome. A variable character would be such a disturbing influence.

The preferences for certain action alternatives and the number of tolerated witnesses are important variables of the character. The preferences indicate, which action alternative is preferentially selected to fulfil a certain goal. The experiences, observations and narrations influence the selection of action. Each agent has a more or less strong innate dislike against witnesses, who observe its cheating or robbing. If an agent is known as a cheater fewer agents will trade with it. The number of tolerable witnesses is uniformly distributed in the starting population.

3.4. *The Offspring*

As mentioned above a sexual reproduction is skipped. On the other hand human being's life is finite. The agents have therefore a limited, randomly determined life span. As soon as an agent exhausted its life span, two offsprings are produced and it is removed. With the death of the ancestor, the offsprings are produced as "adult" agents, to reduce the model complexity.

The character of the offspring is a mixture of genetic determination and learned behaviour. No predicate is made whether action preferences of humans are innate or not. The preferences are a result of an educational process. At its end innate and educated preferences are no more separated.

One of the two offsprings starts on the position of its ancestor and the other on a randomly chosen cell. Everyone has a randomly determined supply of food. They take over the character – with small mutations – and the memories from their ancestor as narrations. The number of accepted witnesses is taken over unchanged.

All remaining variables are chosen randomly for the start population. The model is implemented in the object-oriented language Delphi.

4. Results

The Rational-Choice-Theory is checked in two scenarios. The first scenario tests the emergence of norms (robbery is disabled). In the second scenario robbery is enabled. Because of space I will only describe the first scenario and summarise the results of the second one.

At the beginning of a simulation run 200 agents are randomly distributed over the grid. A run takes 1000 turns and for every scenario 10 runs are executed. The results are equal in all runs, therefore I will only show one run as an example.

Definition: Conjunct, proscriptive norm

"Norms are generally valid and understandable regulations for human acting, which orientate themselves directly or indirectly at widespread value conceptions and intend these to transfer into the reality. Norms seek to determine human behaviour in situations, in which it is not already determined. Thus they create expectations. They are secured by sanctions." [BAH 94, p. 49 translation by author]. The group that benefits from a norm must have an interest in its existence and developing [COL 86, pp. 56]. The group which benefits from a norm, is identical with the group, whose behaviour is controlled [COL 91, pp. 318].

According to this definition conjunct, proscriptive norms are behaviour regulations, which orientate themselves directly or indirectly by values. The existence of conjunct, proscriptive norms depends on the sanctions and on their acceptance by people. Agents on Dreamscape are not able to deal with values and sense, so this part is skipped in the definition for the model. The asterisks "*" indicate the model specific definition of sociological terms.

Definition: Conjunct, proscriptive norm*

A conjunct, proscriptive norm* has emerged concerning the goal U at Dreamscape

– if in 50% of the choices action A_i is selected out of a set of actions alternatives $A_1...A_n$,

– if sanctions exist and are used and

– if all agents have an advantage of the existence of the conjunct, proscriptive norm*.

Agents have sanction capabilities in the trade. They can cheat as retaliation or evade further trade relations. The trade can be regarded as a special form of the two-person prisoners' dilemma [for details see e.g. AXE 84]. Here observations and communication are possible. In contrast to Sugerscape the price is fix. All other action alternatives (talking, robbing, collecting, sleeping, and being lazy) are not prisoners' dilemmas.

Simulations show that agents mostly interact only once, i.e. the probability of remeeting is small however larger than zero. In contrast to the prisoners' dilemma agents observe and talk about the behaviour of other agents. Therefore they often know the strategies of other agents before the first interaction. The observer or listener of narrations cannot punish the cheater itself. Nevertheless it is able to reject any further trading with the cheater. Therefore, in contrast to the prisoners' dilemma, *all* agents are able to punish the cheater. Clearly every agent has an advantage if cheating is forbidden.

Agents reject trading offers, because of observed or listened cheating. For the cheater this is costly because it is not able to balance its supply according to its needs. Figure 1 shows a reduction of cheating. The low probability of remeeting is less important than the observations and narrations.

Result 1: The conjunct, proscriptive norm* "Don't cheat!" has emerged.

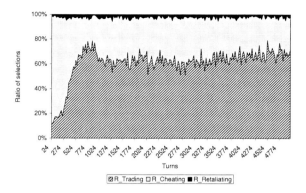

Figure 1. *Development of the action selections with trading over 5000 turns. Emergence of a conjunct, proscriptive norm* "Don't cheat!". Each point is a mean of 25 measurements*

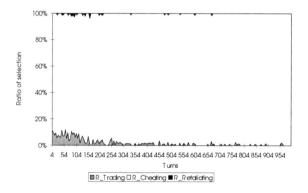

Figure 2. *Development of the action selections with trading. Constant witness dislike of four over the time. (targets: everything; Alternative one: everything without robbery). Each point is a mean of 5 measurements*

Retaliation is not a successful sanction because the probability of remeeting is too small. But rejecting of trade offers by observers is much more powerful. It seems that communication is less important than observation. A reason is situated in the fact that each agent can always observe. However talking requires the action selection of two agents, taking place more rarely.

The probability of cheating depends on the number of known witnesses. Each agent tolerates a number of witnesses. Each additional witness reduces the utility of cheating. An agent prefers cheating without any witness. At the beginning of the simulation the values of the tolerated witnesses are uniformly distributed in population out of the interval of zero to seven. After 1000 turns the value of zero for all agents has evolved.

Rejecting of trade offers is not a direct sanction, but result of gain calculation. The victim gains nothing, so it will avoid being cheated. Therefore cheating without witnesses is advantageous, thus cheating will never disappear completely (Figure 1). This situation is similar to the simple prisoners' dilemma.

During "birth" an offspring takes over the value for tolerated witnesses unchanged. If the value is selected uniformly greater than zero for all agents – also for the offsprings –, then trading disappears nearly complete (Figure 2). In this case no conjunct, proscriptive norm* develops, because as soon as cheating becomes the generally selected action alternative no agent attains an advantage.

Result R2: Rejecting of trade offers by observers is a much more powerful sanction, than retaliation from the victim.

In the scenarios indicated above immigration is not permitted. Further investigations have shown that by immigration the emergence of the conjunct, proscriptive norm* is obstructed. Because immigrants have a randomly distributed witness dislike value, which is usually greater than zero. The higher the number of the average immigrants per time unit, the more weakly the conjunct, proscriptive norm* is.

5. Discussion

The observed conjunct, proscriptive norm* represents a behaviour regularity in the force-free agent population. It is common, because many agents follow it, as the first condition of the definition required. Because of the missing consciousness the agent do not recognise the behaviour regularities. However the agents behave in a way, as if they have recognised the norm. Due to missing consciousness the question about the origin of a conjunct, proscriptive norm* does not arise. With the exception of the missing foundation the results are valid for the sociological term "norm".

The term "norm" focuses on the general application of an action, not on the action itself. The action alternative trading is built in the model, but its common selection develops. The results 1 and 2 therefore lead to the following final result:

Final result: The Rational-Choice-Theory can explain the emergence and maintenance of conjunct, proscriptive norms.

In the second scenario – robbery is allowed – a conjunct, proscriptive norm* does not emerge. At the beginning a dramatic reduction of the population size takes place because of robbery. In the rest of the run interactions are very rare. Because of the small number of agents on the grid a meeting of two agents occurs very rarely.

However, these meetings go often out deadly for an agent, so that the population size remains unchanged.

Final result: As soon as robbing is allowed as an action alternative, the Rational-Choice-Theory is not able to describe the emergence of social order.

The agents have maximised their utility and have killed themselves in a hobbesian fashion. The Rational-Choice-Theory seems to be incomplete if actors are able to kill each other. In the literature a lot of suggestions for a solution are mentioned. Vos [VOS 91] for example examined the role of altruism. So far none of these suggestions solves the problem – for different reasons. In my opinion institutions play an important role. This can be observed daily in collapsing states [see e.g. AI 97]. Therefore further investigations for the emergence of norms and other institutions are necessary within the Rational-Choice-Theory. Castelfranchi et al. [CAS 98] and Saam et al. [SAA 99] took first steps in this direction. The simple solution – excluding deadly violence from the Rational-Choice-Theory – is impossible because of the requirement of the general applicability.

Acknowledgements

The author thanks Sandra Knur and Simone Weichert for their valuable advice.

6. References

[AI 97] AMNESTY INTERNATIONAL, *Jahresbericht 1997*, Fischer Taschenbuch Verlag, Frankfurt am Main, 1997.

[AXE 84] AXELROD R, *The Evolution of Cooperation*, Basic Books Inc. Publishers, New York, 1984.

[AXE 97] AXELROD R., "Advancing the Art of Simulation in the Social Sciences", *Simulating Social Phenomena*, 1997, p. 15-40, Springer, Berlin.

[BAH 94] BAHRDT H.P., *Schlüsselbegriffe der Soziologie*, C.H. Beck, München, 1994, 6. Edition.

[CAS 98] CASTELFRANCHI CH., CONTE R., PAOLUCCI M., "Normative reputation and the costs of compliance", *Journal of Artificial Societies and Social Simulation*, vol. 1, n°. 3, 1998, URL: http://www.soc.surrey.ac.uk/JASSS/1/3/3.html, Last visit: 1999-07-07.

[COL 86] COLEMAN J.S., "Social Structure and the Emergence of Norms among Rational Actors", *Paradoxical Effects of Social Behavior – Essays in Honor of Anatol Rapoport*, 1986, p. 55-83, Physica-Verlag, Heidelberg.

[COL 91] COLEMAN J. S., *Grundlagen der Sozialtheorie*, vol. 1, Oldenbourg, München, 1991.

[EGG 97] EGGER M., DE CAMPO A., "Was Sie schon immer über das Verhalten in sinkenden U-Booten wissen wollten", *Kölner Zeitschrift für Soziologie und Sozialpsychologie*, vol. 49, 1997, p. 306-317.

[EPS 96] EPSTEIN J., AXTELL R., *Growing Artificial Societies*, MIT Press, Cambridge, 1996.

[ESS 91] ESSER H., *Alltagshandeln und Verstehen*, Mohr / Siebeck, Tübingen, 1991.

[ESS 96] ESSER H., "Die Definition der Situation", *Kölner Zeitschrift für Soziologie und Sozialpsychologie*, vol. 48., 1996, p. 1-34.

[GIL 99] GILBERT N., TROITZSCH K.G., *Simulation for the Social Scientist*, Open University Press, Bukingham, 1999.

[HAL 73] HALL E.T., *The Silent Language*, Anchor Books Edition, 1973.

[HOB 76] HOBBES TH., *Leviathan*. Everyman's Library, London, 1976.

[KEL 95] KELLE U., LÜDEMANN CH., "'Grau, teurer Freund ist alle Theorie'. Rational Choice und das Problem der Brückenannahmen", *Kölner Zeitschrift für Soziologie und Sozialpsychologie*, vol. 47, n°. 2, 1995, p. 249-267.

[KUN 97] KUNZ V., *Theorie rationalen Handelns*, Leske und Budrich, Opladen, 1997.

[LEP 99] LEPPERHOFF N., "Dreamscape. Eine Analyse des Rational-Choice-Ansatzes von Hartmut Esser mittels Computersimulation", Internal Report No. SYS-5.99. Department of Computer Science, University of Dortmund, Germany, 1999.

[LÜD 96] LÜDEMANN CH., ROTHGANG H., "Der 'eindimensionale' Akteur", *Zeitschrift für Soziologie*, n°. 4, 1996, p. 278-288.

[MIL 94] MILLER M., "Ellenbogenmentalität und ihre theoretische Apotheose. Einige kritische Anmerkungen zur Rational Choice Theorie", *Soziale Welt*, vol. 45, 1994, p. 5-15.

[OPP 83] OPP K.-D., *Die Entstehung sozialer Normen. Ein Integrationsversuch soziologischer, sozialpsychologischer und ökonomischer Erklärungen*, Tübingen, 1983.

[SAA 99] SAAM N., HARRER A., "Simulating Norms, Social Inequality, and Functional Change in Artificial Societies", *Journal of Artificial Societies and Social Simulation*, vol. 2, n°. 1, 1999, URL: http://www.soc.surrey.ac.uk/JASSS/2/1/2.html, Last visit: 1999-07-07.

[SCR 92] SCRUBAR I., "Grenzen des 'Rational Choice'-Ansatzes", *Zeitschrift für Soziologie*, vol. 21, n°. 3, 1992, p. 157-165.

[VOS 91] DE VOS H., "Altruism and Group Boundaries", *Modellierung sozialer Prozesse*, 1991, p. 397-416, Informationszentrum Sozialwissenschaft, Bonn.

Multi-Agent Modelling of Resource Systems and Markets

Theoretical consideration and simulation results

Frank Beckenbach

University of Kasssel
Nora-Platiel-Str. 4
34109 Kassel
Germany
Beckenbach@wirtschaft.uni-kassel.de

ABSTRACT: *In section 2 the importance of mas for the modern debate in non-canonized economic theory is sketched. Taking resource constraints, bounded rationality and local interaction as basic features of such a debate a mas architecture in which these features are present is provided in section 3. In section 4 conclusions are drawn and lines of further research are outlined.*

KEY WORDS: *Multi-Agent System, Resource system, "Sugarscape", Simulation, Bounded rationality*

Figure 1. *A. Bosse, Illustration for Hobbes' "Leviathan"*

1. Introduction

The conscience that social and/or political constructions are possible which are more than the sum of their parts is well founded in the history of social sciences (cf. fig. 1).[1] But to back such a conscience with a scientific model is an ongoing challenge especially in the social sciences where explaining by models is the domain of economics; but the formalisms used in economics are not very appropriate to explain how the interaction of simple elements creates a *new* whole.[2]

Nevertheless the possibilities to meet this challenge have improved recently. This is due to new modelling 'technologies' (like multi-agent systems (mas)) coming from the field of distributed artificial life on one side and due to an erosion of the canon of economics by investigating rationality constraints and coordination failures on the other side. The basic conviction of the following elaboration is that these two

---

[1] In the figure the "more" of the whole is of different shape: it is the head of the sovereign. For further analysis of the role such composite bodies in public illustrations at the beginning of modern times cf. BREDEKAMP (1999, 76ff).

[2] Rather the formalisms in economics are appropriate to explain how sophisticated elements are able to create a trivial sum total.

developments can fertilize each other. If a synthesis is possible, a new true bottom-up modelling methodology can be introduced to economics.

In the *section 2* the importance of mas for the modern debate in non-canonized economic theory is sketched. Taking resource constraints, bounded rationality and local interaction as basic features of such a debate a mas architecture in which these features are present is provided in *section 3*. In *section 4* conclusions are drawn and lines of further research are outlined.

2.Economic modelling with mas

In the present context mas will be used as a descriptive modelling tool. This is different from the use of mas as an instrumental tool, which is the case if there is an exogenously defined task in a complex environment to fulfil. The descriptive orientation is also different from the use of mas as a normative tool to specify the initial conditions and agent architecture that is required to achieve a predefined desired macroscopic state (like an "equilibrium" or an optimum). Rather the mas is used here as an experimental method either to investigate the macroscopic order that will be created, if the agents as well as the coordinating mechanisms of their actions are defined in a 'realistic' (i.e. more or less observable) manner. Or - the other way round – it helps to specify possible settings for the agents that lead to observable macroscopic data.

In such a context the autonomy of the agents is portrayed in economic terms. Basically the agents require some means of survival (e.g. food ore money income). Then the agents have to find out the options to meet these requirements and carry out the option they consider most advantageous for them. The boundary condition for this accessing the means of survival is that the latter are "scarce". This simply means that not all options can be realized simultaneously *given the constrained agent's abilities to get information or to act*; it does not necessarily imply that the means of survival are scarce from a perfectly informed global perspective. It is sufficient that the means of survival are scarce relative to the endowment constraint of the agents.

Usually the agents looking for the scarce means of survival are considered as homogenous in that they are similar in their behaviour ("methods" in terms of object oriented programming) but differ in their actual states. This is required if a conclusion as regards to the overall (macroscopic) result of their interaction shall be drawn; this stylised representation of the agents is either required for arriving at a desired order of their actions or for drawing conclusions about the time dependent development of a variable which is an aggregation of individual actions. Contrary to that in the frame work of mas both the states *and* methods of agents may differ. Therefore a population of heterogeneous agents is the 'natural' starting point for mas.

It can be studied, how different types of agents can acquire the scarce means of survival. In such an economic process the population is changing in size and composition due to two mechanisms: selection und learning. The better the learning capacities of the agents, the minor the importance of selection.

According to the specificity of the mas-approach to assume agents, which are not globally intelligent (cf. section 2.1 above), the agents are – in terms of economic theory – "bounded rational".[3] The bounded character of their rationality is due to limitations in accessible information, in their calculating capacities, and in their ability to understand what has been perceived and calculated. Hence a common denominator of all types of agents contained in the population is their internal cognitive structure by which they transform the information which is available for them into action terms. The steps of this cognition-action process of bounded rational agents are the perception by which the range of possible actions is framed, the set of actions itself and the pay off realised by executing an action. The core of the cognitive capacity of the agent is built by two feed back processes: (i)an internal mental model of the world i.e. the environment of the agent (including expectations of what other agents will do) which is determined by the results of perception und determines perception via the selection of information; (ii)an evaluation model for the action's pay off which determines procedures for adaptation (switch to another known action) as well as innovation (search for new actions). A scheme of bounded rational action comprising these elements is given in figure 2.

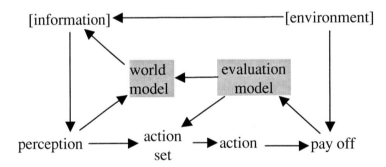

Figure 2. *Scheme of bounded rational action*

The following basic types of bounded rationality of economic agents are discernible:[4]

- bounded rational choice,
- rule rationality and

---

[3] Cf. CONLISK 1996 for an overview.
[4] For a further specification of these types of bounded rationality cf. BECKENBACH 2000.

- skill rationality.

The actual composition of a given population of theses types of bounded rational agents is the *first* important factor influencing the working of the aforementioned mechanism of selection and learning. A *second* important factor for the way the mechanisms of selection and learning works is the type of coordination between the agent's actions. This coordination is neither simply an act of choice nor is it once and for all given; rather it is a variable, depending on the past experience with a given coordination mechanism. But this variable is "slow" compared with the actions of the agent and their internal cognitive structure.

The coordination of bounded rational agents takes place via an environment (i.e. the ensemble of other agents and other objects an agent can perceive; this ensemble comprises by definition of mas only a part of the total amount of agents and objects). This environment is influenced by an agent' s actions and at the same time the environment shapes the options available for this agent. According to the postulate of bounded rationality in mas there is not only one type of such an environment-induced coordination. Rather there is a plurality of price and non-price coordination types (auction, posted price; frequency dependent activation of actions, externalities, imitation etc).[5] Hence the population thinking (and the ordering role of selection) applies to the coordination mechanisms as well.

The crucial feature of modelling the coordination process in a mas frame work is a compatibility postulate between the capabilities of agents and the coordination requirements: only what is within the realm of an agent's cognitive capabilities can be part of the coordination. Any backward construction from a desired coordination result to auxiliary constructions for producing such a result is avoided. This is contrary to the manner coordination is usually reflected in economic theory: there is only one type of coordination via price and the vector of equilibrium prices is either known in advance or is learnt rather easily.

Finally the appropriateness of mas for economic modelling is given by its integration of micro and macro points of view. Contrary to the 'schism' between microeconomics and macroeconomics in a mas microscopic and macroscopic variables are observable at the same time and their interdependencies can be studied. Any (spatial or temporal) regularity in the macroscopic variables is called "order". Such an order may have a complicated microfoundation. If this order cannot be deduced from knowing the initial conditions as well as the transformation algorithms for these conditions, it is called an "emergent" order. In mas the observable order of macrovariables is often emergent due to lack of mathematical understanding on one side and due to calculation constraints in the huge state space on the other side.

The interdependency between microscopic and macroscopic variables is established by a hierarchical structure. The lowest level of this hierarchy is the agent. Depending on how bounded rationality is captured, a subsumtion architecture, a

---

[5] Cf. KIRMAN 1997 and MIROWSKI/SOMEFUN 1998 for an overview.

production system or a mas itself can define the internal structure of the agent (cf. FERBER 1999, 125ff). The next level consists of the coupling of a subset of all agents. Basically this coupling is given via the perceivable environment of every agent (neighbourhood). This 'local' coupling is normally determined by the internal behavioural rules of the agent (corresponding to its internal cognitive architecture) and the external coordination rules. Another way of coupling of agent's actions is given by the introduction of organisations (e.g. firms) which have special internal behavioural and coordinating rules for those agents which are members of it (cf. FERBER 1999, 87ff). All the levels of this hierarchy (agent, neighbourhood, organisation) are defined by their states and methods. The whole system based on the interaction of these levels is multi-scaled in that generally states are changing faster than methods and states and methods of lower levels change faster than states and methods of higher levels.

3. The starting point: the "sugarscape"-mas and its development

3.1. Basic features

In the "sugarscape"-mas of EPSTEIN/AXTELL (1996) a 50x50 lattice with continuous border conditions (torus) is considered. On this lattice there are *firstly* - in a fixed order - renewable resources (N_R) which are different in quality and reproduction. *Secondly* there is - in random distribution - a population of agents (N_A) the elements of which are able to move on the lattice according to their moving rules. While there is at least one element of a resource in each cell of the lattice, the number of agents is minor than the number of lattice cells.

By this a system of objects and a system of agents is combined. For each agent there are different neighbourhoods of objects and agents. Each agent processes information about objects (resources) and agents in his neighbourhood. In the present model this processing of information presumes neither a special language nor a physical medium for the transfer of information. Hence the communication system is not explicitly dealt with.

In the following specification of mas only reactive agents are considered.[6] The agents follow predefined rules (for moving and trading). Given the internal states of the agents in terms of available information and required resources as well as the endowments (resources, money) the rules define the possibilities of action for the agent and at the same time a discrimination procedure between these options as regards to the goals of that agent.

---

[6] Cf. DORAN (1996, 384f) for typifying agents in mas.

The relation of an agent to its neighbourhood is specified threefold: (i)by assuming that the local character of the interaction of agents is spatial;[7] (ii)by assuming that "first come, first served", i.e. the property of a resource is founded by finding the resource[8] and (iii)the possibility to overcome a resource scarcity by trade[9] Two different neighbourhoods correspond to these assumptions: a resource neighbourhood which is given by the agent's vision (i.e. ability to perceive) and a neighbourhood of trade partners which are the von Neumann neighbours to every perceivable point on the lattice.

The following specification of agents and trade differs from EPSTEIN/AXTELL (1996). In their model there are only two types of resources, the agent discriminate between their options with the help of a given preference order,[10] and the exchange takes place in the form of barter. In the specification presented here, there are four different resources, the agents discriminate between their options by referring to more or less biologically determined reproduction requirements and the trade is mediated by money. Furthermore in the present model two different types of information availability and two different types of agents according to their goal functions are taken into consideration.

3.2. Resource system

Four different types of resources are distributed on the lattice in such a way, that on every point of the lattice, there is at least one element of one resource. According to this distribution of the resources different overall resource landscapes follow. If the distribution has a hill pattern (cf. fig. 3, (a)-(d)), then multi-peaked or single-peaked landscapes follow (cf. fig. 3, (e), (f)); if the distribution is random, the landscape is also random (cf. fig. 3, (g)).

---

[7]The economic rationale for this hypothesis is that often a direct relation between spatial distance and transaction costs and moving costs exists so that the probability of interaction is inverse to the spatial distance.

[8]The economic rationale for this hypothesis is that there are no predefined property rights as regards to resources on cells of the lattice.

[9]The economic rationale for this hypothesis is the necessity to surmount the required "double coincidence of wants" in the case of simple barter exchange.

[10]Technically this preference order is derived from a Cobb-Douglas utility function (cf. EPSTEIN/AXTELL 1996, 97ff)

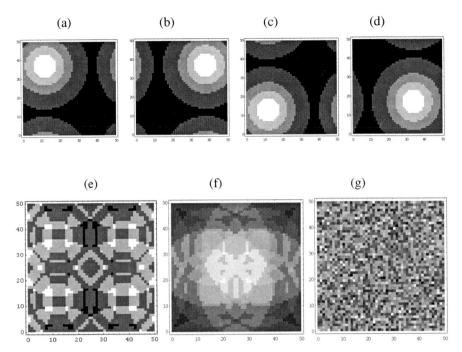

Fig. 3: Contour diagram of resource landscapes (dark is low, pale is high)

If a resource on a cell of the lattice is appropriated by an agent, it regenerates on that cell. Is a the index for the type of resource, l its location, α the regenerated amount of that resource and c the maximum amount at l, then the time dependent regeneration function is given by:

$$N\_R_a^l(t) = \min(N\_R_a^l(t-1) + \alpha, c);$$
$$a = 1...4,$$
$$l = 1...2500.$$

[1]

3.3. Agent system

According to the scheme of a bounded rational agent in section 2.2 the agent is internally defined by its world model and its evaluation model and the rules derived from these models. The *world model* of the present specification is rather simple: instead of making information about all resources and all agents available for the agent only a subset of both is perceivable. In terms of economic theory: the information is "imperfect". This information constraint is implemented in two variants: In the *first* (directional vision; fig. 4(a)) the agent can see only in the four cardinal points of the compass. This maps a cognitive framing effect. Additionally the agent is constrained in the distance he/she can survey. In the *second* variant (circular vision; fig. 4(b)) the agent is able to see all cells of the lattice within a given radius around his location. In both cases all agents situated in the immediate (von Neumann-)neighbourhood of the observable cells can also be seen by the agent.

(a)   (b)

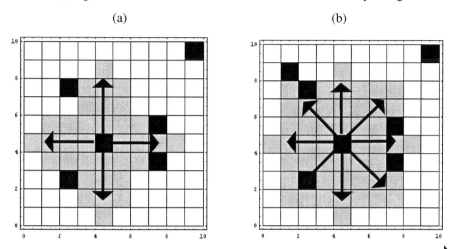

Figure 4. *Local vision of agents (a)directional vision (b)circular vision* ■ *agents;* ➤ *range of resource information;* ▨ *range of market information)*

Compared with the approach of EPSTEIN/AXTELL the *evaluation model* is fundamentally altered. There is no ambitious evaluation apparatus in terms of continuous indifference curves (and the corresponding marginal rates of substitution) applied because *firstly* in such a frame work utmost the emergence of bilateral exchange relations (using the technique of an Edgeworth box) is explainable and *secondly* the calculative and cognitive capacities required for such a procedure seem hardly compatible with the assumption of bounded rationality. This assumption given, a separated medium for expressing exchange relations is required if more than two resources are given. Therefore money - apart from resources - is a component of the initial endowment of agents.[11] The utility function is substituted by a survival aspiration. This is a time span (s) for which the agent wants to have a survival guarantee taking the resources required per time step ("metabolism") as well as the resource endowment for that agent as given. If w_a^A is the endowment with a different resources, m_a^A is the metabolism for agent A per time step for the different resources, then the survival aspiration is given by:

---

[11] This implies, that the articulation of demand and supply is made in money terms; barter is excluded. In the given specification of the model money is simply treated as an object. It is an

$$\frac{w_a^A}{m_a^A} \geq s_a^A, \forall a. \tag{2}$$

The survival aspiration is different for each agent; it is randomly generated over the interval $[s_{min}, s_{max}]$. Two additional components are part of the evaluation model: on one side there is a different parameter for the trade affinity of the agents. This means that the number of observable trade partners - weighed with this parameter (for agent A: λTP^j with $j \in vis_A$, vis_A being the vision of agent A) - is influencing the location of an agent. On the other side there are two different types of agents according to their goals: a (risky) 'resource maximizer', oriented towards the maximum number of available resources and a (risk-averse) 'survival maximizer', oriented towards the composition of available resource, which maximizes his/her survival time. These elements are part of the *movement and appropriation rule* (M) for agent A:

(i)Gather all information within the vision.

(ii.1)Is there an a for which $\dfrac{w_a^A}{m_a^A} < s^A$ holds, inspect if there is an

unoccupied lattice position[12] for which $\dfrac{w_a^A}{m_a^A} \geq s_a^A, \forall a$ is true.

(ii.11)If this is the case and if A is a resource maximizer, go to the

position for which holds: $\max(\lambda^A TP^j + \sum_{a=1}^{r} N\_R_a^j).$

(ii.12)If this is the case and if A is a survival maximizer, go to the

position for which holds:[13] $\max(\lambda^A TP^j + \min_a[\dfrac{N\_R_a^j}{m_a^A}]).$

(ii.13)If this is not the case, go to the position for which holds:[14]

$$\max(\left|\left\{a \left| \frac{w_a^A + N\_R_a^j}{m_a^A} > s^A \right.\right\}\right| + \lambda_A TP^j).$$

---

additional constraint for the exchange rule. Hints for further specification of the role of money are given in section 4.

[12] Confining the moving possibilities to non-occupied positions excludes predation.

[13] The second term in the bracket denotes the most scarce resource for the agent.

[14] The agent accumulates resources which are not scarce for him expecting that there will be a possibility to acquire scarce resources via trade in the future.

(ii.2)If $\dfrac{w_a^A}{m_a^A} > s^A$, $\forall a$ it holds:

(ii.21)If A is a resource maximizer, go to the position for which the

condition: $\max(\lambda^A TP^j + \sum_{a=1}^{r} N\_R_a^j)$ is fulfilled.

(ii.22)If is a survival maximizer, go to the position for which the

condition: $\max(\lambda^A TP^A + \min_a[\dfrac{N\_R_a^A}{m_a^A}])$. is fulfilled.

(iii)Appropriate all the resources on the new position.

The most important elements of the moving and acquisition rule and its dependencies are shown in fig. 5.

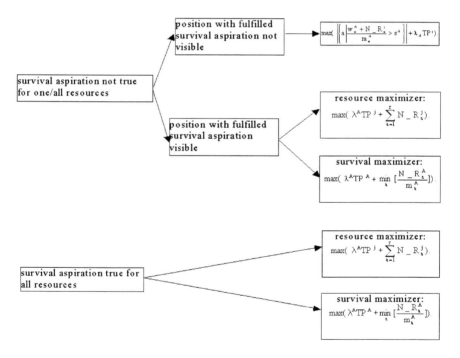

Figure 5. *Scheme of movement and appropriation rule*

If the agent has moved according to **M** an exchange between resources takes place according to a *trade rule* (T). T describes a trading procedure which is similar to the tâtonnement process analysed by WALRAS (1984, 153ff) and which is in a stylised form part of modern general equilibrium theory (cf. ARROW/HAHN 1971, 263ff).

(i)Determine the total demand for every resource for all agents in a neighbourhood i (n_i): $\sum_{A=1}^{n\_i} s_a^A\, m_a^A$.

(ii)Determine the the endowment with resources for all agents in a neighbourhood i: $\sum_{A=1}^{n\_i} w_a$.

(iii)Calculate the equilibrium price for neighbourhood i:

$$\frac{\sum_{A=1}^{n\_i} s_a^A\, m_a^A}{\sum_{A=1}^{n\_i} w_a} = p_a^i .$$

(iv)Determine the excess demand for agent A in neighbourhood i:[15]

$$z_a^A(p_a^i) = s_a^{A}\, m_a^A p_a^i - w_a^A p_a^i .$$

(v)If G_A is the money holding of agent A and if $z_a^A(p_a^i) > 0 \wedge z_a^A(p_a^i) < G_A$ holds, then A buys one element of the most scarce resource from a (randomly chosen) neighbour of A who offers that resource until the survival aspiration for all resources is fulfilled. If there is an exchange of resources, p_a^i is adjusted according to (i)-(iii).

(vi)If $z_a^A(p_a^i) > 0 \wedge z_a^A(p_a^i) > G_A$ holds, then resources which are abundant for the given survival aspiration are offered by A (in an order which is analogous to the degree of abundance). If there no such resources for A or if there is no demand for such resources, s_a^A is reduced.[16] If there is an exchange of resources or if s is changed, p_a^i is adjusted according to (i)-(iii).

(vii)If $z_a^A(p_a^i) \leq 0$ and $s_a^A < s_{a\_max}$ hold, s^A is reduced.

---

[15] Steps (i)-(iv) are based on the assumption that the required information is costless observable in a given neighbourhood (common knowledge assumption).
[16] This means that the demand is reduced and that the supply is augmented.

(viii) Repeat (v)-(vii) for all agents in the neighbourhood of A until no further trade is possible.

Taking the case of a positive amount of demand for resources T can be expressed by the schema given in fig. 6.

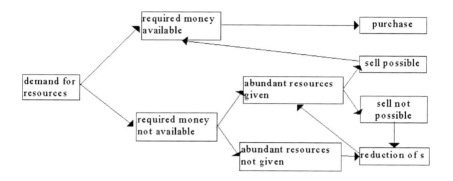

Figure 6. *Scheme of trade rule*

Although there are similarities between the walrasian market clearing procedure and T, some substantial differences should be emphasized:

- T is a decentralized procedure for economic neighbourhoods and not a centralized procedure for the whole economy. Taking the economy as a whole, the prices for a given resource are heterogeneous.

- T operates in a bilateral sequential manner, making the results of the market process dependent on the time path it takes. There is no guarantee that in every neighbourhood in every time step a total market clearing takes place (although the latter is approximated).

- The agents are not homogenous entities well equipped with all necessary information and calculating capacities in terms of continuous indifference curves or individual supply und demand functions; rather they are heterogeneous in terms of metabolism, survival aspiration and goals and discriminate between trade alternatives in a context dependent way.

- Money is not simply a "numéraire" (i.e. an ideal medium for expressing exchange relations) but a real medium of exchange.

Now it is possible to specify the general scheme of the agent's internal architecture (cf. fig. 2) for the version of the "sugarscape"-system presented here (cf. fig. 7). The observation feedback process (perception→world model→information→perception) is structured simply by the type of vision (directional or circular) and the constraints for available information about objects and other agents given by this. No distinction is made between the external information and its internal interpretation according to a mapping and filtering effect of a specific internal world view hold by the agent. The evaluation feedback process (set of alternatives→ activation→z→evaluation model→set of alternatives) is structured by the (agent-specific) metabolism, the (agent-specific) survival aspiration, the (agent-specific) trade affinity and the general rules M and T. The set of alternatives is given by the possibilities to move, to buy and to sell. Depending on what type the agent is (resource maximizer or survival maximizer) the outcome of the agent's action is related to a different goal.

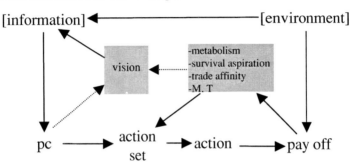

Figure 7. *Scheme of bounded rational action in the present "sugarscape"-system*

3.4. *Total system*

Given the distribution of resource over the lattice according to a landscape type, this resource landscape is accomplished by a (randomly distributed) population of agents with an agent specific vision, metabolism, survival aspiration and trade affinity. The coupling of agents by their actions is realized in a local neighbourhood, which at same time is influenced by the agent's actions and influencing the latter. This recursive interaction is based on a *coupling rule* (C):

(i)Select an agent by making a draw out of the set of all agents (**N_A**) with the probability of $pb = \dfrac{1}{\overline{n}}$ for each agent to be drawn ($\overline{n}$ being the number of agents not yet drawn).

(ii)Execution of M and T by the selected agent.

(iii)Consumption the of resources the requirement of which is fixed by the metabolism und calculation of the available resources afterwards.

(iv)Check if the agent has survived; if this is not the case reduce the total number of agents (n) by one unit.

(v)Repeat (i)-(iv) until $\bar{n} = 0$.

(vi)Set $\bar{n} = n$ and repeat (i)-(v) t times (t being the time step).

This coupling of (heterogeneous) agents acting in a local and sequential manner produces a macroscopic order which is neither explainable by analysing a single agent nor by simply aggregating the agent's state variables. For such an explanation the whole system structure of parameters, microscopic and macroscopic state variables is needed (cf. fig. 8 for an overview of the system's structure).

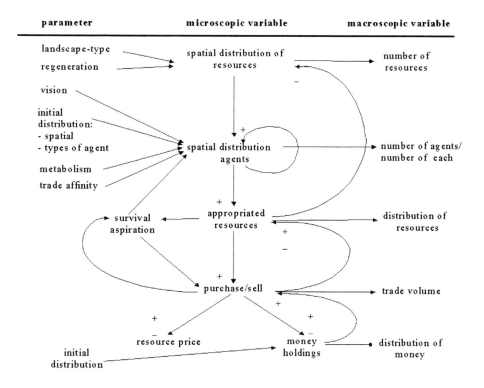

Figure 8. *Parameters and variables of the total "sugarscape"-system*

This simple specification of a mas is different from a cellular automata approach in several respects (cf. FERBER 1999, 188):

- Assuming lattice cells which are not occupied by agents allows them to move on the lattice and to choose the neighbourhood they act upon/by which they are influenced respectively.

- Agents have internal states. The actual value of these states are always compared with the goals of the agent (which correspond to biological and social requirements) and this leads to a situation-specific transformation of the actual states into new states.[17]

- Agents are different as regards to internal states, attitudes and goals. Hence the transformation rules are agent-specific itself.

3.5. A simulation example

The following simulation example demonstrates *firstly*, that with the introduction of trade the allocation of scarce means of survival is modified in such a way that the number of agents who are able to survive increases.[18] This means that without hurting the principle of bounded rationality the "carrying capacity" as regards to agents can be improved by institutional sophistication. *Secondly* the example shows how a macroscopic order is produced by disordered microscopic behaviour.

The assumed resource lattice is a multi-peak landscape (cf. fig. 3(e)) in which a population of 800 agents is randomly distributed. The only difference between agents is their initial endowment; their internal attributes (type and range vision, metabolism, survival aspiration, trade affinity, type of goal) are the same.[19]

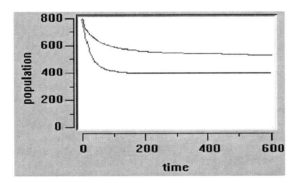

Figure 9. *Population over time in a multi-peak resource landscape (a)without trade (lower line) and (b)with trade (upper line)*

---

[17] The distinction between internal states and goals is also a starting point for a modification of the transformation rules by the agent itself (learning). In the present mas specification this is not yet implemented.
[18] This is only true as long as the parameter for the trade affinity is below a critical level, beyond which a local overcrowding takes place.
[19] In the present simulation the vision is vis=20 lattice cells, the metabolism is m=(1,1,1,1), the survival aspiration is s=0 or 60, the parameter for the trade affinity is λ=0 or 100 and the type of agent is a survival maximizer.

Fig. 9 shows the time-dependent development of the agent population over 600 time steps without trade (fig. 9 (a))[20] and with trade (fig. 9(b)). It clearly shows that the carrying capacity is enhanced by introducing trade.[21] Fig. 10 shows the location of agents after 1 and 600 time steps respectively. It reveals that the location of agents without trade is confined to those areas of the resource landscape where all resources occur at least with one unit (sustainable areas)(fig. 12(a))[22]. If trade is allowed (s > 0, $\lambda > 0$ and G > 0) the possible locations are enhanced around the sustainable resource islands; it is in these additional areas where the trade takes place (cf. fig. 10(d)). Differences in the spatial path of the agents reflect their inhomogeneous resource endowment.

(a)   (b)

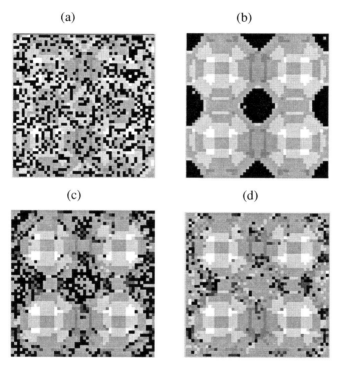

(c)   (d)

Figure 10. *Spatial distribution of agents (black) (a)in time step t=1, (b)in t=600 without trade, (c)in t=600 with trade (d)spatial distribution of trading agents in t=600*

---

[20] There is no trade if the trade affinity, the initial money endowment and the survival aspiration are all zero.

[21] This type of carrying capacity is different from the usual top-down determination of the carrying capacity in that the constrained access of agents to resources (due to information constraints) is acknowledged (bottom-up perspective).

[22] The sustainable area for agents with $m_a^j = (1, 1, 1, 1)$ is given by locations for which the condition $N\_R_a^j > 0, \forall a$ holds. Due to continuous border conditions, there are four such sustainable areas in the present resource-scape example.

The macroscopic order is characterised by the distribution of the visiting frequency over the lattice cells (cf. fig. 11). The histogram demonstrates, that the visiting frequency is higher in sustainable areas but that non-sustainable areas are also visited less frequently due to explorations combined with trade operations.

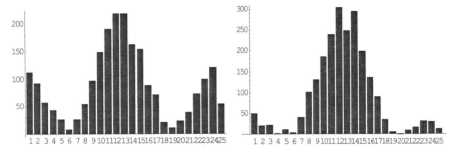

Figure 11. *Visiting frequency of selected agents in terms of the x-coordinate and y-coordinate of the landscape respectively*

The findings for the microscopic movement (movement of single agents) are that agents stay for a more or less longer time in a sustainable area but are irregularly induced to undertake explorations in other sustainable areas (cf. fig. 12). So their moving profile is an irregular change between short-distance and long-distance moves. Due to constrained vision only the sustainable areas which are horizontal or vertical neighbours are visited and very seldom the diagonal neighbour. Hence an erratic microscopic moving process with small and long distance jumps lies behind the concentration of nearly all agent in or nearby the sustainable areas in every time step (after a transient phase).

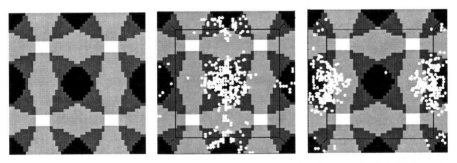

Figure 12. *Sustainable areas in a multi-peak resource landscape (dark is high, pale is low sustainability) and the visited places by two different agents (white) over time*

3.6. Comparing the original and modified "surgarscape"-system

The common feature of the original and modified sugarscape-system is the attempt to portray the decentralised resource gathering and resource exchange activities of a multitude of agents. Hence the broad qualitative results are about the same in the two variants:

- Generally the activities of agents lead to welfare improving states without ever reaching the global Pareto optimality due to decentralised information endowments and "false trading".

- Because the resource endowment is endogenously changed in every time step and the adjustment processes need time, the systems remains in states far from equilibrium.

- The carrying capacity is higher in a system including trade than in a system without trade. But to include trade implies more "injustice" in that the distribution of resources is more skewed in the former case.

- In both variants the phenomenon of "horizontal inequality" occurs: individuals with identical endowments in terms of resources, metabolism and vision end up on different welfare levels. This reflects the path-dependency of the processes going on in the respective systems.

Considering specific quantitative results, the variants are different. The *first* difference is, that there is no general tendency for the standard deviation of the average resources price(s) to decrease in the modified variant contrary to the simulation results for the original version if the vision is not too low (cf. EPSTEIN/AXTELL 1996, 109f, 117f). The *second* difference is that in the original version there is no macroscopic spatial regularity resulting from the erratic movements of individual agents (cf. e.g. EPSTEIN/AXTELL 1996, 100). This is the case in the modified version (cf. section 3.5 above).

Both differences follow from the additional constraints imposed upon the agents in the modified version. Enlarging the number of resources to four means to reduce the amount of sustainable options for the individual agent in every time step. This is only partly compensated by additional trading options because (i) – contrary to the 2-ressource case of the original version – there is no symmetry in terms of preferences and metabolism between the agents (cf. EPSTEIN/AXTELL 1996, 108) in the 4-ressource case and (ii) trade requires real money (either as an initial endowment or as a result of a preceding sell of resources). Due to these additional constraints for a viable system there is a need for a spatial overlapping of resources. This overlapping spatial resource structure is the main reason for the spatial macroscopic regularities which are observable in the modified version after a transient phase. Due to these additional constraints the exchange process remains more erratic and the the standard deviation of the average resource prices are hindered to decrease.

4. Conclusions and perspectives

In the present version of the "sugarscape"-system resource constraints, bounded rationality and local interaction are combined to a simple economic model. How the spatial distribution of agents intermingle with appropriation, selling, and purchasing of resources can be studied on an elementary level within such a frame work.

Based on a constrained vision and on given rules the bounded rational agents interact in a local and sequential manner. But to give the agents such a constrained vision is only a very limited way to endow the agents with a world model mentioned in section 2.2. No difference between information and perception is allowed for, there is no room either for costly information gathering strategies or for the forming of expectations about the future environment.

Another shortcoming of the model presented above is, that the evaluation model is simple in that the rules of the agents are fixed. Therefore in dealing with the scarcity of the means of survival only the selection mechanism is implied (selection of agents) and learning is absent (cf. section 2.2). A first step to alter this would be to give an agent more than one rule (e.g. to behave as a resource maximizer *or* a survival maximizer, to follow different trading rules etc.) and let the activation of a rule depend on the success (pay off) realized with a given rule in the past.

To conclude: the "sugarscape"-system is useful as a starting point for the integration of more complicated topics of the debate about a non-canonical economic theory.

Acknowledgements

I like to thank R. Briegel, M. Strickert and N. Weigelt for their assistance in developing the simulation software.

References

ARROW, K.J./HAHN, F.H. 1971. General Competitive Analysis. Amsterdam: North-Holland.

BECKENBACH, F. 2000. Beschränkte Handlungsrationalität und Theorie der Unternehmung, in: Pfriem, R./Beschorner, T. (Hrsg.), Evolutorische Ökonomik und Theorie der Unternehmung, Marburg: Metropolis.

BREDEKAMP 1999. Thomas Hobbes visuelle Strategien. Berlin: Akademie-Verlag.

CONLISK, J. 1996. Why Bounded Rationality?. Journal of Economic Literature, 34, S. 669-700.

DORAN, J. 1996. Simulating Societies Using Distributed Artificial Intelligence. In: Troitzsch, K. G. e. al. (Hg.): Social Science Microsimulation, S. 381-93, Berlin: Springer.

EPSTEIN, J. M. & AXTELL, R. 1996. Growing Artificial Societies: Social Science from the Bottom up. Cambridge/Mass.: MIT Press.

FERBER, J. 1999. Multi-Agent Systems: An Introduction to Distributed Artificial Intelligence. Reading/Mass.: Addison-Wesley Publishing Company.

KIRMAN, A. P. 1997. The Economy as an Interactive System. In: Arthur, B. e. al. (Hg.): The Economy as an Evolving Complex System II, Reading/MA: Addison-Wesley Publishing Company.

MIROWSKI, P. & SOMEFUN, K. 1998. Markets as Evolving Computational Entities. Journal of Evolutionary Economics, 8, S. 329-356.

WALRAS, L. 1984. Elements of Pure Economics or Theory of Social Wealth, London: Allen and Unwin.

The Interplay of Power on the Horizon

José Castro Caldas[*] – Helder Coelho[**]

*DINAMIA / ISCTE
Av. das Forças Armadas
1600 Lisboa, Portugal
jmcc@iscte.pt

**Universidade de Lisboa
Bloco C5, Piso 1, Campo Grande
1700 Lisboa, Portugal
hcoelho@di.fc.ul.pt

ABSTRACT: The research in multi-agent systems, like the one in economics, has paid little attention to the question of power. This is perhaps due to the fact that power is a hard topic to tackle from the methodological individualistic perspective that has influenced both disciplines. A dependence network built upon a simple concept of dependence is used as a simulation model aimed at exploring the consequences of power on a preliminary basis. Three questions are addressed: (a) in what ways the power relations impose structure upon society?; (b) how they structure groups internally?; (c) how they differentiate groups and individuals in relation to their conditions of existence?.

RÉSUMÉ: La recherche sur les systèmes multi-agents, tout comme la recherche en economie, a dédié trés peu d'attention à la question du pouvoir. La raison en est peut-être que le pouvoir est matiére difficilement saisissable à partir d'une perspective d'individualisme methodologique, perspective commune aus deux disciplines. Un graphe de dépendance, construit sur une conception relativement simplifiée de dependance, est ici utilisé comme modèle de simulation pour l'exploration préliminaire des conséquences du pouvoir. Trois questions sont traitées: (a) Comment les relations de pouvoir imposent-elles une struture à la societé ? (b) Comment ces relations façonent-elles la structure interne des groupes ? (c) Comment ces relations diffèrencient-elles les groupes et les individus quand à leurs conditions d'existence ?

KEYWORDS: Multi-Agent Simulation, Socio-economic Simulation, Power, Dependence, Dependence Networks.

MOTS-CLES: Simulation Multi-Agent, Simulation Socio-économique, Pouvoir, Dépendance, Graphe de Dépendance

1. Introduction

Power is a point still missing in most multi-agent systems (MAS) [CAS 90], and particularly in MAS applications to economics. One reason for this is that it is a difficult topic. Another reason, is that both MAS and economics have been under the predominating influence of methodological individualism, or, as it is currently referred to, "the bottom up approach". Since the "bottom up" point of departure in agent-based modeling and in economics is the individual [EPS 96], this view demands that the existence of lower level actors be taken as given [AXE 94], i.e. as independent of their place within the social network. Consequently, the macroscopic social structures should be explained as *ex-post* results of the interaction between those given individuals. Power, however, shapes the social network and places the agent within it. What the agent is, depends on where he stands, and therefore the system may be hard to approach from in a "bottom up" fashion.

Modern mainstream economics avoids the topic of power through a separation of the political and economic spheres. The political institutions, on the one hand, are viewed as results of a static hobbesian social contract, a rational device aimed at avoiding the war of all against all, through the protection of the individual property rights. The agents interacting in perfect markets, on the other hand, are powerless. As Negri's work on Spinoza [NEG 89] clearly shows, this perspective has been challenged since the XVII century by an alternative concept of power, according to which the civil state is not fundamentally different from the state of nature, in the sense that the institutions are not neutral in relation to power, and the only source of power, is power itself, not reason. In our opinion this spinozian alternative is closer to an open ended and dynamic concept of power that would be worth exploring both in MAS and economics.

While the philosophic debate is instructive and helpful for anyone trying to capture the real meaning of power and politics, the purpose of this research is much more limited. Power is a hard topic and the understanding of the importance of the power dimensions of socioeconomic interaction is therefore a goal we set on the horizon. Meanwhile, since we believe that multi-agent simulation may help us to move forward in that direction, we decided, as a first step, to put together some partial insights on the subject, and explore their consequences with a very simple dependence network, which is in fact the most basic MAS involving power relations we could think of. Our purpose with this model is to clarify: (a) in what ways the power relations impose structure upon society; (b) how they structure groups internally; (c) how they differentiate groups and individuals in relation to their conditions of existence (the resources that they control and the means of action that are available for them).

This research, however, is only part of a broader program around autonomous agents living in a society, that has been going on for some years, and making progress along the following lines of inquiry: How can we design better agent architectures (more tuned with real applications) by adopting a (agent-based methodology) table of mental states [COR 98a, 98b]? How can we improve the agent decision making by using values (the Belief-Value-Goal architecture) to guide the choice machinery [ANT 1999]? How can we build social power structures during the negotiating process for choosing adequate partners (coalitions) and persuasive proposals so as to convince the others to collaborate in particular and coordinated manners [DAV 99]? How can emotional states govern and balance rational decision making in organizations and also improve the agents' personality [BOT 99]? What is the relation between choice and institutions in economic settings [CAL, 99]?

2. The Advent of social machines

A basic non-social notion of power, such as, *power of* (personal power) defined as an agent's capability of performing a given action and/or achieving a given goal [CAS 2000] is helpful. However, it is debatable whether it may be developed within a strict "bottom up" framework. In fact, as soon as agents are allowed to interfere with each other, every agent's capabilities, not to speak of beliefs and goals, depend on his position in the social network. When we pass from personal power to *dependence* this point becomes clear. *Dependence* arises from lack of power [CAS 2000]. Agents need each other to achieve their personal goals. Agent A may lack power to achieve his goal p while B has this power. In this case B will have *power over A*. Dependence may be *reciprocal* implying that A depends on B for his goal p, and that B depends on A for his goal q and it may also be, and generally is, an unbalanced relationship with room for *differential power*, leading, as in the case of unilateral dependence, to a *power* of one agent *over* the other.

It is now clear that *dependence* and *power over* are intrinsically social notions. They are objective social relations that hold independently the agents' consciousness, and they constitute the basis of social interaction [CAS 2000]. Dependence and power over depend on the agents relative position in society, the amount of resources they can command and the social influence that they can exercise.

The problem with the "bottom up" perspective in connection with power and dependence is that the existence of the lower level agents may not be taken as given. What the agent is and what he can do, depends on where he stands in the dependence network. This has long been realized. Solomon Ash (quoted in [HOD, 98]) wrote in 1952: "the unit is not the individual but a social individual, one who has a place in the social order ... To understand the individual we must study him in his group setting; to understand the group we must study the individuals whose interrelated actions constitute it."

The micro-macro relationship is still a difficult problem in social science and in MAS. The solution is easy to state (we can agree with Ash's formulation) but difficult to formulate, in particular in MAS. We know that "the simulation would ... have to model both the emergence of societal level properties *from* individual actions and the effect of societal level properties *on* individual actions" [GIL 98], but we do not know how to do it. We do not have a convincing example of such a dream social machine. Meanwhile, we have chosen to start this research with a model that is built upon a social relation (dependence), not on individual agents or macroscopic social structures. Since we wish to concentrate on the dynamics of the configuration of the social network that is induced by a dependence relation that holds independently of the agents' goals and means of action, the agent is modeled as a mere automaton plugged into a pre-existing structure, the future prospect being, of course, to animate this agent.

3. The dependence network

The relationship that shapes the dependence network is unbalanced. If agent *A* *depends on* agent *B*, agent *B* will have a degree of *power over* agent *A* even if *B* also depends to some lesser extent on *A*. In the dependence network that will be used for simulation, this relationship is constrained, in the sense that it assumes an institutional setting where one agent may depend on one, and only one agent, for all of his life time. An agent may depend on himself, being in this case independent. Besides reciprocal, dependence can also be intransitive. If *A* controls resource *a*, and B controls resource *b*, *A* depends on *B* for *b* and *B* depends on *A* for *a*. *A* and *B* will have a degree of power over each other. It is also possible that *A* depends on *B*, *B* of *C* and *C* of *A*.

If a population and the dependence relationship is represented in a graph where the nodes stand for agents and the arcs for dependence, and if a group is defined as a connected subgraph in this graph, we may have a partition of the population in different groups.

Depending on the environmental setting chosen these groups may engage in collective activities that originate a benefit to be apportioned among all group members according to some rule. However, given *dependence* and *power over*, it is not hard to assume that a part of the individual benefit of the dependent agents will tend to be transferred to those who have *power over* them. As in Axelrod [AXE 94] tribute model we will assume therefore that if *A depends on B*, *A* will pay a *tribute* to *B*.

3.1. *The environmental setting and the dependence network model*

The environmental setting for the simulation with the dependence network involves a population with a fixed number of economic agents, engaged in the production of a good in a sequence of market periods. An agent is a mere 4-tuple,

‹*name, age, capacity, dependent on*›,

where *age* stands for the number of market periods the agent has lived, *capacity*, is a figure that is initially randomly generated and that determines the agent's production and supply decisions (being updated in every market period), and *dependent on* is initially set randomly and fixed for the agent's lifetime.

The amount produced and supplied to the market in each period is given by the total productive capacity of all agents. Given this amount, the price of the good is computed by a mechanism represented by a negatively sloped demand function that sets a single price for all transactions:

$$price = \frac{A}{\sum_i capacity[i]}$$

An agent's individual benefit (his payoff in a market period) is a function of his capacity (amount produced and supplied), price and unit cost:

$$payoff[i] = capacity[i] \times \left(price - unit\ cost\right)$$

However, the unit cost for agent i, is not constant, depending on the aggregate capacity of the group, J, of which agent i is a member. This might be due to external effects of aggregation, with economies up to a certain group capacity, and diseconomies beyond this threshold. The unit cost for group J would be given by:

$$unit\ cost[J] = B + \left(\frac{C - \sum_{i \in J} capacity[i]}{D}\right)^2$$

The net tribute of each agent is the sum total of the tributes received deducted of the tribute paid by i to the agent i depends on:

$$net\ tribute[i] = t \times \sum_{l \in D} payoff\,[l] - t \times payoff\,[i],$$

where D is the set of all agents that depend on i, and tribute is a fixed percentage (t %) of the respective payoffs (in case the payoffs are positive).

After each market period each agent's capacity is updated according to the following rules:

$$capacity'[i,t+1] = capacity[i,t] + net\ tribute[i]$$

$$capacity[i,t+1] = capacity'[i,t] - a \times capacity'[i,t] + b \times payoff\,[i,t]$$

It is therefore assumed that capacity will erode with time (in each market period $a\%$ is lost) and that it is increased at a rate of $b\%$ of payoff (when the agents experience positive results), decreasing at the same rate otherwise.

A survival condition is defined for all agents: if capacity falls below a critical threshold c, the agent will be replaced by a new one with the same name, but with age zero and with new (randomly set) initial capacity and dependence.

The simulation is initialized by the random definition of dependence and capacity. Dependence will be a uniformly distributed integer between one and *popsize* (population size) and capacity a real valued number between *mincap* and *maxcap* (minimum and maximun capacity). In each market period the following steps are executed: (a) computation of the market price; (b) computation of the unit costs for each group in the population; (c) computation of individual payoffs; (d) computation and transfer of tributes; (e) adjustment of capacities; (f) survival test with replacement of agents; (g) age updating.

4. Results of the simulation

Different simulations can be run using different random generator seeds and different parameter sets. For the parameter set in table 1 we ran a large number of simulations (figures 1 to 4 exhibit the initial and final configuration of the dependence networks for two of these simulations).

A	B	C	D	t	a	b	c	popsize	mincap	maxcap
88	0.5	22	50	5%	1%	20%	1	16	1	10

Table 1. *Simulation parameters*

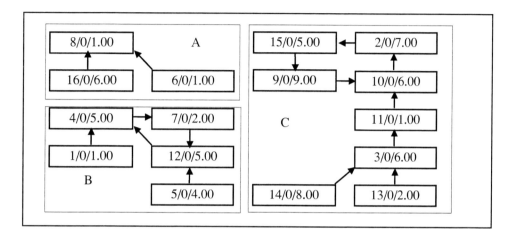

Figure 1. *Simulation 1; initial configuration of the network, agents (name/age/capacity) and groups A, B and C, delimited by broken lines*

Looking at the randomly generated initial network structures (see Figures 1 and 3) it is easy to identify the three basic group structures that may exist within a network: hierarchies, rings, single-agent groups; and the composite structure ring-hierarchy. In Figure 1 we find the initial configuration of a network that contains three groups: *A, B, C. A* is a small hierarchy, part of *C* is a ring (agents 15, 2, 9 and 10), and *C* as whole is a composite ring-hierarchy.

During the simulation there tends to emerge an equilibrium quantity and price. In all simulations (for the set parameters) after an adjustment period that may last for one thousand to three and a half thousand market periods, aggregate supply averages 141 units and price 0.62. The total capacity of groups averages 35 units, a figure that can be easily understood since it corresponds (for the equilibrium price) to the point of zero growth on group capacity.

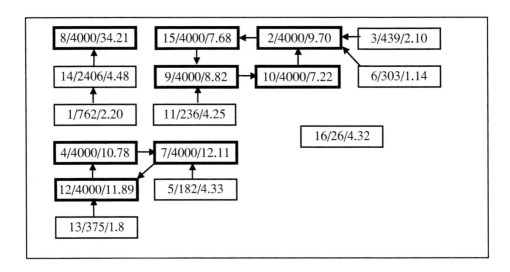

Figure 2. *Simulation 1; configuration of the network in market period 4000; old agents delimited by bold lines*

When the initial configuration of the networks is compared with the final configurations (in market period four thousand) we can find (see Figures 2 and 4) that in some simulations the final configuration has some elements of similarity with the initial one. For instance in simulation 1 (see figures 1 and 2) the ring structures in groups *B* and *C* survived the entire process. But in other simulations the initial and final configurations were very different, as in simulation 2 (see Figures 3 and 4).

However, in every case, and irrespective of the differences in the initial conditions, there are striking common features: (a) the locus of old agents tend to be at the top of hierarchies, and within ring structures; (b) the distribution of capacity in the final networks is comparatively even within rings, and unbalanced in hierarchies, with larger agents at the top and small ones at the bottom. It is clear that this uneven distribution of collective benefits must originate higher mortality rates at the bottom of hierarchies and the corresponding constant replacement of agents by new ones.

The fact that all three types of group structures are present in the final configuration of the networks must therefore be complemented by the observation that only rings (and single agent groups) may be stable structures, since the composition of hierarchic structures tend to change through time with the constant replacement of agents placed at the bottom.

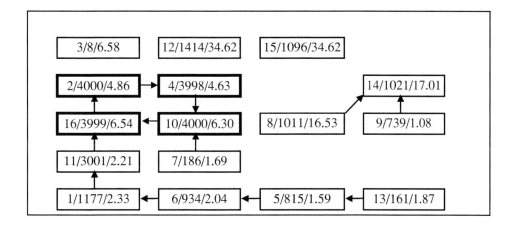

Figure 3. *Simulation 2; initial configuration of the network*

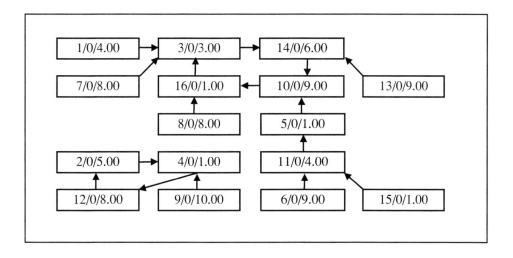

Figure 4. *Simulation 2; configuration of the network in market period 4000*

5. Conclusion

Even though this dependence network was intended only as a first step in the design of more general and ambitious simulation models, it has the interesting features of other more complex MAS. It exhibits a comparatively complex behavior, out of simple local rules, leading to results that are useful, and which could hardly be analytically deduced. They are somehow related to reality and help to understand it better.

Dependence generates groups. In the chosen environmental setting, for the chosen parameters and irrespective of the initial configuration of the network, different group configurations emerged, each with an aggregate supply close to the optimum value. Those groups however had different internal configurations. We identified hierarchies, rings, single-agent groups and the composite structure ring-hierarchy. More importantly we found that the distribution of capacity is balanced inside rings and highly unbalanced within hierarchies. Therefore only rings and single-agent groups are stable structures, in the sense that the composition of hierarchies is highly variable with high mortality rates at the bottom and low ones at the top.

The simulation was based on a notion of dependence as an objective social relation that a single agent cannot overcome. This is clearly an underestimation of the degree of autonomy and freedom of the agent, but it is not totally unrealistic. As far as there may be some empirical correspondence in this notion, the simulation suggests clearly the reason the agents' being depends on where they stand. Starting with a random distribution of capacity resources, the dependence relations induce a distribution that is strictly correlated with the position of the individual within the group and with the configuration of the group. The individual power, his means of action, what he sets as a goal and what he believes he may achieve can not be taken as given, they depend on where he stands in the social structure.

Even if we should avoid the danger of premature and unfounded application, it is hard to resist the comparison of the overall pattern of the results with real networks of economic agents. For instance, if we bear in mind real networks of outsourcing (or distribution), the unstable nature of hierarchies, with high mortality rates at the bottom and uneven distributed size, seems to be very familiar. The same might be said for the stability of ring structures, which reminds us of industrial districts and other non-hierarchical networks of interdependent firms.

Acknowledgments

We thank Project PRAXIS XXI 2/2.1/TIT/1662/95 SARA and DINAMIA for the support given. A short stay at the Santa Fe Institute by one of the two authors, as research visitor, allowed to better clarify some of the ideas presented herein.

References

[ANT 99] ANTUNES, L., COELHO, H., "Decisions Based upon Multiple Values", *Proceedings of EPIA99, Lecture Notes in AI 1695*, Berlin, Springer-Verlag, 1999, p. 297-311.

[AXE 94] AXELROD, R. "A Model of the Emergence of New Political Actors", in E. Hillebrand and J. Stender (eds.), *Many-Agent Simulation and Artificial Life*, Amsterdam,

IOS Press, 1994.

[BOT 99] BOTELHO, L., COELHO, H., "Adaptive Agents: Emotion Learning", *Proceedings of the Workshop on Grounding Emotions in Adaptive Systems, Fifth International Conference of the Society for Adaptive Behavior 98 (SAB 98)*, Zurich, 21 August 1999, p. 19-24.

[CAL 99] CALDAS, J. C., COELHO, H. "The Origin of Institutions, Socio-economic Processes, Choice, Norms and Conventions", *Journal of Artificial Societies and Social Simulation*, vol. 2, no. 2, 1999, ⟨http://www.soc.surrey.ac.uk/JASSS/2/2/1.html⟩.

[CAS 90] CASTELFRANCHI C., "Social Power: A Missed Point in Multi-Agent, DAI and HCI, in Y. Demazeau, J. P. Muller (eds.), Amsterdam, 1990, Elsevier, p. 49-62.

[CAS 2000] CASTELFRANCHI C., "All I Understand About Power (and something more)", Position paper presented at SARA II Workshop, Lisbon, 11 February 2000.

[COR 98a] CORRÊA, M., COELHO, H., "Agent´s Programming from a Mental States Framework", in H. Coelho (ed.), *Progress in Artificial Intelligence - IBERAMIA 98, Lecture Notes in AI 1484*, Berlin, Springer Verlag, 1998, pp. 64-75.

[COR 98b] CORRÊA, M., COELHO, H., "From Mental States and Architectures to Agents´Programming", in Flavio M. Oliveira (ed.), *Advances in Artificial Intelligence, 14th Brazilian Symposium on AI, SBIA'98, November 1998, Lecture Notes in AI 1515*, Berlin, Springer Verlag, p. 31-39

[DAV 99] DAVID, N., SICHMAN, J. S., COELHO, H., "Extending Social Reasoning to Cope with Multiple Partner Coalitions", *Proceedings of the MAAMAW'99, Lecture Notes in AI 1647*, Berlin, Springer-Verlag, 1999, p. 175-187.

[EPS 96] EPSTEIN, J. M., AXTELL, R., *Growing Artificial Societies - Social Science from the Bottom Up*, Cambridge, MA, The MIT Press, 1996.

[GIL 98] GILBERT, N., "Simulation: an emergent perspective", 28th of July 1998, ⟨http://www.soc.surrey.ac.uk/research/simsoc/tuturial.html⟩.

[HOD 98] HODGSON, G. M., "Institutional Economic Theory: The Old Versus the New", in D. L. Prychitko (ed.), *Why Economists Disagree*, New York, State University of New York Press, 1998.

[NEG 89] NEGRI, A., *The Politics of Subversion, A Manifesto for the Twenty-first Century*, Cambridge, Uk, Polity Press.

ECONOMICS

INDIVIDUAL DECISIONS AND GAMES

The "mind or no-mind" dilemma in agents behaving in a market

Pietro Terna

Dipartimento di Scienze economiche e
finanziarie G.Prato - Università di Torino
corso Unione Sovietica 218bis
10134, Torino, Italia
terna@econ.unito.it

ABSTRACT: *In computer simulation models based upon agents, what is the degree of sophistication that we have to put into the agents? Should we provide them or not with a "mind"? The answer ranges from Axelrod's simplicity principle to the use of full BDI (Beliefs, Intentions, Desires) cognitive agents. To discuss the subject we introduce here three models: one with "no-mind" agents that operate in an unstructured market, the second with "minded" agents assuring some stability to an emerging unstructured market and, finally, the third with no mind agents, that show a sophisticated outcome in a structured market. No generalised results come from this presentation, but many useful doubts.*

RÉSUMÉ: *Quel degré de complexité faut-il introduire dans un modèle de simulation fondé sur des agents? Doivent-ils disposer d'un "esprit"? Nous présentons ici trois modèles qui utilisent des agents, avec et sans "esprit", et ou les résultats obtenus sont très différents suivant la structure du marché dans lequel opèrent les agents.*

KEY WORDS: *economic simulation, agent based models, Swarm*

MOTS-CLÉS: *simulation économique, modèles fondés sur agents, Swarm*

1. Introduction

According to [GIL 00]: Ostrom [OST 88] proposed that there are three different "symbol systems" available to social scientists: the familiar verbal argumentation and mathematics, but also a third way, computer simulation. Computer simulation, or computational modelling, involves representing a model as a computer program. Computer programs can be used to model either quantitative theories or qualitative ones. They are particularly good at modelling processes and although non-linear relationships can generate some methodological problems, there is no difficulty in representing them within a computer program.

The logic of developing models using computer simulation is not very different from the logic used for the more familiar statistical models. In either case, there is some phenomenon that we as researchers want to understand better. This is the "target". We build a model of the target through a theoretically motivated process of abstraction (this model may be a set of mathematical equations, a statistical equation, such as a regression equation, or a computer program). We then examine the behaviour of the model and compare it with observations of the social world. If the output from the model and the data collected from the social world are sufficiently similar, we use this as evidence in favour of the validity of the model (or use a lack of similarity as evidence for disconfirmation).

The question now is: if our computer simulation model is based upon agents (e.g. built with Swarm[1], as the models presented here), to what extent must our agents be sophisticated? Should we provide them with a "mind"? The answer ranges from Axelrod's simplicity principle [AXE 97] to the use of full BDI (Beliefs, Intentions, Desires) cognitive agents. To discuss the subject we introduce here, in Section 2, a model with rigidly "no-minded" agents that behave in an unstructured market, with unrealistic cycles and chaos; in Section 3 a model with learning "minded" agents, that assure some stability to the emerging unstructured market; finally, in Section 4, we present no mind agents operating in a structured market, with a sophisticated outcome. No generalised results come from this presentation, but many useful doubts. See Section 5 for a comment about the necessity of integrating the different cases treated here in a unique framework, to improve the possibility of comparing the different situations.

2. Chaos from agents: "no-mind" agents in an unstructured market

This first simulation comes from [TER 98], and is based upon agents that apply mechanically their rules, without learning or adaptive capabilities; the market in which they behave is completely unstructured. The experiment shows the emergence

---

[1] See http://www.swarm.org

of chaotic price sequences in a simple model of interacting consumers and vendors, both equipped with minimal rules[2]. (We are not seeking to produce chaos: it emerges as a side effect of the agents' behaviour.)

2.1. *Technical details*

We have consumers and vendors. Each agent is capable of reacting to messages, for example deciding whether it should buy at a specific offer price. We use a shuffler mechanism to change the order in which the agents operate and to establish random meetings of the members of the two populations. At every simulation step, artificial consumers look for a vendor; all the consumers and vendors are randomly matched at each step. An exchange occurs if the price asked by the vendor is lower than the level fixed by the consumer. If a consumer has not been buying for one (if the sensitivity parameter is set to 1) or more than one (if the sensitivity parameter is set to 0) step, it raises its price level by a fixed amount according to the counter rule and the sensitivity parameter introduced below. It acts in the opposite way if it has been buying and its inventory is greater than one unit. A simulated vendor behaves in a symmetric way (but without a sensitivity parameter): it chooses the offer price randomly within a fixed range. If the number of steps for which it has not been selling is greater than one, it decreases the minimum and maximum boundaries of this range, and vice versa if it has been selling.

In all the experiments, the result is that the mean price behaviour emerges as cyclical, with chaotic transitions from one cyclical phase to another. From a methodological point of view there are two kinds of emergence.

- Unforeseen emergence: while building the simulation experiment, we were only looking for the simulated time required to obtain an equilibrium state of the model with all the agents exchanging nearly at each time. The appearance of a sort of cyclical behaviour was unexpected (the inventory cycle having been undervalued).

- Unpredictable emergence: chaos is obviously observable in true social science phenomena, but it is not easy to make a reverse engineering process leading to it as a result of an agent based simulation.

2.2. *Results*

We have now to summarise the parameters used in the experiments reported in the Figures of this paragraph. Parameters: "theLevel" is the initial price below which consumers buy (it changes independently for each consumer while the simulation evolves); "agentNumber" is the number of consumers and vendors; "minStartPrice" and "maxStartPrice" are the initial limits within which vendors choose their selling

---

[2] The Swarm code of this experiment can be obtained directly from the author, it is named ABCDE, from "Agent Based Chaotic Dynamic Emergence".

price (they change independently for each vendor while the simulation evolves); the "reactivityFactor" is a multiplying factor that enhances the fixed values used by consumers and vendors to modify their prices or range of prices; "sensitivity" is zero or one, with the meanings introduced above. The series reported in the Figures are the mean of global prices (all prices offered in each day or cycle) or the min. or max. within global prices. (The "alternative way" of the title is related to an internal calculus problem).

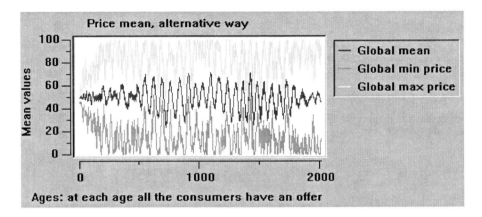

Figure 1. *Starting with a balanced situation, low reactivity and low sensitivity*[3]

The experiment reported in Fig.1 starts from a balanced situation of the buying and selling prices[4]. With a low reactivity factor and a low sensitivity parameter in the behavioural choices of the consumers, we have a relevant amplitude of the fluctuations, with chaotic appearance of the global mean of the prices offered in each cycle.

Technically: the FFT[5] of the series of data shows only one peak, related to the constant value; Lyapunov exponents are in the range 0.6-0.7 and both capacity and correlation dimensions are less than 5. Also the experiment reported in Fig.2 starts from a balanced situation: the high reactivity factor improves the cyclical effect and the presence of the sensitivity parameter reduces the amplitude of the fluctuations; anyway, chaos appears.

---

[3] theLevel=50; minStartPrice=45; maxStartPrice=55; reactivityFactor=1; sensitivity=0.

[4] Starting from an unbalanced situation the emergence of the cyclical behaviour and the chaos appearance are improved, with the presence of strange attractors in the singular value decomposition space

[5] Fast Fourier Transformation.

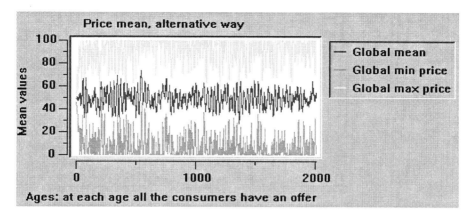

Figure 2. *Starting with a balanced situation, high reactivity and high sensitivity*[6].

The FFT shows the same results as above; Lyapunov exponents are in the range 0.5-0.8 and both capacity and correlation dimensions are less than 5.

2.3. *Comments to the experiment*

A general comment about chaos in these experiments: we are here in presence of endogenous chaos, emerging from agent interaction. We know, by construction, that here chaos is not related to a well specified structure, but to collective behaviour, which we are not able to describe ex ante in an analytical form. The price memory is diffused in the agents, having a collective effect of synchronisation or heterogeneous behaviour in the agents' reaction to the exchange prices.

The more interesting thing here, from the point of view of the "mind or no-mind" dilemma, is the rigidity of the cycles, without any form of stability in the market: our agents are performing their tasks without the aid of any form of adaptation; moreover, in a market that is not provided with any operating mechanisms.

3. Equilibrium from agents: minded agents in an unstructured market

The second model is a more sophisticated one, involving learning agents provided with goals, and able to develop an internal consistency between the actions they perform and the guesses on their effects [TER 00a][7].

---

[6] theLevel=50; minStartPrice=45; maxStartPrice=55; reactivityFactor=3; sensitivity=1.

In the Hayek sense of individualism and economic order [HAY 49] we are here dealing with agents behaving on a strictly individualistic basis, without the over-simplification of an artificial auctioneer market. A market with stable prices anyway emerges, with an empirical quasi-equilibrium. Note that we explicitly exclude from our model any form of prior description of this kind of equilibrium and that the agents have no knowledge about the mean price, which is only used by the observer to externally describe the experiment.

3.1. Technical details

To develop our agent based experiments, we introduce the following general hypothesis (GH): an agent, acting in an economic environment, must develop and adapt her capability of evaluating, in a coherent way, (1) what she has to do in order to obtain a specific result and (2) how to foresee the consequences of her actions. The same is true if the agent is interacting with other agents. Beyond this kind of internal consistency (IC), agents can develop other characteristics, for example the capability of adopting actions (following external proposals, EPs) or evaluations of effects (following external objectives, EOs) suggested from the environment (for example, following rules) or from other agents (for examples, imitating them). Those additional characteristics are useful for a better tuning of the agents in making experiments.

To apply the GH we are employing here artificial neural networks; we observe, anyway, that the GH can be applied using other algorithms and tools, reproducing the experience-learning-consistency-behaviour cycle with or without neural networks.

An introductory general remark: in all the cases to which we have applied our GH, the preliminary choice of classifying agents' output in actions and effects has been useful (i) to clarify the role of the agents, (ii) to develop model plausibility and results, (iii) to avoid the necessity of prior statements about economic rational optimising behaviour [BEL 96]. Economic behaviour, simple or complex, can appear directly as a by-product of IC, EPs and EOs. To an external observer, our Artificial Adaptive Agents (AAAs) are apparently operating with goals and plans. Obviously, they have no such symbolic entities, which are inventions of the observer. The similarity that we recall here is that the observations and analyses about real world agents' behaviour can suffer from the same bias. Moreover, always to an external observer, AAAs can appear to apply the rationality paradigm, with maximising behaviour.

---

[7] The Swarm codes - named bp-ct and ct-hayek - can be downloaded from the Swarm site (see <http://www.santafe.edu/projects/swarm/users/user-contrib.html>), or can be requested directly to the author.

We are considering learning agents, from the point of view of the bounded rationality research program [ART 90].

> In designing a learning system to represent human behaviour in a particular context, we would be interested not only in reproducing human rates of learning, but also in reproducing the style in which humans learn, possibly even the ways in which they might depart from perfect rationality. The ideal, then, would not simply be learning curves that reproduce human learning curves to high goodness-of-fit, but more ambitiously, learning behaviour that could pass the Turing test of being indistinguishable from human behaviour with its foibles, departures and errors, to an observer who was not informed whether the behaviour was algorithm--generated or human-generated.

In one sense our agents are even simpler than those considered in neoclassical models, as their targets and instruments are not as powerful as those assumed in those models. From another point of view, however, our agents are much more complex, due to their continuous effort to learn the main features of the environment with the available instruments.

3.2. The algorithm

The name cross-targets (CTs) comes from the technique used to figure out the targets necessary to train the ANNs representing the artificial adaptive agents (AAAs) that populate our experiments. Following the GH, the main characteristic of these AAAs is that of developing internal consistency between what to do and the related consequences. Always according to the GH, in many (economic) situations, the behaviour of agents produces evaluations that can be split in two parts: data quantifying actions (what to do) and forecasts of the outcomes of the actions. So we specify two types of outputs of the ANN and, identically, of the AAA: (i) actions to be performed and (ii) guesses about the effects of those actions.

Both the targets necessary to train the network from the point of view of the actions and those connected with the effects are built in a crossed way, originating the name Cross Targets. The former are built in a consistent way with the outputs of the network concerning the guesses of the effects, in order to develop the capability to decide actions close to the expected results. The latter, similarly, are built in a constant way with the outputs of the network concerning the guesses of the actions, in order to improve the agent's capability of estimating the effects emerging from the actions that the agent herself is deciding.

We choose the neural networks approach to develop CTs, mostly as a consequence of the intrinsic adaptive capabilities of neural functions. The AAA has to produce guesses about its own actions and related effects, on the basis of an information set. Remembering the requirement of IC, targets in learning process are: (i) on one side, the actual effects - measured through accounting rules - of the actions made by the simulated subject; (ii) on the other side, the actions needed to match guessed effects. In the last case we have to use inverse rules, even though some problems arise when the inverse is indeterminate. For further technical explanations on the CT method see [BEL 96] or [TER 00a].

Some definitions: we have (i) short term learning, in the acting phase, when agents continuously modify their weights (mainly from the hidden layer to the output one), to adapt to the targets self-generated via CT; (ii) long term learning, ex post, when we effectively map inputs to targets (the same generated in the acting phase) with a large number of learning cycles, producing ANNs able to definitively apply the rules implicitly developed in the acting and learning phase.

A remark, about both external objectives (EOs) and external proposals (EPs): if used, these values substitute the cross targets in the acting and adapting phase and are consistently included in the data set for ex post learning. Despite the target coming from actions, the guess of an effect can be trained to approximate a value suggested by a simple rule, for example increasing wealth. This is an EO in CT terminology. Its indirect effect, via CT, will modify actions, making them more consistent with the (modified) guesses of effects. Vice versa, the guess about an action to be accomplished can be modified via an EP, affecting indirectly also the corresponding guesses of effects. If EO, EP and IC conflict in determining behaviour, complexity may emerge also within agents, but in a bounded rationality perspective, always without the optimisation and full rationality apparatus.

3.3. The hayekian market arising from the experiment

The experiment structure is briefly described below (a detailed definition of the structure is reported in the code ct-hayek, which is the adaptation of bp-ct to the specific experiment).

The consumer agent has the following information set: the expense of the previous period; the requirement of the previous period; the price of the unique good, as proposed by the agent in the previous period; the agent buying proposal in the previous period. The producer agent has in input: the revenue of the previous period; the production stream requirement of the previous period; the price of the unique good, as proposed by the agent in the previous period; the agent selling proposal in the previous period.

The production process is undefined; the producers are simply supposed to offer the quantity that they are producing in each time unit; consumers and producers meet randomly each "day". The exchange is possible if the producer proposed price is less or equal to the price proposed by the consumer; the price used in the exchange is that proposed by the producer and the quantity is the minimum between the consumer proposal and the producer proposal; if the exchange is not possible the reference price (used in the determination of the mean price of the day) is that of the consumer and the quantity is 0.

We introduce also external objectives (EOs) which are explained in detail in the distributed ct-hayek code. In the consumer case, the effect Expenditure is trained with a lowering target; the effect Requirement is trained with a constant target.

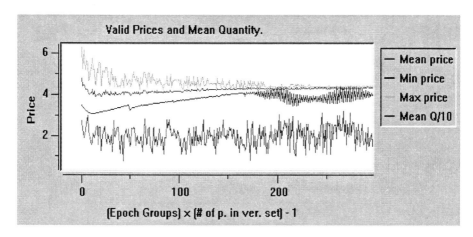

Figure 3. *Long term learning, without EOs*

The CT consequences are modification of the price guess, remembering that the EOs modifies the outputs of the effect side of the underlying ANN, but via CT also the action side. In the producer case we act symmetrically, increasing the Revenue target and keeping constant the other one; ProductionStream can be interpreted as the adequate production related to an existing fixed capital structure.

We have to read the lines of the graphics of the Figures as (bottom up): (i) mean quantity of the exchanges (divided by 10 for a scale necessity); (ii) Min price; (iii) mean price; (iv) Max price. Prices are obtained by the p variable described above. A market spontaneous equilibrium emerges immediately in our runs of the model. In the case with heavy relearning, reported in Fig. 3, we can see a robust equilibrium, with some individuals differentiating their behaviour. Operating simultaneously to diminish expenditures, raise revenues, stabilise requirements and production streams, we stabilise the market, with low oscillations in quantities, mainly when the agents are able to operate globally, after long term learning, as in Fig. 4.

3.4. *Comments to the experiment*

The more interesting thing here, from the point of view of the "mind or no-mind" dilemma, is the flexibility and adaptation ability of the agents that, while developing the internal consistency between guesses about their actions and guesses about the effects (of those actions), behave in a way that stabilise a market not provided with any form of operating mechanisms, as the previous one.

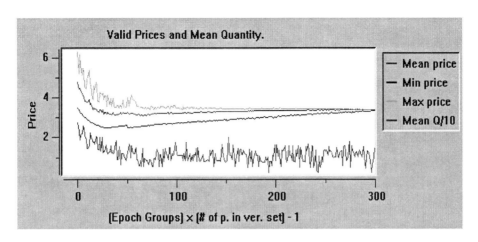

Figure 4. *Long term leaning, with EOs*

4. Bubbles and crashes from agents: "no-mind" agents in structured market

We are using here "no-mind" agenthat operate in a rigid market mechanism. The Surprising (Un)realistic Market (SUM) model [TER 00b], deals with the micro-foundations of a stock market[8]. We avoid any artificially simplified solution about price formation, such as to employ an auctioneer to clear the market; on the contrary, our model produces time series of prices continuously evolving, transaction by transaction.

4.1. Technical details

The core of the model is represented by a computational structure that reproduces closely the behaviour of the computerised book of a real stock market. The agents send to the book their buy and sell orders, with the related limit prices. The book executes immediately the orders if a counterpart is found in its log; otherwise, it records separately the buy and sell orders, to match them with future orders. The book is cleared at the beginning of each day.

---

[8] The Swarm codes - temporary named SUM - can be requested directly to the author.

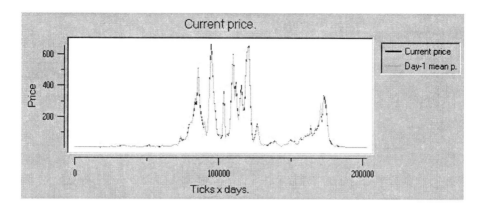

Figure 5. *Bubbles and crashes produced by no-mind agents*

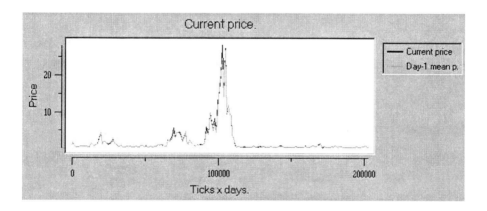

Figure 6. *Bubbles and crashes produced by no-mind agents, with a floor price*

Our (un)realistic market emerges from the behaviour of myopic agents that: (i) know only the last executed price, (ii) choose randomly the buy or sell side and (iii) fix their limit price by multiplying the previously executed price times a random coefficient, as shown in Fig. 5 and 6.

In Fig. 6 we introduce also the rule of buying with a fixed probability (here $p = 0.2$) if the price falls below a specific floor. A bubble emerges again, but the market is more stable than in the first case.

4.2. *Comments to the experiment*

This structure generates increasing and decreasing price sequences with relevant volatility. Also bubbles and crashes appear in this market, generated within the market structure, without the need of exogenous explanations, as a consequences of the rules of the market.

From the "no-mind" in agents perspective, we show here that it is possible to generate complex patterns (as bubbles) without using BDI agents, if the structure of the market is highly sophisticated, and consequently able to generate internally sequences of prices linked to the agents' actions in a non linear way.

5. Conclusions and further developments

The following statements may constitute a tentative conclusion:

- first of all we can fully accept the Axelrod simplicity principle, since it is easily shown that also very simple agents can generate complex emerging structures;

- more complicated agents facilitate the emergence of theoretical results, as the hayekian market;

- finally, external constraints are as strong as a mind proxy (the CT scheme) in determining the emergence of hard to explain patterns, like bubbles in a stock market.

Are human agents so far from the complexity of the economic system, as ants are from their anthill?

Further developments may arise, within the framework introduced in Section 4, relaxing hypothesis (i) for a small quota of the agents, in order to investigate the consequences of the presence either of subjects using technical trading rules to forecast the future market prices and of cognitive agents capable to learn from their experience. In some way, the last ones can correspond to the artificially intelligent agents behaving as econometricians proposed by Sargent [SAR 93], with the interaction of minded agents and structured environments or markets.

The framework of Section 4.1 is the natural candidate to develop the unified environment suggested in the Introduction, with the goal of comparing directly - in a unique structure - the four extreme situations of (i) no-mind agents behaving in an unstructured environment, (ii) minded agents behaving in an unstructured environment, (iii) no-mind agents behaving in a structured environment and (iv) finally minded agents behaving in a structured environment (this last case is not treated in this paper).

6. References

[ART 90] ARTHUR W.B., A Learning Algorithm that Mimics Human Learning., *Santa Fe Institute Working Paper* 90-026, 1990.

[AXE 97] AXELROD R., Advancing the Art of Simulation in the Social Sciences, in R.Conte, R.Hegselmann and P.Terna (eds), *Simulating Social Phenomena*, Lecture Notes in Economics and Mathematical Systems 456, pp.21-40, Springer-Verlag, 1997.

[BEL 96] BELTRATTI A., MARGARITA S., TERNA P., *Neural Networks for Economic and Financial Modelling*, ITCP, London, 1996.

[GIL 00] GILBERT N., TERNA P., How to build and use agent-based models in social science, *Mind & Society*, no. 1, 2000.

[HAY 49] HAYEK F.A., *Individualism and Economic Order*, London, Routledge, 1949.

[OST 98] OSTROM T., (1988) Computer simulation: the third symbol system. *Journal of Experimental Social Psychology*, vol. 24, 1998, pp.381-392.

[SAR 93] SARGENT T.J., *Bounded Rationality in Macroeconomics*, Oxford, Clarendon Press, 1993.

TER 98] TERNA P., ABCDE: Agent Based Chaotic Dynamic Emergence, in J.Sichman, R.Conte e N.Gilbert (eds), *Multi-Agent Systems and Agent-Based Simulation*, LNAI series, vol. 1534, Berlin, Springer-Verlag, 1998.

[TER 00a] TERNA P., Economic Experiments with Swarm: a Neural Network Approach to the Self-Development of Consistency in Agents' Behavior, in F. Luna and B. Stefansson (eds.), *Economic Simulations in Swarm: Agent-Based Modelling and Object Oriented Programming*. Dordrecht and London, Kluwer Academic, 2000.

[TER 00b] TERNA P., *SUM: a Surprising (Un)realistic Market - Building a Simple Stock Market Structure with Swarm*, forthcoming, 2000.

Variable Payoffs in the Minority Game

Robert Savit* — Yi Li* — Adrian VanDeemen**

Physics Department and Center for the Study of Complex Systems
University of Michigan, Ann Arbor, MI 48109
savit@umich.edu
lliyi@umich.edu

**University of Nijmegen, Nijmegen, Netherlands*
a.vandeemen@bw.kun.nl

ABSTRACT: *In the standard minority game, each agent in the minority group receives the same payoff regardless of the size of the minority group. Of great interest for real social and biological systems are cases in which the payoffs to members of the minority group depend on the size of the minority group. This latter includes the fixed sum game. We find, remarkably, that the phase structure and general scaling behavior of the standard minority game persists when the payoff function depends on the size of the minority group. There is still a phase transition at the same value of z, the ratio of the dimension of the strategy space to the number of agents playing the game. We explain the persistence of the phase structure and argue that it is due to the absence of temporal cooperation in the dynamics of the minority game. We also discuss the behavior of average agent wealth and the wealth distribution in these variable payoff games.*

1. Introduction

The minority game is a game played with heterogeneous agents which seeks to model a situation in which agents adaptively compete for a scarce resource.[1] In the simplest version of this model, each agent, at each time step of the game joins one of two groups, labeled 0 and 1. Each agent in the minority group is rewarded with a point, while each agent in the majority group gets nothing. An agent makes his decision about which group to join by using one of several strategies in his strategy set. The strategies use as input a set of common information. This model has a most remarkable structure:[2,3] Most notably, the system has a phase transition as a function of the ratio of the amount of information used the by the agents' strategies to the number of agents playing the game. In the region near the phase transition the system also evidences an emergent coordination among the agents' choices which lead to an optimum utilization of the scarce resource, in a well-defined sense. This transition is remarkably robust, and persists even when the nature of the information used by the agents changes,[4] when the information becomes exogenous rather than endogenous,[5] and when the agents' strategies are allowed to evolve over time.[6]

In most studies of the minority game, the payoff to the agents is very simple, namely, each agent that is in the minority group is awarded one point, and each agent that is in the majority group is awarded nothing. Another important aspect of the game to study is what happens when the game is modified so that the payoffs to the agents (and attendant modifications of the rankings of the agents' strategies) depend on the size of the minority group. In real social and biological systems, there may be various kinds of rewards for being in the majority, or for being innovative. It is easy to imagine situations in which the members of the minority group share a fixed amount of resource (a fixed-sum game): For example, a number of children are collecting soft drink cans on a beach to return for the deposit money. A remote, seldom-visited part of the beach has a large pile of cans from a party the previous night. Several children search this remote site. The number of cans at the site is fixed, so that the smaller the number of children, the more cans there are for each child. Note that in this story, there would be no payoff at all from the cans at this site if no children went to this remote section of the beach, i.e. if there were not a minority group, since the site is in a "seldom-visited" part of the beach. It is

[1] D. Challet and Y.-C. Zhang, *Physica A*, **246**, 407 (1997).
[2] R. Savit, R. Manuca and R. Riolo, Phys. Rev. Lett. **82**, 2203 (1999).
[3] R. Manuca, Y. Li, R. Riolo and R. Savit, *The Structure of Adaptive Competition in Minority Games.*, to appear in Physica A.
[4] Y. Li, R. Savit and R. Riolo, in preparation.
[5] A. Cavagna, *Irrelevance of memory in the minority game*, Phys. Rev. E, **59**, R3783 (1999).
[6] Y. Li, R. Riolo and R. Savit, *Evolution in Minority Games I: Games with a Fixed Strategy Space*, to appear in Physica A. Y. Li, R. Riolo and R. Savit, *Evolution in Minority Games II: Games with Variable Strategy Spaces*, to appear in Physica A.

furthermore not difficult to generate scenarios in which total resources available to a minority group increase or decrease in various ways as the size of the minority group decreases, resulting in payoffs to members of a minority group that depend, in various ways, on the size of the minority group. The most obvious example is that of a simple market in which there is a simple supply-demand relation for the price of some object. If the minority group at a certain moment is sellers, then the smaller the minority group, (i.e. the fewer number of sellers relative to buyers) the higher the price will be and the greater the rewards for the sellers. So in this case, agent payoff increases as the size of the minority group decreases. Another example, in which agent payoff may increase as the size of the minority group grows is given by the story of a prospector who finds a particularly rich mine (heretofore unknown). His ability to mine the ore will be very limited unless he enlists the aid of partners. Working together they may be able to mine more per miner than each one could separately. This example also indicates that the issue of variable payoffs in the minority game is associated with the more general question of cooperation versus competition at different levels of organization. In the case of the miner, cooperation with his mining partners accounts for the increasing payoff with increasing size of the minority group, while competition with other miners in the discovery of the mine leads to the possibility of any payoff in the first place.

Aside from their interest for specific social and biological systems, minority games with different payoff functions are interesting from the point of view of the fundamental dynamics of emergent cooperation. In this context, games in which an individual's payoff increases as the size of the minority group decreases are particularly interesting. Studies of the minority game, heretofore, have shown that the dynamics of the game leads to situations in which the size of the minority group is maximized, so that, in some sense, social utility is maximized. This was most clearly demonstrated when evolution was added to the game. If one imposes payoffs that explicitly favor the formation of small minority groups, it is not *a priori* clear how the dynamics will proceed. Will the phase transition persist? Will the system seek to maximize the size of the minority group, or will it seek to maximize agent wealth? To begin to address this question, I will first present a brief review of the minority game, and will then present some results for games in which agent payoff depends on the size of the minority group. We will find, surprisingly, that even with payoff functions that favor the formation of small minority groups, the fundamental phase structure of the game as a function of the amount of information available to the agents is unchanged: There is still a phase transition at the same critical parameter value as in the standard minority game, and at that transition the size of minority groups are maximized. Other measures of utility such as mean agent wealth and the wealth distribution among agents vary in an understandable way. I will argue that this phenomenon is intimately related to the absence of nontrivial *temporal* coordination in the usual statement of the minority game.[7]

2.   Description of the Game and its Modifications

2.1. *General Features of the Standard Minority Game*

The minority game is a simple competitive game. The rules of the game are as follows: At each time step of the game, each of N agents playing the game joins one of two groups, labeled 0 or 1. Each agent that is in the minority group at that time step gains some reward, while each agent belonging to the majority group gets nothing. In the commonly studied version of the game, the reward for each agent in the minority group is fixed at one point, independent of the size of the minority group. An agent chooses which group to join at a given time step based on the prediction of a strategy. A strategy is a look-up table which returns a prediction of which group will be the minority group during the current time step of the game, given the value of a piece of data. In general, different agents use different strategies, but the data used by the strategies is commonly available to all the agents. That is, at each point in the game, each agent receives the same information (signal), and his strategies respond to that signal with a prediction. In the original game, the signals given to the agents are the list of m 0's and 1's that denote which were the minority groups for the past m time steps. Thus, a strategy of memory m is a look-up table of 2^m rows and 2 columns. The left column contains all 2^m combinations of m 0's and 1's, and each entry in the right column is a 0 or a 1. To use a strategy of memory m, an agent observes which were the minority groups during the last m time steps of the game and finds that entry in the left column of the strategy. The corresponding entry in the right column contains that strategy's prediction of which group (0 or 1) will be the minority group during the current time step. In this version of the game, the strategies use (the publicly available) information from the historical record of which group was the minority group as a function of time. Other versions of the game have been studied, including the interesting case in which the signals provided to the agents are exogenous IID integers between 0 and 2^m-1.[5] The gross phase structure of the system is the same in these cases. In all cases, the controlling variable is $z \equiv D/N$, where D is the dimension of the strategy space from which the agents draw their strategies. (I.e., D is the number of different values that the publicly available signal can take on.) In the case in which the agents are given the m-history of the minority groups, $D=2^m$. In Fig. 1 we present a graph which shows how the system behaves as a function of z. The vertical axis is σ^2/N, where σ is the standard deviation of the number of agents belonging to (say) group 1. A small

---

[7] A more detailed discussion of the minority game with variable payoffs can be found in Y. Li, A. VanDeemen and R. Savit, *The Minority Game with variable payoffs*, University of Michigan, Center for the Study of Complex Systems preprint no. PSCS-2000-002 (1999). To appear in Physica A.

value of σ means that the minority groups are typically large, so that the scarce resource (membership in the minority group) is used near its limiting value. It is clear that as a function of z, the best resource utilization occurs at $z=z_c\approx0.35$, which is also the point at which the system evidences a phase change. Note also the remarkable scaling properties of these results.[2,3]

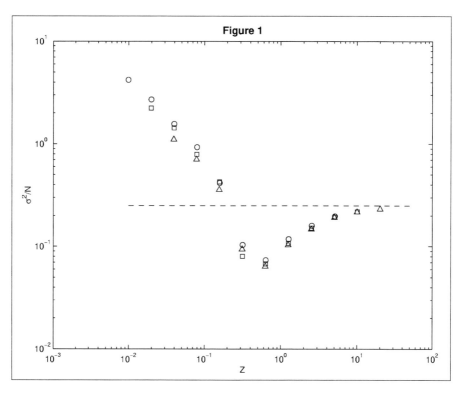

Figure 1. *σ^2/N as a function of $z=2^m/N$ for standard minority game. Each point represents an average value over 32 runs of 10,000 time steps apiece. Triangles indicate the results of games played with N=51 agents, squares correspond to N=101 agents, and circles indicate the results of games played with N=201 agents.*

2.2. The Minority Game with Variable Payoffs

The robustness of the general phase structure of the minority game is remarkable. But the payoff structure of the standard minority game is neutral with respect to the size of the minority group. It is not clear whether the same structure will obtain if the payoff functions are changed. In particular, it is not clear what the nature of the phase structure will be if the payoff structure to individuals does not favor the formation of large minority groups. In a fixed sum game, or in a game in which individual payoffs increase more rapidly as the size of the minority group decreases, we might expect qualitative changes in the phase structure of the system.

To address this question, we will study games in which we alter both the payoff to the agents, as well as the way in which the strategies are ranked. For simplicity, we will consider games in which the information used by the strategies is, as in the standard game, the list of which were the minority groups for the past m time steps. In the games we shall discuss, all strategies used by all the agents have the same value of m. At the beginning of the game each agent is randomly assigned s (generally greater than one) of the 2^{2^m} possible strategies of memory m, with replacement. For his current play the agent chooses from among his strategies the one that currently has the highest rank. In the original version of the model, a strategy is awarded one point for every time step in the past in which that strategy would have predicted the correct minority group.[8] In the cases we shall consider, the payoffs will generally depend on the size of the minority group. So, a strategy that would have successfully predicted the minority group at a given time step will be rewarded by an amount equal to the payoff given to each of the agents in the minority group at that time step.[9] Following each round of decisions, the cumulative performance of each of the agent's strategies is updated by comparing each strategy's latest prediction with the current minority group. Because each agent has more than one strategy, the game is adaptive in that agents can choose to play different strategies at different moments of the game in response to changes in their environment; that is, in response to new entries in the time series of minority groups as the game proceeds. Although this system is adaptive, the versions we analyze here are not, strictly speaking, evolutionary. The strategies do not evolve during the game, and the agents play with the same s strategies they were assigned at the beginning of the game.

To cover a range of possibilities, we shall consider both power law and exponential payoff functions. Let n be the population of the minority group, and let r=n/N. Then, we consider payoff functions of the form $A(r) \sim r^{-\alpha}$, and $A(r) \sim e^{-\gamma r}$.

---

[8] Here we consider the dynamics in which strategies are ranking according to whether they would have predicted the correct minority group without taking into account the fact that playing that strategy might have changed the composition of the minority group, or even changed which was the minority group. Such agents have been referred to as "naïve" agents. See, for example, M. Marsili, D. Challet, and R. Zecchina, LANL e-print, cond-matt/9908480 v3 (1999); Phys. Rev. Lett. **84**, 1824 (2000).

[9] Again, the games considered here are those with naïve agents. Thus, the reward to a strategy that was not played at a given time step, but which would have predicted the correct minority group (absent the changed membership of the agent in question) will be rewarded with a payoff equal to the payoff actually received by the agents belonging to the minority group at that time step.

Here $A(r)$ is the award made to each member of the minority group[10] when the minority group has a population, $n=rN$. The special case $\alpha=1$ is the fixed sum game, while the limits $\alpha \to 0$ or $\gamma \to 0$ recover the standard minority game. In addition to examining the behavior of overall resource utilization, σ, we will also study the wealth distribution among agents by looking at mean agent wealth and measures of the width of the wealth distribution. We choose to let A depend on r rather than on n since the results have a nicer scaling behavior, as we shall explain below. It is obvious that the results of games in which A depends explicitly on n can be obtained from our results by a simple rescaling of overall normalization or of γ.

3.   Results

Here we present only the most important of our results on the variable payoff games. Further details can be found elsewhere[7]. Each of the simulations reported in this paper were run for 10,000 time steps. Values of N used were 51, 101, and 201 agents, and eight realizations of each experiment were preformed. In Fig. 2a-e, we present σ^2/N as a function of $z=2^m/N$ for several different games with different pay-off functions. Fig. 2a is the result for the game with exponential payoff and $\gamma=4.0$, thus strongly favoring the formation of small minority groups. Fig. 2b is the result for the game with power law payoff and $\alpha=2$, also favoring small minority groups, and in particular, very strongly favoring the formation of very small minority groups. Fig. 2c shows the result for the fixed sum game, $A(r)=r^{-1}$. Figs. 2d and 2e show the result for games which weakly and strongly favor formation of large minority groups, namely, $A(r)=r^2$ and $A(r)=e^{0.1r}$, respectively. In all these graphs we see the same general behavior of σ^2/N as a function of z that we saw in the standard minority game, Fig. 1. In particular, as in the standard game, all results appear to fall on the same universal scaling curve, and there appears to be a phase change in the system at the same value of z as in the standard game. At the phase transition we have the best overall resource utilization in the sense that the typical minority group is largest. Note also the remarkable fact that the actual values of σ^2/N do not seem to depend on the form of the payoff in these graphs. The only exception to this is that σ^2/N in the standard game is somewhat lower for small enough z than in the games with other payoff functions. We shall explain this effect below. This same picture obtains for games with more than two strategies per agent. Here also, the general behavior of σ^2/N as a function of z does not materially depend on $A(r)$.

To check further that the nature of system and its phase change is as in the standard minority game, we have also computed the conditional probabilities $P(1|u_m)$, which are the probabilities to have the minority group be group 1 following some specific string, u_m, of m minority groups, in the game played with memory m.

---

[10] We have also studied the case in which the payoff function depends on the difference between the minority and majority groups. Results of that study are qualitatively consistent with the results presented here, and did not present any very interesting new structure.

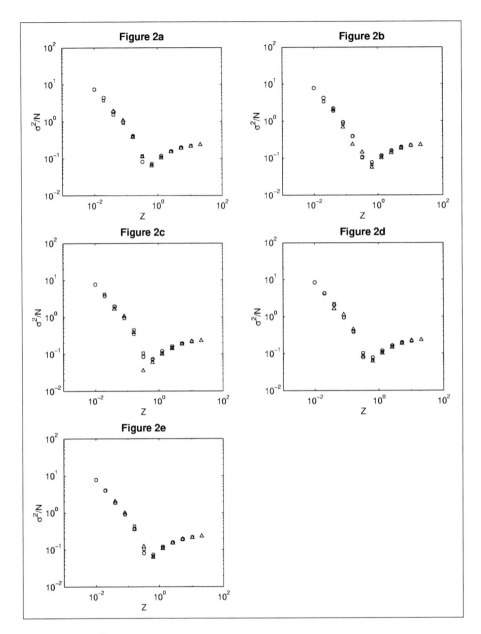

Figure 2a-e. σ^2/N *as a function of* $z=2^m/N$ *for several different games with different pay-off functions. Each point represents an average over 8 runs of 10,000 time steps apiece. In all these figures, triangles indicate the results of games played with N=51 agents, squares correspond to N=101 agents, and circles indicate the results of games played with N=201 agents. 2a)* $A(r) = e^{-4r}$, *2b)* $A(r) = r^{-2}$, *2c)* $A(r)=r^{-1}$ *(fixed sum game), 2d)* $A(r)=r^2$, *2e)* $A(r)=e^{0.1r}$.

As in the standard game, we find that for $z < z_c$ the histogram of $P(1|u_m)$ is flat at 0.5 for all u_m, while for $z \geq z_c$ it is not flat. This verifies that the phase transition in the games with different $A(r)$ is of the same type as in the standard minority game, and may be thought of as a transition from an informationally strategy-efficient phase to a strategy-inefficient phase.[2,3]

We have also studied[7] the mean wealth of the agents as a function of z for the five cases studied in Figs. 2a-e. There are a number of interesting features discussed in that reference, but for our purposes, the most important point is that changing $A(r)$ does affect the qualitative behavior of average agent wealth as a function of z. In particular, if $A(r)$ falls off fast enough with r (as in, for example, Figs. 2a and b), then average agent wealth will have a local minimum at the phase transition. Thus, the phase structure of the minority game is universal against changes in $A(r)$, but agent wealth is not.

Changing the payoff function does not seem to materially affect the overall utilization of resources, in the sense that the curve of σ^2/N as a function of z is not substantially different than in the standard minority game. And while different payoff functions do alter details of agent wealth such as the mean of wealth and the nature of its distribution among agents, these changes are easily understandable, given the fact that σ^2/N as a function of z is not altered. To test further the notion that changing the payoff to the agents does not change the fundamental phase structure of the system, we have constructed an artificial payoff function that strongly favors the formation of minority groups of a specific size. In particular, we have considered[7] a game played with N=101 agents and the payoff function $A(r) = 1$ for $r \neq r_o$, and 10 for $r=r_o$. We have plotted σ^2/N as a function of z for several different choices of r_o corresponding to favored minority groups of size n_o=49, 45 and 43. Again, this curve is substantially the same as in the standard minority game, and in particular, shows a minimum and a phase change at $z=z_c$.[11]

4. Discussion of the Results

The most significant result of this paper is the observation that the behavior of σ^2/N as a function of z is not materially altered when the payoff function is changed. σ^2/N still shows the same remarkable scaling behavior and phase structure that it had in the original, standard minority game.[2] One might have supposed that the behavior of σ^2/N would have been strongly affected by varying $A(r)$, and in particular, by allowing $A(r)$ to be large for small r. Then, it should have been possible for agents to arrange their choices so that an average agent would have been in the majority group well over 50% of the time, but when in the minority group that minority group would be small. In principle, this can lead to greater agent wealth (and high ranking

---

[11] There are, of course, changes in mean Agent wealth and in the wealth distribution as a function of z, but these are not important for us here.

for the appropriate strategy) if the payoff for small minority groups is sufficiently high. It is somewhat surprising that this does not happen, and that the curve of σ^2/N as a function of z is largely unchanged (with the exception of very low z, an effect which is explained elsewhere[7].

One way to understand this, is to recognize that an agent's choice about which group to join is dictated by that strategy that has the highest rank. For values of z not too far from z_c, (and following an initial learning period) most agents have one strategy which has a very high rank, and is used most of the time. Recall that the rankings of the strategies are cumulative over the course of the game, so such rankings represent average strategy performance.[12] Thus, the solution which the system discovers, and which results in large minority groups regardless of A(r), is based on the average performance of the agents' strategies. However, in order for the system to take advantage of A(r)'s that strongly favor small minority groups, requires *temporal* coordination. That is, agents must cooperate in the sense that agents must sacrifice themselves so that they place themselves in the majority group most of the time, and in the minority group only seldom. Given the way in which strategies are evaluated, it is fairly clear that such temporally structured solutions will not, in general, be found. The kind of temporal cooperation necessary to take advantage of an A(r) that favors small minority groups is akin to the successful strategies used in the iterated prisoner's dilemma, and related games.[13] There, players explicitly use the information that the game will continue in order to develop strategies that are sub-optimal locally in time, but perform much better over time. The question of modifying the minority game to allow agents to develop temporally coordinated strategies in order to generate mutually beneficial small minority groups will be discussed elsewhere.

In the context of a statistical mechanical description of the minority game, one might suppose that A(r) is something like an irrelevant operator. In ordinary statistical mechanical systems, irrelevant operators do not affect the critical exponents at second order phase transitions. However, our numerical results suggest that much more of the structure of the minority game is unaffected by changes in A(r), in particular, the shape of the curve of σ^2/N as a function of z and the value of z_c. In the context of a field theoretic approach to statistical mechanics, A(r), therefore, appears to play the role of a total derivative operator, the addition of which does not affect the dynamics of the system. If this is the case, then it should be possible to transform the minority game played with a non-trivial A(r) into the standard minority game by a canonical transformation.[14] On the other hand, it is unlikely that the phase transition observed at $z=z_c$ is a simple second order phase

---

[12] This argument holds even if the strategy rankings are determined by credit that is discounted far into the past. See Ref. 3 for more details.

[13] See, for example, R. Axelrod, *The Evolution of Cooperation*, (Basic Books, 1984).

[14] One of us (RS) thanks R. Akhoury for enlightening discussions on this point.

transition. It is more likely that the minority game is analogous to a spin-glass, and that the phase transition is analogous to that seen in spin-glass-like systems.[15] One must be cognizant of this essential complication. Of course, if the dynamics of the minority game were generalized sufficiently to allow for the temporal coordination described above, then A(r) would presumably cease to be a total derivative.

Finally, it would be most interesting to perform analysis of the minority game with evolution and with different payoff functions, A(r). According to the arguments we have presented, we expect that the system will evolve. As in Reference 6, to states in which the size of the effective strategy space is consistent with a value of z $\Box$ z_c, and the size of the typical minority group is very close to N/2.

5.   Conclusion and Summary

We have shown that the main results of the minority game, in particular, σ^2/N as a function of z, is materially independent of the payoff function to the agents. The system continues to have a phase transition at the same value of z, and the two phases have the same characteristics. We have also studied the behavior of average agent wealth and the wealth distribution, and we have shown[7] above that those functions were understandable given the payoff function and the fact that σ^2/N as a function of z is materially the same as in the standard game. Finally, we discussed what we believe to be the fundamental dynamical reason for the persistence of this result, namely, the absence of nontrivial temporal cooperation among the agents.

Our results provide another important piece of information that points to the surprising robustness and universality of the phase structure of minority dynamics, at least for those systems in which there is an absence of temporal cooperation. And because different social and biological systems manifest different payoffs, our results strongly suggest the relevance of these dynamics to a wide range of complex adaptive systems. Indeed, in very simplified terms, different payoff functions, A(r), can arise from different detailed cooperative dynamics within groups. Thus, these games can be considered to be very simple models that capture some of the consequences of cooperation within groups.   Understanding, in more detail, how minority dynamics manifests itself in specific social and biological systems is likely to lead to a deeper understanding, not only of those specific systems, but of the structure of complex adaptive systems in general.

Acknowledgements
We thank Rick Riolo for very helpful conversations. This work was supported in part by the US National Science Foundation under grant no. DMI-9908706.

---

[15] This possibility was first suggested in Ref. 2. The work cited in Ref. 8, by M. Marsili, et al. has explored this possibility further.

Cooperation in an Adaptive Network

M.G. Zimmermann[1,2], V.M. Eguíluz[1,3], M. San Miguel[1], A. Spadaro[4]

Abstract: We study the dynamics of a set of agents distributed in the nodes of an adaptive network. Each agent plays with all its neighbors a weak prisoner's dilemma collecting a total payoff. We study the case where the network adapts locally depending on the total payoff of the agents. In the parameter regime considered, a steady state is always reached (strategies and network configuration remain stationary), where co-operation is highly enhanced. However, when the adaptability of the network and the incentive for defection are high enough, we show that a slight perturbation of the steady state induces large oscillations (with cascades) in behavior between the nearly all-defectors state and the all-cooperators outcome.

Keywords: Social organisation, Networks, Game theory, Agent based models, Weak Prisoner's Dilemma

[1]Instituto Mediterráneo de Estudios Avanzados IMEDEA(CSIC-UIB), E07071 Palma de Mallorca, Spain. Supplementary information at http:`www.imedea.uib.es`.

[2]Present address: Departamento de Física, Universidad de Buenos Aires, Pabellón I Ciudad Universitaria, 1428 Buenos Aires, Argentina.

[3]Corresponding author email: `victor@delta.ens.fr`. Present address: DELTA (Joint Research Unit CNRS-ENS-EHESS), 48 Bd Jourdan, 75014 Paris, France.

[4]DELTA (Joint research unit CNRS-ENS-EHESS) and Department of Economics and Business, Universitat de les Illes Balears, E07071 Palma de Mallorca, Spain.

Résumé : Nous étudions la dynamique d'un groupe d'agents distribués dans les noeuds d'un réseau. Chaque agent joue avec tous ses voisins un Faible Dilemme du Prisonnier en collectant un pay-off total. Nous étudions le cas d'un réseau qui s'adapte localement selon les pay-off des agents. Premièrement, un état stationnaire est toujours trouvé pour les paramètres étudiés, où la fraction d'agents qui coopère est stationnaire. Pour quelques paramètres même on a trouvé un état presque complètement coopérative. Cependant, quand l'adaptabilité du réseau et l'incitation á la défection sont assez grands, on montre que'une petite perturbation de l'état stationnaire induit des grandes oscillations (avec cascades) dans le comportement entre 1 état quasi-tout-defection et quasi-tout-cooperation.

Mots-clés : Organisation sociale, Réseaux, Théorie des jeux, Models d'agents, Faible Dilemme du Prisonnier

1. Introduction

A subject which has intrigued many economists is how the organization of an economy arises and evolves. Agents interact in multiple ways, as for example information transmission in financial markets[5], or firms competition or collusion in an oligopoly[6]. These interactions can be described by a set economic agents which sit in the nodes of a network. Among other approaches (for a review see [KIR 99]), the mechanisms of interactions and the emergence of collaboration in a group of agents have been analyzed by the use of evolutionary game theory [WEI 96]. Using the Prisoner's Dilemma (PD) game, [AXE 81] and [AXE 84] showed how cooperation may be sustained by a population of agents meeting repeatedly and having certain degree of rationality. Strategies were allowed to mutate and reproduce in proportion to the difference between the agent's payoff and the population's average payoff. Cooperation was shown to be sustained by the use of the evolutionary stable strategy Tit-For-Tat. This approach assumes that the game is carried out by randomly matching a pair of agents from a fixed population. This assumption seems plausible for systems with a large number of agents where the probability of playing several times with the same agent is extremely low, and for systems where the agents cannot create links or preferences between them.

However, in many social and economic environments this assumption does not hold, and each agent interacts only with a small subset of the whole population[7]. One reason for this might be that agents have imperfect information on the whole population, except for a small subset which can be considered as "the neighbors".

---

[5]See for example [BAN 92], [KIR 93], [CON 99], [EGU 99].

[6]See for example [FER 98], [GOY 99].

[7]For a deep study of the dynamics of a PD game with different strategies, evolution of the strategies and networks see [COH 99].

In this paper we introduce a spatial Weak Prisoner's Dilemma (WPD)[8] model played on an endogenously adaptive network where cooperation is promoted and sustained by local interactions *and* the adaptation of the network. To simplify matters we do not allow the strategies to evolve and consider only zero-memory strategies, *i.e.* all-C [all-D] strategy means doing C [D] *all* the time irrespective of the outcome.

Each agent plays the same strategy either C (cooperate) or D (defect) with all its local neighbors, as in [NOW 92]. Each agent revises his strategy at each iteration of the game and imitates the strategy of the neighbor with highest aggregate payoff. Finally we consider the adaptation of the network by allowing the possibility of changing the neighborhood whenever an agent was unsatisfied and imitated its best local neighbor. Specifically, if this best local neighbor is a D-neighbor, the imitating agent cuts the link with the D-neighbor, with some probability, and establishes a new link selecting randomly a new agent to become its neighbor from the whole population of agents.

As possible scenarios where these cooperative networks might arise we can mention a network of individuals or firms that have some agreements among them but with some risk involved in the cooperation. The agreements correspond to the links in the network, and respecting their agreements results in playing Cooperation (C), while not respecting their agreement corresponds to Defection (D). An interesting application might be a network of firms which share their research and development outcome. Another application might be a network of scientist which agree to collaborate in different projects.

We have determined from numerical experiments the following main results. First, for the range of parameters studied, the network always reaches a steady state where the fraction of cooperating agents (C-agents) is high. In these states the network remains stationary. However, most of the agents are unsatisfied and thus are continuously imitating their best neighbor's strategy, which is the same strategy they are using. This does not change the local payoffs and thus it remains in a stationary state. We find also that although the dynamics always converges to a steady state, when the incentive to defect is sufficiently high, a perturbation may induce large oscillations in the fraction of C-agents together with a large reorganization of the network. These oscillations stretch between the *quasi*-all C-agents, to the *quasi*-all D-agents networks. We stress the fact that these are transient and they last for some time before a new steady state is reached. In most cases high cooperation is again reached, but there is a small probability to reach the *quasi*-all D-network. Thus we show that although cooperation is greatly enhanced by such a network update, the system may organize in a state where an exogenous or stochastic perturbation

---

[8]We will explain in the next section the difference between the classical Prisoner's Dilemma and the WPD we use in this paper.

may produce drastic changes on a finite time. The oscillations can be triggered by a change of strategy of a single agent with a large number of links. This identifies the importance of the highly-connected agents which play a leadership role in the collective dynamics of the system. Finally, it is interesting to study the characteristics of the network that emerges from the interaction between agents. Such structure is far from trivial in the sense that presents a given pattern.

The paper is organized as follows. The next section defines the adaptive model. Section 3 deals with the conducted numerical experiments. First the case of a fixed network is revisited, and then the full adaptive network is presented and discussed. Finally, in Section 4, we discuss our results and open problems.

2. The model

We consider an adaptive game where N agents play a WPD game on a network Γ. Each agent is located in a *node* of the network (and there is a single agent per node). Two agents are *neighbors* if they are directly connected by *one* link. We define the *neighborhood* of agent i as the subset of Γ which are neighbors of i, and we represent it as neigh(i); its cardinal is k_i. Each agent plays only with those other agents connected by one link[9]. If N_l is the total number of links and k_i is the number of links of node i, then the *average connectivity* of a network, k, is defined as the average number of links per node

$$k = \frac{\sum_{i=1}^{N} k_i}{N} = \frac{2N_l}{N} .$$
[1]

In this paper we consider two different kind of initial networks on which the agents start the game: regular lattices in two-dimensions and random networks. A two-dimensional regular lattice correspond to a Manhattan-like grid, where the nodes are the intersections of streets and avenues. We will consider first-neighbor interaction that corresponds to the four possible moves a chess King can make (thus $k_i = 4$, $\forall i$ and $k = 4$), while the 2nd-neighbor interaction corresponds to the 4 extra neighbors which will complete a square around the King (thus $k_i = 8$, $\forall i$ and $k = 8$)[10]. Random networks of average connectivity k are formed by distributing $N_l = kN/2$ bidirectional links between pairs of nodes (i, j), with the constraint that $(i, j) = (j, i)$ (bidirectional links). The resulting distribution of the number of links in the network is Gaussian with the maximum located at the average connectivity k.

---

[9]We assume that the links are bidirectional. More general situations can be considered with uni-directional links, but we do not explore this further.

[10]Previous results of PD game in regular lattices are investigated in for example [NOW 92].

Let us denote by $s_i(t) = \{0, 1\}$ the strategy of agent i at time step t, where $s_i = 1$ corresponds to play cooperation (C), and $s_i = 0$ corresponds to defection (D). These will be referred to as C-agents or D-agents, respectively. The payoff matrix for a 2-agents game is:

	C	D
C	σ, σ	$0, b$
D	$b, 0$	δ, δ

where we take $b > \sigma > \delta > 0$, and $b/2 < \sigma$ for a Prisoner's Dilemma game. In this paper we study the case of a Weak Prisoner's Dilemma (WPD): a Prisoner's Dilemma is Weak when $\delta = 0$. In a standard Prisoner's Dilemma there exists a unique Nash equilibrium (D, D) while in WPD either a (C,D), (D,C) or (D,D) may be attained as a Nash equilibrium.

We use in this Paper the WPD for which the analysis is much simpler, taking into account that [NOW 92, LIN 94] showed that, at least for a fixed regular network, the results do not change qualitatively when using $1 \gg \delta > 0$.

We consider the situation in which agents always tries to maximize their utility, and therefore seeks the largest possible benefit from their local interactions in the network Γ. We assume each agent plays the same strategy with all its neighbors neigh(i) and only with them. The game is played *synchronously*, *i.e.* the players decide their strategy in advance and they all play at the same time. The strategy update of agent i is as follows:

1. Each agent i plays the WPD game with each neighbor using the *same* strategy s_i and collecting a total individual payoff Π_i.

2. Agent i revises its current strategy at each iteration of the game (i.e., at every time step), and updates it by *imitating* the strategy of its neighbor with a highest pay-off. Agent i is said to be *satisfied* if his pay-off is the maximum of its neighbors; otherwise it will be *unsatisfied* and it will revise its strategy.

3. The agents have also the possibility of an extra action which adapts its neighborhood. Namely we consider:

   Network Rule: *if agent i is unsatisfied and imitates from a D-agent j, then with probability p, i breaks the link with j and establishes a new link with another agent chosen randomly in the network Γ.*

This rule leads to a time evolution of the local connectivity of the network, leaving the global connectivity k, as defined in Eq. 1, constant. For each agent i which imitates a D-agent j and decides to break the link and choose a new agent β, neigh(i) changes by replacing $j \to \beta$ and $k_i(t+1) = k_i(t)$. However j will lose a link, $k_j(t+1) = k_j(t) - 1$, and the new agent β will increase its local connectivity $k_\beta(t+1) = k_\beta(t) + 1$. Thus, the network adaptation introduces a diversity in the agents local neighborhoods.

Agreements between satisfied agents do not change. This does not mean that new agreements with other agents are not possible (these agents may always receive new links), but those which exist remain untouched. The same is true for unsatisfied C-agents imitating another C-agent. However neighborhoods of D-agents that have the maximum pay-off in the neighborhood could change abruptly in just one iteration.

The network rule can be understood as a risk minimization. If agent i is a D-agent and is unsatisfied he minimizes the risk of cooperation by taking chances and selecting a new neighbor from the whole network. In the context of game theory, this can be seen as a retaliation, because is highly unlikely that he will play with those agents in the future.

The probability p represents a transaction cost of breaking *one* agreement *and* establishing a new agreement with a new partner. It can also be understood as a measure of the tolerance of being exploited. We would like to stress that the transaction cost has two components: first, the cost of breaking an agreement and second, the cost of finding a partner and that this new partner accepts the agreement[11]. The case $p = 0$ corresponds to an infinite transaction cost for breaking the link, while $p = 1$ corresponds to the limiting case of no transaction cost. It is clear that breaking at the same time more than one link, and finding their respective partners is more unlikely. The probability p is also a measure of the adaptability of the network to the results of the game at each iteration.

It will be useful to define the *looking function* of agent i which will be denoted by $l(i)$. This function points to i's neighbor with highest payoff, including himself; thus if i is not imitating any neighbor then $l(i) = i$. From this we can define an agent being a *local maximum* in payoff as the one which satisfies $i = l(i)$ and at least one of its neighbors is looking at it.

Suppose that at a given time step there is a D-agent which is a local maximum. This implies that at the next time step, the D-strategy will be replicated on all of its neighbors, *and* its links will be destroyed with probability p. Thus, a D-local maximum at one time step, is an unstable situation where the agent looses a fraction p of all its links on the next time step, and these links will be replaced by new neighbors.

With the network rule implemented in this Paper *the total number of links*

---

[11]One could separate these two costs, and would have a process of breaking links (with a given probability q) and another process of generation of links (with a probability r). This line of research is not explored in this paper.

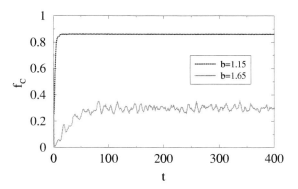

Figure 1: Time evolution of the fraction of C-agents f_C for a non-adaptive network $p = 0$, in a two-dimensional regular lattice with second-neighbors interaction ($k = 8$: (top trajectory) asymptotic periodic trajectory for $b = 1.15$ and (bottom trajectory) chaotic trajectory for $b = 1.65$. Payoff matrix: $\sigma = 1$, $\delta = 0$.

in the network Γ is conserved. We do not take into account more complicated network dynamics as spontaneous creation or destruction of links, that will break the conservation of total number of links.

3. Numerical studies

We have characterized numerically the model described above using as parameter the incentive to defect b. We have used as initial networks random networks with an average connectivity $k = 4$ and $k = 8$ and two-dimensional regular lattices with first- ($k = 4$) and second-neighbor ($k = 8$) interaction. We have also fixed the adaptability $p = 1$. The statistical measures that we have studied are:

- The fraction (normalized to the whole population N) of cooperating agents (C-agents), denoted by $f_C = (\sum_{i=1}^{N} s_i)/N$.

- The average payoff per agent $\Pi = (\sum_{i=1}^{N} \Pi_i)/N$ of the whole network.

- The probability of having a link between two C-agents, p_{CC}, between a C-agent and a D-agent, p_{CD}, and between two D-agents, p_{DD}. These probabilities satisfy:

$$1 = p_{CC} + 2p_{CD} + p_{DD} \qquad [2]$$

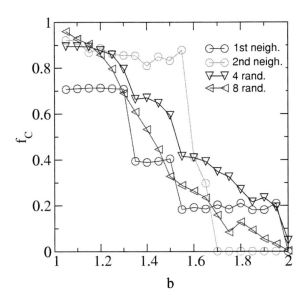

Figure 2: No network adaptation ($p = 0$). Average fraction of C-agents, f_C, vs. defecting incentive, b, in 1st and 2nd neighbors regular lattices, and in random networks with $k = \{4, 8\}$.

In the numerical simulations we maintain fixed the parameters $\delta = 0$ and $\sigma = 1$ of the payoff matrix and we vary b in the range $1 < b < 2$. Finally, in most simulations we take $N = 10000$ agents, and we start with an initial population of $0.6N$ C-agents randomly distributed in the network Γ.

The game in a fixed network ($p = 0$) and regular lattices, has been previously studied by [NOW 94, NOW 92, NOW 93]. Typically the behavior of the fraction of C-agents, f_C, can show different features. The simplest is an asymptotic stationary or periodic state, where f_C remains stationary or fluctuates periodically. A more complex behavior is the spatio-temporal chaotic regime, where f_C fluctuates in time around an average value while the spatial distribution of C- and D- agents present evolving patterns at each iteration. Finally, if the incentive to defect b, is high enough the asymptotic state of the system is all D-agents. Also the introduction of elements that disrupt the spatial correlations present when the game is played in a regular lattices (e.g., random lattices, noise and errors in the imitating process), was shown to destroy the periodic fluctuations and regular patterns observed, as expected.

One of the main result of these studies is that partial cooperation can be sustained by *local interactions*, together with a very simple choice of strategies which does not include memory. This can be illustrated by studying the average fraction of C-agents for an increasing value of the incentive to defect b (see

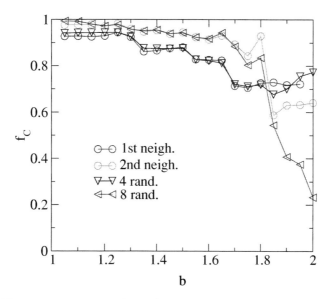

Figure 3: Network adaptation ($p = 1$). Fraction of cooperative agents vs. b in different initial networks.

Fig. 2). We have extended previous results by explicitly considering random networks, which is a more natural assumption in an economic context.

The numerical results also show that increasing the average size of the neighborhood, *i.e.* average number of links per agent, k, the average fraction of C-agents f_C decreases faster with b. Several extensions of this model have been studied in the literature: introducing asynchronous updates [HUB 93] or introducing errors in the imitation process [MUK 96], where the basic results shown above persist [NOW 94].

It is also worth noting that the fraction of C-agents depends strongly on the network. As can be seen from Fig. 2, both the regular lattice with first neighbor interaction and the random network with $k = 4$ have the same average connectivity, however f_C behaves differently with b. Same applies for the regular lattice with second neighbor interaction and random network with $k = 8$.

In Fig. 3, we plotted the averaged asymptotic value of f_C for the fully adaptive network $p = 1$ and for different initial networks. The average is over 10 different random initial conditions with a density of 0.6 C-agents. Unlike the non-adaptive case, the fraction f_C seems to be quite independent of the incentive to defect b, and the initial network chosen (regular or random). Only the average connectivity k seems to play a role for determining the asymptotic

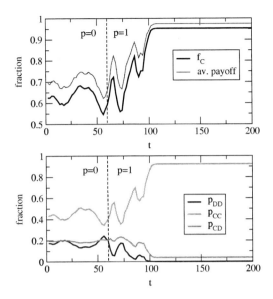

Figure 4: (Top) Time series of C-fraction f_C and average payoff in a random network: without network adaptation ($p = 0$) for $t < 60$, and thereafter in the full adaptive network ($p = 1$). (Bottom) Corresponding time series of the different link probabilities: two C-agents (p_{CC}), a C and a D-agent (p_{CD}), and two D-agents (p_{DD}) having a link. Parameter values: $b = 1.35$, $k = 8$.

fraction of cooperation. To illustrate how cooperation is enhanced against the non-adapting network, we show in Fig. 4 a simulation where the system first evolves with $p = 0$ until at $T = 60$ time iterations the adaptation is switched on ($p = 1$). It is clear from the figure that the fraction of C-agents is highly enhanced with respect to the static network.

One of the most interesting features encountered when the network is able to adapt with the game ($p = 1$), is that throughout the whole range of parameters studied ($1 < b < 2$), the dynamics settles onto a *steady state* after some transient time. Figure 4 also shows the time series of the different links probabilities (p_{CC}, p_{CD}, p_{DD}). The steady state corresponds to a stationary network structure and individual payoffs Π_i. Notice how the network adaptation clearly favors having links between C-agents. Most agents are unsatisfied[12] in this steady state and they continuously imitate the strategy of their neighbors with highest payoff (all of them C-agents). Also note that at the steady state, the probability of having a link between a C and a D-agent p_{CD} is finite, while for two D-agents $p_{DD} \to 0$. This shows that D-agents end up without

---

[12]In a weak sense, after all they are benefiting from cooperation.

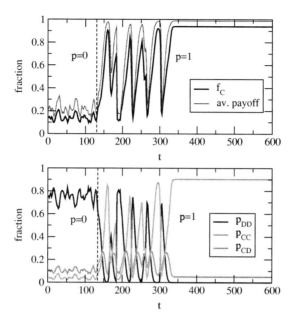

Figure 5: Time series for high b. During $0 < t < 120$, the network is left fixed $(p = 0)$, while for $t > 120$, $p = 1$. Below the corresponding time series of the link probabilities p_{CC}, p_{CD}, p_{DD}. $b = 1.75, k = 8$.

links to other D-agents and exploiting other C-agents. Also note that when $p_{DD} = 0$, there is no D-agent which will change their neighborhood, so the system may reach a stationary state. In this case D-agents will be satisfied "passive" local maxima, in the sense that nobody is imitating their strategy[13].

A stationary situation with individual payoffs Π_i may arise with a number of agents forming, what we shall denote a *chain*, such that: $s_{l^m(i)} = s_{l^{m-1}(i)} = \ldots = s_{l(i)} = s_i = 1$, where $l^m(i)$ is the only agent which is satisfied. All others in the chain are actually unsatisfied, but as they imitate the same strategy they were playing on the previous step, they never change their relative payoff, and the chain becomes a steady state.

An interesting result arises when one looks at the time series for large values of p $(p \sim 1)$ and a high value of the incentive to defect b. Before reaching the asymptotic steady state, one observes that *large oscillations* occur for different choices of initial conditions. Figure 5 shows an example of the dynamics starting from the fixed network. From other initial conditions, similar oscillations are observed. The time evolution of the system before the network is allowed to

---

[13] A highly unlikely situation where two D-agents are neighbors in a steady state would occur if they have exactly the same payoff.

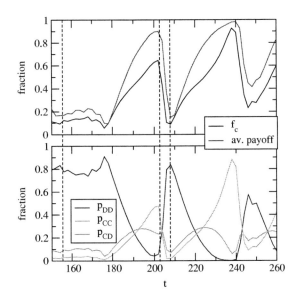

Figure 6: Blow-out of a time series showing avalanches. Parameter values as in Fig. 5.

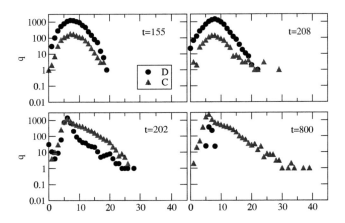

Figure 7: Histogram of number of links, q, for a C and D-agents, at different time steps (from time series in Fig. 6) during large oscillations. $t = 155$ corresponds to the distributions of the initial random network with $k = 8$. $t = 202$ corresponds to the maximum of p_{CC}, while at $t = 208$ to the maximum of p_{DD}. Finally at $t = 800$ the distributions of the asymptotic steady state are shown.

adapt is governed by the high reward of D-agents. However, when the network starts the adaptation ($p = 1$ for $t > 120$) the dynamics promotes the creation of more links between C-agents, while decreasing dramatically the links between D-agents, as can be seen at time step $t \sim 150$. However, first attempts to build a global cooperative behavior are unsuccessful because the system frustrates. The defecting behavior is so rewarding, that the cooperation has to be built in a specific network configuration in order to be robust against eventual changes of strategy. This correspond to the successive oscillations shown in Fig. 5. The systems reaches a similar fraction of C-agents as in the stationary solution, but several oscillations occur before the stationary regime settles.

In Fig. 6 we show a blow-out of two oscillations. Note the drastic change in the connectivity between C and D-agents. To quantify this phenomenon we determined the distribution of links for the population of each strategy at different time steps as shown in Fig. 7. The initial distribution $(t = 155)$ shows a Gaussian distribution around the starting $k = 8$ value. Then at the maximum of p_{CC} $(t = 202)$ it is observed that the tails of both distributions extend up to 28 links. Then very rapidly the network switches to the almost defective solution $(t = 208)$. However there are a small number of C-agents with a large payoff, which permits the gradual build-up of cooperation. Finally for large times $(t = 800)$, the D-agents distribution shrinks to a very narrow distribution, while the C-agents distribution displays a long exponential decay. The stationary network configuration is thus dominated by a few C-agents with a large number of links (the tails of the histogram of links for C-agents). These highly-connected agents dominate the collective behavior of the network.

To illustrate the relevance of the highly connected agents we have built a numerical experiment in which after the system reaches a steady state, the best connected agent, that is the one with a largest number of links switches strategy (from C to D). Figure 8 shows the resulting oscillations, before the system reaches again a (possibly different) steady state. This makes very clear the dominant role of these best connected agents.

4. Discussion

The main results of this work are the following. We have introduced a model of cooperation on an adaptive network, where the cooperation is highly enhanced. The network adaptation involves exclusively the D-agents, which in some sense are allowed to "search" for new neighbors, in the hope of finding C-agents to exploit. However our study reveals that this mechanism benefits in the long run cooperators. The asymptotic state reached by the system is a steady state in which the network structure and the average payoff Π remain stationary. However, most agents are unsatisfied, and continuously imitate the strategy of their neighbors with highest payoff (most of them C-agents). Also

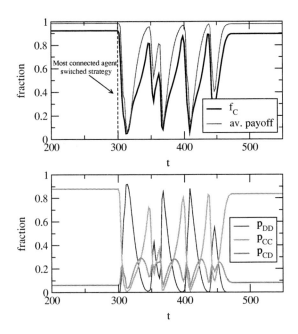

Figure 8: Time series of f_C, where at $t = 300$ the agent with most links changes strategy from C to D. Parameter values: $b = 1.75$ and $k = 8$.

the structure of the stationary network presents interesting characteristics. The distribution of links for C-agents has a long exponential tail, with a very few number of highly connected C-agents having up to 4 times the average number of the links in the whole network. These agents dominate the cooperative network structure.

We have also obtained that, for sufficiently high values of the incentive to defect b, the induced network structure may suffer large reorganizations. These manifest themselves as large oscillations in the fraction of C-agents, where the network visits for a short time the nearly full cooperative regime, followed by a short time of nearly full defecting regime. In the current dynamical model, these large oscillations are long lived transients, but the system reaches a final stationary state. The interesting aspect is that these large oscillations might be easily triggered by the spontaneous change of the strategy of a highly connected agent.

Acknowledgment.   We acknowledge useful discussions with D. Cardona-Coll, P. Battigalli, A. Kirman and J. Weibull. M.G.Z., V.M.E. and M. S. M acknowledge financial support for DGYCIT (Spain) project PB94-1167.

References

[AXE 81] R. AXELROD AND W. D. HAMILTON. The evolution of cooperation. *Science*, 211:1390–1396, 1981.

[AXE 84] R. AXELROD. *The Evolution of Cooperation*. Basic Books, New York, 1984.

[BAN 92] A. BANNERJEE. A simple model of herd behaviour. *Quarterly Journal of Economics*, 108:797–817, 1992.

[COH 99] M. COHEN, R. RIOLO AND R. AXELROD. The emergence of social organization in the prisoner's dilemma: how context-preservation and other factors promote cooperation. Santa Fe Institute Working Paper 99-01-002, 1999.

[CON 99] R. CONT AND J. P. BOUCHAUD. Herd behavior and aggregate fluctuations in financial markets. *Macroeconomic Dynamics*, 1999. In press.

[EGU 99] V. M. EGUILUZ AND M. G. ZIMMERMANN. Dispersion of rumors and herd behavior. Los Alamos e-print archive (www.lanl.gov): cond-mat/9908069, 1999.

[FER 98] C. ALÓS FERRER, A. B. ANIA AND F. VEGA-REDONDO. An evolutionary model of market structure. Preprint from http://merlin.fae.ua.es/fvega/#rp, 1998.

[GOY 99] S. GOYAL AND S. JOSHI. Networks of collaboration in oligopoly. Mimeo, 1999.

[HUB 93] B. A. HUBERMAN AND N. S. GLANCE. Evolutionary games and computer simulations. *Proc. Natl. Acad. Sci. USA*, 90:7716–7718, 1993.

[KIR 93] A. KIRMAN. Ants, rationality and recruitment. *Quarterly Journal of Economics*, 108:137–156, 1993.

[KIR 99] A. KIRMAN. Aggregate activity and economic organisation. *Revue Economique des sciences sociales*, 113:189–230, 1999.

[LIN 94] K. LINDGREN AND M. G. NORDAHL. Evolutionary dynamics of spatial games. *Physica D*, 75:292–309, 1994.

[MUK 96] A. MUKHERJI, V. RAJAN AND J. R. SLAGLE. Robustness of cooperation. *Nature*, 379:125–126, 1996.

[NOW 92] M. A. NOWAK AND R. M. MAY. Evolutionary games and spatial chaos. *Nature*, 359:826–829, 1992.

[NOW 93] M. A. NOWAK AND R. M. MAY. The spatial dilemmas of evolution. *Int. Jour. of Bif. and Chaos*, 3(1):35–78, 1993.

[NOW 94] M. A. NOWAK, S. BONHOEFFER AND R. M. MAY. Spatial games and the maintenance of cooperation. *Proc. Natl. Acad. Sci. USA*, 91:4877–4881, 1994.

[WEI 96] J. WEIBULL. *Evolutionary Game Theory*. MIT University Press, 1996.

Generalized Lotka-Volterra (GLV) Models of Stock Markets

Sorin Solomon

Rakah Institute of Physics, Hebrew University of Jerusalem

ABSTRACT. *The Generalized Lotka-Volterra (GLV) model:*

$$w_i(t+1) = \lambda w_i(t) + a\bar{w}(t) - c\bar{w}(t)w_i(t) \quad , \quad i = 1, ..., N$$

provides a general method to simulate, analyze and understand a wide class of phenomena that are characterized by power-law probability distributions:

$$P(w)dw \sim w^{-1-\alpha}dw \quad (\alpha \geq 1)$$

and truncated Levy flights fluctuations $L_\alpha(\bar{w})$. We show how the model applies to economic systems.

1. Introduction

Many natural and man-made phenomena are known to involve power-law probability distributions (e.g. Pareto 1897; Zipf 1949; Mandelbrot 1961, 1951; Bouchaud et al. 97; Cahalan and Joseph 1989; Mantegna and Stanley 1994, 1995, 1996, 1997; Stanley et al. 1995; Sornette et.al. 1997; Zhang et al 1997).

Power-laws are common in systems composed of units that have no characteristic size, and in systems made of auto-catalytic elements (Yule 1924; Champernowne 1953; Simon and Bonini 1958; Ijiri and Simon 1977, Anderson 1995). Moreover it has been shown that in systems which are not separable into energetically independent parts, the power laws naturally take the place of the usual exponential (Boltzmann) distribution (Tsallis 1988).

It has been shown both theoretically (Solomon 1998; Solomon and Levy 1996) and numerically (Biham et al. 1998) that the Generalized Lotka-Volterra (GLV) model produces power-law distributions, without suffering from the problems and limitations of previous similar models. Since the GLV requires only a few reasonable conditions, it may be expected to be widely applicable.

The GLV involves three scalar parameters, and a probability distribution, each with a clear role in the model's interpretation. Certain model properties are "universal", i.e.

independent of some of the model's parameters. This conceptual simplicity makes the GLV easily adaptable to different systems.

The features listed above make the GLV a candidate for a general method to simulate, analyze and understand a wide class of phenomena which are characterized by power-law probability distributions and multi-scale fluctuations.

The aim of this paper is to provide a practical introduction to GLV modeling. We describe the basic theory, how to construct a numerical simulation of the GLV, and applications to practical interesting systems.

For didactic reasons we will present a few previous and simpler models before introducing the GLV. This will nicely partition the topics involved into more manageable parts. The models described in this paper are:

– Single-agent random multiplicative process without barrier eq. (7).
– Single-agent multiplicative process with fixed lower barrier eq. (20).
– Multiple agent process with barrier coupled to the mean eq. (40-42).
– Single-agent linear (stochastic multiplicative/additive) process eq. (50)
– Generalized Lotka-Volterra (autocatalytic competing) agents eq. (52).

2. Some basic concepts

Microscopic representation or agent-oriented simulation is a relatively new way of generating and expressing knowledge about complex systems (see Solomon 1995 for a physicist review and Kim and Markowitz 1989 for early pioneering work in finance and ZhangWB 1991 for a synergetically inspired view).

One idea this document will try to convey is the basic difference between the standard methods of explanation, which are based on a global parameterization of a macroscopic dynamics and alteranate methods of explanation, based on "microscopic representation".

To illustrate the usual methods, consider the textbook problem of computing the trajectory of a stone under the influence of gravity. The stone is treated as a point mass (global parameterization), and we use Newton's Laws (macroscopic dynamics).

Such an explanation is not always useful. For instance, in order to study the cracking and crumbling of the stone under pressure, one would have to consider its structure composed of clusters of (of clusters ...) of smaller stone parts. In many physical, economic etc situations, we find it is most natural to regard the system under study as a collection of "microscopic" similar units (or "agents"), which interact among themselves in some well-defined way and (co-)evolve in time.

Experience has shown that even simple dynamics, when applied to a system consisting of many similar interacting agents, may produce interesting macroscopic effects. The properties which arise from the collective behavior of many similar elements are called emergent properties.

Some examples of systems with emergent properties are the following:

Animal (and human) populations (cities/countries) are composed of individuals who are constantly born (and die), and who compete with other members of their species (for food, mates etc).

It is specifically in order to model the time evolution of such populations $w(t)$ that the classical (scalar) Lotka-Volterra system:

$$w(t+1) = (1 + \text{birth} - \text{death}) * w(t) - \text{competition} * w(t)^2 \qquad [1]$$

was invented. We will show that its straightforward multi-agent generalization (eq.(2)), which treats the population as a collection of sub-populations w_i, has emergent properties very different from the eq. (1), which treats the entire population as a single variable.

The system eq. (1) can also be interpreted as a stock market model where the market index $w(t)$ is proportional to the capitalization (total worth of the money invested) in the traded equities. For a fixed amount of shares, this is a measure of the price of the shares traded in the market. Such global models which treat the index/share price $w(t+1)$ as a single entity whose time evolution is governed by stochastic differential equations were introduced in the past (Baillie and Bollerslev 1990) The microscopic representation method models the market index $\bar{w}(t)$ as an collective quantity emerging from the interactions of a macroscopic number of traders.

More precisely, the "microscopic representation" of the stock market is composed of many investors $i = 1, ..., N$ each having a certain personal wealth $w_i(t)$. Alternatively, one can consider as elementary degrees of freedom the individual stocks i.e. the capitalization $w_i(t)$ of the individual companies i traded in the market.

We are going to use the Generalized Lotka-Volterra (GLV) equation system

$$w_i(t+1) = \lambda(t)w_i(t) + a(t)\bar{w}(t) - c(t)\bar{w}(t)w_i(t) \quad , \quad i = 1, ..., N \qquad [2]$$

to construct a very simple model of the stock market. Despite of being very simple, the model yields (and explains) the (100 years old) Pareto wealth distribution.

Eq. (2) models also the dynamics of cities population if one denotes by w_i the number of individuals belonging to the city i. More precisely, eq. (2) would result from the following assumptions:

- for each of the w_i citizen of a city, there is a λ probability that he will attract (or give birth to) a new citizen. One may include as a negative contribution to λ the probability for the citizen to die or leave the town without preferred destination.

- each of the w_i citizens of a city has a probability c/N to be attracted by one of the $N\bar{w}$ citizens of the existing cities and leave the town i.

- the citizens which left own town but are not bound to a particular town, have the probability a to end up in any of the i towns.

Systems made of auto-catalytic (terms λ and a) competing (term c) elements are wide-spread in nature. To make things more concrete, we will often use in the following discussion terminology borrowed from the GLV model of the stock market. However, our results and insights will be quite generic and applicable to other systems. For example, we will often use the term 'traders' i instead of microscopic elements and talk about the 'wealth' w_i of each trader and the "average wealth" $\bar{w}(t)$:

$$\bar{w}(t) = \frac{1}{N} \sum_i w_i(t) \qquad [3]$$

This nomenclature should be suitably altered when used in other contexts.

3. Probability Distributions as Predictive Output of Modeling

Modeling the stochastic evolution in time $t = 1, ..., T$ of a system of equations type (1) produces a lot of raw data. It is not very useful to produce more and more sequences of numbers

$$w(t); \quad t = 1, ..., T$$

without subsequent data analysis.

A natural way is to collect numerous sequences and analyze them statistically. A way to look at it is to imagine a large set of (uncoupled) traders w_i, $i = 1, ..., N$, subject to the same stochastic dynamics, and to compute their distribution. More precisely, assuming each data sequence i produced by eq. (1) describes the evolution of one trader i

$$w_i(t); \quad t = 1, ..., T$$

we may compute over a large set of traders $i = 1, ..., N$ the number of traders $N_t(w)$ with wealth $w_i(t)$ in the interval $(w, w + dw)$. In the limit of $N \to \infty$ this defines the individual wealth probability distribution

$$P_t(w)dw = N_t(w)/N . \qquad [4]$$

This way of looking at the problem is conducive to a model like eq. (2) in which the various traders **do** interact, e.g. through terms including their average $\bar{w}$. As we will see, this is a key ingredient in solving some of the problems with the one-agent models of the type eq. (1) and renders the model more realistic.

4. The general shape of the probability distributions

It may be a little surprising, but under certain conditions, even for non-stationary interacting non-linear dynamical systems of the type eq. (2), we may predict (without performing any computer runs) what the wealth distributions $P_t(w)$ produced by our models will look like.

Before going into a more detailed analysis, we list here some obvious properties which the probability distribution has to obey.

– The distribution vanishes for negative values.

$$P(w) = 0 \; for \; w < 0$$

This property follows from the way we choose the initial wealth values, and from the nature of the dynamics. In practice, this corresponds to the fact that population sizes, capitalization of companies, cloud sizes, etc. assume only positive values.

– The value zero usually has vanishing probability distribution, $P(0) = 0$. This follows from the continuity of the distribution, and from the previous characteristic.

– The distribution has a tail which may or may not obey a power-law

$$P(w) \sim w^{-1-\alpha} \qquad [5]$$

In either case, distributions must decay to zero at infinity:

$$\lim_{w->\infty} P(w) = 0 \qquad [6]$$

otherwise the probability to have finite w_i values would vanish.

– The distribution has a maximum since a continuous and non-negative function has always a maximum between two zeroes (in our case the function vanishes at zero and at infinity).

The remaining non-trivial issues are:

– The functional form of the tail, in particular whether it decreases as a power-law (eq. (5)), log-normal, exponential, etc.

– The location and height of the maximum

– The behavior of the rising part

– The relation between the tail shape and the parameters of the model. We will see that in certain conditions, the tail behavior is quite universal in as far as it is quantitatively independent of most of the parameters and it is preserved even in generically non-stationary conditions.

In this article, we will be interested mainly in the shape of the tail of the probability distribution $P(w)$, in particular whether it is a power-law (eq. (5)) or not.

The importance of the power laws is far from purely academic: the power laws are the bridges between the simple microscopic elementary laws acting at the individual level and the complex macroscopic phenomena acting at the collective level. They ensure that the dynamics covers many scales rather than acting only at the smallest and/or largest scales of the system.

Moreover, power laws ensure that the dynamics of the intermediate scales of the system is largely independent of both the microscopic details and the macroscopic external conditions constraining the system. Consequently, the macroscopic complexity is not the direct and linear result of the microscopic details but rather a generic consequence of the self-organization taking place in systems with many interacting parts and inter-related feedback loops.

As a result, one may hope to extract macroscopic and mesoscopic laws which hold for large classes of microscopic laws in a universal way.

This unifying and predictive power of power laws has resulted in their paramount importance in many branches of science beginning with quantum field theory continuing with statistical mechanics and extending to ecology and economics.

One can say that the emergence of the power laws is a *sine qua non* condition for the emergence of the macroscopic world out of local microscopic elementary laws of nature. As such, it has become itself a fundamental natural law.

The present paper shows that power laws emerge generically in the most simple and natural models which were considered in the past in the modeling of chemical, biological and social systems.

5. Multiplicative random dynamics and log-normal distributions

Power-law probability distributions (eq. (5)) with exponent -1 (i.e. $\alpha = 0$), can be obtained analytically from a multiplicative process (Redner 1990; Shlesinger 1982):

$$w(t + 1) = \lambda(t)w(t) \qquad [7]$$

where the random variables $\lambda(t)$ are extracted from a fixed probability distribution $\Pi(\lambda)$ with strictly positive finite support.

Indeed, in order to obtain the distribution of $w(t)$ in the large t limit, one takes the logarithm on both sides of eq. (7) and uses the notations $\mu = \ln \lambda$, $x = \ln w$. Using these notations, eq. (7) becomes:

$$x(t + 1) = \mu(t) + x(t) \qquad [8]$$

The respective probability distributions $\rho(\mu)$ and $\mathcal{P}(x)$ for μ and x are related to the distributions for λ and w by the identities:

$$\rho(\ln \lambda)d(\ln \lambda) = \Pi(\lambda)d\lambda \qquad [9]$$

and

$$\mathcal{P}(\ln w)d(\ln w) = P(w)dw \qquad [10]$$

which mean that

$$\rho(\mu)d\mu = (\exp \mu)\Pi(\exp \mu)d\mu \qquad [11]$$

and

$$P(x)dx = (\exp x)P(\exp x)dx \qquad [12]$$

The interpretation of eq. (8) is that $x(t+1)$ is the sum of the constant $x(0) = \ln w(0)$ with the t random variables $\mu(t) = \ln \lambda(t)$ extracted from the fixed distribution $\rho(\mu)$. Under the general conditions of the Central Limit Theorem (CLT) we get for $x(t)$ at large t the normal (Gaussian) distribution:

$$\mathcal{P}_t(x) \sim \frac{1}{\sqrt{2\pi\sigma^2_{\ln \lambda} t}} \exp -\frac{(x - <x>)^2}{2\sigma^2_{\ln \lambda} t} \qquad [13]$$

where

$$<x> = tv \equiv t < \ln \lambda > \qquad [14]$$

and

$$\sigma^2_{\ln \lambda} = < (\ln \lambda)^2 > - < \ln \lambda >^2 \qquad [15]$$

Note that the width of the normal distribution $\mathcal{P}_t(x)$ (the denominator of the expression in the exponential in eq. (13)) is

$$\sigma^2_x = t\sigma^2_{\ln \lambda} \qquad [16]$$

and increases indefinitely with time. This means that the distribution $\mathcal{P}_t(x)$ becomes independent of x

$$\mathcal{P}_t(x) \sim \frac{1}{\sqrt{2\pi\sigma^2_{\ln \lambda} t}} \qquad [17]$$

in an ever-increasing neighborhood of $<x>$ (where the exponential is close to 1).

Transforming eq. (17) back to the w variables by using eq. (10) one obtains

$$P(w)dw = \frac{1}{\sqrt{2\pi\sigma^2_{\ln \lambda} t}} d(\ln w) \qquad [18]$$

i.e.

$$P(w)dw \sim 1/w\ dw \qquad [19]$$

Graphically, this means that as time goes to infinity, $P(w)$ is an ever "flattening" distribution approaching w^{-1}.

6. Non-interactive multiplicative processes with fixed lower bound

In order to obtain power-law probability distributions $P(w) \sim w^{-1-\alpha}$ with exponent $\alpha > 0$, the multiplicative process eq. (7) has to be modified (Yule 1924, Champernowne 1953, Simon and Bonini 1958, Ijiri and Simon 1977) in such a way that the variation of $w(t)$ under eq. (7) will be constrained by a lower bound w_{min}

$$w(t) > w_{min} \qquad [20]$$

In terms of $x(t) = \ln w(t)$, eq. (8) becomes supplemented by the lower bound:

$$x(t) > x_{min} \equiv \ln(w_{min}) \qquad [21]$$

More specifically, the dynamics consists in the updating of $w(t) \to w(t + 1)$ by eq. (7) (or - equivalently - eq. (8)) **except if** this results in $w(t + 1) < w_{min}$ (or, equivalently $x(t + 1) < x_{min} = \ln(w_{min})$), in which case the updated new value is $w(t + 1) = w_{min}$ (respectively $x(t + 1) = x_{min}$).

These modifications are obviously not consistent with the applicability of the Central Limit Theorem. Consequently, the derivation in the previous section which led to the log-normal distribution (eqs. (13)(19)) does not hold.

Instead, intuition can be gained on the modified system eq. (7)(20) through a physical analogy: In fact the system (eq. (8)) with the constraint eq. (21) can be interpreted as the vertical motion of a molecule in the earth's gravitational field above the earth surface. In this case the "earth's surface" is x_{min}, the gravitationally-induced downward drift is $v = <x>/t = <\ln \lambda>$, and the diffusion per unit time is parametrized by the squared standard deviation $\sigma^2_{\ln \lambda}$.

For $v < 0$ this is the barometric problem which has the static solution:

$$P(x) \sim \exp -x/kT, \qquad [22]$$

which when re-expressed in terms of w becomes (cf. eq. (10)):

$$P(w)dw \sim e^{-(\ln w)/kT} d\ln w \qquad [23]$$

i.e.

$$P(w) \sim w^{-1-1/kT} \qquad [24]$$

In order to estimate the value of the exponent

$$\alpha = 1/kT \qquad [25]$$

one substitutes the probability distribution eq. (24) into the master equation which governs the time evolution of the process (eq. (7)). The master equation expresses the flow of probability between the various values of w as $w(t)$ is updated to $w(t + 1) = \lambda w(t)$. More precisely, the probability for $w(t + 1) = \lambda w(t)$ to equal a certain value w is the integral over λ (weighted by $\Pi(\lambda)$) of the probability that $w(t) = w/\lambda$. Assuming that for assymptotically large time values the probability distribution converges to a fixed shape, leads to the relation:

$$P(w) = \int \Pi(\lambda)P(w/\lambda)d(w/\lambda) \qquad [26]$$

Substituting (24)(25) into eq. (26):

$$w^{-1-\alpha} = \int \Pi(\lambda)(w/\lambda)^{-1-\alpha}d(w/\lambda) \qquad [27]$$

and dividing both members by $w^{-1-\alpha}$ one obtains:

$$1 = \int \lambda^\alpha \Pi(\lambda) d\lambda \qquad [28]$$

This means that the value of α is given by the transcendental equation: (Solomon and Levy 1996):

$$< \lambda^\alpha > = 1 \qquad [29]$$

One may wonder why this equation does not hold for the problem in the previous section (the system eq. (11) without the lower bound eq. (20)) since the lower bound w_{min}, does not seem to appear in the formula eq. (29). The answer is that in the absence of the lower bound, there is no stationary equation (26) as the system evolves forever towards the non-normalizable solution $P(w) \sim w^{-1}$. In fact, formally, $\alpha = 0$ is a solution of eq. (29). This "solution" is in fact the relevant one in the case $< \ln \lambda >> 0$.

Another nontrivial fact is that the limit $w_{min} \to 0$ leads to $\alpha \to 1$ rather than $\alpha \to 0$ (which is the value in the total absence of a lower bound). This nonuniform behavior of the limits $N \to \infty$ and $w_{min} \to 0$ is related to the non-trivial thermodynamic limit of the system (Biham et al. 1998).

One of the problems with the solution to eq. (29) is that while it is independent of w_{min}, it is highly dependent on the shape and position of the distribution $\Pi(\lambda)$ of the random factor $\lambda(t)$, and consequently it is highly dependent on changes in the dynamics (eq. (11)).

In the systems introduced in the following sections, the situation will be the opposite: the characteristics of $\Pi(\lambda)$ will be largely irrelevant and the lower bound eq. (20) will play a central role.

In particular, the distribution of the social wealth $P(w)$ and the inflation $(d\bar{w}/dt)$ of the system will depend on the social security policy, i.e. on the poverty bound w_{min} below which individuals are subsidized (Anderson 1995). The relevant parameter is the ratio

$$q = w_{min}/\bar{w} \qquad [30]$$

between the minimal wealth w_{min} and the average wealth:

$$\bar{w} = 1/N \sum_i w_i \qquad [31]$$

In the presence of inflation, it is q rather then w_{min} which has to be fixed since a fixed minimum wealth independent of changes in the average wealth would not be very effective or politically viable for long periods of time.

We will extend the formalism to these more realistic conditions in later sections. To this effect, we will need the expression of $\alpha = 1/kT$ in terms of q (eq. (30)) which we deduce below.

Such a relation can be obtained by using in eqs. (24)(25) the facts that:

- the total probability is 1:

$$\int_{w_{min}}^{\infty} P(w)dw = 1 \qquad\qquad [32]$$

i.e.

$$Const. \int_{w_{min}}^{\infty} w^{-1-\alpha}dw = 1 \qquad\qquad [33]$$

- the average of w is $\bar{w}$:

$$\int_{w_{min}}^{\infty} wP(w)dw = \bar{w} \qquad\qquad [34]$$

i.e

$$Const. \int_{w_{min}}^{\infty} w^{-\alpha}dw = \bar{w} \qquad\qquad [35]$$

By extracting $Const$ from eq. (33):

$$Const = \alpha w_{min}^{\alpha} \qquad\qquad [36]$$

and introducing this value in eq. (35), one obtains the relation:

$$\alpha w_{min}^{\alpha}[-w_{min}^{1-\alpha}/(1-\alpha)] = \bar{w} \qquad\qquad [37]$$

By dividing both sideas of the equation $\bar{w} \frac{\alpha}{1-\alpha}$ one obtains:

$$-w_{min}/\bar{w} = 1/\alpha - 1 \qquad\qquad [38]$$

Considering the definition eq. (30) this reads:

$$\alpha = 1/(1-q) \qquad\qquad [39]$$

This is a quite promising result because for the natural range of the lower bound ratio ($0 < q < 1/2$) it predicts $1 < \alpha < 2$ which is the range of exponents observed in nature (and which is far from the log-normal value $\alpha = 0$).

The main problem with the power-low generating mechanism based on the single-agent dynamics (eq. (11)(20)) is that it works only for negative values of $< \ln \lambda >$ (the barometric equation does not hold for a gravitational field directed upwards).

This means that, (except in the neighborhood of w_{min}), $w(t+1)$ is typically smaller than $w(t)$. This is not the case in nature in which populations and economies may expand.

Moreover, the exponent α of the power law is highly unstable to fluctuations in the parameters of the system. In particular, large changes in $\bar{w}$ imply large fluctuations of

q and consequently (cf. eq. (39)) large variations in the exponent α. This again is in disagreement with the extreme stability of the exponents α observed in nature.

We will see later how the multi-agent GLV solves these problems. The key feature is to introduce interactions between the individual elements w_i through the inclusion of terms (or lower bounds) proportional to $\bar{w}$.

7. Multiplicative processes coupled through the lower bound

In the previous section we showed that power-laws eq (24) can be obtained from multiplicative stochastic dynamics with lower bounds in the same way that the exponential laws eq. (22) can be obtained in additive stochastic dynamics eq. (8) bounded from below eq. (21).

The problematic points were: the instability of the exponent α to variations in the average wealth/population and the fact that the mechanism accounts only for "deflating"/"shrinking" of w.

However, the solution of these difficulties is already apparent in eq. (39): we consider a system of N degrees of freedom w_i (with $i = 1, ...N$) which is governed by the following dynamics:

at each time t, one of the w_i's is randomly chosen to be updated according to the formula:

$$w_i(t + 1) = \lambda(t)w_i(t) \qquad [40]$$

while all the other w_i's are left unchanged. At each instance, the random factor λ is extracted anew from an i-independent probability distribution $\Pi(\lambda)$.

The only exception to this prescription (eq. (40)) is if, following the updating $w_i(t) \to w_i(t + 1)$ (eq. (40)), $w_i(t + 1)$ (or other w_k's) end up smaller then a certain fixed fraction $0 < q < 1$ of the average $\bar{w}$:

$$w_i(t + 1) < q\bar{w}(t) \qquad [41]$$

The prescription, should eq. (41) be valid, is to further update the affected w_j's to:

$$w_j(t + 1) = q\bar{w}(t). \qquad [42]$$

The wonderful property of the system (eq. (40–42)) is that when re-expressed in terms of the variables

$$v_i(t) = w_i(t)/\bar{w}(t) \qquad [43]$$

it leads to a system very close to the system eq. (7),(20):

$$v_i(t + 1) = \tilde{\lambda}(t)v_i(t) \qquad [44]$$

$$v_i(t + 1) > q \qquad [45]$$

where the effective multiplicative factor in eq. (44) is such that:

$$< \bar{v}(t) >= 1 \qquad [46]$$

at all times t. Note that this solves the problem of $< \ln \lambda >> 0$ because the multipli-cation with the "renormalized" factor $\tilde{\lambda}$ ensures automatically that the v distribution never diverges.

Another way to see how this solves the problems with the single "particle" dynam-ics (eqs. (7)(20)) is to realize that in this situation, even if the average $\bar{w}(t)$ diverges, the lower bound trails it in such a way as to insure a stationary value of α.

Indeed, according to eq. (24), the v_i dynamics eq. (44–45) leads to a v_i distribution

$$P(v) \sim v^{-1-\alpha} \qquad [47]$$

which in turn implies

$$P(w) \sim w^{-1-\alpha} \qquad [48]$$

Since we do not have a closed analytic formula for $\tilde{\lambda}$ eq. (46) in terms of the model parameters, the transcendental equation (eq. (29)) is not useful here.

However, since $\bar{v} = 1$ by definition, one calculates according eq. (39) the follow-ing close formula for the exponent α:

$$\alpha = 1/(1-q) \qquad [49]$$

This means that even for significantly time-varying distributions $\Pi_t(\lambda)$ in eq. (40), the exponent of the power law remains invariant.

The above results are quite non-trivial insofar as they predict the stochastic behavior of highly interactive and time non-stationary systems eqs. (40)-(42) by relating them formally to non-interacting static statistical systems eqs. (7)(20).

We will extend this line of thought in the following sections an reduce the highly nontrivial GLV system to a rather simple single-agent linear stochastic equation.

8. The single-agent linear stochastic equation

The discrete equation below is a more elaborate version of the single-agent model introduced in Section 6. Here the lower bound is effectivelly supplied by an additive random term ρ, instead of by an explicit barrier eq. (20):

$$w(t+1) = \lambda(t)w(t) + \rho(t) \qquad [50]$$

The equation (50) may (crudely) describe the time-evolution of wealth for one trader in the stock market. In this context w may represent the wealth of one trader who performs at each time-step a stock transaction. $w(t)$ is the wealth at time t, and $w(t+1)$ is the wealth at time $t+1$.

λ and ρ are random variables extracted from positive probability distributions. λ may be called the "success factor", and ρ is a "restocking term", which takes into account the wealth acquired from external sources (e.g. using state-built infra-structure, subsidies etc).

The dynamics (eq. (50)) leads to a power-law distribution $P(w) \sim w^{-1-\alpha}$ if $< \ln \lambda > < 0$. More precisely, the $P(w)$ has a power-tail for values of w for which $\rho(t)$ is negligible with respect to $\lambda(t)w(t)$. If $< \ln \lambda > >> 0$ the distribution is a log-normal expanding in time, which in the infinite time limit corresponds to a power-law with exponent $-1 - \alpha = -1$. This implies that the mechanism eq. (50) does not explain expanding economies with $\alpha > 0$.

Since the distributions (and initial values of w) are positive, the $\rho(t)$ term keeps the value of $w(t)$ above a certain minimal value of order $\bar{\rho}$. Therefore, for large enough values of w the dynamics is indistinguishable from our previous model, the multiplicative process (7) with fixed barrier (eq. (20)).

It is therefore not surprising that it can be rigorously proven (Kesten 1973) that eq. (50) leads to a power law eq. (24) with exponent α given by the transcendental equation (29):

$$< \lambda^{\alpha} > = 1 \qquad [51]$$

It is again notable that (as in the case of the w_{min} lower bound), the exponent α is totally independent of the distribution of the additive term ρ while it is highly sensitive to the shape and position of the $\Pi(\lambda)$ distribution. We will see that in GLV the situation is reversed.

9. The Generalized Lotka-Volterra system

The GLV (Solomon and Levy 96) implements more complex dynamics than eq. (50). The advantages, however, overweight the difficulties:

– The GLV model ensures a stable exponent α of thepower-law $P(w) \sim w^{-1-\alpha}$ even in the presence of large fluctuations of the parameters.

– The value of $< \lambda >$ and the average $\bar{w}$ can vary during the run (and between runs) without affecting the exponent α of the power-law distribution.

– λ may assume values both larger or smaller than 1.

The GLV is an interactive multi-agent model. We have N traders, each having wealth w_i, and each w_i is evolving in time according to:

$$w_i(t + 1) = \lambda(t)w_i(t) + a(t)\bar{w}(t) - c(t)\bar{w}(t)w_i(t) \qquad [52]$$

Here $\bar{w}$ is the average wealth, which supplies the coupling between the traders:

$$\bar{w} = (w_1 + w_2 + \ldots + w_N)/N \qquad [53]$$

λ is a positive random variable with a probability distribution $\Pi(\lambda)$ similar to the λ success factor we used in eq. (50). The dramatic difference is that in this case, λ may systematically assume values larger than 1 and its distribution may be time-dependent (including time intervals with $< \ln \lambda >$ both greater or less than 0).

The coefficients a and c are in general functions of time, reflecting the changing conditions in the environment.

The coefficient a expresses the auto-catalytic property of wealth at the social level, i.e. it represents the wealth the individuals receive as members of the society in subsidies, services, and social benefits. For this reason it is proportional to the average wealth.

The coefficient c originates in the competition between each individual and the rest of society. It has the effect of limiting the growth of $\bar{w}$ to values sustainable in the current conditions.

10. Reducing GLV to a set of independent equations (50)

Summing the GLV eq. (52) over i, and taking the local time average one gets for the local time average $< \bar{w} > (t)$ an equation similar to the scalar LV equation (eq. (1)).

$$N < \bar{w} > = < \lambda > N < \bar{w} > + < a(t) > N < \bar{w} > - < c(t) > N < \bar{w} >^2 \quad [54]$$

which gives :

$$< \bar{w} > = \frac{-1 + < \lambda > + < a(t) >}{< c(t) >} \quad [55]$$

Neglecting the fluctuations of the average $< \bar{w} > (t)$ during the updating of a single individual i, one may replace $< \bar{w} > (t)$ by $\bar{w}$ in the last term of eq. (52) and regroup the terms linear in w_i:

$$w_i(t+1) = [1 + \lambda(t) - < \lambda(t) > - < a(t) >]w_i(t) + a(t)\bar{w}(t) \quad [56]$$

Introducing wealth values normalized by the average wealth: (as in eq. (43)):

$$v_i(t) = w_i(t)/\bar{w}(t) \quad [57]$$

equation (56) becomes:

$$v_i(t+1) = [1 + \lambda(t) - < \lambda(t) > - < a(t) >]v_i(t) + a(t) \quad [58]$$

where we have again neglected the fluctuation of $\bar{w}$ during the time $t \to t+1$ and set $\frac{\bar{w}(t)}{\bar{w}(t+1)} = 1$. This can be justified rigorously for $\alpha > 1$ in the large N limit as the size of the largest w_i is (cf. Solomon 1998) of order $O(\bar{w}N^{1-\alpha}) << 1$ and therefore the changes in $\bar{w}(t)$ induced by updating any single w_i are negligible to leading order (in N). In finite systems $N < \infty$ and for $\alpha < 1$, there are (computable) corrections.

The key observation now is that the system eq. (58) assumes the form of N **decoupled** equations of the form (50) with the effective multiplicative stochastic factor

$$\tilde{\lambda} = 1 + \lambda(t) - <\lambda(t)> - <a(t)>$$ [59]

This implies that the results of the single linear stochastic agent model eq. (50) can be applied now to the $v_i(t)$ in order to obtain

$$P(v) \sim v^{-1-\alpha}$$ [60]

which in turn yields

$$P(w) \sim w^{-1-\alpha}$$ [61]

with the exponent α dictated by the equation eq. (51)(59):

$$<[1 + \lambda(t) - <\lambda(t)> - a(t)]^\alpha> = 1$$ [62]

This demonstrates that the wealth distribution in a economic model based on GLV is a power law. In addition, it is easy to see using (58) that the elementary steps in the time variations of the average wealth are distributed according to a (truncated) power law. Consequently, it was predicted that the market returns will be distributed by $L_\alpha(\bar{w})$ a truncated Levy distribution of index α (Solomon 1998). This turned out to be in accordance with the actual experimental data (Mantegna and Stanley 1996).

Note that similarly to the passage from the single agent system eq. (7)(20) to the many agents system coupled by the lower bound eq. (40)(41), here too, the **formal** reduction of the GLV to a single agent system implies very different properties in the actual "physical" system.

In particular, while in the single agent system the average of λ was crucial in the fixing of the exponent α and had to have an average less then 1, in the multi-agent model, the average value of λ cancels in the expression (59) for $\tilde{\lambda}$. On the other hand, while the additive term in eq (50) had no role in the fixing of α, the corresponding term a is one of the crucial factors determining α in GLV (cf. eq. (62)). Moreover, while the parameters in the eq. (50) model permitted time variations in the $\bar{w}$ only at the price of variations in the exponent α, in the GLV system, one may arbitrarily change the ecological/economic conditions c to vary the total population/wealth by orders of magnitude (cf. eq. (55)) without affecting either the power law or its exponent: indeed, $\bar{\lambda}$ is independent on c and so is the solution of $<\bar{\lambda}^\alpha> = 1$.

11. The Financial interpretation of GLV

In this section we discuss the various terms appearing in the equations, their interpretation in the financial markets applications, their effects and their implications for the phenomenology of the financial markets.

We first discuss the assumption that the individual investments/gains/losses are proportional to the individual wealth:

$$w(t + 1) = \lambda w(t)$$

This is actually not true for the low income/wealth individuals whose incomes do not originate in the stock market. In fact the additive term $a\bar{w}$ tries to account for the additional amounts originating in subsidies, salaries, and other fixed incomes. However, for the range of wealth where one expects power laws to hold ($w > \bar{w}$), it is well documented that the investment policies, the investment decisions, and the measured yearly income are in fact proportional to the wealth itself.

The statistical uniformity of the relative gains and losses of the market participants is an expression of the weak form of market efficiency. It implies the lack of arbitrage opportunities: one cannot obtain systematically higher gains $\lambda - 1$ than the market average without assuming higher risks. For instance, if the distribution of λ were systematically larger for small-w-investors, then the large-w-investors would only have to split their wealth in independently managed parts to mimic that low-w superior performance. This would lead to an equalization of their λ to the λ of the low-w investors. Consequently in the distribution $\Pi(\lambda)$ will end up w-independent as assumed in GLV.

Almost every realistic microscopic market model we have studied in the past shares this characteristics of w-independent $\Pi(\lambda)$ distribution.

Turning to the terms relevant for the lower-bound w region, the assumption that the average wealth contributes to the individual wealth $a\bar{w}$ and the alternative mechanism assuming a lower bound proportional to the average $q\bar{w}$ are both simplified mechanisms to prevent the indefinite reduction of wealth.

In practice they might be objectionable: it is not clear that the state subsidies can be invoked to save bankrupt investors (though this happens often when large important employers are at risk or when their collapse would endanger the stability of the entire system). In any case, the term $a\bar{w}$ appropriately takes into account the arbitrariness of the money denominations. More precisely, assume that (by inflation or by currency renaming) the nominal value of all the money in the economy becomes 10 times larger. Then the subsidies term $a\bar{w}$ will become 10 times larger preserving in this way the actual absolute value. So to speak, multiplying a quantity by $\bar{w}$ expresses it in "absolute currency".

The mechanisms controlling the lower bound behavior of the system may be considered as just parametrizations of the continuum flow of investors/capital to and from the large-w investor ranges relevant for the financial markets trading. It is however possible that the subsidies to the very poorest find their way (through the multiplicative random walk) into the middle class and end-up in the large-w scaling region in the way our models suggest.

More theoretical and experimental research is necessary in order to discriminate between the various alternatives (or to recognize them as different aspects of the same phenomenon).

For instance one can look at the relation between q and α as essentially kinematic in the sense that given the power law, it is unavoidable that the lower bound $q\bar{w}$ would govern the exponent of the power law.

It would still be interesting to study in detail how the wealth pumped at the lower-bound barrier makes its way to the large w tail and or, alternatively in the case of stationary $\bar{w}$, to find the way in which the additive subsidies to the low-w individuals in our models are covered by the "middle classes".

For instance in the $q\bar{w}$ lower-bound model, the dominant mechanism of extracting wealth from the middle class seems to be accelerated inflation. More specifically, the updating of the individual w_i's induces changes in $\bar{w}$ which in turn induces changes in the position of the lower bound $q\bar{w}$. This, in turn, leads to the necessity to subsidize immediately all the w_i's situated between the old and the new poverty line. Finally, this leads to the increase of $\bar{w}$ and to the completion of the positive feedback loop. When looking at the normalized wealth $v_i = w_i/\bar{w}$, this accelerated inflation is effectively a proportional tax which reduces the λ gains to smaller relative gains $\tilde{\lambda} = \lambda w(t)/w(t+1)$.

In the case of the GLV model, there is no inflation (for constant c, $\bar{w}$ is - modulo local fluctuations - constant in time). The extraction of funds from the middle class for subsidies is quite explicit ¿From the way the subsidies term $a\bar{w}$ is affecting negatively $(-a)$ the λ gain value eq. (39) it is clear that the subsidies are partially gathered in this model on the expense of the growth of the middle class. However most of the loss in λ eq. (39) comes from the term $(- <\lambda >)$. This means that it is due mainly to the competition between the large traders $-cw_i\bar{w}$.

It would appear that the government has the choice of either enforcing such a proportional tax and keep $\bar{w}$ roughly constant, or just printing the money which it dispenses to the poor and letting the inflation tax the other classes. One can of course make compromises between these 2 extremes by allowing both taxation and inflation. In any case, the net result can be only variations in the relative size of the middle class (variations of α) as the generic emergence of the power law will be very difficult to avoid.

A government may try to get a more equalitarian distributions (increasing α) by increasing q. However this would reduce an even larger population to the neighborhood of the poverty line. This would require more and more frequent subsidies to enforce and consequently (according to the analysis above) higher taxes and/or faster inflation.

Fearing this, another government might decide for low values of α. This would not only mean an increase of the ratio between the richest and poorest which might be morally questionable but also lead to dramatically unstable fluctuations in the market (e.g. in $\bar{w}$). Indeed, one can show that typically the largest trader owns $O(N^{1-\alpha})$ of the total wealth. For finite N and very low q, α may be shown to drop below 1 (in contrast to eq. (49)). This would imply that almost all the wealth is owned by the largest w_i. It is well know however that the single agent discrete logistic map eq. (1) leads generically to chaotic unstable dynamical regime (May 1976).

In between these extremes it may be that there is not much choice of dynamically consistent α values outside the experimentally measured range $1.4 < \alpha < 1.7$. These values correspond (through eq. (49)) to poverty lines between $0.3 < q < 0.4$. Larger values of q would imply that almost everybody is subsidized while significantly lower values would mean the poorest cannot literally live: the average wages in an economy are automatically tuned as to ensure that a family of 3 can fulfill the needs considered basic by the society on a one-salary income. Somebody earning less than $\frac{1}{3}\bar{w}$ will therefore have serious problems to live a normal life. In fact, such a person might be exposed to hunger (even in very rich economies) since even the prices of the basic food are tuned to the level of affordability of the average family in the given economy.

Far from implying a fatalistic attitude of the economic facts of life, the analysis of our simplified models might lead in more realistic instances to ideas and prescriptions for dynamically steering the social economic policies to optimal parameters both from the technical/efficiency and from the human/moral point of view.

They might help transcend (through unification) the traditional dichotomy by which science is only in charge of deciding true from false while humanities are only in charge of discerning good from bad.

12. Further Economics applications of GLV

As mentioned a few times, the GLV systems can be applied to many power laws.

Even within the financial framework there are a few apparently different realizations of the GLV dynamics and of the power laws.

For instance, one can consider the market as a set of companies $i = 1, \ldots, N$ whose shares are traded and whose prices vary in time accordingly.

One can interpret then w_i as the capitalization of the company i, i.e. the total wealth of all the market shares of the company.

The time evolution of w_i can still be represented by eq. (2). In this case, λ represents the fluctuations in the market worth of the company. For a given total number of shares, λ is measured by the change in the individual share price. These changes take place during individual transactions and are typically fractions of the nominal share price (measured in percents or in points).

With such an interpretation, a represents the correlation between the worth of each company and the market index. This correlation is similar for entire classes of shares and differences in the a's of various economic sectors result in the modern portfolio theory in "risk premia" which affect their effective returns $\tilde{\lambda}$ in a way similar to our formulae in a previous section (low correlation a corresponds to larger effective incomes).

The coefficient c represents the competition between the companies for the finite amount of money in the market (and express also the limits in their own absolute worth). We do not need to consider c a constant. Temporal increases in the resources may lead to lower values of c which in turn lead to increases in $\bar{w}$. However, as seen before, such changes do not affect the exponent of the power law distribution.

In this interpretation, the GLV model will predict the emergence of a power-law in the probability distribution of company sizes (capitalization). In particular, this would imply that the weights of the various companies composing the S&P 500 are distributed by a power law. This would imply in turn that the S&P fluctuations follow a truncated Levy distribution of corresponding index.

Yet another interpretation is to consider w_i as the size of coordinated trader sets (i.e. the number of traders adopting a similar investment policy) and assuming that the sizes of these sets vary self-catalytically according to the random factor λ while the a term represents the diffusion of traders between the sets. Such an autocatalytic dynamics for the trading schools is not surprising as their decision processes involve elements similar to the use of common language, common values, which are central in the dynamics of languages and nations (which fulfill power laws). The nonlinear term c represents then the competition between these investing schools for individual traders membership. In fact if a and c fulfill the relation $a/c = \bar{w}$, the corresponding two terms in GLV taken together represent (in "absolute currency" $\bar{w}$) the act of each of the schools loosing (shedding) a certain c fraction of its followers which are then spread uniformly between the schools.

Such an interpretation of the GLV would predict a power-law in the distribution of trader schools sizes (similar to countries sizes). Again, such a distribution would account for the truncated Levy distribution of market fluctuations (with index equal to the exponent of the power-law governing trader sets sizes).

It would be interesting to discriminate between the validity of the various GLV interpretations by experimentally studying the market fluctuations and the distributions of respectively individual wealth, companies capitalization and correlated investors sets. It is not ruled out that some of these interpretations may be consistent with each other. This in turn would be consistent in turn with the modern portfolio theory claim on the existence of a "market portfolio" (stochastically) common to most of the traders.

Further developments of the GLV model will include introducing variable number of agents N, studying the role of the discretization of the w_i changes (due to indivisible units like people, shares, etc), taking into account the influence of the history of $w(t)$ on λ etc..

13. Acknowledgements

The research was supported in part by the Germany-Israel Foundation. My thinking on the subject has been influenced by many colleagues who share similar ideas (see refs.): P. W. Anderson, A. Agay, P. Bak, J-P. Bouchaud, R. Cont, F. Fucito, K. Illinsky, H. Levy, M. Levy, T. Lux, G. Mack, R. Mantegna, M. Marsili, S. Maslov, R. Savit, D. Sornette, H.E. Stanley, D. Stauffer, A. Weigend, G. Weisbuch, Y-C. Zhang.

I benefited also from many illuminating discussions on the subject with Prof. Shlomo Alexander who will be always remembered as a brilliant scientist, a broad intellectual, and a symbol of the eternal youth.

14. References

P. W. Anderson, J. Arrow and D. Pines, eds. The Economy as an Evolving Complex System (Redwood City, Calif.: Addison-Wesley, 1988);

P. W. Anderson in The Economy as an Evolving Complex System II (Redwood City, Calif.: Addison-Wesley, 1995), eds. W. B. Arthur, S. N. Durlauf, and D. A. Lane

R.Baillie and T.Bollerslev, Rev. of Econ. Studies 58 (1990) 565

P. Bak, M. Paczuski and M. Shubik, Physica A 246, Dec. 1, No 3-4, 430 (1997).

O. Biham, O. Malcai, M. Levy, S. Solomon, Phys. Rev. E **58**, 1352 (1998)

Blank A., Sorin Solomon cond-mat/0003240 Power Laws and Cities Population

R. Cahalan and J. Joseph, Monthly Weather Review **117**, 261 (1989)

D. G. Champernowne, Econometrica **63**, 318 (1953) Hellthaler T.,Int. J. Mod. Phys. C, vol 6, (1995) 845

Ijiri Y. and H. A. Simon, *Skew Distributions and the Sizes of Business Firms* (North-Holland, Amsterdam, 1977)

H. Kesten, Acta Math. **131**, 207 (1973)

Kim G.R. & Markowitz H.M. (1989) J. Portfolio Management, Fall 1989, 45.

Louzoun Y, Sorin Solomon, Henri Atlan, Irun. R. Cohen nlin.AO/0006043 Microscopic Discrete Proliferating Components Cause the Self-Organized Emergence of Macroscopic Adaptive Features in Biological Systems

T. Lux "The Socio-Economic Dynamics of Speculative Markets: Interacting Agents, Chaos, and the Fat Tails of Return Distributions", in: Journal of Economic Behavior and Organization Vol. 33 (1998), pp. 143 - 165

"Time Variation of Second Moments from a Noise Trader/Infection Model", in: Journal of Economic Dynamics and Control Vol. 22 (1997), pp. 1 - 3

"The Stable Paretian Hypothesis and the Frequency of Large Returns: An Examination of Major German Stocks", in: Applied Financial Economics Vol. 6 (1996), pp. 463

"Long-term Stochastic Dependence in Financial Prices: Evidence from the German Stock Market", in: Applied Economics Letters Vol. 3 (1996), pp. 701 - 706

R. N. Mantegna and H. E. Stanley, Phys. Rev. Lett. **73**, 2946 (1994)

R. N. Mantegna and H. E. Stanley, Nature **376**, 46 (1995)

R. N. Mantegna and H. E. Stanley, Nature **383**, 587 (1996)

R. N. Mantegna and H. E. Stanley, Physica A **239**, 255 (1997)

B. Mandelbrot, Comptes Rendus **232**, 1638 (1951)

B. Mandelbrot, Econometrica **29**, 517 (1961)

M. Marsili, S. Masvlov and Y.-C. Zhang: Dynamical optimization thery of a divesified portfolio, Physica A 253 (1998) 403-418

S. Galluccio, G. Caldarelli, M. Marsili, Y.-C. Zhang: Scaling in currency exchange, Physica A 245 (1997) 423-436

G. Caldarelli, G. Marsili, Y.-C. Zhang: A Prototype Model of Stock Exchange, cond-mat/9709118, Europhysics Letters 40, p479

R.M. May, Nature 261 (1976) 207

Moss De Oliveira S., P.M.C de Oliveira, D. Stauffer; Springer-Verlag Sex, Money, War and Computers: Nontraditional Applications of Computational Statistical Mechanics; 1998

V. Pareto, Cours d'Economique Politique, Vol 2 (1897)

S. Redner, Am. J. Phys. 58 (3)

M. Shatner, L. Muchnik, M. Leshno, S. Solomon cond-mat/0005430 A Continuous Time Asynchronous Model of the Stock Market; Beyond the LLS Model

M. F. Shlesinger and E. W. Montroll, Proc. Nat. Acad. Sci. USA (Appl. Math. Sci.) **79**, 3380 (1982)

Shnerb N.M., E. Bettelheim, Y. Louzoun, O. Agam, S. Solomon cond-mat/0007097 Adaptation of Autocatalytic Fluctuations to Diffusive Noise

Shnerb N.M., Yoram Louzoun, Eldad Bettelheim, Sorin Solomon adap-org/9912005 The Importance of Being Discrete - Life Always Wins on the Surface to appear in Proc.Nat.Acad.Sci

H. A. Simon and C. P. Bonini, Amer. Econ. Rev. **48**, 607 (1958)

S. Solomon, Ann. Rev. Comp. Phys. II p243 (World Scientific 1995) ed. D. Stauffer

S. Solomon and M. Levy, J. Mod. Phys. C **7**, 745 (1996); adap-org/9609002

S. Solomon, Computational Finance 97 (Kluwer Academic Publishers 1998) eds. A.P.-N. Refens A.N. Burgess and J.E. Moody

Solomon S, Moshe Levy cond-mat/0005416 Market Ecology, Pareto Wealth Distribution and Leptokurtic Returns in Microscopic Simulation of the LLS Stock Market Model in Proceedings of Complex behavior in economics: Aix en Provence (Marseille), France, May 4-6,2000

D. Sornette and R. Cont , J. Phys. I France 7 (1997) 431

D. Sornette and A. Johansen, Physics A, vol 245 (1997) 411

D. Sornette: Multiplicative processes and power laws (1998) Phys. Rev. E 57, p 4811-4813

D. Stauffer and D. Sornette: Log-periodic oscillations for biased diffusion on random lattice Physica A 252 (1998) 271-277

H. E. Stanley, Europhys. Lett. **49**, 453 (1995) and M. H. R. Stanley, L. A. N. Amaral, S. V. Buldyrev, S. Havlin, H. Leschhorn, P.Maass, M. A. Salinger, and H. E Stanley; Nature 1996, vol 379, p 804.

Takayasu H., Miura H., Hirabayashi T. and Hamada K.: Statistical properties of deterministic threshold elements - the case of market price, Physica A 184 (1992) 127

Takayasu H., Sato A.-H. and Takayasu M.: Stable infinite fluctuations in randomly amplified Langevin systems, Phys. Rev. Lett. 79 (1997) 966

Takayasu H. and Okuyama K.: Country dependence on company size distributions and a numerical model based on competition and cooperation, Fractals 6 (1998) 67

Fractals in the Physical Sciences H. Takayasu J. Wiley & Sons Chichester 1990

C. Tsallis, J. Stat. Phys. **52**, 479 (1988).

N.Vandewalle and M.Ausloos: Coherent and random sequences in financial fluctuations, Physica A 246 (1997) 454

N. Vandewalle, M Ausloos: Multi-affine analysis of typical currency exchange rates, The European Physical Journal B 4 (1998) 257-261

N. Vandewalle, M. Ausloos, Ph. Boveroux and A. Minguet: How the financial crash of october 1997 could have been predicted, The Eur. Phys. J. B 4 (1998) 139-143

N. Vandewalle, P. Boveroux, A. Minguet, M. Ausloos: The crash of October 1987 seen as a phase transition: amplitude and universality, Physica A 255 (1998) 201

N.Vandewalle and M.Ausloos: Sparseness and Roughness of foreign exchange rates, Int. J. Mod. Phys. C 9 (1998) 711

N.Vandewalle and M.Ausloos: Extended Detrended Fluctuation Analysis for financial data,Int. J. Comput. Anticipat. Syst. 1 (1998) 342

U. G. Yule, Phil. Trans. B. **213**, 21 (1924)

Zhang W.B. (1991) *Synergetic Economics*. Springer, Berlin-Heidelberg.

G. K. Zipf, Human Behavior and the Principle of Least Effort (Addison-Wesley Press, Cambridge, MA, 1949)

Psychological factors affecting market dynamics: the role of uncertainty and need satisfaction

Marco A. Janssen[*] — Wander Jager[**]

[*] *Department of Spatial Economics*
Vrije Universiteit, De Boelelaan 1105
1081 HV Amsterdam, The Netherlands
m.janssen@econ.vu.nl

[**] *Centre for Environmental and Traffic Psychology*
University of Groningen, Grote Kruisstraat 2/I
9712 TS Groningen, The Netherlands
w.jager@ppsw.rug.nl

ABSTRACT: *Markets can show different types of dynamics, ranging from stable markets dominated by one or a few products, to fluctuating markets where products are frequently being replaced by new versions. This paper explores the dynamics of markets from a psychological perspective using a multi-agent simulation model. The behavioural rules of the artificial consumers, the consumats, are based on a conceptual meta-theory from psychology. The artificial consumers have to choose each period between different products. Products remain on the market for as long as their market share exceeds a minimum level. If not, it will be replaced by a new product.*

Simulation experiments are being performed with a population of consumats having different preferences. Results show that the dominating type of cognitive (choice) process has large consequences for the resulting market dynamics. Moreover, the size of the social network affects the market dynamics too.

KEYWORDS: *social networks, consumer behaviour, market dynamics*

1. *Introduction*

In daily life consumers act on many different markets. Some markets are stable and are dominated by one or a few product, whereas other markets are fluctuating, where new products frequently replace old ones. Not only prices affect the market dynamics, but also psychological factors and processes, such as habits, imitation and the identity value of products. These factors may explain why the market in e.g., daily food products is relatively stable, whereas markets of e.g. clothing and toys show fashion and fad dynamics. In this paper we will demonstrate how the cognitive processes underlying product choice explain such differences in market dynamics. Moreover, attention will be given to the size of the social network in which consumption takes place.

We will present a multi-agent simulation model in which artificial consumers, called consumats, choose every time-step which product to consume. The cognitive process that dominates this choice process depends on their level of need satisfaction and uncertainty. The needs refer to the individual preferences the consumats have for products (individual need), and how many neighbours in their social network consume the same product (social need). We explore the consequences of different degrees of uncertainty tolerance and different minimum levels of satisfaction. As a sensitivity test we explore the consequences of connectiveness of social networks.

The paper is built up as follows. The structure of social networks is discussed in Section 2. Section 3 describes the conceptual framework to simulate artificial consumers, the consumats. The simulation model is described in Section 4 and the experiments with the model are reported in Section 5. Section 6 concludes.

2. *Structure of social networks*

Social networks refer to the links between people in a large population. Social networks are characterised by two effects, namely the small-world effect and the clustering effect [NEW 99]. The small-world effect refers to the experience that despite the large population, the map of who knows whom is such that we are all very closely connected to one another. An interesting example is the analysis of the properties of the network of hyperlinks between documents on the World Wide Web. Despite about a billion of documents on the web, the average distance between documents was estimated only to be about 19 hyperlinks [ALB 99]. Social networks seem to be structured in such a way that information can be spread fast. Another aspect of social networks is the existence of clusters. People's circles of acquaintance tend to overlap to a great extent. Your friend's friends are likely also to be your friends.

[WAT 98] proposed a model for social networks that fits very well on both small-world and clustering characteristics. Their suggestion was to build a model that is a regular lattice having some degree of randomness in it (Figure 1). They construct the network by taking a lattice of periodic boundary conditions, and go through each of the links on the lattice (causing the clustering effect). With some probability s that link is being rewired by moving one of its ends to a new randomly chosen position (causing the small-world effect). More formal discussions on the characteristics of these types of networks can be found in [WAT 98] and [NEW 99].

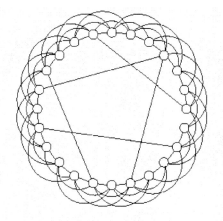

Figure 1. *A Watts-Strogatz model of social networks*

3. *The consumat approach*

Many behavioural theories, like theories about human needs, motivational processes, social comparison theory, social learning theory, theory of reasoned action and so on, all explain parts of the processes that determine consumer behaviour. Social psychology is often discussed to be in a pre-paradigm state. According to some scholars there is a need for a meta-theory of human behaviour [VAL 94]. The consumat approach is based on a comprehensive conceptual model of consumer behaviour (Figure 2), and as such tries to offer such a meta-theory [JAG 00]. Based on this conceptual model, a multi-agent simulation model has been developed. In most multi-agent models the decision rules of the agents have not been developed on the basis of psychological theory. The consumat approach has been developed to provide a broad framework for introducing psychologically validated rules in agent rules.

The consumat approach starts with the driving forces at the collective (macro) and the individual (micro) level, which determine the environmental setting for the consumat behaviour. The collective level refers to technical, economical, demographic, institutional and cultural developments, and thus describes the world the consumats are living in. The individual level refers to the consumats, which are equipped with needs which may be more or less satisfied, are confronted with opportunities to consume, and that have various abilities to consume the opportunities. Furthermore, consumats have a certain degree of uncertainty, depending on the difference between expected and actual outcomes of their behaviour.

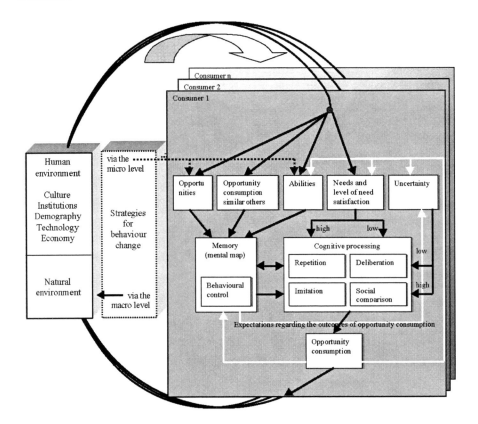

Figure 2. *A conceptual model of consumer behaviour*

The consumats may engage in different cognitive processes in deciding how to behave, depending on their level of need satisfaction N and degree of uncertainty U. Consumats having a low level of need satisfaction and a low degree of uncertainty are assumed to *deliberate*, that is: to determine the consequences of all possible decisions given a fixed time-horizon in order to maximise level of need satisfaction. Consumats having a low level of need satisfaction and a high degree of uncertainty are assumed to *socially compare*. This implies the comparison of own previous behaviour with the previous behaviour of consumats having about similar abilities, and selecting that behaviour which yields a maximal level of need satisfaction. When consumats have a high level of need satisfaction, but also a high level of uncertainty, they will *imitate* the behaviour of other similar consumats. Finally, consumats having a high level of need satisfaction and a low level of uncertainty habitually *repeat* their previous behaviour. When consumats engage in reasoned behaviour (deliberation and social comparison) they will update the information in their mental map, which serves as a memory to store information on abilities, opportunities, and characteristics of other agents.

After the consumption of opportunities, a new level of need satisfaction will be derived, and changes will occur regarding their abilities, opportunities and the social and physical environment, which will affect the consumption in succeeding time steps. In the following section we will formalise the consumat approach for a dynamic market with a fixed number of products.

4. The model

A simple dynamic market system is developed in which a large number of consumats consume one product on each time-step [JAN 00]. Products are assumed to differ from each other on two dimensions, d_1 and d_2, which are defined for a range from 0 to 1. For simplicities sake 10 products are assumed to be available on the market. The products have randomised product characteristics for d_1 and d_2. When a product j is introduced on the market it gets an introduction period t_j to be able to built up a market share. After this introduction period the product must have a minimum market share of m_{min} in order to survive. When a product does not have a market share of m_{min} after the introduction period, the product drops out of the market and a new product, with randomised product characteristics, is being introduced.

The survival of products on the market thus depends on whether consumats consume the products. The cognitive process the consumat engages in determines the choice for a particular product. Here the level of need-satisfaction and uncertainty play an important role.

The level of need satisfaction depends on a personal need and a social need. The personal need is assumed to be the preference of the consumat. Each consumat has a specific preference for each of the two dimensions of the product. The level of need satisfaction for the personal need depends on the difference between the dimensions of the consumed product j and the preferred characteristics by the consumat i, p_{1i} and p_{2i}:

$$N_{pi} = 1-[(p_{1i}-d_{1j})^2 +(p_{2i}-d_{2j})^2]^{0.5}/2^{0.5} \qquad [1]$$

The satisfaction of the social need depends on how many neighbouring consumats consume the same product. The social network, which indicates who ones neighbours are, is implemented in line with the Watts-Strogatz model (Figure 1). A market share m can be calculated indicating how many neighbours in the social network consume the same product. We assume that consumats prefer to consume the same as their neighbours as to stress their group identity. The level of need-satisfaction for the social need N_s is higher the more neighbours (on the average 7) consume the same product. A more detailed model of alternative implementations of social needs, such as consumats who prefer to consume a different product than their neighbours can be found in [JAN 00]. More detailed description of the consumat rules and the psychological rationale behind them can be found in [JAG 99] and [JAG 00]. The assumed formulation of social needs results in a level of satisfaction of the need identity equal to the market share of the product j that is consumed by the consumat and their neighbours.

$$N_{si} = m_j \qquad\qquad [2]$$

The total level of need satisfaction is equal to

$$N_i = \beta_i * N_{si} + (1-\beta_i) * N_{pi} \qquad\qquad [3]$$

Where β_i weights the influence of the social need and the personal taste need.

Uncertainty, U_i, is defined as the difference between expected N, which is assumed to be equal to N at time t-1, and the actual N:

$$U_i = (N_i - N_i(t-1)) \qquad\qquad [4]$$

The threshold parameters N_{min}, the minimum level for satisfaction, and U_T, the uncertainty tolerance level, are given. Given the values of N_i and U_i the type of cognitive processing of the consumat can be defined.

- Repetition ($N_i > N_{min}$; $U_i < U_T$)

The consumat continues to consume the product it consumed last time step.

- Deliberation ($N_i < N_{min}$; $U_i < U_T$)

The consumat will evaluate the expected N of each product, and will consume the product with the highest score. When more than one product have the highest score, the choice is at random between the candidate products.

- Imitation ($N_i > N_{min}$; $U_i > U_T$)

The consumat evaluates the product that is being consumed the most in the previous time-step by the other consumats in its social network. This product will be chosen for current consumption. In case two or more products are consumed equally, the choice is at random between the candidate products.

- Social comparison ($N_i < N_{min}$; $U_i > U_T$)

The consumat compares the expected N_i of consuming the same product as in the previous time-step with the expected N_i for the product that is consumed the most in the previous time-step by the other consumats in its social network. The consumat will choose the product with the highest expected N_i. If more products have the same expected N_i, the choice will be at random.

A complicating factor is the fact that products may disappear from the market. When a consumat engages in repetition, but the product has disappeared from the market, it will engage in deliberation to choose a new product for consumption. When a consumat engages in social comparison, and the product that the comparison other consumed has disappeared form the market, the consumat cannot consider this product as a candidate for adoption.

5. Experiments

Consider a market of 100 consumats and 10 products. The minimum market share for survival is defined as 10%, and the introduction period is equal to 5 time steps. A Watts-Strogatz social network is defined where agents are connected with their four nearest neighbours and randomly to each possible other agents, using a probability of 1%. This results in a one-dimensional circle as depicted in Figure 1, where consumats have 7 contacts on the average. The value of β_i, weighting the two needs, is drawn randomly for each consumat from a uniform distribution between 0 and 1. The preferences of the consumats for dimensions 1 and 2 are also drawn from a uniform distribution between 0 and 1. The same holds for the two characteristics of the 10 products.

We will first present the results of two simulation runs involving different conditions regarding the values of N_{min} and U_T: (i) $N_{min} = 0.1$ and $U_T = 0.1$; (ii) $N_{min} = 0.9$ and $U_T = 0.1$. The values in these two conditions are chosen as to derive a variety of different types of cognitive processes. If U_T would be much higher, the consumats would not engage in social processing and the resulting market dynamics would be of less interest for this paper. More detailed discussion of these conditions can be found in [JAN 00]. In Figures 3 and 4 we depict the market shares (3a and 4a) of the ten products and the average distribution of cognitive processes (3b and 4b) for 100 time-steps.

In Figure 3a we observe a typical local lock-in occurring, where a few products end up dominating a local part of market [JAN 99]. Because the consumats are easily satisfied ($N_{min} = 0.1$), but also very quickly uncertain ($U_T = 0.1$), they are mainly engaging in imitation during the first time steps (Figure 3b). This imitation causes that, after about 10 time steps, clusters of consumats have emerged that consume the same product, thereby pushing the alternative products out of the market. Because this clustering causes uncertainty to drop, the consumats become to 'feel' certain. Moreover, the chosen products become more attractive because of their higher social need satisfying capacity. As a consequence the overall level of need satisfaction increases. Being certain and satisfied, the consumats exclusively engage in repetition after time-step 20, thereby creating a stable market.

Examples of such locked-in markets refer typically to dominance of products in local domains of social networks, such as the choice for certain brands of cola, the choice for computer systems (Microsoft versus Apple) and software, and the choice for places to go out and meet other people (e.g., bars, dancings).

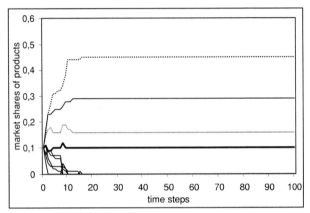

Figure 3a. *Market shares for various products in case $N_{min}=0.1$ and $U_T=0.1$*

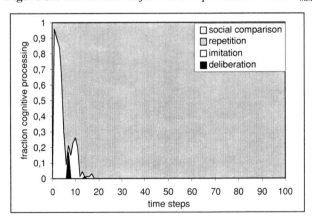

Figure 3b. *Fractions of cognitive processes in case $N_{min}=0.1$ and $U_T=0.1$*

In Figure 4a we observe large oscillations in the market. Here, the consumats are very hard to satisfy (N_{min} = 0.9), and very quickly uncertain. As a consequence, the consumats engage primarily in social comparison and deliberation, as can be seen in Figure 4b. What can be clearly seen is that different products replace each other in having a leading market position. Here, the social comparison process causes that many consumats are starting to consume the same product, because it yields a higher N_i than the product they consumed before. The more consumats consume the same product, the lower uncertainty gets, thereby stimulating the consumats to engage in deliberation. As a consequence, the consumats immediately perceive new attractive products, which, when attractive enough, may dispel the 'old' opportunity from the market. Because the consumats in networks will experience a high level of need satisfaction for identity when they are consuming the same product, the overall N is very high during the periods in which a product dominates the market.

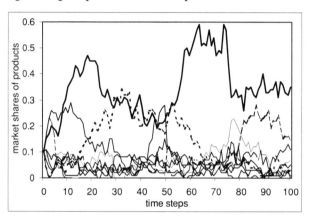

Figure 4a. *Market shares for various products in case N_{min}=0.9 and U_T=0.1*

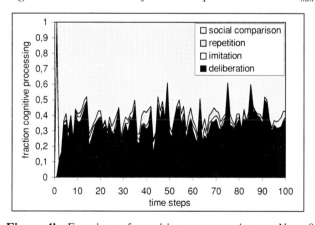

Figure 4b. *Fractions of cognitive processes in case N_{min}=0.9 and U_T=0.1*

This type of market typically resembles fashion markets for products that are bought repetitively (clothing, Pokémon cards, hair-cuts), where people are frequently uncertain regarding what is in vogue, and think it is very important that they consume in a fashionable manner. Especially the consumptive behaviour of young adolescents, who are often very uncertain regarding their developing identity, may display such fashion effects.

The two above presented conditions show the different possible types of market dynamics. To test if these results are robust we will perform 100 simulation runs for each of the two conditions. In the default case we use a social network with $s = 1\%$, indicating that each consumat has a chance of 1% to be linked to an arbitrary other consumat, additional to the four local neighbours each consumat is linked to. An indicator of the type of market that emerges is the number of products that have a market share higher then 10% after the introduction period of 5 years. In case of a lock-in of one product, this amount of products will be close to one, but in case of unstable markets this can go up to 40 products in a simulation period of 100 time steps.

For the two conditions we present the average number of products of 100 runs (Table 1). The results confirm the earlier examples. In condition (i) we observe on the average four products that survive the introduction period. This low number is explained by local lock-ins of the products. In condition 2 (ii) we observe a much higher numbers of products.

To perform a sensitivity analysis, we replicated the previous two conditions, only this time with a s of 0% and 10%. A s of 0% implies that information can only be transferred via local links, which implies a slower spreading of information in comparison to the default runs. A s of 10% implies more random links, indicating a faster information spreading than in the default runs.

Table 1. *Number of products which penetrate the market in a period of 100 time steps, for the default case (s=1%), two alternative degrees of social networks and different assumption on status needs, for different assumptions on N_{min} and U_T*

	N_{min} (Low) U_T (Low)	N_{min} (High) U_T (Low)
Default s = 1%	4.3	16.7
s = 0%	4.1	17.9
s = 10%	1.1	8.2

Table 1 shows that, in general, the more links in the social network (a higher s), the lower the amount of products that have survived (Table 1). This implies that when consumats have a low uncertainty tolerance, and therefore engage more in social processing, larger networks lead to faster dominance of one or a few products.

To derive an indicator of the degree to which consumption has locked-in, we determine for each neighbouring pair of consumats (100 pairs on the circle of Figure 1) if they consume the same product or not. If all pairs consume the same product, the value of the indicator is 0, indicating a global lock-in. A value close to 1 indicates that a small fraction of the pairs consume the same product, indicating that consumption is random.

Table 2 shows that under the condition of a low N_{min} and low U_T the indicator values are lower than in the condition with a high N_{min} and low U_T. This suggests that when consumats imitate a lot (in the early stages), the chances on a locked-in consumption pattern increase. Only within the low N_{min} and low U_T condition we observe an effect of the number of links between the consumats. This indicates that the small-world effect has only an impact if the consumats engage mainly in imitation (in the first time-steps). Here it can be seen that when there are more links between the consumats, they all become to consume the same due to a global lock-in.

Table 2. *Fraction of closest two neighbouring pairs consuming a different product at time-step 100, for different assumptions on N_{min} and U_T*

	N_{min} (Low) U_T (Low)	N_{min} (High) U_T (Low)
Default s = 1%	0.34	0.74
s = 0%	0.33	0.73
s = 10%	0.00	0.71

6. Conclusions

It appears that cognitive processes are an important determinant of market dynamics. The experiments presented in this paper demonstrated that uncertainty in consumats may cause very different market dynamics, depending on the minimum level of need satisfaction they aspire. If uncertain consumats have a low aspiration level, a stable market emerges where a few products survive. A high aspiration level of uncertain consumats yields a very unstable market, where products push each other away in dominating the market.

When we realise that uncertainty also plays an important role in the decision of consumers in their daily lives, especially when it concerns expensive and nonroutine consumer goods, the above described dynamics may be helpful in understanding real market behaviour. Empirical research that includes the decision process of consumers should be performed to obtain some validation for the market dynamics as discussed above. This also notifies that especially the combination of empirical research with simulation experiments may be very fruitful in studying dynamical effects. The hypotheses that result from the simulation experiments may help to identify promising research questions for (experimental) empirical studies, whereas the latter in its turn may provide validation for dynamical effects.

As regards the simulation model that has been used to obtain the results presented in this paper, one of the main omissions is the inadequate modelling of the production side. Important aspects of the model that can be improved are the inclusion of firms and their strategic behaviour to influence the market in order to maximise their profits.

Acknowledgements

We thank Gérard Weisbuch for his comments on an earlier version of this paper, and Jasper Noordam for his contributions on a precursor of the presented model. For more information on the consumat approach we refer to http://go.to/consumats

References

[ALB 99] Albert, R., Jeong H., Barabási, A.-L, "Diameter of the world-wide web", *Nature* , vol. 401, 1999, p. 130-131.

[JAG 00] Jager, W., *Modelling consumer behaviour*, PhD thesis, University of Groningen 2000.

[JAG 99] Jager, W., Janssen, M.A., C.A.J. Vlek, Consumats in a commons dilemma: Testing the behavioural rules of simulated consumers, COV report no. 99-01, 1999, Centre for Environment and Traffic Psychology, University of Groningen, http://www.ppsw.rug.nl/cov/staff/jager/simpaper.pdf.

[JAN 99] Janssen, M.A., Jager, W., "An integrated approach to simulating behavioural processes: A case study of the lock-in of consumption patterns", *Journal of Artificial Societies and Social Simulation,* vol. 2, no. 2, 1999, www.soc.surrey.ac.uk/JASSS/2/2/2.html

[JAN 00] Janssen, M.A., Jager, W., Adoption of new products in a market of changing preferences and social networks, Research Memorandum, 2000, Vrije Universiteit, Amsterdam

[NEW 99] Newman, M.E.J., Small Worlds – The Structure of Social Networks, Santa Fe Institute working paper, 99-12-080, 1999, Santa Fe, NM

[VAL 94] Vallacher, R.R., Nowak, A., The chaos in social psychology, In: R.R. Vallacher, A. Nowak (eds.), *Dynamical systems in social psychology*, San Diego: Academic Press, Inc., 1994

[WAT 98] Watts, D.J., Strogatz, S.H., "Collective dynamics of "small-world" networks", *Nature*, vol. 393, 1998, p. 440-442.

Competition, training, heterogeneity persistence, and aggregate growth in a multi-agent evolutionary model

Gérard Ballot* — Erol Taymaz**

*Université Paris II and ERMES-CNRS
ERMES, Université Paris II, 92, rue d'Assas 75006 Paris France
ballot@u-paris2.fr
**Middle East Technical University, 06531 Ankara, Turkey
etaymaz@metu.edu.tr

ABSTRACT: We use the framework of a multi-agent based macroeconomic model to analyse the possibility in the long run of the coexistence of two alternative types of firm behaviour towards the accumulation of human capital, training and poaching, and its aggregate outcomes. Besides R&D, we assume that firms need workers endowed with general human capital (or competencies) in order to innovate but also, although to much lower extent, in order to imitate innovations. Firms can either train workers or poach trained workers. Firms are assigned a type, and experiments compare the outcomes of the change of key parameters. The main results are: i) the coexistence of trainers and poachers is possible in the long run, and can even be beneficial to the economy when poachers raid inefficient trainers, ii) trainers fare somewhat better than poachers do, iii) mobility costs have a major negative impact on aggregate performance.

RESUME : Nous utilisons le cadre d'un modèle macroéconomique à base d'agents pour analyser la possibilité à long terme de la coexistence de deux types alternatifs de comportements d'entreprises vis à vis de l'accumulation de capital humain, la formation continue et le débauchage. Outre la R&D, nous supposons que les firmes ont besoin de salariés dotés de capital humain pour innover, mais aussi, bien qu'à un degré bien moindre, pour imiter les innovations. Les firmes peuvent ou bien former ou débaucher des salariés formés. Un des deux comportements est affecté à chaque firme, et les simulations permettent de comparer les effets des changements de paramètres -clés. Les résultats importants sont que i)la coexistence des deux types est possible à long terme, et peut même être bénéfique à l'économie quand des firmes débauchent des salariés des firmes formatrices inefficientes, ii)les formateurs ont des performances un peu supérieures iii)les coûts de mobilité ont un impact majeur négatif sur la performance agrégée.

KEY WORDS : multi-agent model, evolutionary economics, training, growth

MOTS-CLES : modèle multi-agent, économie évolutionniste, formation continue, croissance

1. Introduction

Endogenous growth theory has emphasised the role of human capital for aggregate growth with the very influential contribution of Lucas [LUC 88] . Human capital is an input in the aggregate production function. *Growth* of human capital is required to obtain the *growth* of productivity. Without a positive accumulation of human capital, decreasing returns set in and the economy reaches a stationary state. However another, indirect, mechanism has more recently been developed to explain how human capital can increase the ability to innovate, as well as the ability to imitate and adopt an existing innovation. An important difference with the previous story is that here the *level* of the stock of human capital determines the flow rate of innovation, and therefore the *growth* rate of productivity and GNP. The seminal model dates back to Nelson & Phelps [NEL 66], but is now receiving increasing attention in endogenous growth theory along a approach which labels itself Schumpeterian because of its emphasis on innovation as the necessary condition for growth. Human capital and R&D appear as complementary factors. Aghion & Howitt [AGH 98] formulate some models and clearly distinguish the two theories. The empirical tests on aggregate data by Benhabib & Spiegel [BEN 94] tend to validate the second theory. Our modelling of the firm adopts a synthetic approach. It considers specific human capital as an input in the firm production function, in the Lucas' tradition. For general human capital, it follows the Nelson-Phelps view which offers rich insights.

Lucas focused on certain types of human capital: education and learning by doing. However training of employees (paid by the firm or not) is an important type of human capital and should have the same effects, but its particularity is that the decision is made by the firm, and not by the individuals or the government. Training is therefore an intentional investment made by the firm, and a strategic variable for its performance.

2. Firms heterogeneity, training and poaching, and growth

The firms should then invest in training with the only restraint that their resources are limited, even if they can borrow or issue equities. There are also alternative uses of resources, such as investment in physical capital, R&D, or advertising which compete with training expenditures. However the preceding reasoning considers a representative firm. In fact firms are heterogeneous, and, at a certain date, are endowed with certain stocks of specific and general human capital, and a certain technology, which constrain their behaviour. There is path dependency. Therefore those with a low level of human capital should innovate less, and make less profits, have less resources, invest less in training. A vicious cycle sets in and leads to decline and possibly failure. Firms with a high human capital should undergo a virtuous cycle and grow. In the long run there should remain only firms with a high human capital and high training investments, or a distribution of firms according to their level of human capital and profits, with a higher probability of exit for the firms with a low human capital. This is an evolutionary story, but the conclusion is the same as for the reasoning in terms of a representative firm. The firms should invest in training up to an optimal level.

However, a more realistic look at the labour market considers the possibility of poaching to acquire human capital rather than training. A firm needs only to offer a wage a little higher to a worker to induce him to quit a training firm and benefit from the skills of this worker without paying for the investment, if mobility costs are negligible. In reaction to this behaviour firms should not train. This is the neoclassical story initiated by Becker [BEC 75] for general human capital, defined precisely by its tranferability. Firms should only invest in specific human capital, and workers should share this investment and undergo all the general training expenditures (or the government should supply it).

However several studies such as Barron, Black and Lowenstein [BAR 89] or Bishop [BIS 91] show that firms undergo some general training expenditures. Several recent theories have recently been built to explain this behaviour.

We develop here further an explanation we have called training for the rent [BAL 94]. It incorporates the effect of the general human capital level on the flow of innovations in the line of Nelson-Phelps. First we should emphasise that general human capital is the only type of human capital which generates radical innovation. This contrasts with small (incremental) innovations which can be generated by both general and specific human capital. Firms can accumulate human capital either by investing in general training or by hiring educated workers from other firms or unemployment, since general human capital is transferable. Firms which invest in general training (the trainers) increase their probability of doing big innovations, and stochastically increase their profits for some time, since an innovation gives them a temporary monopoly or monopolistic power. This allows them to raise the wages to retain the trained workers. However some other firms succeed in poaching i.e. attracting workers who then quit their current firm. More precisely they poach workers from firms which have invested in general training (and R&D) and have not innovated, hence have not been able to pay higher wages. However the poachers are not without their own difficulties. Since the trainers impose a technological competition, the poachers must also spend on R&D. This investment, even with the help of poached workers, takes some time to induce technical progress for the poaching firm. The lag means that this type of firm may not get any profit if the innovation is of a process type, and may only share the new market if it is of a product innovation type. Poaching firms may prefer to adopt existing innovations. This behaviour does require some absorptive capacity as emphasised by Cohen and Levinthal [COH 90]. This capacity is based on technological capital and human capital, but the stocks needed should be less important than for innovation.

This story hints at the possibility for trainers and poachers to coexist in the long run. Trainers spend high amounts of resources in general training and R&D, and obtain a temporary rent as a return. Poachers obtain some general skills by poaching, and do some limited R&D. They adopt and improve existing innovations, and also gain some profits. The coexistence is a possibility, but not certain. Poachers could eliminate trainers, or the reverse.

The distribution of firms between trainers and poachers may have an important macroeconomic impact. If trainers dominate, the aggregate investment in training should be high, and growth of output should be also high. The reverse is true if poachers dominate. Some features of the labour market may also interact with this distribution to affect growth, notably mobility costs and the possibility that trainers lower individually their investment as a response to quits. The paper will investigate these questions within an agent based macro model. Such a model is able to investigate the macroeconomic effects of the heterogeneity of firms behavior, whilst at the same time examining the possibility of the persistence of such an heterogeneity. We now summarise the model.

3. The model

MOSES (Model of the Swedish Economic System) has been constructed primarily to analyse industrial evolution on the basis of firms' decisions, and is designed to reproduce the effects of this evolution on the macro accounts as well as on some distributional patterns concerning firms. It is a micro based endogenous growth model initially built be Eliasson [ELI 77] and continuously improved and updated since[1]. Manufacturing is modelled both at the level of the individual firm and at the sectoral or market level, whereas in other models of the aggregate economy the sector is the basic unit. The manufacturing sector is divided into four industries (raw material processing, intermediate goods, durable goods, and consumer non-durables). Each industry produces an homogenous product and consists of a number of firms - 225 in total in the base year - of which 154 are real and the others synthetic, to sum up to the national accounts. The firms take decisions on all markets (products, labour, and capital), and these decisions are based on adaptive expectations. The decision process is based on bounded rationality principles and uses rules. Markets are explicitly represented, and transactions occur with little or no iteration of decisions, hence markets do not clear in general. Firms then find themselves with unused capacity, undesired stocks, unfilled vacancies. The time period is the quarter. Firms revise decisions, but sometimes they are unable to avoid losses, and they are eliminated by competition. However profits in an industry lead to the birth of new firms.

---

[1] A set of manuals give a full description of MOSES before the introduction of human capital and technological change: Albrecht et al. [ALB 89], and Taymaz [TAY 91]. A synthesis is given by Eliasson [ELI 91].

At the aggregate level the sectors interact through an eleven sectors Leontieff type input-output structure which evolves with the relative weight of the firms and with the (endogenous) technological progress which affects process innovation. However in manufacturing, firms individually buy from other sectors and sell to other sectors. There is an aggregate household sector with a Keynesian consumption function, and saving. There is also a Government that levies taxes, and buys in the markets, distributes subsidies, and hires people. The economy is open, with the foreign product prices and the foreign interest rate exogenous. Finally the model is calibrated to reproduce roughly the evolution of the main macroeconomic Swedish variables since 1982 [TAY 91].

In the base version described above, the model appears already as embodying some of the most important ideas of J.Schumpeter and the more recent evolutionary school[2]. Recent developments of the model by Ballot and Taymaz [BAL 96][BAL 97] [BAL 98] have introduced different forms of process innovation and, simultaneously, expenditures on training by firms. Innovation modelling choices in MOSES differ in important ways from the standard approach followed in both game theoretical models and in other evolutionary models based on bounded rationality[3]. The standard approach focuses on R&D and, sometimes, learning-by-doing as the determinants for innovation. The innovation-technology module in MOSES implements the fundamental hypothesis expressed in section 2, i.e. that the level of the general human capital of the labour force in the firm is crucial for three purposes: the discovery of innovations, the imitation of innovations of other firms, and the acquisition of specific human capital. The first two purposes correspond to an effect of a stock on the growth of the technological level and productivity. The latter is important for the economic exploitation of these innovations. General human capital reduces the cost of specific human capital, an input in the production function.

Innovations are embodied in investment, if we keep aside learning-by-doing, which is disembodied. There are radical and incremental innovations. Incremental innovation is done through search for better technologies. We use genetic algorithms. Starting from existing technologies it has experimented, the firm recombines them, and adopts the one that has the highest fitness value in terms of productivity. It may also modify one of the technologies (mutation) or recombine one of its technologies with a technology of another firm (imitation[4]). The move of the economy towards a new technological paradigm characterised by a set of related radical innovation is favoured by the decreasing returns to incremental innovations,

---

[2]See Andersen [AND 94] for an excellent synthesis.

[3]See Reinganum [REI 89] for the first approach, which focuses on the determination of R&D expenditures in the patent race. Silverberg, Dosi and Orsenigo [SIL 88] is a good example of the second approach.

[4] This is therefore never a pure imitation. The firm modifies and adapts the other firm's technology.

but its success depends on the willingness of many firms to follow the first firm which has ventured into the new paradigm. There are increasing returns to adoption as described by Arthur [ART 88]). This means that better paradigms might not develop if the returns to the current paradigm are satisfactory to individual firms which decide in a non-cooperative manner. Several paradigms may also share the manufacturing sector for a long time, involving lock-in effects (Ballot and Taymaz [BAL 98]).

To summarise, firms, in order to make profits or simply survive, must allocate resources on different accounts. First they must invest in physical assets since they embody new technologies, and also simply because they depreciate. Second, they may spend on training. Trainers invest in general as well as specific training, but poachers invest only in specific training which means that they are unable to make radical innovations or imitations unless they poach workers well endowed with general human capital[5] (see appendix for specifications). Finally firms benefit from spending on R&D, but they must then choose or find a balance between incremental and radical R&D. Profits result from the market process, and the precise relation with any of the mentioned expenditures is far too complex to be fully understood by a firm. Consequently the firms' decisions are modelled as boundedly rational rules.

The labour market is decentralised, each firm setting its wage rate at the beginning of the quarter, on the basis of expectations about the wage that will prevail. Since workers are not explicitly represented, only an employment level, one wage and two average (per head) levels of human capital, general and specific, are determined for each firm. When a firm needs to hire, it selects randomly between the unemployment pool and the other firms, with a probability to tap the unemployment pool which increases with the unemployment rate, and negatively with the level of the firms human capital. The unemployed accept any wage offer, but they have less human capital. If the firm chooses to raid other firms, it selects the attacked firm by a random draw among firms with a probability increasing in their size and levels of human capital, and decreasing in their wage rate.

When a firm plans to hire in order to meet its needs in manpower, it starts by adjusting partially its wage to the wage it expects to be set on the market. If the poacher offers a wage higher than the wage set by the attacked firm plus the mobility cost, it hires part of the workers of that firm. If the raid fails because the offered wage is too low, the poacher increases its wage by a certain amount, which can be limited by its financial capacity. The poacher may then succeed or fail. The process is iterated a certain number of times (four) before final wages are set, and hires, quits, and employment determined for the different firms (see Appendix B). If the raided firm looses too many workers so that its employment level falls under its planned employment level, then it will enter the same process of hiring and raising the wage next period.

---

[5] Trainers also poach in order to fulfil their needs in manpower. The exact difference between poachers and trainers is that the poachers do not invest in general training.

4.Experiments

For this first piece of research we do on this topic, we have designed only simple experiments. Firms are assigned randomly one of the two types, trainer or poacher, at the beginning of a simulation run, and cannot change type. However the proportion of each type is endogenous at the end of a run, through exit of unsuccessful firms.

We have explored the outcomes of the economy along three different sets of assumptions. A first set deals with the different initial proportions of poachers: 0%, 25%, 50%, 75%, and 100%. A second set concerns the behaviour of training firms: either quits have no effect on trainers investment decisions, or quits have a strong negative impact on trainers investment decisions (1 percentage point increase in the quit rate decreases the training expenditures by 20%). Mobility costs assumptions constitute a third set. If they are substantial, a poacher must offer a wage premium which is high enough to compensate for that cost, and poaching is more difficult. We consider two possibilities: no mobility costs, high mobility costs (20% of the current annual wage).

If we consider the interactions of the three criteria, initial proportion of poachers, effect of quits, mobility costs, we obtain twenty different experiments. For each experiment, we have run 20 simulations with a different seed number for the pseudo-random numbers generator, in order to average out the stochastic variations. A simulation runs over 60 years, i.e. 240 periods. We have run 400 simulations in total, and each simulation takes 25 minutes on a powerful PC. This is a reason for not running the model for centuries. Another and better reason is that it is meaningless to run an economic model with several important fixed institutions and rules (tax rates, estimated consumption functions…) for more than a few decades. These institutions naturally change, and they do so in response to the evolution of the economy. We will study successively the aggregate outcomes and the difference in outcomes between trainers and poachers. Some selected experiments are described in annex A.

4.1. *Aggregate outcomes*

First we make a broad comparison of the effects of the three criteria of differentiation on the performance of the economy after 60 years, as measured by the manufacturing output (table 1). Some results emerge when we change one parameter at a time.

% poachers	0	25	50	75	100
No quits effect, No mobility costs	1.085.384	1.045.297	868.160	895.804	1.035.379
No quits effect, High mobility costs	447.193	672.113	564.604	348.097	188.746
High quits effect, No mobility costs	1.091.257	989.687	1.092.934	790.444	650.664
High quits effect, High mobility costs	514.649	355.982	477.522	242.801	184.310

Table 1. *Level of manufacturing output after 60 years (Millions SEK 1982)*

First mobility costs have a major negative impact on aggregate performance. Poachers, in order to obtain workers, are compelled to bid the wage much higher than is the case in the experiments with no mobility costs. Wages are higher for all experiments with mobility costs. Labour costs are then a burden for firms. This affects negatively the allocation of resources to training, hence innovation and growth. Another mechanism goes through the coefficient of variation of wages which is higher. Wage differentials allow poor performers to survive by paying low wages and this also affects negatively the allocation of resources.

Secondly, the effect of quits on training investment does not have the general negative impact that could be expected. A negative impact on output appears in the case of mobility costs, when the percentage of poachers ranges from 25% to 75%. Trainers invest much less in general human capital, and less in specific human capital. Poachers have difficulties in obtaining the trained workers they need. A *contrario* when mobility costs do not exist, the macroeconomic outcome is good even if quits affect training. This surprising result may be caused by evolutionary mechanisms. Inefficient or unlucky trainers cannot avoid quits, because they cannot pay high wages, and therefore reduce their training expenditures. However efficient poachers are then able to raid the workers they need. They build high levels of general and specific human capital, and R&D, and innovate or adopt innovations. Technological change benefits poachers which even reach a higher average technological level than trainers in the cases of 25 and 50% poachers.

Thirdly the initial proportion of poachers has a negative effect on aggregate performance, but essentially when the percentage rises over 50%. The decline in manufacturing output above 50% is easily explained in terms of a decline in human capital. The good performance for percentages up to 50% can be interpreted again in terms of an efficiency role played by poachers, provided they are not too numerous. They obtain human capital at low cost from some inefficient trainers who are unable to retain them. The poachers which raid are those which grow, need manpower, and can be considered as efficient. *A mix of the two types then appears as efficient.*

An exception to the rule of the decline of output when the proportion of poachers increases over 50% is the experiment with a 100% poachers, no effects of quits and no mobility costs. This economy is peculiar, and the model has not been designed and calibrated so as to obtain a viable system. Yet it is viable, and consistent. It has an extremely low level of general human capital, but a substantial level of specific human capital accumulated through learning by doing, and a low technological level. The unemployment level is then much lower than in all the other experiments (1.3% to compare with the next best 9.1%), since technical progress in the model saves labour but does not stimulate demand, product innovation being absent.

4.2. *Trainers and poachers*

The main result is that trainers and poachers coexist on average at the end of experiments for the initial proportions of poachers we have tried, i.e. from 25 to 75%. However we can observe some stable differentials between the outcomes of the two types.

Intangible capital stocks are lower in poachers. This is true for general and specific human capital, and for R&D. For the general and specific human capital, it results from the definition of poachers, since they do not invest in general human capital, and general human capital is an input in the production of specific human capital. For R&D, the reason is behavioural, since the financially unconstrained demand for R&D has general human capital as one of its determinants (see annex B). In spite of these unfavourable endowments, the technological level of poachers at the end of the experiments is not always lower than the level of trainers. This is due to the imitation and improvement of the technologies of other firms. Poaching builds the minimum capacity to absorb innovators' technologies.

Some variables indicate that poachers fair somewhat not as well as trainers. Their market share at the end of the experiments is always lower, by 3 to 15%, to the exogenous initial share. The technological lead of trainers is a part of the explanation, but the difficulties of raiding may be another element. The average rate of return of poachers is also lower by 1 to 4 per cent. These rates of return show no global trend when year 60 is compared to year 50. Poachers do not appear to be doomed to long term extinction.

5. Conclusions

The behaviour of the firms in the experiments presented here does not include a learning process about the success of this behaviour. Firms are assigned a type, trainer or poacher, and do not change it. In spite of this limitation that we intend to remove in later work, the experiments have offered some results of interest on the coordination and performance of an economy with heterogeneous agents, and on the persistence of this heterogeneity.

First the coexistence of trainers and poachers is possible in the long run, for all the sets of experiments we have made, starting with an initial proportion of poachers from 25 to 75%. Trainers fare somewhat better than poachers because they are technological leaders and poaching is not always easy. Yet the differential is not high enough to lead to the elimination of poachers.

Second we are able to obtain a paradox i.e. a result which contradicts the received result of neoclassical theory on human capital. While neoclassical theory shows that poaching precludes general training completely, with underinvestment and bad aggregate performance, the best performance in terms of manufacturing output is obtained for a set of simulations in which there is an equal proportion of trainers and poachers. The advantage of the model over a very abstract pure competition model lies in the presence of heterogeneity of firms (technology, human capital, rules). Some firms are more efficient than others, and earn higher profits. This Schumpeterian competition process then allows high performance firms to raid trained workers from low performance trainers and benefit from technological spillovers. Poaching then is an allocation process that makes the labour market function efficiently.

This result is reinforced by the bad outcomes we obtain when mobility costs block the process. At the same time the process takes some time so that trainers can often innovate and raise their wages to keep their workers. This contrasts with the timeless neoclassical model in which they loose their workers immediately. A dynamic and agent based model such as the one we have developed then entails results which are totally opposed to the standard model, and much closer to the firms behaviour as it is observed in econometric work such as [BAL 99] or direct surveys.

Annex A

Selected experiments

This annex A presents in more detail some experiments (table 2). A reference experiment is the case with no poachers, no effect of quits on the training investment, and no mobility cost, in the first column. It gives almost the highest output, with the case which has the same first two characteristics, and high mobility costs, and the case of 50% trainers, no effect of quits on training, and high mobility costs.

It was expected that this reference experiment would yield a high growth of manufacturing output and a high level of GNP. The levels of general and specific human capital are specially high, as well as the level of R&D. The technological level is the highest. The quit rate is relatively low. Few firms exit but more new firms are created than in any other experiment, due to the growth of the economy. Unemployment is substantial (11.8%) since process innovations spare labour.

We then introduce poachers, and examine three cases with an equal initial proportion of poachers. We consider first the case in column 2 in which quits do not effect training and there are mobility costs. Mobility costs have a very negative influence on manufacturing output.

Then we examine the case in the fourth column which differs from the previous one simply because quits now affect training negatively. The macroeconomic results are worse, and some firms exit.

Finally we look at column 3, the opposite case of column 2, in which quits affect training but there are no mobility costs. The macroeconomic situation is good. This comes as a surprise. The average wage is low, since poachers need not bid much to obtain employees. Our interpretation is that efficient poachers obtain the manpower they need, from inefficient or unlucky trainers (which do not innovate lose it) . The allocation of human capital is efficient, and as a result, the macroeconomic outcome is good.

Experiment	NN		NH		HN		HH	
Effect of quits	No		No		Yes		Yes	
Mobility costs	No		High		No		High	
% poachers	0		50		50		50	
Manuf. Output	1,085,384		564,604		1,092,934		477,522	
GNP	3,444,000		2,074,000		3,443,000		1,852,000	
Unemp. Rate	11.8		10.9		19.4		20.5	
Firms category	T	P	T	P	T	P	T	P
No employees (Thousands)	919	/	341	346	559	389	342	313
Sales revenue	28,922	/	8,074	6,314	18,758	10,415	7,295	5,328
Market share	100	/	56.1	43.9	64.3	35.7	57.8	42.2
Rate of return	27.1	/	27.9	25.1	27.4	23.1	27.6	21.7
General HC	478	/	171	24	451	59	132	23
Specific HC	349	/	130	99	293	216	107	91
R&D stock	51	/	28	24	52	41	8	6
Techno.level	2.1	/	1.7	1.6	1.6	2	1.7	1.5
Average wage	1,980	/	2,737	2,682	1,777	1,782	2,609	2,587
Wage diff.	.190		.221		.175		.226	
Quit rate	.33	/	1.20	.50	.29	.24	.80	.82
Entering firms	23	/	10.8	12.2	10.8	10.8	10.5	11.3
Exiting firms	.5	/	0	0	.3	.3	.2	.8

Table 2. *Selected experiments (average values of 20 runs for year 60)* T= Trainers P=Poachers

Manufacturing output, GNP and sales revenue are in Million SEK (1982 prices), General and Specific human capital, R&D are in Thousands SEK (1982 prices). Entering or exiting firms is the number of firms concerned by entry or exit during the past ten years.

Annex B

Specifications of the model for training, R&D activities, and the labour market

Investment in training

The trainers' accumulation of human capital is modelled as follows. Desired total investment in training is:

$$TR^{des} = f(q, K^e/K^{elim}, S, L*H^{gen}, L*H^{spec}) \qquad [1]$$

$$\partial TR^{des}/\partial q < 0, \; \partial TR^{des}/\partial(K^e/K^{elim}) < 0, \; \partial TR^{des}/\partial S > 0, \; \partial TR^{des}/\partial L > 0,$$

$$\partial TR^{des}/\partial H^{gen} > 0, \; \partial TR^{des}/\partial H^{spec} > 0$$

where q is the quit rate, K^e the maximum output, when infinite amounts of labour are used, K^{elim} the maximum level of K^e when specific human capital is infinite, L the number of employees, H^{gen} general human capital stock per employee, and H^{spec} specific human capital stock per employee, S sales revenue.[6]

The level of desired investment in training depends on three variables: existing stocks of knowledge and specific skills, (the inverse of) the rate of utilization of potential capacity (K^e/K^{elim}) and sales revenue. Firms tend to increase the stock at a certain rate and to spend a part of their sales revenue on training. If the (K^e/K^{elim}) ratio is low, the firm will spend more on training since a low value of that ratio indicates that the firm is not able to use efficiently its productive capacity because of the lack of specific skills.

The real training expenditures are obtained after the firm has set all the types of desired expenditures mentioned above and compared the sum to its budget constraint, borrowing possibilities being taken into account. Rationing may take place. The distribution between real general (I^{GT}) and specific (I^{ST}) training per employee is determined by a distribution parameter and the (K^e/K^{elim}) ratio.

Poachers do not invest in general training. Therefore, the desired investment in training for poachers is adjusted by reducing the part that would be spent on general training.

The stock of specific human capital is determined by:

$$H_t^{spec} = H_{t-1}^{spec}(1 - \rho_s) + L_{t-1}^{EFF}l(Q_{t-1}/L_{t-1}, I_{t-1}^{ST}) \qquad [2]$$

---

[6] Firm and time subscripts are dropped in some equations to simplify the notation.

The stock of general human capital is determined by:

$$H_t^{gen} = H_{t-1}^{gen} * (1 - \rho_g) + I_{t-1}^{GT} \tag{3}$$

where ρ_s and ρ_g are depreciation parameters respectively. $l(..)$ is an exponential function, which expresses the increase of specific human capital as a result of past production per employee (learning by doing). L^{EFF} is the efficiency of the investment in specific human capital, which depends on the stock of general knowledge. The depreciation rate (or the obsolescence rate) of the stock of specific skills, ρ_s, is a function of the rate of improvement in the case of incremental innovations. A different (and much higher) value is used for radical innovations. General knowledge, once created, is applicable in all firms and, therefore, transferable. If employees with a high level of general human capital move to another firm, they will increase the stock of general knowledge of the new firm as follows:

$$H_{i,t}^{gen} = H_{i,t-1}^{gen} * L_{i,t-1} + H_{j,t-1}^{gen} L_{ij,t-1} \tag{4}$$

where $L_{i,t-1}$ is the number of employees in Firm i at time t-1, $H_{i,t-1}^{gen}$ the general human capital stock in Firm i at time t-1, $H_{j,t-1}^{gen}$ the general human capital stock in Firm j at time t-1, and $L_{ij,t-1}$ the number of employees transferred from Firm j to Firm i. Thus, the stock of general knowledge can be increased by general training *and* the hiring of highly trained workers from other firms.

Investment in R&D

The desired level of investment in R&D depends on the stock of general knowledge, sales revenue, and the emphasis on radical innovations:

$$RD^{des} = f(H^{gen}, S, s^{rad}) \tag{5}$$

$$\partial RD^{des}/\partial H^{gen} > 0 , \partial RD^{des}/\partial S > 0, \partial RD^{des}/\partial s^{rad} > 0,$$

where s^{rad} is the ratio of radical R&D expenditures in total ($s^{rad} = RD^{rad}/RD^{rad} + RD^{inc}$). The firm allocates more resources on radical R&D if its technological level is higher and if the learning rate is lower:

$$s^{rad} = s(P^F, lr^T, lr^k) \tag{6}$$

$$\partial s^{rad}/\partial P^F > 0 \; , \; \partial s^{rad}/\partial lr^T < 0 \; , \; \partial s^{rad}/\partial lr^k < 0$$

where P^F is the technology used by the firm, and lr^T and lr^k the (weighted average of recent changes) in T^{new} and k^{new} parameters, respectively.

In addition to training and R&D, the firm calculates its desired level of investment in physical capital and liquid assets. Then, given the level of net cash flow, the firm decides on the level of desired borrowing (desired total investment *minus* net cash flow). The actual level of borrowing depends on the resources of the bank and total demand for borrowing. Finally, after the level of borrowing has been set in the credit market, the firm allocates its resources (net cash flow *plus* net borrowing) among four different assets (training, R&D, physical capital and liquid assets) in proportion to its desired levels.

The labour market

At the beginning of a quarter, firms set the planned output and corresponding employment levels on the basis of their sales forecasts, expected prices and wages, and target levels of profit margins. Before entering the labour market, firms determine the planned change in employment, $\Delta L_t = L_t^{plan} - L_{t-1}$, and adjust their wages towards expected levels.

$$w_t^{in} = \kappa^+ w_t^{exp} + (1-\kappa^+)w_{t-1} \text{ if } \Delta L_t > 0 \qquad [7]$$
$$w_t^{in} = \kappa^- w_t^{exp} + (1-\kappa^-)w_{t-1} \text{ if } \Delta L_t =< 0$$

where w_t^{in} is the initial wage offering at the time the firm enters the labour market, w_t^{exp} the expected wage rate at time t, w_{t-1} the wage rate at time t-1, and κ^+ and κ^- adjustment parameters, $0 < \kappa^+ < \kappa^- < 1$ (in experiments reported in this pqper, $\kappa^+ = .77$, $\kappa^- = .90$).

After setting the initial wage rates, firms are ranked in order of the planned relative change in employment, $\Delta L_t/L_{t-1}$. Each firm that has a positive planned change in employment is allowed to "attack" another firm or the pool of unemployed, chosen at random. The probability for a certain firm to be attacked is defined as follows:

$$p_i^{att} = p(L_i, H_i^{gen}, w_i) \qquad [8]$$
$$\partial p_i^{att}/\partial L_i > 0, \; \partial p_i^{att}/\partial H_i^{gen} > 0, \; \partial p_i^{att}/\partial w_i < 0$$

where p_i^{att} is the probability that i^{th} firm will be attacked, L_i the number of employees of the ith firm, H_i^{gen} general human capital stock per employee, and w_i the current wage rate. For the pool of unemployed, L is the number of unemployed workers, H^{gen} is the average general human capital stock of unemployed workers, and w the average wage rate for the manufacturing industry. The average general human capital stock changes over time as a result of depreciation, quits and lay offs, and entry of young workers to the labour force. Probabilities are adjusted so that

$$\Sigma_{i \neq j} p_i^{att} = 1$$

where j is the index for the attacking firm, and i the index for the rest of firms and the pool of unemployed.

The attack is successful if the firm attacks the pool of unemployed. The firm gets the desired number of employees from the unemployed. If the firm attacks another firm, the attack is successful if the wage rate in the attacking firm is greater than the wage rate in the attacked firm *plus* the cost of mobility. In this case, the firm hires workers from the attacked firm (the number of workers hired cannot exceed a certain proportion of the workers in the attacked firm). After the transfer of workers, the desired change in employment in both firms is re-calculated.

If the attack is not a success, then the attacking firm will raise its wage rate to be successful in attacking in the next iteration. The wage rate for the unsuccessful firm is determined as follows:

$$w_j^{itn} = max\{w_j^{max}, \xi(w_i*(1+mc))+(1-\xi)*w_j\} \tag{9}$$

where w_j^{itn} is the wage rate for the attacking firm at iteration n, w_j^{max} the maximum wage that make profit margin equal to zero, mc the mobility cost (as a percentage of the wage rate), ξ the adjustment parameter, $0 < \xi < 1$ (in our experiments mc $= .2$, $\xi = ;13$).

The interactions in the labour market (the part after Equation 7) are iterated a predetermined number of times (4 in our experiments). In each iteration, a firm that has a positive desired change in employment has a chance to attack others. At the end of iterations, wages and employment are determined for all firms. If a firm has lost too much of its labour force, or could not meet recruitment plans, its production plan is revised. If a firm has more employees than its planned level, i.e., if the planed change in employment is negative, the firm will start laying off a part of the labour force.

Acknowledgements

Erol Taymaz is grateful to the University Paris II for an invitation as guest professor in January 2000 which made the research possible.

References

[AGH 98] Aghion P., Howitt P., Endogenous Growth Theory, Cambridge, Mass. : MIT Press.

[ALB 89] Albrecht J.W. et al., Moses Database, Stockholm : IUI and Almquist & Wicksell.

[AND 94] Andersen E.S., Evolutionary Economics. London : Pinter Publishers.

[ART 89] Arthur W.B., "Increasing Returns and Path Dependence in the Economy", Economic Journal 99, March, 116-31.

[BAL 94] Ballot G., " Continuing Education and Schumpeterian Competition. Elements for a Theoretical Framework" in R. Asplund (ed) Human Creation in an Economic Perspective, Heidelberg : Physica-Verlag, p.160-171.

[BAL 96] Ballot G., Taymaz E. "Firm Sponsored Training, Technical Progress and Aggregate Performances in a Micro-macro Model" in A. Harding (ed), Microsimulation and Public Policy, North Holland, Amsterdam, pp 421-449.

[BAL 97] Ballot G., Taymaz E., "The Dynamics of Firms in a Micro-to-macro Model with Training, Learning and Innovation", Journal of Evolutionary Economics 7 (4),.435-457.

[BAL 98] Ballot G., Taymaz E., "Human Capital and Endogenous Change in the Technological Paradigm: Dynamics of the Firms and the Economy in a Schumpeterian Model", in G. Eliasson, C. Green and C. McCann (eds.), Microfoundations of Economic Growth : A Schumpeterian Perspective. Ann Arbor: University of Michigan Press

[BAL 99] Ballot G., Fakhfak F., Taymaz E., "Firms' Human Capital, R&D and Performance: A Study on French and Swedish Firms", ERMES working paper.

[BAR 89] Barron J.M., Black D.A. & Lowenstein M.A., "Job Matching and On-the-job Training", Journal of Labor Economics, 5 (1), 76-89.

[BEC 75] Becker G.S., Human Capital. New York: Columbia University Press.

[BEN 94] Benhabib J., Spiegel M.M., "The Role of Human Capital in Economic Development: Evidence from Aggregate Cross-Country Data" Journal of Monetary Economics 34(2), 143-173.

[BIS 91] Bishop J., "On-the-job Training of New Hires", in D.Stern & J.M.M. Ritzen (eds) Market Failure in Training? Berlin: Springer Verlag.

[COH 90] Cohen W.M., Levinthal D.A., "Absorptive Capacity: A New Perspective on Learning and Innnovation" , Administrative Science Quaterly 3: 128-152.

[ELI 77] Eliasson G., "Competition and Market Processes in a Simulation Model of the Swedish Economy", American Economic Review (67), 277-281.

[ELI 91] Eliasson G., "Modelling the Experimentally Organised Economy", Journal of Economic Behaviour and Organization (16), 163-182.

LUC 88] Lucas R.E., "On the Mechanics of Economic Development". Journal of Monetary Economics 22 (1), 3-42.

[NEL 66] Nelson R., Phelps E., "Investment in Humans, Technological Diffusion, and Economic Growth", American Economic Review (61), 139-162.

[REI 89] Reinganum J., "The Timing of Innovation: Research, Development and Diffusion", in R. Schmalensee and R. Willig (eds) Handbook of Industrial Organisation, vol 1, Amsterdam: North Holland.

[TAY 91] Taymaz E., MOSES on PC. Manual, Initialization and Calibration. Stockholm: IUI and Almquist & Wicksell.

[SIL 88] Silverberg G., Dosi G., Orsenigo L. "Innovation, Diversity and Diffusion,: A Self-organisation Model", The Economic Journal (98), 212-221.

[ULP 96] Ulph D., "Dynamic Competition for Market Share and the Failure of the Market for Skilled Labour", in Booth A. & Snower D. (eds), Acquiring Skills, Cambridge: Cambridge University Press.

Modeling creation vs. diffusion of structured knowledge

Nicolas Carayol

Lirhe-Cnrs
University of Toulouse 1
31 042 Toulouse Cedex
France
carayol@univ-tlse1.fr

ABSTRACT: *The paper is mainly dealing with the dilemma between knowledge creation incentives and knowledge diffusion. Knowledge is modeled as a structure, which is expanding through agents' creation behaviors, and becomes "locally" available to other agents once it is disclosed. An agent taken randomly at each period of the discrete time is choosing between the acquisition of an accessible piece of knowledge and the creation of one. Knowledge value being a decreasing function of the number of agents sharing it, a higher (exogenous and tunable) rate of disclosure decreases the incentives to create (in increasing the diffusion speed). Using simulations, we show that there is, for each set of values of the different parameters, a non null optimal rate of disclosure (maximizing the collective performances of the set of agents) and discuss the effect of some of the structural parameters on it.*

RESUMÉ: *Le papier traite principalement du dilemme entre incitation à la création de savoir et diffusion des connaissances. Le savoir est modélisé comme une structure qui s'étend à travers les comportements de création des agents, et qui devient localement accessible aux autres agents une fois la connaissance divulguée. Un agent tiré aléatoirement à chaque période du temps discret, choisit entre acquérir une pièce de savoir parmi celles qui lui sont accessibles et en créer une. La valeur d'une connaissance étant une fonction décroissante du nombre d'agents qui la partagent, un taux de divulgation (exogène) plus élevé) décroît les incitations à créer (en accroissant la vitesse de diffusion). Au moyen de simulations, nous montrons qu'il existe, pour chaque ensemble de valeurs des paramètres, un taux de divulgation optimal non nul et nous discutons de l'effet de certains paramètres sur celui-ci.*

KEY-WORDS: *knowledge structure, knowledge creation incentives, knowledge disclosure, knowledge diffusion.*

MOTS-CLÉS: *structure de connaissances, incitations à la création de savoirs, divulgation, diffusion.*

1. Introduction

The production, the mastering, and the diffusion of advanced knowledge recently appeared as essential factors of the modern economies performances ([MAC 84]). In order to describe such economies where knowledge has a central importance, David and Foray proposed the notion of "knowledge based economy" [DAV 95], and Lundvall and Foray the notion of "learning economy" [LUN 95] (so as to insist on its dynamic character, and in particular, on the agents' cognitive capacities of knowledge acquisition).

As a matter of fact, knowledge has for long been of a central importance in economic processes, and has also been a central category in many powerful economic analyses (Smith, Hayek, Schumpeter...). In reality, the main difference between modern economies and old ones seems rather to lie in the fact that some processes dealing with cognitive issues are becoming critical ones. These processes are the followings: knowledge creation ([ARR 62], [HIR 71]), knowledge disclosure ([DAS 94]), knowledge diffusion ([DAV 92]), search ([STI 61]), learning, and knowledge codification ([SAV 98], [COW 97]). Being critical in modern economies, economic literature has to take them into account, knowing, in addition, that they may interact the ones on the others at both the individuals' level (search permits learning, learning favors creation...) and at the aggregated level (disclosure favors or permits diffusion, codification favors diffusion...).

At the latter level of analysis, a complex and problematic interaction exists between knowledge creation incentives and knowledge diffusion. In the one hand, diffusion has very interesting economic properties, but in the other hand, it tends to mechanically decrease creation incentives in various situations, in which either the enforcement of the intellectual property on knowledge is impossible or the nature and the rhythm of innovation render intellectual property protection non effective (because, then, the sharing of a piece of knowledge is diminishing its private returns). In this situations, we do not know if we should relatively favor knowledge diffusion or knowledge creation incentives, both opposite public policy orientations having their advocates. The first is expressed in [DAV 95], and the latter corresponds to the standard assumption which considers that the only way to ensure that a socially valuable research project is undertaken is to remunerate it at the level of the social value it generates. The paper is trying to deal with this well known dilemma, taking into account most of the economic processes exposed above, plus one fundamental property of knowledge, namely its "cognitive local character".

This idea comes from Boulding's assumption highlighting both that "knowledge must itself be regarded as a structure" ([BOU 55], p. 103) [1], and that this constitutes the main difference between knowledge and information. This idea is expressing the

---

[1] Or as "a correlational structure" in [SAV 98].

evidence that there exists some cognitive proximities (or, on the contrary, cognitive distances) between different pieces of knowledge. A cognitive proximity between two pieces of knowledge simply expresses that an agent is able to pass from the mastering of one to the mastering of the other. We will model knowledge structure using Graph Theory, as double set of pieces of knowledge and links between them. The density of this connected and undirected graph indicates the degree of knowledge codification, which, as it is commonly accepted, facilitates knowledge acquisition. We will then introduce agents with heterogeneous endowments of elements of these two sets, who are able either to acquire pieces of knowledge or to create new ones. Its is only once the piece of knowledge is disclosed through an exogenous and tunable process, that it becomes globally available to other agents. But the agents will be only able to acquire a piece of knowledge that is at a given distance (in the model we will restrict our analysis at distance 1) from what they already know [2].

The model differs from already existing ones within the field of knowledge diffusion. Usually, knowledge diffusion is modeled as operating through a given exogenous structure (more or less specified), using a given diffusion rule ([DAV 92], [COW 99]) or a search process (an "adaptive walk" in [LOB 99]). Here knowledge diffusion (arising through knowledge acquisition) takes place in a structure that is itself evolving because of the agents' creation behaviors [3], which enables us to expose the co-evolution of a set of agents and the structure in which they behave. The process is of a sequential nature: each playing agent is modifying the way others will behave and so on. This framework being too complex to be solved analytically, we will mostly obtain our results using computer simulations.

We will also explicitly introduce knowledge value and its endogenous evolution. The problem of information value is far from being new in social sciences, and is a quite difficult one: the only use of an information may then reveal it and this way avoid or at least diminish its intrinsic value ([ARR 62]). So the knowledge value, revealed by the market process, seems rather impossible to determine. Even some institutional settings (patents, copy rights, trade secrets) which are dedicated to the protection of the creator do not really permit the total appropriation of the surplus generated. In order to treat this delicate problem, we will assume that knowledge pieces have intrinsic heterogeneous value functions which give the one period payoffs generated by their possession from the number of agents sharing it and from the realization of a random variable. Moreover, knowledge value will be a decreasing convex function of the number of agents sharing it, and such that the social value generated by a given piece of knowledge will always increase with the number of agents sharing it. Then, first of all, the creation of a piece of knowledge

---

[2] The agents learn *from* what they already know, and *through* the cognitive proximities existing between pieces of knowledge. This idea is related to Cohen and Levinthal's notion of "absorptive capacity" [COH 90].

[3] The diffusion networks are assumed to be totally resumed by the agents' knowledge endowments. But this doesn't change anything on the model's technicalities.

will exhibit positive externalities, but only in enlarging the acquisition opportunities of the others. Secondly, knowledge acquisition will have negative externalities on the agents already possessing this piece of knowledge (but always a positive social effect). Each pair of knowledge pieces will exhibit some extra stochastic value expressing various complementarities existing between the two pieces of knowledge. Then, idiosyncratic endowments in knowledge pieces will also generate idiosyncratic complementarities. It should be noted that consequently, the value of a given piece of knowledge will be different among agents due to various complementarities they can exploit between the acquired knowledge and the ones they already possess.

Since the disclosure of a piece of knowledge is be a necessary condition for its acquisition, the determination of the constant exogenous per period rate of disclosure of all undisclosed pieces of knowledge (τ) will be of a critical importance. The main issue will be to find the appropriate balance between the two types of behaviors, by tuning τ. As a matter of fact, various institutional settings in economic activity may modify the rate of disclosure. They are among others: knowledge transfer institutions, the density of personal networks, geographic proximity, and "high velocity labor markets". The latter has been emphasized as one of the main reasons of the Silicon Valley's "regional advantage". In weakening the laws on trade secrets, firms' secrecy protecting behaviors were restricted and then knowledge diffusion were greatly improved (emphasized in [SAX 94] and [HYD 98] which are path-breaking contributions in the too weak literature on trade secrets). Known by the agents, the value of the structural parameter τ will modify their anticipations on the speed of the sharing process of a piece of knowledge they may create. The agents will be able to evaluate *ex ante,* through a "naive best response strategy", the value of knowledge creation. Comparing this value with the expected returns from the acquisition of each of the accessible pieces of knowledge (and taking into account the fixed costs of each possible action), they will decide how to behave. The tuning of the parameter τ will modify (in opposite ways) both the diffusion process and the incentives to create. We will then determine by adjustment the optimal setting of τ in order to maximize collective efficiency for different values of the other parameters, that is for different features of the innovation regimes.

The paper is built as follows: we will expose the modeling of knowledge structure and knowledge value (2), the agents' possible behaviors and the terms of their choice (3), and the way the agents are anticipating the sharing process and are then fixing the expected value of knowledge (4). We will then present the simulations' results, which demonstrate that a non null level of knowledge disclosure may be collectively profitable, and which expose the influence of the various parameters on the optimal value of τ (5).

2. Knowledge structure, endowments, and payoffs

2.1. *Knowledge structure and endowments*

The knowledge structure can be formalized as two sets: the first being constituted of elementary and separable pieces of knowledge $K = \{k_i\}$ with $|K| = K$, and the second being constituted of the links existing between elements of the first set $E = \{e_{ij}\}$ with $i \neq j$, $k_i, k_j \in K$ and $|E| = E$. The knowledge structure is then a graph denoted $KB = (K, E)$. It is supposed to be undirected ($(e_{ij}) = (e_{ji})$), and connected (there is a path between any two pieces of knowledge of the graph: $\forall k_i, k_j \in K, \exists \{e_{il}, e_{lh}..., e_{mj}\} \subset E$). It can be characterized by its density $d = E / K$ which may represent the degree of knowledge codification.

Each agent $a = 1...A$ of the set of all agents ($a \in \Omega$) is characterized by a knowledge base KB_a which is an idiosyncratic endowment of knowledge pieces and links between them denoted $KB_a = (K_a, E_a)$, that is formally a the double subset of the sets of all pieces and links: $K_a \subset K$ and $E_a \subset E$. The agents knowledge bases are also assumed to respect the connectivity property. Each piece of knowledge and each link of the knowledge structure KB is at least part of the knowledge base of an agent, that is: $K = \bigcup_a K_a$ and $E = \bigcup_a E_a$. The agents' knowledge bases can be characterized by their scope $|K_a|$ and their density index $d_a = |E_a|/|K_a|$.

We define the social knowledge base as the structured set of knowledge pieces that are globally available (but only locally accessible) to the agents. It is the structured (but not necessarily connected) set of disclosed piece of knowledge. The social knowledge base is a double subset of the sets of all pieces and links: $KB_s = (K_s, E_s)$ with $K_s \subset K$ and $E_s \subset E$. It is also characterized by its scope $|K_s|$, and its density $d_s = |E_s|/|K_s|$. The agents endowments and the social knowledge base are defining an immediate knowledge neighborhood for each agent N_a, which is the set of knowledge pieces $\{k_j\}$ such that: $\forall k_j \in K_s$ (with $k_j \notin K_a$), if $\exists k_i \in K_a$ and if $\exists e_{ij} \in E_s$, then $k_j \in N_a$. We then have $N_a \subset K_s$ and $N_a \cap K_a = \emptyset$.

2.2. *Knowledge value*

Let's now assume that the value generated, during a given period of time, by the possession of a given piece of knowledge k_i is given by the function $r_i(\cdot)$. It is defined such as $r_i(n_i) \equiv \hat{\varepsilon}_i r(n_i)$, that is both function of the number of agents sharing it $n_i \in \{1...A\}$, and function of the realization ($\hat{\varepsilon}_i$) of a random variable ε_i. All ε_i

being independent, identically distributed and non null positive random variables which are normalized such that their mean expected value $E(\varepsilon_i) = 1$. Moreover, the function $r(\cdot)$ is assumed exhibit the three following very intuitive properties. First of all, it is a decreasing function of n_i, that is the private returns from the mastering of a given piece of knowledge decrease when the number of agents increases. Secondly, it is also convex: when the number of agents sharing a piece of knowledge increases, the sharing costs (i.e. the payoffs decrease of an agent who was already possessing it, due to the sharing of the piece of knowledge by one more agent) decrease. Third property: $(n+1)r(n+1) > nr(n)$ whatever is $n \in \{1,..., A-1\}$, so that the social payoffs of a given piece of knowledge are always increasing with the number of agents sharing it. Then, even if the payoffs captured by some agent(s) from the possession of a given piece of knowledge may decrease quite fast with its sharing by one more agent, the total payoffs captured by all will be higher than in the prior situation.

The possession of each pair of nodes is also assumed to generate an idiosyncratic extra value expressing complementarities (or intranalities) existing between different pieces of knowledge: there may be some pieces of knowledge that are more or less interesting to possess together. Let the complementarities between k_i and k_j, be given by the realization $\hat{\varepsilon}_{ij}$ of a simple random variable ε_{ij}. These random variables are assumed to be mutually independent, independent of the ε_i and, identically distributed with mean expected values such as: $E(\varepsilon_{ij}) = E(\varepsilon_i)/\alpha = 1/\alpha$. The parameter α is expressing the relative value of nodes over the complementarities one's. If α is very high, there is no increasing returns in knowledge.

Let specify the value function of the nodes in the following way:

$$r_i(n_i) \equiv \hat{\varepsilon}_i(\mu + \beta e^{-n_i}) \tag{1}$$

with μ the range of use of knowledge (such as $\mu \geq \overline{\mu} = e^{-2}$ the sufficient condition for $r_i(\cdot)$ to respect the properties exposed above), and β the degree of products' substitutability such as $0 < \beta < 1$. μ, which is increasing the value of knowledge whatever is its sharing situation, is expressing the idea that a piece of knowledge may be of a relevant use in markets of different sizes or in several ones. β is increasing the value of knowledge when it is shared by relatively few people, and is sharpening its decline with the number of sharing. It expresses the fact that novelty has a higher value when product substitutability is high because the share of the market captured is then higher. Let's observe that knowledge pieces values are never null because, even if a piece of knowledge is shared with many agents, it is still important to possess it in order to avoid possible coordinating problems.

The agents' one period outcomes are assumed to be linearly constituted of the intrinsic payoffs of their knowledge base elements and their complementarites:

$$R(KB_a) \equiv \sum_{k_i \in K_a} r_i(n_i) + \sum_{i \neq j} \varepsilon_{ij} \tag{2}$$

3. The agents' behaviors: knowledge acquisition vs. creation

At each period of the discrete time, on agent is randomly chosen and has the opportunity either to acquire or to create a piece of knowledge in order to improve its payoffs. Let us examine both actions and the choice issue.

3.1. *Knowledge acquisition*

In order to improve the payoffs generated by their knowledge base, the agents can first of all acquire a piece of knowledge. It is then new from the playing agent point of view, but not at the social level. To be acquired, the knowledge piece must have been disclosed, that is be part of the set of disclosed elements of the knowledge structure previously denoted K_s. Knowledge acquisition is operating *on* the "cognitive structure". Indeed, knowledge acquisition is local in nature: agents learn *from* what they already know (i.e. their own knowledge base), and *through* the cognitive proximities existing between what they already know and what is accessible. In our model, highlighting the importance of the local character of knowledge acquisition, we assume that the agents can only acquire a disclosed piece of knowledge which is at geodesic distance equal to one from a piece of knowledge they already have, that is, which was part of the agent's cognitive neighborhood in the previous period N_a^{t-1}. Moreover, we will assume that the agents' information is very high in the local environment of their knowledge base: they are able to identify all the knowledge acquisition possibilities (all the elements of their neighborhood) and, they are also able to evaluate correctly their payoffs (which means they know both the number of agents possessing it [4] and see the realization of the random variables). Nevertheless, the agents are supposed to be totally ignorant of the situation beyond their direct knowledge neighborhood. If an agent is deciding to acquire a piece of knowledge, he is supposed to always acquire the one he expects to be the most profitable one, that is the one that maximize his expected benefits. When an agent is acquiring a node, he is assumed to also acquire all the edges relying it to the nodes he already possesses.

So formally, if any agent undertakes an acquisition, at the beginning of a period t, his knowledge base will be improved in the following way:

$$KB_a^t = \left(K_a^t, E_a^t\right) = \left(K_a^{t-1} \oplus (k_j), E_a^{t-1} \oplus \{e_{ij}\} \,\middle|\, \max \Pi_a^t(n_j); k_i \in K_a^{t-1}, k_j \in N_a^{t-1}, \forall (e_{ij}) \in E^{t-1}\right) \quad [3]$$

with $\Pi_a^t(n_j)$ the actualized expected benefit of acquiring the knowledge piece k_j (that we shall expose in the next section). In this case KB is left unchanged.

---

[4] The number of agents possessing a given piece of knowledge does integrate the concerned agent if he decides to undertake the action.

3.2. Knowledge creation

The agents may also decide to create a piece of knowledge which will then be new both at the agent's level and at the social level. If knowledge acquisition is done *on* the social knowledge structure, knowledge creation works quite differently. Instead of depending of the knowledge structure, it tends to make it expand. Then the creation action consists formally in both operations:

$$KB_a^t = \left(K_a^t, E_a^t\right) = \left(K_a^{t-1} \oplus (k_j), E_a^{t-1} \oplus \left\{\varepsilon_{ij}\right\} \Big| \; k_i \in K_a^{t-1}, k_j \notin K^{t-1}\right)$$

$$KB^t = \left(K^t, E^t\right) = \left(K^{t-1} \oplus (k_j), E^{t-1} \oplus \left\{\varepsilon_{ij}\right\} \Big| \; k_j \notin K^{t-1}\right) \qquad [4]$$

Creation provokes the addition of a node and of a random number of edges relying this node to some other(s) of the agent's knowledge base chosen at random. The mean expected value of the number of edges created is equal to the density of the knowledge structure (d), and the non null integer $\left|\left\{\varepsilon_{ij}\right\}\right|$ is its realization. So the implicit assumptions here are both that the agents can't decide where from (which node(s)) they will create a piece of knowledge, and that there is a density conservation of the whole knowledge base (KB), admitting local specifications (the graph is not regular).

It has to be noticed that, as a creator, the agent can only estimate the values of the random variables ε_i and ε_{ij}, while, as an acquirer, he can observe their realizations $\hat{\varepsilon}_i$ and $\hat{\varepsilon}_{ij}$. Then, the higher the variances (σ_i^2 and σ_{ij}^2) of the random variables (ε_i and ε_{ij}), the higher the informational advantage (disadvantage) of acquisition (creation) behavior.

3.3. Choice between creation and acquisition

Given the one period payoffs of a given node k_i (in [1]), an agent a can deduce, at the beginning of a given period t, the actualized expected payoffs generated by the possession of this node denoted $V_{a,i}^t(n_i)$, and the expected benefits of undertaking a given action (with creation as a specific case characterized by $n_i = 1$) such as:

$$\Pi_{a,i}^t(n_i) = V_{a,i}^t(n_i) - C^t(n_i) \qquad [5]$$

with $C^t(n_i)$ the fixed costs of creating or acquiring a given piece of knowledge, that can be specified in the following way:

$$C^t(n_i) \equiv \begin{cases} c & \text{if } n_i = 1 \\ s \cdot \dfrac{A - n_i}{A - 2} & \text{if } n_i \geq 2 \end{cases} \qquad [6]$$

where the creation cost is a given constant c, and knowledge acquisition cost is a linearly decreasing function of the number of agents sharing it, which is equal to zero for $n_i = A$, and equal to the parameter s for $n_i = 2$. The shape of the cost function expresses the intuitive assumption that, the more a given piece of knowledge is shared, the less it is difficult to acquire it. Moreover, and as it is also intuitively accepted, there is a tunable gap between creation and acquisition costs (c/s). Then, the expected benefits for a to undertake a given action becomes:

$$\Pi_{a,i}^t(n_i) = \gamma \varepsilon_i \beta e^{n_i} + \lambda \left(\varepsilon_i \mu + \sum_{j \neq i} \varepsilon_{ij} \right) - C^t(n_i) \qquad [7]$$

with ε_i and ε_{ij} being estimated at their mean expected value when $n_i = 1$ and observed otherwise. λ and γ are the actualization terms. The first being the normal

one such as: $\lambda = \lambda(i,T) = \dfrac{1 - \left(\dfrac{1}{1+i}\right)^{T+1}}{1 - \dfrac{1}{1+i}}$ with i the discount rate and T the optimization

period. The latter $\gamma = \gamma(i,T,\tau,p_a^t)$ being the actualization term taking also into account the agent's expectations (as we shall see in the next section) on the speed of the sharing process of the knowledge he may create or acquire.

As long as the agent is choosing the action that he expects to be the most profitable, creation arises when $\Pi_a^t(1) > \Pi_a^t(n_i)$, $\forall k_i \in N_a^{t-1}$, that is when we have:

$$\gamma \left(\frac{\beta}{e} - \hat{\varepsilon}_i \beta e^{-n_i} \right) + \lambda \left((1-\hat{\varepsilon}_i)\mu + \frac{\left|K_a^{t-1}\right|}{\alpha} - \sum_i \hat{\varepsilon}_{ij} \right) > c - s \frac{A-n_i}{A-2}, \quad \forall k_i \in N_a^{t-1}. \qquad [8]$$

and $\Pi_a^t(1) > 0$, which means that the expected value of creating a piece of knowledge is strictly positive and greater than acquiring anyone which is accessible. Otherwise, the agent is acquiring a piece of knowledge under the additional condition: $\exists k_i \in N_a^{t-1}$ such that $\Pi_{a,i}^t(n_i) > 0$. In the third case ($\Pi_a^t(1) \leq 0$ and $\forall k_i \in N_a^{t-1}$, $\Pi_{a,i}^t(n_i) \leq 0$) the agent prefers not to do anything and inaction arises.

4. Knowledge disclosure rate, knowledge diffusion and knowledge expected value

The process of knowledge sharing is a two steps sequential process. First of all, all the created pieces of knowledge are secret and may be disclosed at each period with a constant exogenous and tunable probability τ, called the rate of disclosure. Since it is disclosed, it becomes accessible to others' acquisitions which gives birth to an endogenous diffusion process [5]. When a piece of knowledge is already shared by all agents, it cannot diffuse anymore. In order to determine the expected value of a given action, the agents are anticipating the speed of the sharing process of a piece of knowledge. Then they are affecting a value at the parameter γ and determine the value of $\Pi_{a,i}^t(n_i)$. To do so, the agents both, estimate correctly the number of periods before a piece of knowledge they may create will be disclosed (knowing the value of τ), and anticipate the speed of the endogenous diffusion of the piece of knowledge they may create or acquire. To form the latter anticipation, the agents are supposing that the others will still, in average, behave in the future the same way they did in the near past, and that these behaviors are independent of the knowledge value at the present date.

Let's assume that the agents are quite well informed about the past actions of the other agents. Then, each agent a knows the m past actions of the other agents and stores this knowledge in his memory which is simply a vector updated at the beginning of each period of time t_0: $M_{a,m}^{t_0} = (\phi_1,...,\phi_m)$ with $\phi_i \in \{-1,0,1\}$, respectively if the other agents have done acquisition, nothing or creation in the i'st preceding play of others (one agent and only one is playing at each period). In computing this memory they are assumed to make previsions on the future actions of others in following the rule: they equal the respective proportions of the different types of actions in the past to the probabilities that the others will undertake these different types of actions in the future. Specifically, at period t_0, an agent a is assigning an idiosyncratic probability to the event that, at each future period of time, if another agent than him is playing, he expects that he will acquire a piece of knowledge with probability $p_{a,s}^{t_0} \equiv \frac{1}{m}\Sigma_{\phi_i \in M_{a,m}^{t_0}} \Gamma(\phi_i)$, with $\Gamma(\phi_i)$ the dummy variable which is equal to 1 if $\phi_i = (-1)$, and equal to 0 otherwise.

Let then an agent a deduce, from the probability $p_{a,s}^{t_0}$, the value, fixed in t_0, of the probability that any disclosed piece of knowledge is shared by one more agent at each period of time in the future (denoted $p_a^{t_0}$), in the following way:

$$p_a^{t_0} \equiv P_a^{t_0}(n_i^{t+1} = n_i^t + 1 | n_i^{t_0} \geq 2) = \frac{p_{a,s}^{t_0}(A-1)}{K \times A}, \ \forall t \text{ such that } t_0 \leq t \leq T \qquad [9]$$

which is the probability that another agent will play, that he will choose to acquire a piece of knowledge and finally decide to acquire this given piece of knowledge among all others (the agent considering these three events as mutually independent and independent of the present payoffs generated by the piece of knowledge).

---

[5] In a previous version of this paper we introduced the possibility that unexpected re-creation arises. For simplicity and place requirements we didn't retain this technicality even if it may be of great importance in certain situations.

Since, one can acquire only a disclosed piece of knowledge, we are now able to specify the value the agent is giving to the actualization term γ in the acquisition case ($n_i^{t_0} \geq 2$):

$$\gamma\left(i, T, \tau, p_{a,s}^{t_0} \middle| n_i^{t_0} \geq 2\right) = \frac{1 - U^I}{1 - U} + U^I \frac{1 - Q^{1+T-I}}{1 - Q} \qquad [10]$$

with $U = \dfrac{e^{-p_a^{t_0}}}{1+i}$, $Q = \dfrac{1}{1+i}$ and $I = Int\left(\dfrac{A - n_i^{t_0}}{p_a^{t_0}}\right)$ if $I < T$ and $I = T$ otherwise (to

control the sequentially of the process and its restriction on the optimization period T). The probability the agent is assigning to the event that one more agent will be sharing the piece of knowledge in the future periods of time being constant, the number of periods until all agents will be sharing the piece of knowledge is geometrically distributed with parameter $p_a^{t_0}$ and mean expected value $1/p_a^{t_0}$. Then the estimated period at which the expected number of agents sharing the piece of knowledge will stop increasing (being acquired by all agents) is the nearest integer

of $t_0 + \dfrac{A - n_i^{t_0}}{p_a^{t_0}}$.

Concerning the actualization term γ in the creation case, the agents' expectations about the sharing of the piece of knowledge in the future periods have to also take into account the period of time during which the piece of knowledge will be kept secret. The expected value of this period is only function of the disclosure probability τ. Once the piece of knowledge is disclosed, it enters in the acquisition process exposed above. Then the actualization term becomes in this case:

$$\gamma\left(i, T, \tau, p_{a,s}^{t_0} \middle| n_i^{t_0} = 1\right) = \frac{1 - Q^Y}{1 - Q} + Q^Y\left(\frac{1 - U^{J-Y}}{1 - U} + U^I \frac{1 - Q^{1+T-J}}{1 - Q}\right) \qquad [11]$$

with U and Q the same than in the acquisition case, $Y = Int(1/\tau)$ if $1/\tau < T$ and

$1/\tau = T$ otherwise, and finally $J = Int\left(\dfrac{1}{\tau} + \dfrac{A-1}{p_a^{t_0}}\right)$ if $\left(\dfrac{1}{\tau} + \dfrac{A-1}{p_a^{t_0}}\right) < T$ and $J = T$

otherwise. The agent is ensured to maintain its returns on knowledge creation investment until it is disclosed, and from then we fall in the acquisition process described above. Both events, the number of periods before the piece of knowledge is disclosed and, the number of periods between it is disclosed and it is totally shared are geometrically distributed with parameters τ and $p_a^{t_0}$, and with mean expected values $1/\tau$ and $1/p_a^{t_0}$. Then the estimated period at which the piece of knowledge shall be disclosed is the nearest integer of $t_0 + 1/\tau$ and, the one at which the piece of

knowledge shall be shared by all agents, is the nearest integer of $t_0 + \left(\dfrac{1}{\tau} + \dfrac{A-1}{p_a^{t_0}}\right)$.

5. Simulations' results: the optimal rate of disclosure

We need first of all a criterion in order to evaluate the social efficiency in the different runs. We chose (among other equivalent indicators) the average social payoffs growth over the whole running period (denoted $T^{\max}$) which is simply:

$$\bar{g} \equiv \frac{1}{T^{\max}} \sum_{t=1}^{T^{\max}} \frac{\sum_a R(KB_a^t)}{\sum_a R(KB_a^{t-1})} \qquad [12]$$

We are trying to find out what should be the "relevant" (or optimal) tuning of the rate of disclosure τ^*, in various situations characterized by: the initial settings in term of knowledge endowments, the density d, the relative importance of the nodes values over the complementarities ones α, the range of knowledge use μ, the substituability of products β, the informational advantage of knowledge acquisition over knowledge creation, and the parameters affecting the actions' costs (c and s).

As fixed parameters, we also have to specify the number of agents, the initial number of knowledge pieces, the discount rate and, the actualization period. We have taken 5 agents and 25 pieces of knowledge at the initial period. The discount rate is fixed at $i = 0.01$. Then, each five period round could be considered as one year. Each agent playing in average once each five period, we can then consider that each agent is playing in average once a year. The creation cost (c) is assumed to be four times the acquisition cost when $n_i = 2$ (s). The actualization period is $T = 200$ and the whole run is of $T^{\max} = 1000$ periods. The random variables (ε_i and ε_{ij}) are uniformly distributed. Each simulation run is fully documented, and some of the informations we have on each run are presented in Figure 1.

Directly coming from the model settings, we can infer that there is no need for a rate of disclosure which would be lower than $\bar{\tau} = 1/T$, that is the one that maximizes the creations' incentives, if the time horizon T is finite.

Coming from the overall set of simulations, we observed that, except for very high values of the variance of the random terms of the knowledge value function, the simulations do not exhibit contradictory results but robust ones. It should also be noticed, that, the exact knowledge structure being not under control of the simulator, but only its size and its density, the results have to be considered as robust ones whatever is the exact knowledge structure (relying only on the density index).

From the simulation runs, we obtained the following results (the three first ones are proving that a disclosure rate higher than $\bar{\tau}$ may be useful, and the others are detailing the impact of different parameters on the optimal rate of disclosure τ^*):

Result 1/ Contrarily to the standard assumptions, there are many situations in which a quite high level of disclosure ($\tau > \bar{\tau}$) is socially efficient. Once a certain number of periods attained, the disclosure process permits the "realization" of the positive externalities of previous creations.

Result 2/ On the other side, there is no linear consideration on the rate of disclosure: if the disclosure rate is too high, creation behavior may be no more interesting. The set of available pieces of knowledge is then decreasing dramatically until acquisition opportunities become rare. Then inaction may arise which implies social payoffs stagnation.

Result 3/ For each set of values of the initial settings and of the structural parameters, there is a robust optimal level of τ (Figure 2) which can be determined by adjustment. This result comes from a phase transition phenomenon on disclosure, which permits a sufficient social payoffs increase (without big need to further improve disclosure rate compared to the necessity to preserve creation incentives). That means there is not an identical optimal value of τ for different values of the other parameters. This is confirming the assumption ([HYD 99]) which calls for considering and settling the institutional settings affecting knowledge diffusion and knowledge creation incentives, in different manners depending on the sector and on the technological field concerned.

Result 4/ If the variances of the random variables affecting knowledge value are high, that is the informative advantage of the acquisition behavior is high, then knowledge acquisition becomes more valuable compared to creation behaviors which is then very risky [6]. Consequently, the higher the variances of the random variables, the higher the optimal disclosure rate.

Result 5/ The lower the relative value of the knowledge pieces values over the complementarities ones, the higher is the optimal disclosure rate. When the value of knowledge is combinatorial, acquisition behaviors should be favored in order to permit the valorization of the various complementarities.

Result 6/ The optimal rate of disclosure increases with the range of knowledge use. When μ becomes high, acquisition behavior becomes relatively more profitable and should then be favored in increasing the speed of the diffusion.

Result 7/ When the substituability of products (β) becomes high, creation behavior should be encouraged because of its high private and social returns. Then the optimal rate of disclosure τ^* is lower.

Result 8/ The lower the density d, the higher the risk of divergence [7] which implies a relative stagnation of acquisition possibilities. In order to avoid this risk a higher disclosure rate is required when d is low.

---

[6] Note that in this case, the average growth obtained with the same set of parameters becomes more volatile. But, with a sufficient amount of simulations, the results are still confirmed.

[7] We define a situation of divergence by the co-occurrence of an increase of the social knowledge base and a stagnation (or a weak increase) of the average neighborhood size.

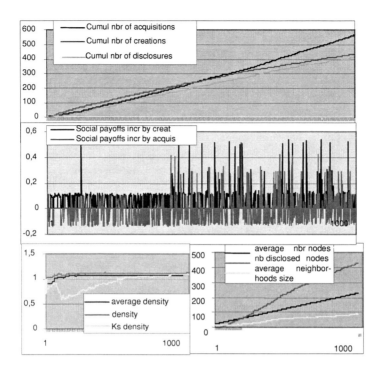

Figure 1. *Some relevant documentation of a single simulation run: the cumulated number of the different types of behaviors and of the disclosures, the social payoffs increase while behaving of the different manners, the evolution of the densities of KB, KB_s and, KB_a and, the evolution of the average neighborhood size compared to total number of disclosed nodes*

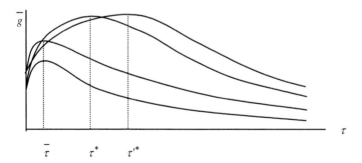

Figure 2. *The various optimal levels of the disclosure rate τ for different sets of values of the other parameters*

6. Conclusion

In this paper, we have presented a model which wishes to take into account most of the knowledge creation and diffusion processes exposed in recent empirical and theoretical literature. The model is built on the assumption that knowledge has a "cognitive local character", and is using Graph Theory to represent knowledge as a structure. The agents have knowledge bases they can improve in choosing between creating or acquiring a piece of knowledge. This choice is function of the fixed costs and expected values of the different actions. Because knowledge value is decreasing with the number of agents sharing it, an increased speed of knowledge diffusion is decreasing the expected value of knowledge. The speed of the sharing process being partly tunable (and partly endogenous) through the determination of the rate of disclosure, we faced a dilemma between encouraging knowledge diffusion or knowledge creation incentives in order to maximize collective efficiency.

Running computer simulations, we showed that there exists, in many situations, a non null optimal rate of disclosure which maximizes the collective performance of a population of agents. The optimal rate of disclosure is varying with the values of the structural parameters. This gives a theoretical justification of some empirical research highlighting the criticality, especially in certain sectors, of knowledge disclosure and diffusion. Discussing the effect of some of the parameters on the optimal rate of disclosure, we showed that a higher rate of disclosure is particularly important in economic configurations characterized by either a high level of uncertainty in knowledge creation, a high level of complementarity between different pieces of knowledge, a high level of knowledge use range, a low level of product substitutability and/or, a low level of knowledge codification.

Bibliography

[ALL 83] ALLEN R., "Collective invention", *Journal of Economic Behavior and Organization*, no. 4, 1983, p. 1-24.

[ARR 62] ARROW K., "Economic welfare and the allocation of resources for invention", in *The Rate and Direction of Inventive Activity: Economic and Social Factors,* National Bureau of Economic Research, Princeton University Press, Princeton, 1962.

[ARR 94b] ARROW K., "Methodological individualism and social knowledge", *American Economic Review*, Richard T. Ely Lecture, vol. 84 n°2, 1994, p. 1-9.

[ATK 69] ATKINSON A.B., STIGLITZ J.E., "A new view of technological change", *Economic Journal*, vol. 79, 1969, p. 573-578.

[BOU 55] BOULDING K., "Notes on the information concept", Exploration (Toronto), vol. 6, 1955, p. 103-112.

[CAR 98] CARAYOL N., "The evolution of scientific knowledge: a self-organization model", *EAEPE conference*, Lisbon, 5 8 November, 1998.

[COH 90] COHEN W., LEVINTHAL D., "Absorptive capacity: a new perspective on learning and innovation", *Administrative Science Quarterly*, vol. 35 no. 1, 1990, p. 128-152.

[COW 97] COWAN R., FORAY D., "The economics of knowledge and the diffusion of knowledge", *Industrial and Corporate Change*, vol. 16 no. 3, 1997, p. 596-622.

[COW 99] COWAN R., JONARD N., "Network structure and knowledge interaction", working paper no. 28, may 1999, MERIT.

[DAL 99], DALLE J.M., JULIEN N., "An economic analysis of Free Software : NT vs. Linux, or some exploration into the economics of creativity", *EMAEE conference*, Grenoble, June 1999.

[DAS 94] DASGUPTA P., DAVID P., "Toward a new economics of science", *Research Policy*, vol. 23, 1994, p. 487-521.

[DAV 92] DAVID P., FORAY D., "Percolation structures, markov random fields and the economics of EDI standard diffusion", discussion paper series no. 326, 1992, CEPR, Stanford University.

[DAV 95] DAVID P., FORAY D., "Distribution and expansion of the scientific and technologic knowledge base", *STI Review*, no. 16, OCDE, 1995, p. 13-73

[FAV 98] FAVEREAU O., "Note sur la théorie de l'information à laquelle pourrait conduire l'économie des conventions", in PETIT P., *l'Economie de l'information. Les Enseignements des Théories Economiques*, 1998, Paris, La Découverte, p. 195-238.

[GAR 99] GARROUSTE P., "Apprentissage, interactions, et création de connaissance", *Revue d'Economie Industrielle*, no. 88, 1999, p. 137-152.

[HIR 71] HIRSHLEIFER J., "The private and the social value of information and the reward to inventive activity", *American Economic Review*, vol. 61, 1971, p. 561-574.

[HYD 99] HYDE A., "The wealth of shared information: silicon valley's high-velocity labor market, endogenous economic growth, and the law of trade secrets", 1999, Rutgers University.

[LOB 99] LOBO J., MACREADY W.G., "Landscapes: a natural extension of search theory", working paper no. 05-37, 1999, Santafe Institute.

[LUN 95] LUNDVALL B.A., FORAY D., "The knowledge based economy. From the economics of knowledge to the learning economy", *Conference La Connaissance dans les Organisations productives*, Aix en Provence, 1995.

[MAC 84] MACHLUP F., K*nowledge: its creation, distribution, and economic significance*, vol. 3, Princeton, Princeton University Press, 1984.

[ROM 93] ROMER P., "Implementing a national technology strategy with self-organizing industry investment boards", in BAILLY M.N., REISS P.C., WINSTON C., *Brooking Papers on Economic Activity. Microeconomics*, 1993, p. 345-399.

[SAV 98] SAVIOTTI P.P., "On the Dynamics of Appropriability, of Tacit and of Codified Knowledge", *Research Policy*, vol. 26, no. 7/8, 1998, p. 843-856.

[SAX 94] SAXENIAN A., *The Regional Advantage. Culture and competition in Silicon Valley and Route 128*, Cambridge (Mass), Harvard University Press, 1994.

[STI 61] STIGLER G., "The economics of information", *Journal of Political Economy*, vol. 69, 1961, p. 213-225.

ECONOMICS

APPLIED MARKET MODELS

Simulating transaction networks in housing markets

Leslie Rosenthal

Department of Economics, University of Keele
Keele, Staffs ST5 5BG, UK

l.rosenthal@keele.ac.uk

ABSTRACT: *Linked networks of transactors attempting to complete both the buying and selling of properties, often termed "housing chains", are conspicuous features within owner-occupied housing markets, often seen as a cause of severe delay to transaction completion. This paper introduces a bounded or limited rationality-based model of housing market transactions and examines the properties and predictions of the resultant system. Agent-based simulation is able to reproduce: a) the existence of chains of buyers and sellers observed in the housing market; b) the delays to transaction completion often noted; and c) the empirical observation that housing price series for first-time buyers and for new or vacant housing serially leads the series for existing, current owner-occupiers.*

KEY WORDS: *Housing: Owner-Occupation: Transactions: Simulation.*

1. Introduction

Owner-occupied housing markets display a unique and, in many ways, a puzzling phenomenon of linked networks of buying and selling transactors, often termed "housing chains". Within such chains, all links must be in place before the final exchanges of any individual pairing can take place. Such features within housing markets are observable wherever owner-occupied housing is common.. Owner-occupier household A, although contracted at an agreed price to sell to household B, finds itself unable proceed with the transaction because B's agreement to sell its own property to C is held up, possibly because of problems further down the line. Transactions can finalise only when a completed chain comes into existence. Quite long networks may form, over many dwellings and contracts (links). The whole process, involving pairs of transactors having to wait for third parties to obtain totally separate contracts before their own contracts can be honoured, can delay substantially the time required for owner-occupier transactions. Clearly, the existence of housing chains depends on markets failing either to provide middle-man arbitrageurs or to provide easily-available short term bridging loans to facilitate temporary ownership of more than a single owner-occupier property.

A model of the owner-occupied housing market is here presented which produces such chains of linked networks of buyers and sellers awaiting each other's housing transaction completion. Agents act according to limited or bounded-rational behavioral rules and an agent-based simulation methodology is used to explore some properties of the system.

Alongside the desire to reproduce both chains and the delays caused by chains, the model is also aimed at allowing an explanation for the empirical observation that price changes within the *existing* owner-occupier sector normally lag those in the first-time buyer and newly constructed properties sectors of the housing market [ROS, 1997]. For a speedy motivation, figure 1 has been constructed. This shows hedonic-price-based, quality-adjusted, monthly housing price indices on first-time buyers and existing owner-occupiers for South-East England (including London) for the period 1986-91. This period covers a major boom and bust cycle in house prices in the UK, and the figure provides graphical justification for the lagging of price changes within the existing owner-occupied sector.

Previous academic literature on the economics of housing chains is sparse. Rosenthal [ROS 97] presents an earlier model, but does not attempt to determine house prices endogenously. With regard to the empirics of housing links, Forrest and Murie present evidence for the UK on housing chains [FOR 94]. Starting from the purchase of new dwellings, they report some ten per cent of chains could be traced back four or more linkages. DETR reports a survey of experiences of buyers and sellers on the UK housing market [DET 98] and notes an average delay, *after contract offers are accepted,* of around three months until transactions complete. Ten per cent of transactions are reported to take over six months more.

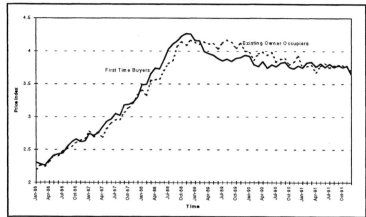

Figure 1. *Housing Price Indices for South-East England 1986-91 Existing Owner-Occupiers and First Time Buyers*

Within the remainder of the present paper, section 2 presents an outline of the model of the housing transactions market, where the price of housing is endogenously determined and pairwise contracts between buyers and sellers are forged. At the end of each market period, the structure of existing contracts is examined to search for fully formed chains, members of which are able finally to complete their transactions. Section 3 discusses the characteristics of the model, and presents the results of a number of simulations. This section also presents the bases for arguments on the existence of lags in prices for the existing owner-occupier sector compared to the other sectors. Section 4 presents some summary comments.

2. The Model

The basic model of the market used here is based on a "simple" rules, limited rational, model of Lesourne ([LES 92]). This forms part of a two-stage process. The first market stage determines the price of housing and forges pairwise contracts. The second stage reviews the system of contracts so that where successful chains have formed final transactions can take place.

The description of the model is divided into several sections:

2.1   Basic Background
2.2   The Market Period and Price Determination
2.3   Chain Completion
2.4   Leftover Agents adjust Reservation Prices and New Agents Enter

2.1. Basic Background

Three mutually exclusive types of agent exist, each trading one-unit blocks of housing: a) "first-time buyers" do not yet own any housing, but wish to purchase a single unit; b) "empty dwelling sellers" wish to sell single units of housing but not buy any; and c) "existing owner-occupiers", who must simultaneously both buy a new unit and sell an existing unit of housing. Decisions to enter the housing market are exogenous and a fixed, arbitrary number of each type of agent enter the market at the beginning of each market period, each with a given, exogenously determined, reservation price. If asked to trade at prices outside this reservation amount, the agents concerned will contract to buy/sell zero units in the period. As we shall see, the number of entering first-time buyers and empty dwelling sellers must be equal unless we are to see a continuous increase in the numbers of one or other of these two types of agent over time.

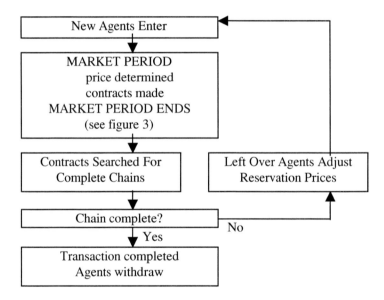

Figure 2. *Basic Schema of Model*

The flow chart on figure 2 shows the overall scheme of the model. New agents of whatever type join any agents left over from previous periods to take part in the contract forging (linkage) process within the market period. At the end of the market period, the networks of contracts now existing are checked for complete chains, and the agents involved in these chains are able to complete their transactions and withdraw from the market. Any agents unable to complete at this stage must await new entrants to the market and/or adjust their reservation price as a new market period ensues.

2.2. *The Market Period and Price Determination*

Inside the market period, buyers (either first-time buyers or existing owner-occupiers) interact with sellers (either empty dwelling sellers or existing owner-occupiers) to determine the price of housing. Both buyers and sellers follow simple rules. Within the market period there are an indeterminate number of "rounds", each round enabling every buyer to look for acceptable contract prices among the sellers. Contracts form and re-form over rounds until a stable state, explained below, emerges. Then putative contracts become binding and the market period ends.

Rules followed by buyers and sellers, and the stable state, are now briefly described, and the reader may find figure 3 a useful aide. Beginning each round, every seller declares a single "announced price" (itself determined by a set of rules as below) at which the seller is willing to accept or renew a contract.

2.2.1. *Buyers*

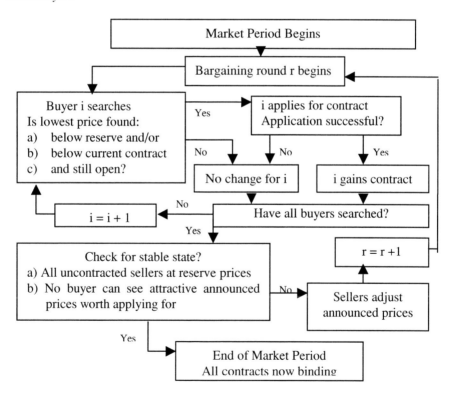

Figure 3. *Schema for the Market Period*

Buyers are taken singly in turn in each round, in random order, to search the announced prices of the sellers. The lowest seller's price found is compared to the buyer's reservation price and the price on any contract the buyer might hold from the previous round. A new contact will be forged, (and any old contract costlessly broken) if: a) a low price is observed, at least equal to the buyer's reservation price, and strictly lower than that on any existing contract; b) the seller concerned has not already closed a deal for the round, and c) the seller concerned is unable to re-contract at the current announced price with the contract holder from the previous round, if one exists.

This process continues through the round, until all the buyers have participated. At the end of the round, the system is checked for whether a stable state exists, as described below, and if not, a new round will commence. Only in a stable state do contracts formed become fully binding.

2.2.2. Sellers

At the end of each round within the market period, if the check for a stable state has failed, each seller declares an announced price applicable for the coming new round. This announced price follows from the seller's situation at the end of the round: a) if a contract to sell has been closed or renewed, for the next round the announced price will be that contract price plus one unit; b) if no contract exists, the announced price will be the current announced price less one unit (until the seller's reservation price is reached).

For contract-making, sellers' actions match those outlined for the buyer: The seller closes a contract either with the first buyer willing to match the announced price in a new contract, or by re-contracting with an existing contract-holder from the last round, who is preferentially allowed to match any new "outside" offer.

2.2.3. Stable State

When no more swaps to the system of contracts between buyers and sellers are forthcoming, a stable state exists. This requires two conditions: a) all sellers without any contract for the current round must have reduced their announced prices to the minimum their reservations allow; and b) when searching, no buyer is able to observe an announced price that makes it attractive to make an application. Hence all announced prices that the buyers can see must be either higher than their reservation, or as high as the price they already face. Compared with their current contract, no actual or potential attractive alternative exists for any of the buyers involved. On the existence of a stable state, all putative contracts held are declared as binding, and the market period is declared to have ended.

2.2.4. *The Market*

In this model, buyers use information obtained from searching the range of sellers to apply if and where prices are more favourable than in existing contracts. Sellers use information, from the existence or absence of applications and contracts, that the announced prices they are demanding may be out of line, and adjust accordingly. The behavioural rules presented for buyers, sellers and for the stable state, are enough to sort the buyers and sellers, so that the N buyers with the highest reservation buying prices are paired, in some way, with the N sellers with the lowest reservation selling prices. At the end of a market period, but for one unit of price, contract prices will be the same in all contracts. The one-unit discrepancy arises from the discrete, integer formulation employed.

Apart from this lumpiness, the outcome is identical to a familiar market demand and supply model. An actual realisation of the system provides one of a number of possible pairwise matchings of the buyers and sellers whose reservation values allow contracts to be formed. Some agents will find that their reservation values are too out of line to participate in any exchange. Such agents are allowed to adjust their reservations and re-participate in the next market period.

The reader will recognise the programmable nature of the system described. This market mechanism specification, based on Lesourne's "simple" rules model, forms the price-determining core of the agent-based simulation model used here. While individual links are forged within this market system, the description of the way that links must form into whole networks of chains follows.

2.3. *Chain Completion*

As a market period ends, some buyers (including the buying side of existing owner-occupiers) and some sellers (including the selling side of existing owner-occupiers) will find themselves without contracts due to their reservation values being out of line. Others, of course, will be holding viable contracts.

The array of binding contracts is now examined to see whether finished networks of chains have come into existence that can enable satisfied agents to leave the market. As existing owner-occupiers are not allowed to buy without selling their existing dwelling, nor to sell an existing one without having re-purchased, it is possible that a first time buyer A, is prevented from buying the dwelling of existing owner-occupier B because B has failed to conclude a contract to buy a dwelling from C, or anyone else. Networks can be incomplete.

Complete networks (successful chains) can be one of two general types. The vast majority will begin with a first time buyer buying at one end of the chain, linking on to an empty dwelling seller selling at the other end of the chain. Such a chain may be a single dwelling traded by empty dwelling seller to first time buyer, but often the chain will have an indeterminate number of existing owner occupiers buying and selling in the middle. Each such successful chain will have *exactly* one first-time buyer and one new dwelling seller at each end. The second type of successful chain, and the only other possibility, is one composed entirely of owner-occupiers going in a "tail-swallowing" circle, with the "last" owner-occupier buying the dwelling of the "first". (The technical possibility of an owner-occupier household buying from and selling to itself is disallowed).

All satisfied agents within complete chains withdraw from the market entirely. Individual contracts which are formed, but which do not link up with other contracts into either type of successful chain, are taken to be fully binding into further market periods, although this restriction is certainly not required. The links, contracts and prices already formed are carried forward alongside any further newly-forming contracts for the determination of new complete chains after the next market period converges. Thus, chains can build bit by bit over a number of periods. Where links have formed but have failed to build into complete chains, agents involved await the inflow of new agents, and the outcome of reservation price revisions, to overcome the bottlenecks faced.

2.4. *Left Over Agents adjust Reservation Prices and New Agents Enter*

Often, agents will fail to find a contract during the market period because their selling reservations values are too high or buying reservations too low. Rather than allow the numbers of frustrated agents to grow indefinitely, the model allows reservation values to be revised. For agents who fail to conclude a contract at the end of the period, sellers reduce their minimum acceptable price by one unit, and buyers increase their maximum acceptable price by one unit.

At the beginning of each new market period, there is an in-flow onto the market of new agents of all three types. As first-time buyers and empty dwelling owners can only exit the system in non-tail-swallowing chains at a rate of exactly one each per chain, entry numbers for these types of agent are also kept equal each period. Agents entering are randomly assigned reservation prices from a uniform distribution of integer values, centered on the average price for contracts formed during the previous market period. The price of housing is able to evolve over time.

3. Characteristics of the Model

The remainder of the paper examines the characteristics of the model set out above, presenting both equilibrium results and simulations of the model.

Stationarity for the model requires the stock of each type of agent existing in the market remains constant over time, so that entry and exit numbers must be equal for types of agent. Complete chains come in two varieties, tail-swallowing (TS) and non-tail-swallowing. The sole means of escape for first-time buyers (FTB) and empty dwelling sellers is to form the closed ends of non-tail-swallowing chains, so these agents exit at the rate of exactly one each per chain. Similarly, for stationarity, the number of new owner-occupiers (OO) entering the system must also equal the number of owner-occupiers exiting.

It is relatively straightforward to derive a number of basic properties of the model, applicable to the stationary equilibrium of the system [ROS 98]. The number of chains completing each market period at stationarity will equal the number of first-time-buyer exits (and entries) plus the number of tail-swallowing (TS) chains:

$$\text{Number of chains} \quad = \quad \text{number of FTB exits} + \text{number of TS chains} \qquad [1]$$

At stationarity, the average length of completing chains (measured in links or contracts) is determined by the relative numbers of entering agents of the different types, and so long as the number of tail-swallowing chains is small (as it is), then it may be shown that:

$$\text{Average chain length} \quad \approx \quad 1 + (\text{OO entry/FTB entry}) \qquad [2]$$

Agents can begin a market period either already contracted (linked) to another agent or not. Becoming part of a complete chain during the period depends upon whether or not the agent is already encumbered by carrying forward a contract to another agent who cannot complete during the current period. Exit probabilities depend on whether such links exist. By type of agent (and the situation of the first-time buyer (FTB) and the empty dwelling seller is identical), the probabilities of exit at stationarity may be shown to be such that:

$$\text{Prob(exit of unlinked FTB)} > \text{Prob(exit of FTB linked to OO)}$$

$$= \text{Prob(exit of OO linked to FTB)} > \text{Prob(exit of unlinked OO)} \qquad [3]$$

An as-yet-unlinked and uncontracted first-time buyer with realistic reservations, will be able to form complete links in the current period either directly with an empty dwelling seller, or with a part chain including an empty dwelling seller. By linking to an owner-occupier, such a household may harm its chances of completing during the period by becoming stuck with an unclosed part-chain containing an owner-occupier who has yet to adjust reservation prices to marketable levels. Owner-occupiers must avoid such problems on both their buying and selling sides to complete. Formal consideration of such arguments leads to the inequalities of equation [3]. By implication, the expected number of periods from entry to exit must be correspondingly longer for owner-occupiers than for the other two types of agent. Similarly, the stationary stock of owner-occupiers must be larger than for the other two types of agent (for equal entry numbers).

Although the number of each type of agent in the market will change stochastically over time, central values must be such that, at the stationary probabilities of exit for each type, the required numbers of exits matches entries. Over time, during periods when there are relatively high concentrations of owner-occupiers, the probability of an open link of a partially formed chain connecting with an owner-occupier, rather than anyone else, is increased. So, when high concentrations of owner-occupiers occur, chains will form with increased numbers of owner-occupiers between the first-time buyer and empty dwelling seller, and longer chains will appear. This mechanism equilibrates the model

Other characteristics of the model's behaviour are much less tractable. This is especially true in regard to the non-stationary dynamics and the distribution of chain lengths produced. To explore these less accessible characteristics and the outcome evolution, some agent-based simulations of the system are undertaken, using the author's own programs.

The specific parameters employed for the simulations reported here are arbitrary, but the model's simulated characteristics are robust to a wide range of values for parameters chosen. For the simulations reported here, 100,000 market periods were allowed, plus an initial 100 periods discarded to help disallow any initial conditions effects. Most runs were for a market with ten-to-thirty buyers (first-time buyers and existing owner-occupiers) and equal numbers of sellers (empty dwelling sellers and existing owner-occupiers) entering the market anew each period, to join buyers and sellers uncompleted from prior periods. Even when computing is cheap, quick and personal, simulation times for larger numbers of agents proved daunting, for no appreciably different results. As noted above, the numbers of entering first-time buyers and empty dwelling sellers are kept equal. Each buyer searches a random sample of eight seller prices during each round within the market period. The reservation values are integers taken from a uniform distribution with a range of plus or minus five units around a central value of the previous market period price[1]. The initial starting price is set at 1000.

Figure 4 shows the number of owner-occupiers and first-time buyers in the virtual market over 300 periods of a typical run of the model. Here, 20 buyers and 20 sellers (10 owner-occupiers, 10 first-time buyers and 10 empty-dwelling sellers) enter every market period. Note how the numbers seem to fluctuate around a long-run average, and how the average number of owner-occupiers exceeds that for first-time buyers. The amplitude of owner-occupier fluctuations also seems to be larger.

---

[1] The number of announced prices that buyers search affects only the number of rounds that the model takes to converge (and the time taken for the simulations to run). The range of the distribution from which reservation prices are taken affects the overall time agents spend within the market, as it affects the number of market periods taken for reservation prices to be adjusted to tradable levels

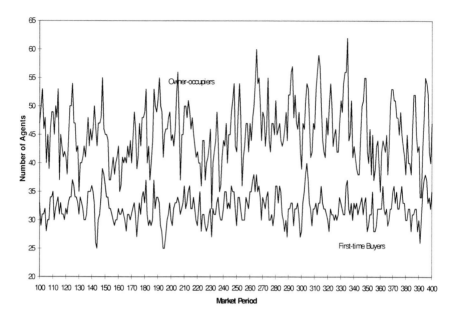

Note: Uses formulation with ten of each type of agent (formulation III). Shows number of owner-occupiers and first-time buyers over 300 market periods.

Figure 4. *Time Series of Numbers of Owner-Occupiers and First-time Buyers*

Table 1 shows a number of relevant statistics for runs of the model for five formulations, which differ only in the numbers of owner-occupiers that newly enter each period. Several noteworthy results emerge in line with the stationary theory results presented above. The simulations produce further results however. The figures in the final few rows show the distribution of the lengths of chains forming and that to grow chains of notable length, relatively large numbers of owner-occupiers are required. So-called "tail-swallowing" chains, containing only owner-occupiers, are clearly rare, appearing only at a rate of about one-half of one per cent of all chains. They are rare because, for a tail-swallowing chain to emerge, one open end of the developing chain must link with the *exact* owner-occupier at the other open end of the chain, in competition with a large number of searching first-time buyers and other closing links.

	Formulation				
	I	II	III	IV	V
Entry Numbers					
First Time Buyers	10	10	10	10	10
Owner Occupiers	1	5	10	15	20
Empty Dwelling Sellers	10	10	10	10	10
Average Stock Numbers					
First-time Buyer	24.82	28.11	31.60	34.72	37.46
Owner-Occupier	3.45	19.70	44.62	73.98	106.85
Periods to Completion					
First-time Buyer	3.46	3.79	4.14	4.45	4.72
Owner-Occupier	4.34	4.68	5.25	5.71	6.10
No of Chains	10.00	10.01	10.03	10.04	10.05
Tail-Swallowing Chains	0.00	0.01	0.03	0.04	0.05
Average Chain Length	1.10	1.50	2.00	2.49	2.98
Length Distribution					
1	9.07	6.62	4.96	3.97	3.31
2	0.87	2.29	2.54	2.42	2.42
3	0.06	0.76	1.29	1.49	1.53
4	0.00	0.24	0.64	0.88	1.00
5 and more	0.00	0.11	0.60	1.28	1.97

Notes: Results averaged over 100,000 periods. Formulations differ in the number of owner-occupiers entering each period, as shown in top rows.

Table 1. *Simulation results*

The table shows that the number of owner-occupied agents in the market remains a larger multiple of owner-occupier entry numbers than obtains for first-time buyers (and empty dwelling sellers), and this implies a longer time is required to exit the system for the owner-occupier than for other agents. This is confirmed elsewhere in the table: for all the results shown the owner-occupier can expect to remain active in the market longer than will the other two types of agent.

The prediction that owner-occupiers will expect to spend more periods in the market has implications for observable phenomena within the housing market. Agreements between buyers and sellers are permanently fixed once settled, at least in this version of the model and owner-occupiers will tend to hold contracts over relatively more periods before completion. If shocks occur, to reservation values or to the numbers of agents entering, causing market prices to change over time, then the price series for the existing owner-occupier section of the housing market will tend to lag that of the other sectors. One motivation for the research reported here was for an explanation for this phenomenon, observed in the UK.

The lag of the existing owner-occupied price series may be shown explicitly in a further simulation shown in figure 5.

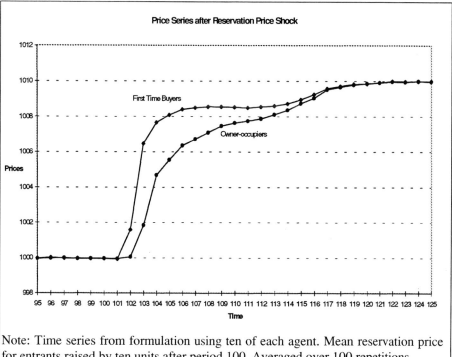

Note: Time series from formulation using ten of each agent. Mean reservation price for entrants raised by ten units after period 100. Averaged over 100 repetitions.

Figure 5. *Profile of prices after an exogenous shock to reservation values*

A once-for-all, exogenous and permanent increase in the reservation values held by entering buyers and sellers is imposed on the agents. The average market price for dwellings over time is then observed. The time profile of average outcome prices, averaged over one hundred repetitions, for one set of parameters (ten owner-occupiers, ten first-time buyers). For each run, after a hundred periods, centre reservation values were increased from 1000 to 1010 on both the buying and selling sides for all entering agents. This change will cause an increase in observed market price of ten units in the long-run. But in the short-run, because some binding pairwise contracts have been previously concluded at lower market prices, exiting chains will include a mixture of contract prices until all the agents holding contracts at the old prices eventually leave the system. As owner-occupiers take longer to leave the system, the owner-occupier price series will contain earlier, lower priced contracts for longer and will therefore lag other agents' series. The effect is clearly shown on the figure, and provides, therefore, an explanation for an otherwise puzzling feature of observed housing markets.

4. Summary and Conclusions

This paper presents a model of transactions within the owner-occupied housing market allowing for the emergence of networks or chains of transacting buyers and sellers, where the final exchange of the product traded will be delayed until completed chains appear. Various theoretic results and agent-based simulations of the model were presented.

One of the predictions of the model is that different types of agent in the market will spend different lengths of time waiting for chains finally to complete. Specifically, existing owner-occupiers will spend longer in the market, and as a consequence, the time series of owner-occupied dwelling prices should lag the time series of dwelling prices for the other types of agents. This prediction provides an explanation for an empirical phenomenon of the UK housing market.

There seem great possibilities for further research in this area. Extending the model to allow spatial considerations may help explain the existence of the leads and lags observed between housing price series in different cities and regions (for example, the UK's "regional ripple" of house price rises). Other features of housing and related markets, where market inefficiencies in the form of leads and lags appear, may be amenable to analysis where the slow build-up of transaction networks play a central role.

Acknowledgments

The research reported here owes much to help and ideas for improvement from Michael Devereux and Gauthier Lanot, and to the original funding of ESRC under grant R000233462.

References

[DET 98] DETR, *Key research on easier home buying and selling*, London, Department of the Environment Transport and the Regions, 1998.

[FOR 94] FORREST R., MURIE A., "The dynamics of the owner-occupied housing market in Southern England in the late 1980s: a study of new building and vacancy chains", *Regional Studies*, vol. 28 no. 3, 1994, p. 275-289.

[LES 92] LESOURNE J., *The economics of order and disorder*, Clarendon Press, Oxford, 1992.

[ROS 97] ROSENTHAL L., "Chain-formation in the owner-occupied housing market", *Economic Journal*, vol. 107, no. 3, 1997, p. 475-488.

[ROS 98] ROSENTHAL L., *Housing chains, the missing link*, Keele Economics Department Discussion Paper 98-10, University of .Keele, 1998.

An artificial market based on agents
with fluid attitude toward risks and returns

Takuya Iwamura — Yoshiyasu Takefuji

Graduate School of Media and Governance, Keio University
5322 Endo, Fujisawa-shi, Kanagawa 252-8520,

it@sfc.keio.ac.jp
takefuji@sfc.keio.ac.jp

ABSTRACT: *The behaviour of traders in a stock market is influenced by their attitude toward the risk of the security. In this research the internal model of the risk-averse and the risk-loving trader is proposed in the context of the artificial market. This model is based on the ideas of the expected utility hypothesis. It is important to model the difference in subjective value of the same stock because this difference enables market activities. The feature of the proposed model is that this model realizes the dynamic aspect of trader's preference in the risk and the return.*

RÉSUMÉ: Dans études déjà établies dans le domaine de Simulation Sociale, les attitudes des opérateurs vers des risques n'étaient pas traitées d'une manière suffisante. D'où la nécessaire création d'un nouveau modele qui tient compte de la diversité de cognition d'un certain risqué. Le modèle présenté dans la thése est destirée à combler cette nécesisité. Par ailleurs, ce modèle est basé sur l'hypothesis de l'utilité attendue.

KEYWORD: *artificial market, expected utility, risk aversion, Genetic Algorithm*

MOTS-CLÉS: *le marché artificielle, l'utilité attendue, l'aversion du risque, l'algorithme génétique*

1. Introduction

The key issue of traders' behaviour in a stock market is their attitude toward the risk of the security. The decision-making in a trade is strongly influenced by traders' feeling about the expected return and risk of a stock. For example, "Bull" traders hesitate to buy a stock which holds a high return but high risk, while "Bear" traders accept the risk and buy it. In this situation, the concept of risk aversion seems one of the possible explanations for this kind of difference in traders' behaviour.

In the theory of financial engineering, the effect of a subjective risk felt by traders is difficult to deal with, because it is not possible to know each trader's preferences with regard to the combination of the risk and the return. On the other hand, the agent-based simulation makes it possible that the personal preferences in a risky stock can be represented as the internal model of each agent. Even in the early studies of agent-based market, there are some works that deal with risks and returns. For example, the agent in the work of Palmer et al. takes returns and risks of securities [PAL 94]. Some studies have been carried out on cognitive aspects of the agents in this field [ARI 94][CHE 99][IZU 99]. The internal model of agents related to risk aversion, however, has received little attention.

In this paper, although the mechanism is rather simplified, we explicitly implement the model of "Bull" and "Bear" traders based on the expected utility theory proposed by Neumann and Morgenstern [NUE 47]. Freedman and Savage first applied expected utility theory to investigate the risk aversion on the part of policyholders of insurance [FRI 48]. Although there are many good research studies in this approach, the weak point of this approach is that it is not possible to describe each person's expected utility function.

The proposed model also represents the preference change in traders. As Lux showed, the herd behaviour which causes bubble is observed without external inference [LUX 95]. This kind of behaviour is investigated by the internal model of the agent.

In the agent-based market approach, the cause of the fluctuation of the value at the macro level can be explained by the value at the micro level. This means, in this research, that the reason for fluctuation of the stock price may be attributed to the shape of each trader's expected utility function on the assumption that the traders' dealing behaviour is influenced by their degree of risk aversion.

The future goal of our research is the forecasting of the price movement, as some of previous research on the artificial market. This paper explains the internal model for risk-aversion and a way to apply an expected utility function. Suppose that the fluctuation of price is influenced by the collective effect of each trader's degree of risk aversion. The shape of expected utility function of each agent can then be estimated by a searching technique.

This paper shows how the psychological aspect of traders is represented in an agent-based market by constructing the model of agents' attitude toward the risk and return. Our work is a very elementary step on the way to realize such a complicated phenomena. At this stage of our research, the agents can detect only trend data, on the assumption that all the information has already been woven into the data fluctuation.

2. Simulation Process

Our research deals with the data of stocks traded at Tokyo Stock Exchange (TSE). This simulation aims at realizing the opening process of TSE, which is called itayose. Although intra-day trade is an interesting subject to analyse, this kind of trade constitutes future work at this stage of the research. The complicated trades in TSE, therefore, are simplified to the limit orders at opening in this simulation. Traders place buy or sell orders with the market where all the orders are stored until clearing time comes.

Traders in this simulation, called agents, trade only once a day. In addition to this constraint, each trader has his or her own fixed trade span. An agent with a long trade span, therefore, holds his position longer than others with short trade span. This reflects the real condition of a market where there are two types of traders, namely long-term traders and short-time traders (ex. Day-traders).

The trades in this simulation are discrete events and time is counted by the "period". Each trader trades at the period corresponding to his trade timing. For example, the agent that has two periods as its trade span trade every two periods (ex. 0,2,4,...) .

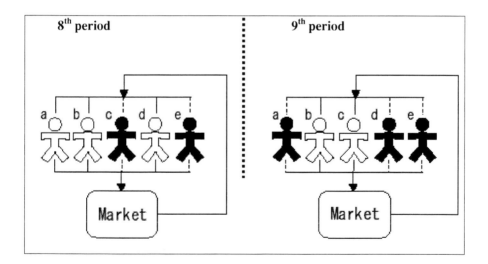

Figure1. *Simulation Process*

Figure 1 shows the process of simulation in this research. This figure depicts the market situation at the 8th period where agents a, b, and d trade while c and e do not. That is because the agent a trades every two periods, b trades every period and d

trades every four periods. On the other hand, the agent c trades every three periods and e trades every 10 periods. As shown Figure 1, the traders who perceive a market situation decide whether they buy or sell according to the utility of the stock. At the next period, namely the 9th period, the traders b and c trade, while the traders a, d and e do not. The utility of the stock is subjective value of the stock price. Each agent reacts variously to the same stock price because each has different attitude to the risk of a stock.

The price of a stock is determined by the result of the traders' order. The markets which show a more similar price fluctuation have more possibilities of being selected. This is on the grounds that the difference in price fluctuation among markets is the constituent of a market, namely traders.

3. Model of traders

3.1. Assumptions about traders' behaviours

We make some assumptions about traders' behaviours, simplifying the pattern of traders' actions for implementation. The assumptions of traders in this research are described below:

– Traders determine their behaviours by the return and the risk of the stock. (1)

– Each trader has their own preferences in the combinations of risk and return. (2)

– Each trader has his or her own trading span. (3)

– Trader tends to neglect the risk of stock when the price keeps rising. (4)

– Trader thinks that a rising price will fall and that the falling price will go up. (5)

Assumptions (1), (2) and (3) mention the static nature of traders, whereas (4) and (5) explain the dynamic aspect of traders' decision-making.

As for assumption (3), different time spans imply that the risk and return in the same stock is also different. It is reasonable to expect the price to fluctuate during a short span, even if in a long span the price has been rising stably.

Assumption (4) means that a trader could be less risk-averse if the price keeps rising, and thereby contribute to the bandwagon effect. On the other hand, assumption (5) indicates that the trader may think the price will fall in the near future in the same situation. These are conflicting assumptions. The inherent reaction speed of individual traders to the market situation differs from one trader to another. The balance of (4) and (5) affects the trader's utility of the expected return of the stock.

3.2. Implementations

An agent trades according to the following trading steps as shown in Figure 2. The process of an agent is composed of the five steps. The contribution of this paper is to describe the internal model in the situation where the information of the market is perceived. The perception process is discussed in many studies. This study aims to implement higher-level information processing, considering the psychological aspect in traders. Unfortunately, in this step of this research, the perception process is considerably simplified, as a consequence of concentrating on an internal model of agents.

When his trading timing comes, an agent perceives the market situation that is, in this research, the information of risk and return of a stock. In the renewal step, the agent expands or narrows his range of the acceptable risk, taking the market situation into consideration. In the calculation step, the agent calculates the utility of the stock according to its internal model. In the decision-making step, the agent decides whether to buy, sell, or keep position and how much to buy or sell. In the placing step, the agent places orders for the stock from the market. After all the steps are completed in a period, the agent waits for his trade span until the next trade timing comes.

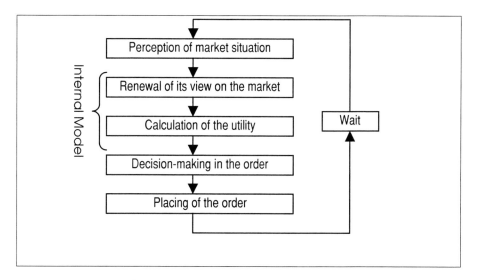

Figure 2. *Trading steps of an agent*

3.2.1. *Internal Model*

We propose a model of traders for an artificial market to deal with the dynamic aspect of their attitude toward risks. The agent reacts to the market situation by expanding or narrowing his acceptable range of risk. For example, some risk-averse agents can trade more boldly when the price has been rising.

The internal model, which represents the character of an agent, is based on the idea of the expected utility hypothesis, especially the subjective expected utility hypothesis proposed by Savage. The mechanism is, however, rather different from the function of these hypotheses. The most distinctive point is that our mechanism is able to represent the transition of the subjective value for the same stock.

Consider two types of tendency in the traders: "bull" and "bear" traders. To implement this distinct variety in the traders, the internal model of the agent is based on the expected utility function. The risk-averse agents are endowed with concave line as their expected utility function, whereas the risk-loving agents are endowed with convex line. This difference in the shape of the utility function strongly influences the preference for the type of stock as seen in Figure 3 and Figure 4.

Figure 3 shows the internal model of a risk-averse agent. This function indicates that this agent's preference is for a secure return rather than for a fluctuating one if the expected return is the same. Note that the agent's utility of a stock depends on the expected lowest value and expected highest value. In Figure 3, u represents the utility of certain (no-risk) value of the expected return, whereas u' represents the utility for the same expected return with variance. As seen in Figure 3, u is greater than u'. That means the agents prefer stocks with certain prices rather than those with uncertain prices even if the expected return from both stocks is the same.

Figure 4 shows the internal model of risk-loving agents. In this case, u' is greater than u. This indicates that this type of agent prefers the stocks with fluctuating return because of possible high returns from uncertain stocks.

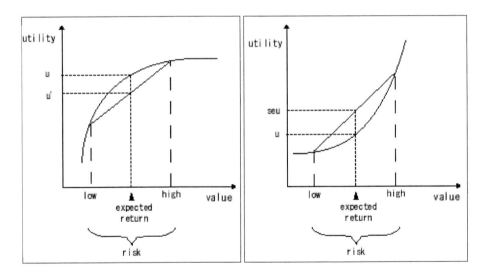

Figure 3. *Risk-averse agent*   **Figure 4.** *Risk-loving agent*

3.2.2. Risk and return

A stock, in this simulation, has only two possible states of price in the point of agent's view. The price will be up or down in the next period (Figure 5). The risk is a variant of a stock, which indicates the percentage of differences between two possible states in the next trade span.

For example, suppose the price of a stock in 100 period is 1000, the trade span of an agent is 5, and the variant of price during an agent's trade span, that is from 95 to 100, is 10%. In this situation the high point is 10% and the low point is -10%.

An agent's utility function takes these high and low points as the input. The agent, then, calculates the utility of the stock to decide whether to buy it or sell it. A risk-averse agent prefers a stock with small variant, because the price is more certain. A risk-loving agent, on the other hand, likes a stock with a large variant in spite of its high risk, because this kind of stock may produce much value.

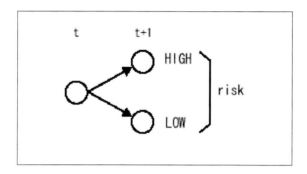

Figure 5. *Two possible states of the price*

3.2.3. Utility

The utility of a stock is defined as the subjective value of that for an agent in this research. Agents buy or sell stocks according to their utility for the stock. If the utility for an agent is high, and then this agent decides to send a buy order. Each agent, therefore, sees the same expected return and risk of the stock differently. As mentioned before, the expected return and risk could also differ according to the agents trade span. (Figure 3)

The utility is calculated as follows. Note that "f(x)" is the expected utility function. seu is the subjective value of the expected stock price, whereas u is the objective value of the same stock price.

$$seu = p \times f(high) + (1-p) \times f(low) \qquad [1]$$
$$u = f(high \times 0.5 + low \times 0.5) \qquad [2]$$
$$0 < p < 1$$

where p is the parameter that represents an agent's subjective belief for the rate of realization of a higher expected price in Figure 4. p decreases gradually as the price keeps rising and vice-versa. In other words, p represents assumption 5). p can be conceptualized as the agent belief in the direction of the price change.

As seen in Figure 4, the utility of the certain stock is higher than the utility of the risky stock when p is 0.5, which means that the agent's belief in the higher price is 50%. If the belief is 90% for the higher expected price, the utility of risky stock rises up to u", then it is higher than u.

Although several equations can be considered as the concave line, we select the following one as utility function [PRA 64].

$$f(x) = 1 - \exp(-1 \times c \times x)$$ [3]

where c is the parameter that represents the degree of risk aversion. The c implements the assumption 4) (Figure 5). If the curve is steep, the utility of the fluctuating price is u', which is much smaller than the certain expected return u. If the curve is gentle, the difference between the fluctuating and certain expected price is much smaller than before. See the difference between u1 and u1'.

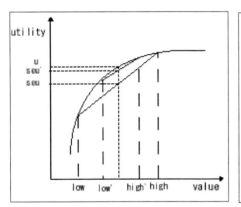   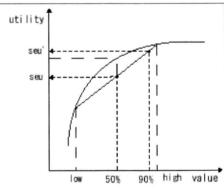

Figure 6. *Preference in risk and return*   **Figure 7.** *SEU of 90% belief and 50% belief*

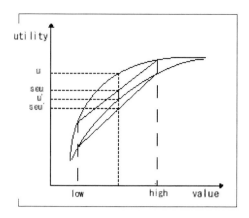

Figure 8. *Difference curve*

3.2.4. *Traits of agents*

Agents in a market have various traits according to the following six values. It is quite important that the differences in agents can be described by a few numbers of values. That is because it is easier to find an appropriate combination of the values if the searching space is smaller.

– The type of expected utility risk averse or risk loving

– Trade span

– The tendency for more risk-averse when the price keeps rising ... a

   – The tendency for less risk-averse when the price keeps rising ... b

– The initial value of the belief for price rising ... p

   – The initial value of the degree of risk-aversion ... c

The traits of the agents depend on these values. The trade span represents whether an agent is a long-term investor or short-term speculator. The tendency toward more risk-aversion is represented by coefficient a in equation [4], whereas the tendency toward more risk-tolerance is represented by coefficient b in equation [5].

$$p_t = p_{t-1} - a \times (price_t - price_{t-1}) / price_{t-1} \qquad [4]$$
$$c_t = c_{t-1} - b \times (price_t - price_{t-1}) / price_{t-1} \qquad [5]$$

3.3. *Order-placing*

The agents place their orders, concerning the subjective utility of the stock as shown Figure 10. An order includes not only buy or sell but also the price and the volume.

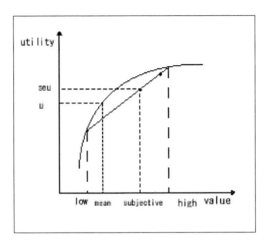

Figure 9. *Order-placing comparing seu with u*

An agent determines to buy or to sell comparing the subjective expected utility of the stock with the utility of the mean price during its trade span. An Agent buys a stock if the subjective expected utility of the stock is larger than the utility of the average prices. The stock is priced in proportion to the difference between these values [6].

$$order = price_t + (price_t - price_{t-1}) \times (SEU - U) / SEU \quad [6]$$

4. Adaptation Mechanism

The markets themselves evolve in the process of adaptation. In other words, those markets which show a more similar price fluctuation have possibilities to be selected. This is on the basis that the differences in price fluctuation among markets are the constituents of a market, namely traders.

As described before, various agents constitute a market. The purpose of adaptation is to find a better constitution of an artificial market where the simulated price fluctuation traces real data. This purpose is on the assumption that the fluctuation is influenced by the collective effect of each trader's degree of risk aversion. In other words, the constitution of a market that is similar to the real market can produce a similar fluctuation.

The adaptation is realized by the searching technique. In this research, the genetic algorithm (GA) is used to optimize the value for every agent's character in the risk aversion [GOL 89].

The targets of selection in GA are markets. The fitness function is, then, the ability to explain the price fluctuation in the real market. That is the market that can trace the fluctuation of real price is selected to make better markets in the next step.

The chromosome that represents the constitution of the market is the set of all agents' traits. The gene that represents each agent's trait is described by 4 value. Then the length of one chromosome is 4 multiplied by the number of agents in a market. Better markets are selected and have a chance to leave their chromosome for new markets.

5.Experiments

The data used by this simulation are the stock prices of certain popular companies on Tokyo Stock Exchange (TSE). This data is daily and its time window is from April 1999 to June 1999. This kind of stock is suitable for our research object because individual traders join the market and their popularity is concentrated in several popular companies, for example IT companies, at TSE in 1999. In this situation, there is more possibility for a situation in which psychological aspects influence price movements.

As seen in Figure 10, the artificial market scores better in the mean fitness as generation descends. The mean fitness is mean value of the fitness among the set of artificial markets in a generation. This simulation result means the situation of an artificial market is getting similar to that of real market.

But this simulation, at the moment, cannot perform well in learning the market's context. It is too stable to show strong fluctuation in the real market.

The reason for high stability is **not** that the introduced model lacks dynamism in nature. As seen in Figure 11, this model rather shows the variability in the response to the same price. This character of the model represents each trader's subjective value for the stock.

The cause of insufficiency of this simulation is due to the mechanism that converts a subjective value to an order. Although the order placing mechanism is not the main theme of this paper, it is needed to apply the internal model to the real market modelling.

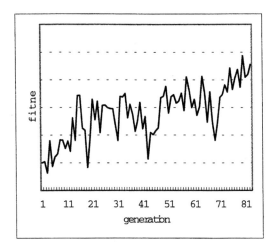

ID	TYPE	PRICE
5	BUY	6833
6	BUY	6847
7	SELL	6799
24	BUY	6842
45	BUY	6842
52	BUY	6833
55	SELL	6797
63	BUY	6847
64	SELL	6796
⋮		

Figure 10. *Mean Fitness through 80 generations*   **Figure 11.** *Variety of orders*

6.Conclusion

In this research the internal model of the risk-averse agents is proposed. This model is based on the mechanism that applies the expected utility function. The highlight is that this mechanism can realize the dynamic aspect of trader's preference toward risk and return.

It is important to model the difference in subjective value in the same stock because this phenomena produces market activities. That is to say, the market cannot serve as the price matching mechanism unless both the sell and buy order are placed. The fact that traders place a sell and buy order for the same stock is the evidence that the subjective value of the stock differs among traders.

In addition, a more important point about subjective value is that the same trader may take quite differently the very similar conditions of a stock. As the price keeps rising, even cautious traders may buy risky stock. This kind of phenomenon is known as a bandwagon phenomenon or a bubble. At the same time, however, other traders feel the situation is quite risky because the price is too high compared with the fundamentals. In other words, traders have two types of tendency toward reactions to the market situation.

As seen before, we define subjective value as the preference toward risk and return. The agent in this research has his own preference and changes the preference according to the market situation. This preference is converted into the expected utility.

The expected utility and the subjective expected utility have been the main theory for long time. At the same time, they have been criticized because of their inconsistency with a real person [CAM 92].

The reason why we take this theory as the base of the internal model is the simplicity of SEU. This research aims at realizing a simple model that deals with changing preference toward risk and return. It is reasonable to apply SEU to the internal model.

We still agree that a more realistic theory is better to represent the psychological aspect of traders' behavior. For example, the research results from experimental economics could be applied as internal models. Especially, it is supposed to be able to capture the effect of the trader's position on its preference. These improvements are left for future works.

7. References

[ARI 94] ARIFOVIC J., "Genetic algorithm learning and the cobweb model", *Journal of Economic Dynamics and Control*, vol.18, pp.3-28, 1994.

[CAM 92] CAMERER C. and MARTIN W., "Recent Developments in Modeling Preferences: Uncertainty and Ambiguity", *Journal of Risk and Uncertainty*, vol.5, pp.325-370, 1999

[CHE 99] CHEN S-H. and TAN C.-W., "Brief signals in the real and artificial stock markets: AN approach based on the complexity function", *In Proceedings of ICAI99*, pp.423-429. CSREA, 1999.

[FRI 48] FRIEDMAN M. and SAVAGE L.J., "The Utility Analysis of Choices Involving Risk", *Journal of Political Economy*, Vol. 56. 1948

[GOL 89] GOLDBERG D.E., *Genetic Algorithms in Search, Optimization, and Machine Learning*. Addison-Wesley. 1989

[IZU 99] IZUMI K. and UEDA. K. Analysis of dealers' processing financial news base on an artificial market approach. Journal of Computational Intelligence in Finance, Vol. 7, pp.23-33, 1999.

[LUX 95] LUX. T., "Herd behavior, bubbles and crashes", *Economic Journal*, Vol. 105, pp.881-896, 1995.

[NUE 47] von Neumann J. and O. Morgenstern., *Theory of Games and Economic Behavior*, 2nd ed. Princeton: Princeton University Press,1947

[PAL 94] PALMER R.G., ARTHUR W.B., HOLLAND J.H., LEBARON B., and Taylor P. "Artificial economic life: a simple model of a stock market". *Physica D*, Vol. 75, pp. 264-265, 1994

[PRA 64] Pratt J.W., "Risk aversion in the small and in the large". *Econometrica*, vol 32, No. 1-2, pp.122-136, 1964

Windows vs. Linux: Some Explorations into the Economics of Free Software

Jean-Michel Dalle* — Nicolas Jullien**

*ENS Cachan & IDHE-CNRS, 61, avenue du Président Wilson -F-94230 Cachan
jmdalle@dir.ens-cachan.fr

** ENST Bretagne & ICI, Technopole de Brest Iroise - F-29285 Brest Cedex
Nicolas.Jullien@enst-bretagne.fr

ABSTRACT: *The article presents an economic analysis of Free Software. We insist on the role played by Public Licenses, which implement a very subtle and efficient way of dealing with positive externalities associated with creativity, in providing the software industry with such a new development methodology and business model, now already challenging some of Microsoft's main products. To test our argument, we turn to a stochastic interaction model to study the current competition between Linux and Windows NT/2000 in the market for Operating Systems, as this model allows us to deal with both local and global positive externalities. Its results enlighten the existence of different diffusion regimes depending on producer strategies, the main question having to do with the redistribution of positive external economies associated with diffusion of new technologies, therefore confirming our suggestion that Free Software might be a superior economic model than proprietary software.*

RÉSUMÉ : *Cet article propose une analyse économique du logiciel libre. Nous insistons sur le rôle joué par les licences libres qui ouvrent la voie à un nouveau modèle de développement et à un nouveau modèle économique pour l'économie du logiciel parce qu'elles gèrent efficacement les externalités positives liées à la créativité des agents. Pour tester ces arguments, nous avons recours à un modèle stochastique d'interaction afin d'étudier la concurrence entre les systèmes d'exploitation Linux et Windows NT/2000, puisqu'il permet d'intégrer les externalités locales et globales. Nos résultats mettent en lumière l'existence de différents régimes qui dépendent de la stratégie du producteur, avec comme point principal la question de la redistribution des externalités positives associées à la diffusion de nouvelles technologies, ce qui tend à confirmer la supériorité du modèle économique du logiciel libre par rapport au modèle "propriétaire".*

KEY WORDS: *Free Software, Externalities, Creativity, Technological Competition, Business Models.*

MOTS-CLÉS : *Logiciel Libre, Externalités, Créativité, Compétition Technologique, Modèles Economiques.*

1. Introduction and overview

Free Software - software distributed with its sources *and* with the right to modify and redistribute them - gradually appears as one of the most fashionable and possibly of the most interesting economic models in today's software industry. It indeed allows users to co-operate - essentially through the Internet - by adding (most of the times marginal) improvements to a given piece of software and to redistribute it once modified: each user this way rapidly benefits from innovations brought by all others. Free Software is thus a very seducing concept, but all the interest it has attracted has not only been theoretical, since it also has to do with pure commercial success: Web server "Apache" is leading its market with no less than 60% market share[1] -, while Linux operating system (OS, from now on) is reported to run more than 25% of Internet servers[2] and its commercial shipments are seen by some analysts to grow faster than any other operating software (25% vs. 10% per year[3]). As a matter of fact, Linux is today the most well-known example of Free Software because it appears as a major challenge to Microsoft's OS Windows NT and 2000[4] (latter called W2000).

Such a success is of course challenging for economists, and this challenge is at least twofold. First, economists have to understand better how Free Software works, i.e. *economics* of Free Software. This is not simple as economists are not well used to studying non-purely market phenomena, specially when they lead to the production of new goods. However, the recent "knowledge-based" approach [DAV95B] and perhaps even more the so-called new "economics of science" [DAS 94, DAV 98A] give us however clues to open such an analysis in the first part of this article. Economic creativity will appear as the main concept here since Free Software licenses and conventions precisely allow developers to fully benefit from positive externalities associated with distributed knowledge. But we will also insist on the fact that the success of Free Software as a production model probably depends more on its ability to become an actual new "business model", closely articulated with markets, than on simple and contingent anti-Microsoft attitudes. Strong incentives indeed arise from reputation earned when participating in free software development projects - with all financial consequences one can anticipate regarding positions in the market for qualified software developers -, but also from direct profit associated with the creation of ancillary businesses selling services dedicated to formerly released Free Software (section 2).

Once the sustainability of such a model has been proved, we have to evaluate the potential of Free Software in the software economy according to its characteristic features. Has Free Software actual chances to win competition against classical

---

[1] See http://www.netcraft.co.uk/Survey/

[2] See http://leb.net/hzo/ioscount/

[3] http://www.idc.com/Data/Software/content/SW033199PR.htm

[4] In a recent internal draft, Free Software was even called a "new development methodology" by Microsoft itself, and seen as a major challenge to Microsoft's products.

proprietary software? This is the question we ask and try to answer in the case of the battle between Linux and W2000 on the market for server OS using a stochastic diffusion model with both local and global positive externalities [DAL 95A, DAV 98B]. It is indeed a very interesting case not only because it is the best-known example of its kind, but also because economists have recently been taught, notably by Arthur [ART 89] and its followers, that standardization is doomed to happen in markets when compatibility issues and positive adoption externalities prevail. Standardization should therefore last "forever" once a technology has become a standard, except perhaps for seldom "major" innovations. Here we argue that increasing returns associated with creativity and their distribution toward end users create sufficiently stronger local and global positive externalities to help Linux reverse current standardization on W2000. More, our simulation studies prove that it is so even when the proprietary software producer tries to adapt its strategy and business model so as to redistribute externalities in a larger extent (section 3).

2. Free Software, a new way of dealing with the creation vs. diffusion dilemma

First of all, Free Software should absolutely not be mistaken with freeware and shareware, as its characteristics and differences from other software types stand as a direct explanation for its commercial success and economic interest. Free Software is software in which not only source and binaries are widely distributed and accessible, usually for free, but also software whose sources can be modified with the supplementary and compulsory need that all derived source code has still to be Free Software[5]. These features, and specially this last one, stem from what is called a "public license", the best known of which being the GNU General Public License[6], and more generally refer to what has been coined as the "CopyLeft" licensing scheme. The CopyLeft scheme is indeed implementing into the software industry a kind of protection that indeed spreads as a "contagious by contact" disease. CopyLeft "protected" programs are economically speaking *non-proprietary*: all Free Software users benefit from each improvement provided by others, and this is the Free Software key feature.

2.1. *Better diffusion for better innovations?*

Free Software sets up a very efficient way to deal with both creation and distribution of knowledge [DAV 95B]. As Eric S. Raymond[7] - a major Free Software advocate - once put it: "From nearly the beginning, [Linux] was rather casually

---

[5] We have chosen here to denote software which present such characteristics as Free Software. Others seem to refer to "Open Source Software" (see for instance Open Source Initiative at http://www.opensource.org/), but we fear this is not a sufficient definition as open sources alone will not provide software with the kind of business model we are to describe here: it does not always guaranties the fact that programs will remain protected by a public license and are not transformed into a proprietary one. As it happens, "Open Source" has more to do with a development methodology than with a business model.

[6] See http://www.fsf.org/copyleft/. GNU is a "recursive " acronym for GNU is Not Unix.

[7] See http ://www.tuxedo.org/~esr/

hacked on by huge numbers of volunteers coordinating only through the Internet. Quality was maintained [... by the] strategy of releasing every week and getting feedback from hundreds of users within days, [...]. To the amazement of almost everyone, this worked quite well." Users also being innovators - and innovators also being users - [VHI 88], such programs are developed to cope with problems which users really face; innovation is also decentralized [COH 83] as numerous developers are able to push their ideas while only the best ones are selected. Both features obviously foster a very high collective efficiency in problem-solving. More, innovation is almost immediately accessible through quicker and better development feed-backs: as soon as a bug is fixed or as a new feature is added, it is released for free and made immediately accessible on the Internet. And Free Software is finally free while being developed by highly trained and efficient developers! On the contrary, proprietary software is more distant from users and has to organize huge marketing studies to decipher their needs; even if competitive teams are implemented inside producing firms, there are much less numerous than in the Free Software model; and feed-backs are also very slow and most of the time included into newer versions of the software which users have to pay for.

Free Software therefore immediately appears as a very powerful way of dealing with *creativity* and its associated positive external economies: as the matter of fact, the fundamental law of economic creativity is that the more creativity is accessible, the more creativity will further occur. Discoveries, innovations, "ideas" - as Romer [ROM 93] would put it -, be they incremental, are eased by previous ones. We believe that this particular property and the importance of economic creativity justify the need for true economics of creativity, and we have in this respect already tried to study the appearance of creative times and places, of creative waves, and also stressed the fact that the economic value of creativity could vary during diffusion processes of new technologies [DAL 98C; DAL 98D]. Here we want to insist more on institutional aspect of the creativity issue, as external economies associated with creativity and associated appropriation issues clearly imply some institutional and/or conventional device to correct the induced lack of individual incentives.

2.2. Incentives for creation and diffusion

Institutions and conventions dealing with economic creativity generally have first to set up conditions for creation and disclosure, which themselves have to do both with incentives and with enforcement procedures. But such institutions and conventions also have to foster distribution, which implies the existence of well-adapted and more or less technological devices, without which the entire system would not function or at least poorly so. As for Free Software, creativity is typically exchanged and pooled through the Internet, i.e. through now extremely general and widely accessible communication means. But technological means such as the Internet do not solve all distributive problems, among which notably the one of co-ordination. Priority rules which characterize both patent and publication systems for instance also ensure that efforts will be more or less coordinated in that they will not too often be duplicated ("split" or "code forking" problems for Free Software), resulting in a global social loss. Free Software has no similar "passive coordination" rule while needing stonger coordination, as it is aimed at becoming a development process for software products. Whilst Free Software communities have already been able to endogenously engender some rather developed and efficient coordination structures such as managing committees and decision rules - a bug fix having for instance to be accepted by a dedicated committee -, it probably explains why Free Software still appears to some analysts as better to fix bugs and re-create existing programs in a free version rather than for creating new ones, as the involved degree of co-ordination involved is in this case obviously lower.

Anyway, the main problem remains on creation and disclosure incentives. Economic creativity indeed implies some kind of a reward, but a difficult one to deal with: while purely non-appropriable creations would fail on the creation side as no one would be interested in creating if he had no return on its creation, purely appropriable ones would also fail on the distribution side as they would never be disclosed and made accessible to others. There is therefore a need here for an adapted institutional or conventional device, which will of course often rely on customized property regimes. This is typically the case for patents, which provide property for a few years while forcing patentees to immediately publish their discovery. Enforcement is provided by dedicated law courts, and incentives of course rely on profit. But the scientific community is also governed by the so-called "convention of Open Science" [DAS 94; DAV 95A], which stipulates that discoveries are made public in scientific conferences and journals, reputation being awarded to the first who publishes. Regulation here is purely conventional, but reputation plays a true appropriation role as reputation governs promotions and access to research grants and credits. Reciprocally, those who act too opportunistically are to lose reputation.

Historically closer to the scientific community[8], Free Software fundamentally appears as a kind of an *anti-patent device,* as property is not granted but *denied.* Denying appropriation paradoxically creates incentives towards creation and disclosure as induced spillovers will of course not be appropriated by the inventor, *but nor by others.* These incentives have indeed proven to be sufficient to motivate large and creative enough Free Software communities to cooperate over many given development project. Free Software potential has indeed much to do with the size and *creative intensity* of associated Free Software communities: if there were too few users, or if there were not able to be innovators and just "passive" users, then creative intensity would not be sufficient to sustain Free Software development. This is of course not to say that all users should be active developers and potential innovators and that Free Software might only work for pure communities of skilled developers. Creative intensity, for which the size of the community of users and the proportion of active developers are important factors, should simply be high enough

---

[8] As software is mostly an intellectual work based on codified knowledge, highly relying on tacit and idiosyncratic skills, as it is also characterized by almost no real "production process " and as complex software needs a large scale of competencies, uneasy (and expensive) to regroup in a single entity, State institutions have indeed historically encouraged co-operation between private and public software research centers. More in Jullien [JUL 99].

to engender a dynamic diffusion scheme. Netscape's recent attempt to open the sources of its Communicator 5 under a specific Public License for instance seems to have largely failed, as it has not been able to attract a sufficient number of interested developers[9].

Apart from subsequent "club" effects, individual incentives have thus generally to be strong enough to attract numerous active developers. The main question here is therefore: are "anti-appropriation" incentives associated with public licenses enough in this respect, or is there a need for other motivations and "cultural" feelings? A few prominent Free Software projects clearly have roots into deep and strong anti-Microsoft or anti-Sun feelings, and such idiosyncratic historical conditions have indeed given momentum to Free Software development: although this is obviously very significant in a path-dependence perspective, as Arthur (1989) and David (1985) have taught us notably with the QWERTY example, it should also be recognized that incentives have now largely ceased to belong to such affective grounding. As a matter of fact, incentives mainly rely now both on reputation and on profit, i.e. both on academic-like and on patent-like phenomena.

Reputation first is gained by developers who fix important bugs or who provide interesting new features: code lines are "signed" by their authors, and knowledge of who made what is widely accessible. And such reputation can easily be transformed in income when used as a reference when applying to a job. It is also more and more often the very "asset" that allows for the creation of business firms selling ancillary services to Free Software and for profit. The importance of this phenomenon should not to be underestimated, as such businesses are indeed most common now: a few of them exist for almost all Free programs, most created by or in association with prominent Free Software developers such as Linus Torvalds for Linux and the Red Hat company, and these partnerships between communities of Free Software developers and ancillary business firms indeed appear as a very efficient way to solve most Free Software problems asociated with the packaging of actual commercial products. Indeed, as there is no reputation associated with the programming of hundreds of lines of uninteresting code, nobody gets appropriate incentives to do so, and programs are therefore not user-friendly enough, all the more so s they are initially targeted toward a community of skilled developers. Ancillary business firms providing appropriate services offer a solution to this dilemma, as they also do for otherwise absent after-sale guaranties, precisely by providing the lacking services, i.e. the software add-ons and the on-line help for users both at the time of the install and afterwards[10]. They might even help a lot for

---

[9] In this case, the program was to remain proprietary, which has certainly contributed to a diminished eagerness to be part of an associated Free Software process. An important lesson indeed for all proprietary software producers interested in fostering Free Software processes associated with some of their products.

[10] As John Ousterhout, creator of the TCL scripting language - another piece of Free Software - and of Scriptics, a firm which sells tools and customer support on TCL, puts it: "The early adopters of an open-source package tend to be like the creator: sophisticated programmers with a particular problem that the package solves. [...]The first products for a

insufficient coordination of the project teams (see above).

The ability of such businesses to deal with an open-source programmer community is to be a core condition of their success: they have to deal with a community of : "geeks", to quote a now much fashionable word even among geeks themselves. As a matter of fact, his topic was indeed listed among main risk factors in Red Hat recent IPO prospectus[11]: "Negative reaction within the open source community to our business strategy could harm our reputation and business [...]. [Some] have suggested that [...] we are trying to dominate the market for Linux-based operating systems and the open source community [...]. This type of reaction, if widely [...], could harm our reputation, diminish the Red Hat brand and result in decreased revenue." The main strategy here is thus to get support from prominent figures of the targeted Free software community, when these prominent developers are not themselves the initiators of these ancillary business: in all cases, reputation gained in Free Software development can this way very rationally be reinvested and transformed into profits.

		Patents	Open-Science	Free Software
Creation and Disclosure	Incentives	Extra Profit and Protection	Reputation by peer effects with associated means	Reputation by peer effects and Profit
	Enforcement	Law courts via infringement trials	Conventional, self regulation of the research community	GPL licenses
Distribution	Device for information exchange and pooling	Patent databases maintained by public agencies	Scientific journals, Conferences, email	Internet (email, mailing lists, web sites, newsgroups)

Table 1. *Different economic devices dealing with creativity*

The creation of service firms by or with former Free Software developers is then a very important element of the Free Software *business model* as it completes very efficiently the incentives structure of the Free Software "institution", first because active developers are now also motivated by reputation and profit, but significantly also because non-sexy work would otherwise not being done due to actually too weak incentives. Together with Public Licenses, these ancillary firms constitute the appropriate conventions and institutions suitable to transform Free Software into a

---

package are typically books and/or training to help people learn the package. [...]The next products [... are] packaged versions of the software and support. [...] Another popular area for commercial products is development tools. " [OST 99].

[11] Thanks to Laurent Kott who attracted our attention to this.

very powerful tool fostering economic creativity in its relevance area (see Table 1). However still under construction, the Free Software model therefore appears as perfectly sustainable. And the question now is: is it really able to truly compete against the proprietary software development model? The role of Free Software in the software economy will indeed not only depend on its sustainability and incentive structure, but also on the ability of Free Software to win competitive situations against proprietary products. This is why we now turn to the direct study of such situations in the case of the well-known OS competition between Linux and W2000: and, as will soon come clear, we suggest that Linux might well succeed once again because the Free Software model implements an original economic model which proves very powerful in dealing with positive externalities associated with creativity[12].

3. Free vs. Proprietary Software: the competition between Linux and NT

To what extent might Free Software competitively succeed against rival proprietary products? We analyze here the on-going competition between Linux and W2000, not only because it is most fashionable today but also, and more importantly so, because OS are specially prone to positive externalities due to compatibility issues. In this case, Linux, a Free Software OS, is invading a market currently dominated by classical proprietary software (Microsoft's NT and now W2000). This situation is all the more interesting as it constitutes a particularly difficult situation for a new entrant facing a prior dominant standard: according even to Arthur's classical results on technological competition [ART 89], lock-in should indeed be irremediable due to network effects [KAT 85] because externalities are strong and a given standard has already won. As a matter of fact, this is not verified empirically since Linux is continuously and consistently gaining new market shares. When reality goes so directly against dominant theory, some new elaborations are needed. Our intention here is firstly to provide an explanation for this phenomenon using a more complete model of technological competition, which typically accounts for both local and global externalities. We will thus follow the recent literature that has stressed both the interest of Arthur's model and some of its significant weaknesses, specifically as it neglects the existence of local interaction structures[13]. Thanks to the tractability of a stochastic interaction model which accounts for heterogeneous agents by making use of a statistical behavioral function, we will even push the analysis further by studying what would happen if Microsoft cared to answer Linux threat by lowering its prices and by changing its business model towards software renting instead of selling[14].

---

12 Not to forget that other factors - such as he size and creative intensity of Free Software communities – might make Free Software comparative advantages over proprietary products vary according to situations and specially depending on different types of software products: a proper analysis has on this respect yet to be done.

13 See e.g. [DAL 95, 97, 98AB], [DUR 93], [DAV 94], [DAV 98B], [KIR 93, 98].

14 However difficult this might prove for as big a company as Microsoft, deeply engaged in

3.1. *Analysis*

Following Kirman's criticism of the representative individual [KIR 92], we consider a population of heterogeneous potential adopters whose decision rules are evidently not the same. Depending on adopters, quality, performance (frequency of errors), availability and variety of dedicated software, easiness of installation and comfort of use, direct and indirect costs (buying, training, maintenance, upgrades, dedicated software), will be more or less relevant parameters as they evaluate the utility of alternative software solutions. As a matter of fact, such valuations will most certainly be very different from a computer hacker to an unskilled computer user or else from an individual user to a major company. Since we are confronted to a very strong form of heterogeneity, we will "simply" adopt here a statistical point of view, accounting for the statistical propensity of a given adopter randomly chosen in a given population to adopt either one of the two competing standards.

But individual valuations are also highly sensitive to both local and global externalities. As is now well-known, global characteristics of products, like quality, performance, availability and variety of dedicated software, price, more or less directly depend on their diffusion level at a given point in time. Products get indeed ameliorated throughout their diffusion processes since producers benefit from external economies associated with diffusion and re-invest a part of the associated profits to lower the price and/or improve the technology. Ancillary products, technologies and services are also increasingly proposed by other firms as a direct function of main product market shares. As a consequence, the statistical propensity of a random adopter to choose a given technology will also be a function of the market share of this technology: and all the more so for pure network technologies for which compatibility issues play a major role. Many individual adopters will simply prefer the dominant technology, because it will allow them to be compatible - to exchange data and programs, in the case of OS - with most other adopters. These compatibility issues are specially prominent within the limited set of other adopters with whom a given adopter often interacts, i.e. *locally*: this is specially true for OS due to regular file exchange among users. And there are yet other major causes for the existence of local externalities: information exchange concerning the relative pros and cons of each available technology are typically mainly local and has a first level influence on many technological choice.

What we therefore have to study is the statistical propensity to adopt each technology in a given population *conditional* on "previous" global and local adoption patterns. *But local and global effects can be very different for different technology independently of each technology's installed base. First, and most important here, global externalities are not redistributed the same way.* An important part of external economies earned by Microsoft as Windows was more and more widely adopted has been appropriated as profit - or monopoly rent! – and has not been reinvested in development of the product and price reduction: as a matter of fact, this is indeed a rational behavior from a monopolist. On the contrary, external

---

long built organizational routines.

economies associated with adoption of Linux have direct consequences for bug corrections and generally for product improvement, as the very core of the Free Software model relies on collaboration in a community. Linux evolutions are therefore constantly accessible on-line and for free, while Windows users have, except for important bugs or minor improvements, to wait generally years until a new version is available, and most of the times have also to *buy* it. Both because of different release models and simply because W2000 is based on a pure profit organization, "redistributed" (to consumers) marginal positive adoption externalities are to be higher for Linux, i.e. for Free Software, than for W2000, i.e. for proprietary software[15].

As a consequence, the most important feature of Linux (resp., Free Software) probably does not lie in its gratuity, but in that it improves "better" and quicker that W2000 (resp. proprietary software): Linux "distributions" provided by ancillary companies the kind of which we have described above are indeed now sold, at the price which is still lower than the one of Windows, but not very significantly low. At first glance, and for the medias, gratuity of "Free" Software might appear as its main advantage and characteristic: it is however particularly wrong and dangerous non only because the potential of Free Software is closely linked to the progressive building of an appropriate and well-adapted business model – or else the non sexy work would never been done and only highly skilled users could simply install Linux – but also because the most important feature of Free Software is not that it is free to buy but that is free to modify and to redistribute, opening the way for a very original model of redistribution of adoption externalities which structurally relies on the creativity of users' communities. The higher indeed the creative intensity of the population of Linux users, the higher global adoption externalities: on the contrary, Microsoft has to attract and to pay for skilled and creative developers and often to buy other firms to have access to many new creative products, therefore experiencing much higher creativity costs, while its advantage for non-sexy work is fading as companies ancillary to Linux have appeared and are developing quickly.

Finally, let us add that Linux is also subject to higher local externalities, essentially due to the proselytism of Linux adopters. There are numerous associations - such as Lugs, for Linux Users Groups - which organize manifestations to promote its use, but there are also dedicated reviews, not to speak of web sites. If we further consider that there are now no more actual differences in access conditions for Linux and W2000 - easy for W2000 due to its huge distribution network, and easy for Linux thanks to the Net and to Red Hat and even now COREL packages -, evaluation of the technologies by future users depends on their relevant neighbors, to make use David's terminology [DAV 88]. And, whereas W2000 users are mainly to remain silent, Linux users are to advertise the quality of their

---

[15] Microsoft, being a monopolist, has specially low incentives to re-invest positive externalities: an explanation perhaps to the fact that a very slow improvement rate and imperfect functioning are quite often reproached to Microsoft, together with very opportunistic release strategies, even more than to other software producers.

technology, while also stressing all the problems experienced by W2000. As a result, propensity to adopt Linux will be higher with a similar level of local positive externalities.

To conclude with this section, it should have become clear why there was such a major flaw in Arthur's model [ART 89] of technological competition under increasing returns: *producer strategies regarding positive externality redistribution are simply not properly taken into account in this model, as emphasis is being mainly put on the demand side rather than on the offer side.* There is a black box in Arthur's model which regards producer strategies: externalities are in a way supposed to be somewhat "magically" re-invested in technological improvement, i.e. redistributed to consumers. It is obviously not always the case, and Arthur's results therefore appear as much too particular and doubtful in this respect. When adoption externalities are not redistributed, even an almost dominant technology might experience some trouble against a new entrant which on the contrary would be highly "generous" as far as marginal adoption externalities are concerned.

3.2. The model

We consider a population of heterogeneous potential adopters, each of them being associated with a local neighborhood (a subset of other potential adopters). We suppose here for tractability reasons that neighborhoods are organized as in a 2-dimensional torus - the "interaction structure" -, i.e. that all adopters have 4 local relevant neighbors[16]. We simulate technological trajectories by choosing a random adopter at discrete times, i.e. a position on the interaction structure and an adoption behavior given local and global environment, according to the following statistical behavioral demand function:

$$\text{Prob}[\textit{Agent A adopts Linux}] = \frac{th\left[a\left((x_l - \alpha x_w) + b(X_l - \beta X_w)\right)\right] + 1}{2}$$

The distribution of probable adoption behaviors, considering both characteristics of technologies and preferences of adopters is obviously a function of U_l - U_w, where U_l (resp., U_w) is Linux (resp. W2000) utility. These utilities are themselves given by:

$$U_{\bullet} = c\, x_{\bullet} + d\, X_{\bullet}$$

where $x_{\bullet}$ and $X_{\bullet}$ stand for the proportion of neighbors who have adopted either technology. As we mentioned above, they indeed depend both on local and global diffusion levels because of compatibility issues but also because the intrinsic utility of a technology is function of the level of diffusion. This level depends of increasing returns and of the fact they have or have not been distributed by producers to users: adoption is all the more probable as a technology has been improved or is cheaper, and it is better or cheaper because it has been previously adopted and because

---

[16] Here for simulation a 30x30 2-dimensional torus (900 potential adopters).

associated increasing returns have been previously redistributed to users or reinvested in further improvements. Utilities of technologies thus essentially depend on the extent of technological diffusion and on the producers' strategies towards redistribution of potential increasing returns. We consider other factors negligible compared to utility improvements allowed by diffusion, even when both technologies are not supposed to be equivalent ex ante.

In the formula above, the various terms of the equation have simply been reorganized and regrouped differently, as the reader will easily verify. Making use of a *th* function, adding *1* and dividing by 2 is just a question of normalization, so that the resulting function increases from 0 to 1 when externalities go from -W to +W, W>0, and is therefore a *probability* of choosing Linux. x_l **(resp. x_w)** is thus the proportion of A's neighbors who have adopted Linux (resp. W2000) while X_l **(resp.** X_w**)** is the proportion of Linux (resp. W2000) adopters in the entire population. *a* estimates the (statistical) preference for standardization: the greater *a*, the more a given potential adopter is driven towards standardization because of compatibility issues; *b* stands as a statistical estimate for the compared influence of preference for global standardization vs. local one. Both a and b characterize technologies and specifically their associated *network effects*. Typically, both a and b will be high for OS. In the limit case, technologies with no associated externalities would correspond to a = 0.

α statistically estimates the *relative* influence of previous local W2000 adoptions as compared to previous local Linux adoptions; β statistically estimates the *relative* influence of previous global W2000 adoptions as compared to previous global Linux adoptions. α and β therefore essentially reflect producers strategies regarding increasing returns, and more generally competing *business models*. As for Microsoft's products, α and β are influenced by the choice of regular release and sale of somewhat improved versions with imperfect compatibility associated issues and by a monopoly pricing strategy, i.e. in both cases by a quasi-monopolistic behavior regarding both quality and price of products: increasing returns are mainly not reinvested and redistributed to users but rather appropriated. As for Linux, α and β are on the contrary very sensitive to the creativity of the associated population of adopters or here community. This is specially true for β since this is mainly a global effect: the higher the proportion of active users able to make use of their skills to correct bugs and improve Linux, the lower β as Linux adoptions will "bring" more externalities. On the contrary, proselytism for Linux – or conversely Microsoft-phobia – will influence α since proselytism is mainly local. Both Microsoft-phobia and improvements due to users creativity characterize Linux's "production method or scheme", say, "business model". Ancillary businesses such as Red Hat or VA Linux (see above) also lower β as they for instance provide increased user-friendliness and after sale support.

As a matter of fact, a major strength of a model as the one we present here lies its ability to take into account for all these very different parameters, both economic and socio-economic, *all of them absolutely crucial and particularly significant* is one is to correctly analyze the Free Software business model. To put it differently, statistical *demand* is more or less *elastic* relative to several characteristics of technologies and of their associated business models. Elasticities here could be measured as partial derivatives of both α and β over different parameters, *including price but in no case limited to price:* Microsoft release strategy, Linux users creativity, Microsoft-phobia, or the development of Linux-dedicated business firms are also relevant parameters.

3.3. Results with passive proprietary software producer.

As local and global externality redistribution are supposed to be higher for Linux than for W2000 (see above), we get : $\alpha < 1$; $\beta < 1$, i.e. a random potential adopter will adopt Linux more frequently than W2000 when the number of previous adopters of Linux and W2000 is the same either in its neighborhood or globally.

We begin with uniform adoption of W2000, which represents a huge installed base, and repeat the algorithm up to 100 000 times while measuring the time needed for Linux to reach 70% market share (possibly infinite). We repeat the entire process for each α and β between 0 and 1 with step 0.1. Figure 1 below gives simulation results for a = 2 and b = 1, which seems appropriate for a technology highly sensitive to standardization phenomena such as OS software.

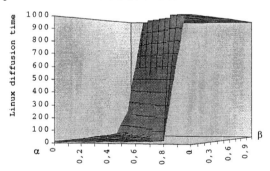

Figure 1. *Linux diffusion time (static α and β parameters)*

The main result here is the existence of a *phase transition*, or the fact that α and β are state parameters associated with a *sharp discontinuity in diffusion regimes*. Above critical values of α and β diffusion is infinitely long - it will never occur in economic time - whereas below them diffusion is almost sure and even rather quick. As a consequence:

• A lock-in situation on W2000 is not irremediable if Linux sufficiently benefits ("more" than W2000) from both local and global externalities: in this case, its diffusion is even rather fast.

• Pure advantage on global externalities is not enough: when $\alpha = 1$, Linux will never diffuse. If local externalities for Linux are not strong enough then the system will never "re-start" into new diffusion dynamics. Linux has to benefit more from both global and local externalities than W2000 to succeed, which implies a high sensitivity to Linux users' proselytic behaviors.

3.4. *Results with reactive proprietary software producer or with reduced Linux user creativity*

These first results imply a more dynamic version of our simulation exercises, to test whether or not they still hold when either Linux users' Microsoft-phobia or creativity diminishes or similarly when the proprietary software producer react[17]. In our framework, all these evolutions are modeled the same way (see above), i.e. though variations of α and β, since in all cases we simply get a variation of the way externalities are re-distributed: for instance, should local pro-Linux proselytism vanish or at least diminish, local Linux adoptions would matter less and α would increase, with consequences on Linux diffusion. Therefore the question is: what does happen when α increases during diffusion due to less Microsoft-phobia? Or similarly: what if there are less creativity in Linux community, or if Microsoft cuts its prices, or if Microsoft changes its business or at least release model, i.e. if β increases?

Since such evolutions are to be pretty rare, as all producers - be they the Linux community - are organizations subject to routines, we study here diffusion dynamics when β is significantly increased during the diffusion process, as soon as the number of Linux users reaches a given threshold defined as a percentage of the entire potential adopter populations[18]. Results are the following:

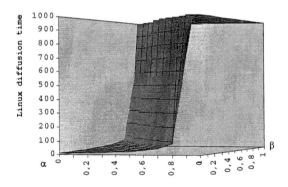

Figure 2. *Linux diffusion time when β varies during diffusion*

Here again a = 2 and b = 1 while plotted variables α and β correspond to their

---

[17] As a matter of fact, Microsoft strategy is from time to time said to evolve towards the software rental with continuous bug correction, improvements being also included in the rental price : this last strategy might indeed sound as Microsoft's answer to the Free Software threat.

[18] We got similar results for decreased Linux proselytism (increase in α).

initial values. As the percentage of Linux adopters reaches 5%, β is increased by 0.2: Microsoft reaction or the decrease in creativity is therefore associated with a very low threshold, while the reaction or evolution itself is pretty strong. Still, Linux diffuses very similarly to what happens without any such reaction or evolution (compare with figure 1). More precisely, when β is increased by 0.2 as the percentage of Linux adopters reaches 5%, diffusion is roughly similar to what would happen with an initial value: $β = β+δ$ with $δ < 0.1$.

Due to non-linear dynamics - a very strong attractor associated to a metastable state in trajectory space -, results thus appear as weakly sensible to possible variations of parameters during diffusion processes[19]. They correspond to "classical" bandwagon effects, or generally to path-dependence phenomena (David, 1985): once diffusion has started, it is difficult to stop. To put it differently, when it is late, it is too late... Historical events do matter, and *Microsoft-phobia might well be playing a similar role for Linux as early technological constraints have played for the QWERTY keyboard*. It might well disappear soon, but it will have permanently oriented the diffusion path. According to our results, and since Linux diffusion has concretely more than started, it might simply be way too late for W2000.

4. Conclusion: Efficient business models can make major innovations!

What is original and surprising according to existing literature on technological competition in both results above is that a minor technological innovation might prove powerful enough to replace a dominant standard when associated with a superior business model. Taken as a technology, Linux is indeed not really superior to Windows, whereas David [DAV 85] and others have proven that even superior technologies might not succeed against existing standards. Here superiority does not come from pure technological arguments, but from a superior *business model* which makes a very powerful use of creativity as soon as it is completed by ancillary business firms which both allow for efficient products and create incentives and reward structures for developers. Non-technological aspects prove to be sufficient to help a non-superior technology to defeat a dominant standard: this a major point, as it confirms not only that standards can be ruled out by alternative technologies but also that parameters which have to do with economic aspects of technologies rather than pure technological features are good candidates to explain such phenomena.

What characterizes technological trajectories is thus closer to persistence [FOR 97] rather than to pure and irreversible path-dependence: *technological diffusion endogenously creates thresholds effects*. Posterior technological candidates have to be "better enough" to get rid of existing standards, i.e. above a previously endogenously created threshold. As we argued elsewhere [DAL 98B], this phenomenon offers *a very straightforward explanation to the classical but mainly*

---

[19] We might have interpreted this phenomenon as a consequence of very strong compatibility incentives (parameter a), but other simulations with lower values result in similar conclusions.

empirical distinction between major and minor innovations: indeed, major innovations are innovations which are sufficiently better to diffuse - above this non-linear threshold -, whereas minor innovations are below this threshold and will therefore never diffuse. As a consequence, major innovations - possibly granted by non-technological means, as for the Free Software business model - have the possibility to be incompatible with existing standards, which is socially optimal as the newer technology is precisely better enough than the existing one to compensate for the enormous collective switching cost. Minor innovations are on the contrary most often to be made compatible by their producers with existing standards as they would otherwise have almost no chance to diffuse: *the existence of diffusion thresholds endogenously creates incentives to compatibility for minor innovations.* As a consequence, the existing standard gets continuously ameliorated instead of getting challenged by poorly alternative candidates, which is also obviously a socially optimal process. To put it differently, there are fewer Linux than there have been minor improvements to Windows.

Finally, technological competition and lock-in are highly sensitive to producer strategies concerning externalities and investments: this should indeed sound reassuring, but it is also an invitation to push further the still preliminary analyses presented in this article. More studies are needed to deal with more complex and realistic strategies. We have for instance supposed here that we could consider W2000 improvements as continuously following adoptions, whereas Microsoft strategies relies upon the periodic release of non perfectly compatible new versions: we should check whether our results hold when improvements are discontinuous. Since the situation presented is a limit case, we conjecture that they will remain similar when timing between releases is small. When it is slower, or when newer versions are not perfectly compatible with previous ones, we also conjecture that the results would be even more favorable to Linux. Anyway, further work is needed to give birth to an improved economic model of technological competition under increasing returns which would not only take local interactions into account, on the demand side, but also producer strategies and business models on the offer side.

The still under construction business model associated with Free Software indeed offers an alternative and original and efficient way to deal with economic creativity. Its pros and cons against other business models have of course to be better understood, specially in a time when software patents have also become fashionable. Let us simply recall that both the scientific community and its convention of "open science" and the intellectual property institutions have certainly done a lot for economic growth since they have appeared. And when they were invented, they were largely different from what they have now become, since "patent letters" used to attract foreign inventors so that they would import technologies which already existed elsewhere [DAV 93] whereas scientists were originally "devoted" to raising princes' reputation, which implied that they render their discoveries public [DAV 95A]. Indeed, institutions also are path-dependent. One should therefore certainly not underestimate what Free Software might gradually bring to the new knowledge-based economies [DAV 95B], or to what Romer has called "economies of ideas"

[ROM 93], *as it is giving birth not only to an appropriate incentive, distribution and reward structure, but also to a new business model for the software economy.* When we forget for once that we have been born in a world where both patents and scientific publications existed for long, we will certainly start to behave differently towards today's still prevailing skepticism towards Free Software.

Acknowledgements

Dalle's understanding of the importance of creativity as an economic concept has considerably benefited from his discussions and work with Dominique Foray and Paul A. David. Both authors also wish to acknowledge the help provided by comments from G. Dang Nguyen, T. Pénard & D. Phan, and from participants at the conferences "Autour du Libre" (Brest, January 29-30 1999), and "Applied Evolutionary Economics" (Grenoble, June 7-9, 1999).

Bibliography

[ART 89] ARTHUR W.B. (1989), Competing technologies, increasing returns and lock-in by historical events, *Economic Journal* 99: 116-131.

[COH 83] COHEN M. D. (1983), Conflict and Complexity: Goal Diversity and Organization Search Effectiveness, *American Political Science Review*, 78 : 435-451.

[DAL 95] DALLE J.-M. (1995), Dynamiques d'adoption, coordination et diversité, *Revue Économique*, 46: 1081-1098.

[DAL 97] DALLE J.-M. (1997), Heterogeneity vs. externalities: a tale of possible technological landscapes, *Journal of Evolutionary Economics* 7: 395-413.

[DAL 98A] DALLE J.-M. (1998), Heterogeneity and rationality in stochastic interaction models, in Cohendet P., Stahn H. (eds), The economics of networks: behaviors and interactions, Springer Verlag: Berlin, pp. 123-145.

[DAL 98B] DALLE J.-M. (1998), Local interaction structures, heterogeneity, and the diffusion of technological innovations, in Orléan A. & Lesourne J. (ed), Self-organization and evolutionary approaches: new developments, Economica: Paris, pp. 240-261.

[DAL 98C] DALLE J.-M., FORAY D. (1998), The innovation vs. standardization dilemma : some insights from stochastic interactions models), in Schweitzer F. & Silverberg G. (eds), Evolution and Self-Organization in Economics, Duncker & Humblot: Berlin, pp. 147-182.

[DAL 98D] DALLE J.-M., FORAY D., NEYMANN A. (1998), L'institution brevet dans une économie fondée sur la connaissance, Rapport for the French "Commissariat au Plan", 117 p., unpublished.

[DAS 94] DASGUPTA P., DAVID P.A. (1994), Towards a new economics of science, *Research Policy* 23: 487-521.

[DAV 85] DAVID P.A. (1985), Clio and the economics of QWERTY, *American Economic Review* (Papers and Proceedings) 75: 332-337.

[DAV 88] DAVID P.A. (1988), Putting the past into the future of economics, Technical Report 533, Institute for Mathematical Studies in the Social Sciences: Stanford University.

[DAV 93] DAVID P.A. (1993), Intellectual property institutions and the Panda's thumb, CEPR publication n°287, Stanford University.

[DAV 95A] DAVID P.A. (1995), Reputation and agency in the historical emergence of the institutions of 'Open Science', paper presented to the National Academy of Sciences Colloquium on the Economics of Science and Technology, held at the Beckman Center, UC Irvine, 20-21 October 1995.

[DAV 98A] DAVID P.A. (1998), Communication norms and the collective cognitive performance of "Invisible Colleges", in, pp. 115-163.

[DAV 94] DAVID P.A., FORAY D. (1994), Percolation structures, Markov random fields and the economics of EDI standard diffusion, in Pogorel G. (ed.), Global Telecommunication Strategies and Technological Change, Amsterdam: Elsevier.

[DAV 95B] DAVID P.A. , FORAY D. (1995), Accessing and expanding the science and technology knowledge base, STI Review 16: 13-68.

[DAV 98B] DAVID P.A., FORAY D., DALLE J.-M. (1998), Marshallian externalities and the emergence and spatial stability of technological enclaves, Economics of Innovation and New Technology 6: 147-182.

[DUR 93] DURLAUF S.N. (1993), Non-ergodic economic growth, *Review of Economic Studies* 60: 349-366.

[FOR 97] FORAY D. (1997), The dynamic implications of increasing returns: technological change and path-dependent inefficiency, *International Journal of Industrial Organization* 15: 733-752.

[JUL 99] JULLIEN N. (1999), Linux, la convergence du monde Unix et du monde PC?, *Terminal* 80-81.

[KAT 85] Katz M.L., Shapiro C. (1985), Networl Externalities, Competition, and Compatibility, *American Economic Review,* vol 75:3, pp 424-440

[KIR 92] KIRMAN A.P. (1992), Whom or what does the representative individual represent?, *Journal of Economic Perspectives* 6: 117-136.

[KIR 93] KIRMAN A.P. (1993), Ants, rationality and recruitment, *Quarterly Journal of Economics* 111: 137-156.

[KIR 98] KIRMAN A.P., (1998), The Economy as an Interactive System, in Arthur W.B., Durlauf S.N. & Lane D (eds), The Economy as an Evolving Complex System II, Addison Wesley: New York, pp. 491-531.

[OUS 99] OUSTERHOUT J. (1999), Free software needs profit, *Communications of the ACM*, 42: 44-45.

[ROM 93] ROMER P. (1993), The economics of new ideas and new goods, Proceedings of the World Bank Annual Conference on Development Economics 1992, World Bank, Washington DC.

[VHI 88] VON HIPPEL E. (1988), The sources of innovations, MIT Press.

Firm Size, Innovation, and Market Share Instability: the Role of Negative Feedback and Idiosyncratic Events

Mariana Mazzucato

Open University
Walton Hall
Milton Keynes
MK7 6AA
United Kingdom

m.mazzucato@open.ac.uk

ABSTRACT: *An evolutionary model is built which uses structural and random factors to account for the emergence of market share instability and industry concentration. The structural factors are studied through the relationship between firm size and innovation (dynamic returns to scale) while the random factors are studied through the effect of shocks on this feedback relationship. We find that market share instability is the highest under the negative feedback regime, when the industry specific level of technological opportunity is intermediate, and when shocks are neither very large nor very small.*

KEY WORDS: *market structure, innovation, dynamic economies of scale, random events.*

1. Introduction

The validity of using a deterministic model to study market structure has been criticized in recent years by contributions in the empirical and theoretical field of industrial organization which emphasize the role of initial conditions and idiosyncratic events [ART 1990, KLE 1990, NEL 1982,]. An idiosyncratic event is an event that could not have been predicted beforehand due to its local and non-structural nature. It could be anything from the trial and error aspect of an innovation (or of an advertising campaign), to the particular personality of a CEO. For example, no one could have predicted the way that the ego-maniac personality of Henry Ford was to influence the market structure of the US automobile industry. The paper develops an evolutionary model which explores the role of such idiosyncratic events under different structural regimes of innovation. The regimes describe different types of feedback between firm size and innovation which have been explored in the Schumpeterian literature on the relative dis/advantages of small and large firms in innovation [SCH 1942, COH 1989] and in the management literature on the relationship between radical innovation by small firms and market instability [ABE 1974, AND 1986, CHR 1997, MAR 1998]. The model thus differs from models that make firm size and market structure solely a function of structural conditions (e.g. cost curves) as well as from those that make firm size solely a function of stochastic shocks (e.g. Gibrat). Our results suggest that *both* "chance" and "necessity" play a role in the emergence of market share instability and industry concentration.

2. Dynamic Economies of Scale

We explore the effect of idiosyncratic events on the relationship between firm size and innovation by developing a stochastic model of *dynamic* returns to scale. Dynamic returns to scale refers to the effect of firm size on the *rate* of cost reduction (i.e. innovation), as opposed to static returns to scale which refers to the effect of firm size on the direction of costs. Dynamic decreasing (increasing) returns to scale describes a negative (positive) feedback mechanism by which an increase in firm size causes the firm's rate of cost reduction to decrease (increase). Economists skeptical of the empirical relevance of the unique equilibrium outcomes associated with *static* decreasing returns to scale have in recent years paid much attention to the role of positive feedback in determining multiple equilibria [ART 1989, DAV 1995; KRU 1997]. These studies have shown that increasing returns to scale causes concentrated markets to emerge and the size of any given firm to be unpredictable ex-ante. Although the theoretical and empirical analyses of positive feedback processes have contributed much to our understanding of disequilibrium dynamics and multiple equilibria, they have indirectly caused all forms of negative feedback, not just the static one, to receive little attention.

The lack of emphasis on negative feedback mechanisms by economists interested in disequilibrium dynamics lies in contrast to the emphasis in management studies on the role of negative feedback in generating market share turbulence. Negative feedback is understood here in the dynamic sense: the penalties incurred by large firms when their large size prevents them from taking advantage of innovation opportunities.   Klein [KLE 1977] claims that market share instability which is characteristic in the early phase of industry evolution, when demand and technology are undergoing great change, is due to the fact that in these periods it is "dynamic efficiency" which determines competitive advantage. Dynamic efficiency refers to the ability of firms to *explore* new frontiers of production. Since small firms are usually more flexible than large firms and hence better able to adapt to new circumstances, periods of dynamic efficiency tend to be characterized by market share instability. Instead periods in which competitive advantage is determined by "static efficiency," i.e. the ability to *exploit* existing techniques of production, are characterized by market share stability due to the "success breeds success" dynamic which favors large incumbent firms[1]. Abernathy and Wayne [ABE 1974] make a similar point regarding the US automobile industry: the benefits (in profit and market share) that the Ford Motor Company reaped from the system of mass production built around the Model T were lost when changes in demand called for more innovative strategies which Ford's large structure was not able to adapt to quickly enough.   Recent contributions in the strategic management literature on "technological discontinuities" and "architectural innovation" also emphasize the effect of negative feedback on market turbulence. Anderson and Tushman [AND 1986] claim that while "competence-destroying" innovations, often initiated by new small firms, cause a shake-up in market shares, "competence-enhancing" innovations, often initiated by large existing firms, cause leaders to remain leaders. In a similar vein, Henderson and Clark [HEN 1990] claim that architectural innovations, i.e. innovations that change the way in which the components of a product are linked together while leaving in tact the core design concepts, tend to destroy the lead of established firms since they destroy the information-processing procedures that established firms are often locked-into. Other studies in the strategic management literature that have linked industry turbulence with the dynamics of small firms and technological change include: CHR 1997, HAM 1998, and MAR 1998.

3. An Evolutionary Model of Dynamic Economies of Scale

In a previous paper we explored the positive and negative feedback mechanisms embodied in the relationship between firm size and innovation through an evolutionary model of dynamic returns to scale [MAZ 1998]. We found that it is indeed when small firms are more innovative, i.e. negative feedback, that market instability emerges, and that this instability is greatest when the average speed of innovation is high. This result confirmed that negative feedback should not be

---

[1] Note that Klein's definition of "static efficiency" is similar to what we call "dynamic positive feedback" and his definition of "dynamic efficiency" is similar to what we call "dynamic negative feedback".

ignored by economists interested in disequilibrium dynamics. Our goal in this paper is to see how those results are altered when we introduce random shocks. This allows us to explore a different set of theories that claim that market share instability is the result of idiosyncratic events on an underlying process of increasing returns to scale [ART 1990, KLE 1990,1996].

Instead of resorting to a model where all change is driven by stochastic events (e.g. models based on Gibrat's law), we retain the structural dynamic embodied in dynamic returns to scale, and ask 'to what *degree* do shocks matter under different structural conditions?'. The study is related to that found in Klepper [KLE 1990, KLE 1996] where regularities concerning entry, exit and concentration are reproduced in a model in which random factors and increasing returns to scale shape market structure at maturity.

Before developing the model of stochastic economies of scale in section 4, we first summarize the underlying deterministic model on which it is based and the results from our previous study [MAZ 1998].

If we take s_i and c_i to denote the market share and cost of firm i respectively, and c to denote the weighted average industry cost, we can describe the evolution of market shares through Eq. [1] which states that the market share of firm i increases (decreases) if its cost is below (above) the weighted average industry cost:

$$\dot{s_i} = s_i(\bar{c} - c_i) \qquad \text{where } \bar{c} \equiv \sum_i c_i s_i \text{ and } \sum_i s_i = 1 \qquad [1]$$

Equation [1] is a replicator equation describing a "distance from mean" dynamic where variety drives change: when $c_i = c$ for all i, there is no change in market shares. The advantage of using replicator dynamics to study market structure is that it allows us to focus on the evolution of *variety* between agents as opposed to the characteristics of one "representative" agent. And a study of market share instability and concentration is indeed a study of the evolution of variety between firms in an industry.

To study the dynamic positive and negative feedback discussed above, the cost terms in Eq. [1] are explored through different assumptions regarding the effect of size on the rate at which firms reduce their costs (e.g. innovation):

$$\frac{\dot{c_i}}{c_i} = -\alpha(1 - s_i) \qquad [2a]$$

$$\frac{\dot{c_i}}{c_i} = -\alpha s_i \qquad [2b]$$

Equation [2a] describes the case of dynamic *negative* feedback: an increase in market share causes a firm's rate of cost reduction to fall. Equation [2b] describes the case of dynamic *positive* feedback. The parameter α is an industry-specific parameter that can be interpreted either as the *degree of technological opportunity* in the industry (ease of innovation) or as the *average rate of cost reduction in the industry*: those industries in which there are more opportunities for innovation are characterized by a higher average speed of cost reduction. The exact rate of cost reduction of any one specific firm depends both on the value of α as well as on its market share via Eq. [1]. The value of α might depend on the "tacitness" of the knowledge base in an industry, on the patent system, or on other industry-specific and technology-specific factors which affect spillovers and diffusion. We can combine the two cost equations into a single equation by putting weights on the different feedback mechanisms[2]:

$$\frac{\overset{\bullet}{c_i}}{c_i} = \lambda \cdot \left(-\beta(1 - s_i)\right) + (1 - \lambda)\left(-\alpha s_i\right) \qquad [3]$$

where $\beta = \dfrac{-\alpha}{n-1}$ and $n =$ the number of firms in the industry. When $\lambda = 1$, costs evolve via dynamic negative feedback, while when $\lambda = 0$, costs evolve via dynamic positive feedback. In what follows we refer to the parameter β for the case of dynamic positive feedback and to the parameter α for the case of dynamic negative feedback.

Figure 1 illustrates the results from the simulation of Eqs. [1] and [3] with $\lambda = 1$ (i.e. only dynamic negative feedback) and with different values of α. In each case, market shares begin equal while costs begin randomly distributed (with mean 1 and variance γ).

---

[2] Because equations (2a) and (2b) embody different average rates of cost reduction, it is necessary, when setting the value for α in the two equations, not to introduce a bias into the model. The average rate of cost reduction for equation (2a) is equal to $-\alpha(n-1)$, while for equation (2b) it is equal to $-\alpha$. To control for this difference, the parameter α must be set differently in the two equations so that for any given value of α in equation (2a), the average rate of cost reduction is the same in the two equations. We do this by replacing the average rate of cost reduction for equation (2b), i.e. $-\alpha$, with the term $-\beta$ and by setting the two average rates of cost reduction equal to each other : $\beta = \alpha(n-1)$. This means that the value chosen for α in the phase of dynamic positive feedback must always be $1/n-1$ times the value chosen for α in the phase of dynamic negative feedback.

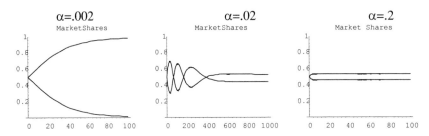

Figure 1. *Negative Feedback: Eq. [1] and [3] for n=2 firms with λ=1, γ = .4*

Figure 2 illustrates the deterministic results from the simulation of Eqs. [1] and [3] with λ = 0 (i.e. dynamic positive feedback) and with different values of β:

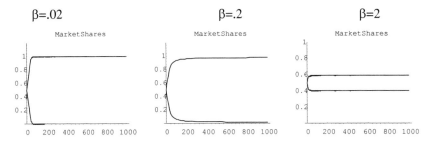

Figure 2. *Positive Feedback: Eq. [1] and [3] for n=2 firms, λ = 0, γ = .4*

The results in Figures 1 and 2 indicate that dynamic returns to scale does not lead to a predictable market structure as does static returns to scale. In this more dynamic conception of returns to scale, even negative feedback leads to multiple equilibria. The particular market structure in each case is sensitive to the industry-specific average speed of innovation (or technological opportunity) and to the variance of the initial random distribution of costs (γ). The results are summarized and interpreted below [for further details see MAZ 1998]:

–   In both the case of dynamic positive and negative feedback, when the average rate of cost reduction is *very low* (i.e. inertia), the market structure which emerges is highly concentrated due to the overpowering effect of selection [Eq. 1]. *This result confirms empirical studies which link market concentration to the intensity of innovation: when the rate of innovation is very slow, innovation tends to lead to a more concentrated market structure [GER 1990, DOS 1987]; concentrated markets are more conducive to innovation in low "technological opportunity" industries in which the science base moves relatively slowly and predictably [COM 1967, SCH 1984]: radical innovation and product innovation tend to produce less concentrated market structures [LUN 1986].*

- In both dynamic positive and negative feedback, with a *very high* value for α, the emergent market structure is less concentrated since the fast speed of convergence between firms weakens the ability of the different feedback regimes to select between firms. In neither of these extreme cases (a high/low α) do market shares undergo changes in rank: the initially most fit firm predictably remains the market leader. *This result confirms the empirical finding that in any given industry, market structure tends to be less concentrated in countries characterized by fast rates of innovation than in those characterized by low rates of innovation (DOS 1984, ACS 1987) and that vigorous innovation tends to be more concentration reducing than increasing (GER 1990, MUK 1985).*

- The case of dynamic positive feedback with an *intermediate* level of α, leads simply to an "in-between" result (as compared to the two extremes), again with the initially most efficient firm remaining the market leader and the exact value of α determining how many other firms co-exist with the leader. In the case of dynamic negative feedback, on the other hand, the results with an intermediate level of α are *qualitatively very different*. A turbulent switching pattern emerges due to the alternating advantages of firms; when a firm's market share increases, the firm becomes less innovative and is surpassed in share by smaller more innovative firms. The final ranking of firms is *unpredictable* since the changes in rank continue until costs reach their lower bound. *This result confirms the empirical finding that market share instability tends to be higher during periods in which small firms have relative advantages in the innovative process, such as the early phase of the life-cycle and in industries characterized by "dynamic efficiency" and radical innovation [ACS 1990, KLE 1977, AND 1986, CHR 1997].*

- The higher is the initial variance of costs, the greater is the degree of market share instability and the longer it takes for market shares to reach an equilibrium value. *This result confirms the empirical finding that low levels of initial asymmetry in firm characteristics allow more firms to compete and a less concentrated market structure to emerge [DOS 1987].*

The results thus confirm the hypotheses found in the management literature cited above on the effect of negative feedback on market share instability: whereas periods characterized by dynamic positive feedback lead to stability and concentration, periods characterized by dynamic negative feedback lead to market share instability. The contribution of the model is to outline *under which conditions* these hypotheses hold.

4. Idiosyncratic events

Recent empirical and theoretical studies have shown that factors governing the early evolution of industries may shape their market structure at maturity. Including a shock to Eqs. 2 and 3 which describe the evolution of costs allows us to partially capture the effect of uncertainty faced by firms in their production and innovation activities. In a non-linear system characterized by positive and negative feedback, shocks may determine early winners and losers and thus have a strong influence on the resulting dynamics:

> "In the real world, if several similar-size firms entered a market at the same time, small fortuitous events - unexpected orders, chance meetings with buyers, managerial whims – would help determine which ones achieved early sales and, over time, which firm dominated. Economic activity is quantified by individual transactions that are too small to observe, and these small "random" events can accumulate and become magnified by positive feedbacks so as to determine the eventual outcome. These facts suggest(ed) that situations dominated by increasing returns should be modeled not as static deterministic problems but as dynamic processes based on random events and natural positive feedbacks, or nonlinearities." [ART 1990, p. 5]

Under such conditions, it is impossible to know apriori which of many different possible market structures will emerge in any given run. Rather, one can:

> "... record the particular set of random events leading to each solution and study the probability that a particular solution would emerge under a set of initial conditions." [ART 1990]

Arthur's analysis of the role of random events in a system characterized by positive feedback is similar to that found in Klepper [KLE 1990, KLE 1996] where market share instability and concentration result from the interaction between the idiosyncratic aspect of firm-specific abilities to innovate and the increasing returns to scale associated with innovation:

> "The result (of increasing returns) is a world in which initial firm differences get magnified as size begets size... If cohorts differ in terms of the distribution of their innovative expertise or if the innovative expertise of incumbents is undermined by certain types of technological changes, then later entrants may leapfrog over the industry leaders and the firms that eventually dominate the industry may not come from the earliest cohort of entrants." [KLE 1996, p. 581]

In both the work of Arthur and Klepper, stochastic shocks have a *qualitative* effect, interacting with the underlying dynamic of positive feedback. This differs from models in which shocks are just "noise" around a systematic trend, i.e. a deviation around average behavior where it is the properties of the latter which are the focus of attention.[3]

---

[3] Normally distributed random terms in econometric models are an example of the latter, allowing the model to embody: "... a systematic component or true value and an 'erratic component' or 'disturbance' or 'accidental error'. The systematic components are assumed to satisfy the regression equation exactly ... the erratic component is taken as error in the literal sense of the word." (KOO 1937, p. 5 cited in MIR 1989)

In this section we test the different feedback regimes explored in section 3 for how robust they are to shocks. Given the results in the deterministic analysis, what do we expect? We expect the period of dynamic negative feedback to be more sensitive to shocks than the phase of dynamic positive feedback since even without shocks the market structure and firm size distribution that emerges from negative feedback is unpredictable (with an intermediate α). The market structure generated from positive feedback is probably more resistant to shocks since the force of selection is strongly biased towards the initially most efficient firm. Yet the presence of shocks should prevent, at least in the beginning, any one firm from getting too far ahead of other firms.

To examine the effect of a stochastic component on costs we embody different size shocks to Eq. [3]:

$$\frac{\overset{\bullet}{c_i}}{c_i} = \lambda \cdot \left(-\beta(1-s_i)\right)\varepsilon_i + (1-\lambda)\left(-\alpha s_i\right)\varepsilon_i \qquad [4]$$

where ε_i is an i.i.d random variable drawn at each moment in time for each firm i from a normal distribution with mean = 1. To study the effect of different size shocks on the model, we vary the variance level (σ) of this distribution. We experiment with values $\sigma = 0$, .05, .1, and .2. If, for example, we increase σ from .05 to .1, this means that the possible size of the shocks has increased although at any moment in time the shock might be small.

For each size shock, the simulations are run with a given initial distribution of costs with mean 1 and variance γ, and with a given speed of cost adjustment parameter (α or β). For each set of parameters ($\alpha,\beta,\gamma,\sigma$), we first calculate the time period (TC) in which market shares settle down to a constant value. This is determined by the period in which the instability index, defined as the sum of absolute market share changes[4], reaches the value .002. The following data is then calculated at that time period: the herfindahl index (HI2), the cumulative instability index (II2: the integral of the instability index from $t = 0\text{-}TC$), the surviving number of firms (n), and the number of times the ranking between firms changed (R). The value of the instability index and the herfindahl index at the mid-way point (TC/2) are also calculated (under the heading II1 and HI1). Market share instability is represented through the instability index and the number of times firm ranking changes. The latter has been used by [GOR 1963]. The values in the table for each of these statistics correspond to the *average* value which emerges from 50 simulation runs using the same set of parameters.

---

[4] The index devised by Hymer and Pashigan [HYM 1962] is defined as:

$$I = \sum_{i=1}^{n}[|\, s_{it} - s_{i,t-1}\,|]\,,$$ where *sit* is the market share of firm i at time t.

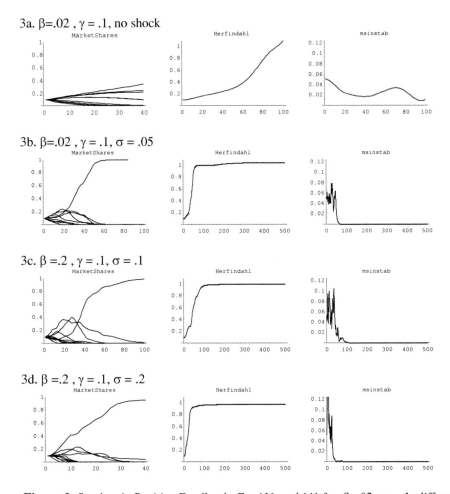

Figure 3. *Stochastic Positive Feedback: Eq. [1] and [4] for β=.02, γ = .1, different σ*

We first add a stochastic component to the case of positive feedback with the objective of observing whether and how the results found in the deterministic simulation of dynamic positive feedback (Fig. 2) are altered. We begin again with the case of a low average rate of cost reduction, recalling that in the deterministic case, a very low β (inertia in costs) causes the force of selection to dominate industry evolution and thus the herfindahl index to always equal 1: the firm with the initially lowest cost always becomes the market leader. Figure 3 illustrates the market patterns which emerge from stochastic positive feedback with a relatively low value of β (=.02), a low variance of the initial cost distribution and different size shocks (σ = 0, .05, .1, .2). For each set of parameters we display three graphs: market shares, the instability index and the herfindahl index. To render the early market share patterns visually more clear, they are illustrated only up to the time period that it becomes obvious which firm will corner the market or maintain its dominant lead (no switching occurs after that period).

	$\alpha=.2,\gamma=.1$	$\alpha=2,\gamma=.1$	$\alpha=6,\gamma=.1$	$\alpha=.2,\gamma=.2$	$\alpha=2,\gamma=.2$	$\alpha=6,\gamma=.2$
$\sigma=0$						
HI1	0.29	0.526	0.248	0.4	0.382	0.42
HI2	1	0.926	0.298	0.489	0.49	0.48
II1	0.019	0.029	0.012	0.023	0.051	0.019
II2	0.002	0.002	0.002	0.002	0.002	0.002
CI1	1.32	1.86	1.2	1.51	1.45	1.55
CI2	2.51	2.4	1.37	1.7	1.73	1.69
R	0	0	0	0	0	1
n	1	1	4	2	2	1
TC	100	100	70	45	35	45
$\sigma=.05$						
HI1	0.47	0.45	0.36	0.565	0.438	0.508
HI2	0.98	0.82	0.46	0.97	0.514	0.66
II1	0.052	0.159	0.02	0.055	0.017	0.272
II2	0.002	0.002	0.002	0.002	0.002	0.002
CI1	1.76	1.5	1.36	1.76	1.56	1.13
CI2	2.48	2.08	1.6	2.3	1.77	1.93
R	2.3	1.5	1	1	0	1
n	1	1.3	2.5	1	2.3	2
TC	63	70	55	44	45	59.6
$\sigma=.1$						
HI1	0.62	0.66	0.33	0.96	0.503	0.538
HI2	0.86	0.84	0.44	0.976	0.623	0.628
II1	0.014	0.022	0.03	0.058	0.021	0.039
II2	0.002	0.002	0.002	0.002	0.002	0.002
CI1	3.2	2.13	1.36	1.83	1.75	1.62
CI2	4.04	2.37	1.61	2.94	1.98	1.79
R	5.3	4.3	3.2	3	1.6	1
n	1.3	1.3	3.2	2	2	2.5
TC	161	66	44	43.5	57.5	42.6
$\sigma=.2$						
HI1	0.88	0.57	0.426	0.565	0.557	0.429
HI2	0.87	0.83	0.53	0.97	0.727	0.725
II1	0.007	0.16	0.01	0.04	0.025	0.051
II2	0.002	0.002	0.002	0.002	0.002	0.002
CI1	2.56	2.02	1.5	2.5	2.03	2.05
CI2	2.6	2.04	1.6	3.3	2.31	2.65
R	3	4.7	2.6	4	3.2	3.5
n	1.3	1.25	2.6	1	1.5	1.75
TC	76	61	45	5	56.5	68

Table 1. *Statistics for stochastic positive feedback*

Figure 3 illustrates that in the stochastic positive feedback case, with a low average speed of cost reduction, it is still a concentrated market structure which emerges (as in the deterministic case), but that the *process* towards concentration is turbulent instead of smooth. This is different from the deterministic case where it was only with negative feedback and with an intermediate average speed of cost reduction that market share instability emerged. The patterns confirm Klepper's [KLE 1996] hypothesis that market share turbulence during the early phase of the industry life-cycle might be the result of idiosyncratic (random) events which disrupt the path-dependent effects of selection under positive feedback. Table 1 shows that as β increases, the final market structure is more concentrated than in the deterministic case: whereas in the deterministic case a very fast average speed of cost reduction causes market shares to converge before the path-dependent selection effects of positive feedback have time to take place, in the stochastic case the instability caused by the shocks causes some firms to get 'shocked-out' of the market. This may imply that in industries in which all firms' costs fall relatively quickly, idiosyncratic events can prevent a relatively competitive market from emerging, as would instead be the case in the absence of those events.

The main result that emerges from the stochastic analysis of positive feedback is that although there is a good chance that the market structure will still be concentrated (as in the deterministic case), it is no longer possible to know ex-ante which firm will become the market leader. We summarize the main conclusions for both positive and negative feedback below:

–   Under stochastic positive feedback with *any* average rate of cost reduction, and under stochastic negative feedback with a *low* average rate of cost reduction, although concentration still tends to emerge (in the former due to path-dependency and in the latter due to inertia), the *process* towards concentration is very different; turbulence precedes concentration, and the final leader is not necessarily the initially most efficient firm.

–   The presence of shocks always renders un-predictable which firms will finally lead the industry: information regarding initial efficiency levels cannot be used to predict the final ranking of firms.

–   When the average rate of cost reduction is very high, the deterministic results are less affected by the presence of shocks because convergence dominates both the process of selection (Eq. 1) as well as the negative/positive feedback process creating variety between firms (Eq. 3). This implies that in industries in which the average rate of cost reduction is very high, idiosyncratic events have less of an impact on industry evolution.

–   Market share instability is highest with *mid*-size shocks since small shocks are not very "disturbing" and large shocks cause too large of a shakeout and hence early concentration. In the stochastic negative feedback case with an intermediate rate of cost reduction, instability is higher than in the deterministic case: shares do not only undergo changes in rank and switching but also experience longer more frequent and jagged ups and downs. Emphasis should thus not be placed only on large radical events affecting change but also and especially on minor events.

–   In the case of stochastic negative feedback with a low α, although the market tends to become concentrated (as in the deterministic case), as the shock size increases, the degree of concentration decreases and the instability index rises. Larger shocks thus make the market more competitive on its way to monopoly.

- In the case of stochastic dynamic positive feedback, a higher variance of the initial cost distribution causes the level of instability to be lower than with a lower variance. This might be because the higher degree of initial differences between firms makes the market structure less vulnerable to shocks due to the stronger force of selection.

- When costs change very slowly, convergence to stability (instability index = .002) takes the longest time to occur with a mid-size shock. This is because large shocks cause many firms to exit, while small shocks cause the selection mechanism to remain strong. Mid-size shocks have the effect of increasing turbulence and hence delaying the time of convergence to a steady state. This result does not hold under negative feedback with a mid-level α, where instead an increase in shock size causes the convergence time to first increase and then to decrease. This is because the intermediate average rate of cost reduction produces market share instability even without shocks so that an increase in shock size causes excessive turbulence causing a severe shakeout to occur very soon.

5. Conclusion and Discussion

A deterministic and a stochastic version of the model were developed separately so that the interaction between structural and random factors could be systematically explored. Economic change occurs in the model due to the *interaction* between initial conditions, shocks and the underlying non-linear dynamic characterizing the relationship between firm size and innovation.

Whereas the deterministic analysis allowed us to gain more insight into the hypotheses that connect market share instability to the innovation activities of small firms, the stochastic analysis allowed us to gain more insight into the hypotheses that connect market share instability to the interaction between random events and increasing returns to scale. In both cases, the point of the model was to explore 'under what conditions' these hypotheses hold. We explored the *degree* to which shocks affect the path-dependent pattern under different types of structural conditions: the type of feedback regulating the relationship between firm size and innovation, the average rate of cost reduction in the industry (or technological opportunity), the size of the shocks, and the different level of initial asymmetry between firms.

The *deterministic* analysis indicated that when small firms are favored in the process of innovation, the market structure tends to be more unstable and less concentrated. When instead it is larger firms that have the innovative advantage (dynamic positive feedback), the emergent market structure tends to be more concentrated and stable (concentration emerges without any switching in firm market shares). The exact patterns are determined by the industry-specific speed of cost reduction and the initial variance between firm efficiencies.

In the *stochastic* version of the model, new results emerge. Under positive feedback, and under negative feedback with a very low rate of cost reduction, although concentration still tends to emerge, the *process* towards concentration is turbulent. Thus observers only interested in the asymptotic level of concentration risk missing important qualitative information regarding industry evolution. Market share instability is the highest when: a) there is negative feedback between firm size and innovation; b) the average speed of cost reduction is neither very fast nor slow; and c) shocks are of an intermediate size.

References

[ABE 1974] ABERNATHY, W.J., WAYNE, K. (1974) "Limits to the Learning Curve", Harvard, Business Review, 52: 109-120

[ACS 1987] ACS, Z.J., AUDRETSCH, D.B. (1987) "Innovation, Market Structure and Firm Size", *Review of Economics and Statistics*, LXIX (4): 567-574

[AND 1986] ANDERSON, P. and M. TUSHMAN (1986), "Technological Discontinuitites and Organizational Environments," *Administrative Science Quarterly*, 31: 439-465.

[ART 1989] ARTHUR, B. (1989),"Competing Technologies, Increasing Returns, and Lock-In by Historical Small Events", *Economic Journal*, 99:116-131

[ART 1990] ARTHUR, B. (1990), "Positive Feedbacks in the Economy", *Scientific American*, February 1990.

[AUD 1995] AUDRETSCH, D.B., (1995), *Innovation and Industry Evolution*, MIT Press, Cambridge, MA

[CHR 1997] CHRISTENSEN, C. (1997), *The Innovators Dilemma: When New Technologies Cause Great Firms to Fail*, HBS Press, Boston, Mass.

[COH 1989] COHEN, W.M., LEVIN, R.C (1989), "Empirical Studies of Innovation and Market Structure", in *Handbook of Industrial Organization*, 2: 1059-1107, Eds. R. Schmalansee and R. Willig, North Holland

[COM 1967] COMANOR, W.S. (1967), "Market Structure, Product Differentiation, and Industrial Research", *Quarterly Journal of Economics*, 85: 524-531

[DAV 1985] DAVID, P. (1985), "Clio and the economics of QWERTY", *American Economic Review*,Proceedings, 75: 332-337

[GER 1990] GEROSKI, P.A. (1990), "Innovation, Technological Opportunity, and Market Structure", *Oxford Economic Papers*, 42 (3): 586-602

[GER 1997] GEROSKI, P., MACHIN, S., WALTERS, C. (1997), "Corporate Growth and Profitability", *Journal of Industrial Economics*, 65:171-189

[GIB 1931] GIBRAT, R. (1931), Les Inegalites Economiques, Paris, Requeil Sirey

[HAM 1998] HAMEL, G. (1998), "Opinion, Strategy Innovation and the Quest for Value," *Sloan Management Review*, Winter: 7-14.

[HYM 1962] HYMER, S., PASHIGAN, P. (1962), "Turnover of Firms as a Measure of Market Behavior", *Review of Economics and Statistics*, 44: 82-87

[KLE 1977] KLEIN, B. (1977), Dynamic Economics, Cambridge: Harvard University Press

[KLE 1990] KLEPPER, S, GRADDY, E. (1990), "The Evolution of New Industries and the Determinants of Market Structure", *Rand Journal of Economics*, 21:24-44

[KLE 1996] KLEPPER, S. (1996), "Exit, Entry, Growth, and Innovation over the Product Life cycle", *American Economic Review*, 86(3): 562-583

[KOO 1937] Koopmans, T.C. (1937), *Linear Regression Analysis of Economic Time Series*, Haarlem, De Erven F. Bohn.

[KRU 1979] KRUGMAN, P. (1979), "Increasing returns, monopolistic competition and international trade", *The Journal of International Economics*, 9: 469-479

[MAL 1996] MALERBA, F., ORESENIGO, L. (1996), "The Dynamics and Evolution of Industries", *Industrial and Corporate Change*, 5(1): 51-88

[MAR 1998] MARKIDES, C. (1998), "Strategic Innovation in Established Companies," Sloan Management Review, Spring, 31-42.

[MAZ 1998] MAZZUCATO, M. (1998), "A Computational Model of Economies of Scale and Market Share Instability", *Structural Change and Economic Dynamics*, 9: 55-83

[MIR 1989] Mirowski, P. (1989),"The Probablistic Counter-Revolution or How Stochastic Concepts Came to Neoclassical Economics", *Oxford Economic Papers*, 41(1): 217-235

[MUK 1985] MUKHOPADHYAY, A. (1985), "Technological Progress and Change in the US: 1963-77", *Southern Economic Journal*, 52: 141-149

[NEL 1982] NELSON, R., WINTER, S. (1982), *An Evolutionary Theory of Economic Change*, Cambridge Harvard University Press

[SCH 1912] SCHUMPETER, J. (1912), *The Theory of Economic Development*, Cambridge, MA: Harvard University Press

[SCH 1942] SCHUMPETER, J. (1942), *Capitalism, Socialism and Democracy*, New York: Harper.

[SIM 1958] SIMON, H.A., BONINI, C.P. (1958), "The Size Distribution of Business Firms", *American Economic Review*, 48(4): 607-617

Exploring the Dynamics of Social Policy Models: A Computer Simulation of Long-term Unemployment

Georg Mueller

Dept. of Social Work and Social Policy
University of Fribourg, Bonnesfontaines 11
CH-1700 Fribourg, Switzerland [1]

ABSTRACT. *This paper focuses on the use of computer models for making inferences about the effects of social policies. In order to improve the reliability of such inferences, the article proposes a new methodology which is based on the systematic search of model output which either confirms or falsifies the aforementioned inferences. The successful use of this new methodology is exemplified by the analysis of a simulation model which describes the dynamics of long-term unemployment.*

KEY WORDS: *Computer assisted inferencing, K. Popper, verification and falsification of propositions, optimization techniques, social policy models, long-term unemployment, labor queues, social discrimination, Switzerland.*

1. The Problem

There is actually a growing number of reforms and propositions which aim at the solution of the crises of the tax and the welfare state by which many Western countries have been hit in the past [MIC 97]. Since the consequences of such plans are often not fully understood, there is also an increasing demand for knowledge about the effects and implications of these reforms. Along with evaluation research [WEI 72: chapters 2, 3; BER 90] social science *microsimulation* [ORC 86; HAR 96] is one of the disciplines which can be used in order to fill these knowledge gaps. In particular, microsimulation models claim

a) to make *conditional forecasts* about the intended and the unintended consequences of policy reforms,

b) to deduce from model output new *theoretical knowledge* about the functioning of economy and society.

The value of these potential contributions to social policy and social science obviously depends on the *reliability* of the conclusions drawn from the simulation runs by which the behavior of a model is explored. Consequently, this paper focuses on the question how the reliability of the inferences from a simulation model can be increased by the use of an appropriate technique for the exploration of a model.

There are of course different factors which may endanger the *reliability* of such inferences. One of them is the *model structure* itself which is never a perfectly isomorphical mapping of social reality and which thus may entail inadequate conclusions about the social phenomena under consideration. Although this is sometimes an important source of errors, we assume in this paper, that the model under discussion has successfully been tested such that it can be considered as suffciently isomorphical to social reality. This assumption will allow us to concentrate on the errors entailing from *model exploration*. They are generally the result of *unsystematic experimentation* with a *limited number* of different values of model parameters by which authors try to explore the behavior of their models. Hanneman e.g. has advocated this type of quasi-experimentation as a third way of knowledge production along with traditional statistical analysis and pure mathematical reasoning [HAN 88; HAN 95a; HAN 95b]. However, the conclusions drawn from such experiments are of course only valid for the very limited set of the tested model parameters and thus cannot be generalized in a meaningful and reliable way. This shortcoming of many model analyses has challenged the author to propose a more reliable method of model exploration [MUE 96; MUE 00] which will be presented in the following of this paper.

2. A New Approach to the Exploration of Models

In the following, the exploration of a model is interpreted as an analysis of the *artificial output data* which the aforementioned model produces by processing the *inputs of varying scenarios* of social reality. For reasons of analogy, it thus suggests itself to have a closer look at the procedures which are generally used in empirical social research in order to test hypotheses with *real observational data*. Commonly this type of empirical hypothesis testing involves the following three steps:

a) The first step is generally the *formulation of a hypothesis* about social reality, e.g. about a correlation between two variables x and y. Often, such hypotheses are inductive generalizations of recurrent patterns of a social behavior. In this paper two important types of such hypotheses will be discussed: Those postulating the *existence* of a social phenomenon in a particular situation, e.g. the equilibrium between supply and demand in a competitive market [SAM 87: p. 482 ff.], and those referring to the *universal validity* of relations between variables in different social settings such as the Phillips curve between inflation and unemployment [SAM 87: p. 247 ff.].

b) The second step in this test procedure is generally the *collection of appropriate data* about the social reality to which the aforementioned hypothesis refers to. Sampling procedures can vary according to the researcher's needs, financial resources and other criteria: Generally there is a strong preference for *statistically representative random samples* for which most of the methods of the inferential statistics have been developed. However, there are also other sampling procedures such as the *analysis of extreme cases* or *theoretical sampling* in grounded theory [STR 87: p. 38 ff.; GLA 67] by which researchers attempt to find examples of empirical evidence either in favor or against the considered hypothesis.

c) In a final step, the collected data are *systematically compared* with the aforementioned hypothesis. If the hypothesis states the *existence* of a phenomenon, it is possible to *directly confirm* it by finding the phenomenon in the data. However, if the hypothesis postulates the *universality* of a phenomenon for all virtual actors and points in time, K. Popper has rightfully argued, that there will never be enough data in order to *confirm* the universality of such a hypothesis [POP 59: p. 70]. In this case, the collected data can only be used in order to demonstrate that there is no empirical counter evidence which could *falsify* the hypothesis in question.

This three-step procedure is generally acknowledged for yielding reliable descriptions of social reality. The author of this paper has thus proposed to apply this procedure also to the artificial data output of simulation models [MUE 96; MUE 00]. In the following it will be shown how the exploration of a model can be conceptualized in very much the same way as the aforementioned empirical test of a hypothesis:

a) In analogy with empirical hypothesis testing, the first step of the proposed model exploration procedure is the *formulation of a hypothesis* about the behavior of the model. This hypothesis can be derived from very different sources such as unsystematic trial runs of the model, the theory on which the model is based on, but also from public discourses about possible consequences of a new social policy. Hypotheses may refer to the existence of phenomena as well as the universality of a social pattern in different social settings.

b) The second step in this procedure is the *generation of model output* that can later be used as *artificial data* in order to test the aforementioned hypothesis. By variation of the input parameters of a model very different samples of model outputs can be generated for this purpose. The usual method of running models for different scenarios [HAN 88; HAN 95a; HAN 95b] corresponds to *convenience sampling* and generally gives results that have been criticized for not being very reliable. Hence we propose to directly look for small samples of *extreme situations* which either confirm or falsify the hypothesis under discussion. There are two approaches in order to construct such samples:

The *first approach* is based on the *algorithmic optimization* [2] of a so-called *correspondence function* which measures the degree of correspondence between the considered hypothesis and an output of the model. Algorithmic optimization starts with an initial estimate of the model parameters and systematically improves them by searching along the gradients of the correspondence function for better parameter values. This process stops if a minimum or maximum of the correspondence function has been identified. It thus yields the best or the worst case values of the parameters in which we are interested in. If the hypothesis postulates the *existence* of a certain model behavior, the correspondence between the model output and the hypothesis has to be *maximized* in order to show the existence of this behavior. However, if the analyzed hypothesis postulates the *universal validity* of a model behavior, the correspondence between the model output and the hypothesis should be *minimized* in order to attempt to *falsify* the hypothesis under discussion [POP 59: p. 70]. If this falsification *fails,* the mentioned hypothesis describes an inference of the model which is *universally valid* for very different social situations.

Algorithmic optimization can fail for various reasons such as numerical inaccuracy, the existence of local minima, or excessive computation time. These problems are especially crucial if big models with many parameters have to be optimized. Hence, we will concentrate in this paper on a *second approach* which starts with the construction of a *random sample* of parameter vectors. These random-scenarios are then processed by the model which thus generates outputs that can be evaluated by the aforementioned correspondence function: Like in the first sampling-approach, the model inputs with the worst or best correspondence values are the ones of interest for the next following step of the model exploration. In order to make shure that this sampling procedure really yields the best or the worst correspondence value, the *size* of the random samples of scenarios has to be *systematically increased* until criteria of convergence make it unplausible that substantially better parameter values can be retrieved.

c) As a third and last step of the proposed exploration procedure, we have to *analyze the degree of correspondence* between the hypothesis and the optimized model output. A hypothesis about the *existence* of a model behavior is confirmed if for the best parameter values the correspondence function nearly reaches its theoretical *maximum.* In this case we obviously have found a model input that "generates" the social phenomenon in which we are interested in. Similarly, a hypothesis about the *universal validity* of a phenomenon is corroborated if the *minimized* value of the correspondence function is substantially higher than its theoretical *minimum* and if we were consequently *unable* to generate a model output which really *falsifies* our hypothesis.

Hence, the proposed exploration procedure promises to solve the reliability problem of the traditional inferencing approach: It systematizes the analysis of the parameter space by introducing the idea of the optimization of the correspondence between the model output and the hypothesis which is being analyzed.

3. An Illustrative Example: The Exploration of a Labor Queue Model of Long-term Unemployment

3.1. *The Model*

In the following, the afore sketched method of optimization based inferencing will be used in order to explore a labor-queue model of long-term unemployment. Among others this will allow us to detail some of the ideas which have been treated in section 2 only in a superficial way. The model used for this purpose is a formalization of ideas of L. Thurow [THU 69: p. 48; THU 75: p. 75 ff.] and others [RES 90: p. 29 ff.] about *labor queues.* They are defined as lines of unemployed job seekers who are sorted according to their *value q* on the labor market: The places at the head of such a queue offer the best chances for reemployment and are occupied by those workers who are e.g. best qualified, have the least cost of on the job training, or the highest labor productivity. Hence, the criteria of stratification of a labor queue depend on the one hand on the economic preferences of the employers. However, the stratification may also be influenced by non-economic aspects such as social discrimination or prejudice against minorities.

According to the model, the composition of the labor queue changes at regular time intervals (see figure 1): The best placed job seekers leave the queue and are reemployed, where the *cut-off point θ_t* of the queue, which defines the segment of the successful job seekers, depends on the number of available job opportunities. At the same time, all those job seekers who are no longer eligible for unemployment insurance benefits leave the labor queue too and become socially marginalized long-term unemployed. In most countries they are irreversibly off the labor market and thus often have to live on poor relief. Finally, the queue is joined by newly laid-off workers and employees who too change the composition of the queue by occupying those places in the line which correspond to their value q on the labor market.

The processes described in figure 1 will in the following be used in order to explain the dynamics of long-term unemployment of pairs of mutually exclusive social groups such as men and women, blue and white collar workers, immigrants and nationals, etc. For this purpose we will assume that the values q of the job seekers on the labor market are for both groups *normally* distributed: From the statistical point of view of the central limit theorem [VAN 69: p. 100 ff.] this is a relatively plausible assumption which takes into account that the value of a job-seeker on the labor market is the sum of very different qualifications. Similarly, it appears as statistically plausible that two mutually exclusive groups which are both *not systematically discriminated* should have *similar means* and *standard deviations* with regard to their labor market values q. Consequently both groups have in the short-run the same chances of reemployment. After a transformation of the labor market values q into a standard normal distribution $N(0,1)$, these job chances can be represented by the *surfaces* O_I and O_{II} right of the cut-off point θ_t of figure 2.

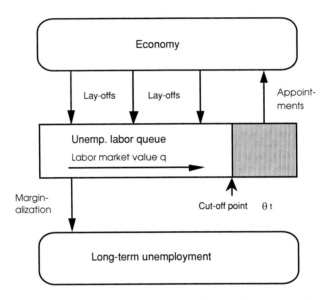

Figure 1. *Population flows between the unemployed labor queue, the economy, and long-term unemployment*

The equal opportunity situation described in figure 2 substantially changes if *group I* is *discriminated* on the labor market on the grounds of ascribed criteria such as gender, race, nationality, etc.: Under these conditions the normal value distribution of the discriminated group I shifts by the amount Δ of the *discrimination* of this group to the left (see figure 3) and thus entails an inequality of job chances: The more discrimination Δ there is, the greater is in figure 3 the inequality $(O_{II} - O_I)$ between the respective *short-term* chances O_I and O_{II}.

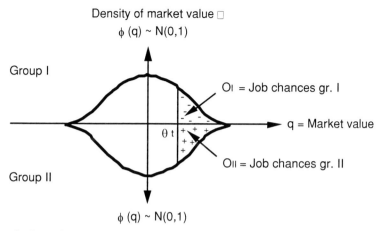

Figure 2. *Distribution of labor market values and short-term job chances of two mutually exclusive groups in an equal opportunity situation*

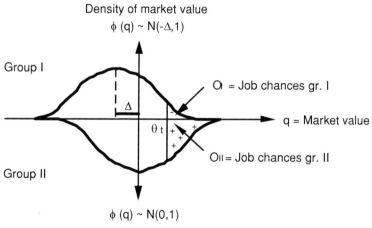

Figure 3. *The influence of the discrimination Δ of group I on the short-term job-chances O_I and O_{II} of two mutually exclusive groups I and II*

As a matter of course, the discrimination Δ also influences the *long-term* job chances of the groups I and II. As a *cohort* of unemployed group members who all lost their job at the *same time t* becomes older, the distribution profile of the market values of those without work gets more and more skewed: After an *unemployment duration d* the density function of q is on the righthand side of the *qualification limit*

$$\varepsilon_{t,d} = \min(\theta_t, \theta_{t-1}, \ldots, \theta_{t-d}) \tag{1}$$

equal to *zero:* Only those members of the cohort are still in the job queue who had at the time points t, t-1, ..., t-d market values below the respective cut-off points θ_t, θ_{t-}

$1, \ldots, \theta_{t-d}$. Figure 4 visualizes this type of distribution profile for the situation where the unemployment duration d has reached the maximum value of the legal duration of *unemployment benefits* δ: Since the *surfaces* U_I and U_{II} obviously represent the risks of the cohort members of the groups I and II for becoming *long-term unemployed*, the *surfaces* J_I and J_{II} can consequently be interpreted as the *long-term job chances* of these two groups. For a given qualification limit $\varepsilon_{t,\delta}$ an increase of the discrimination Δ shifts the qualification distribution of the discriminated group I to the left and thus increases the *inequality of long-term job chances*

$$D = J_{II} - J_I \tag{2}$$

Hence, the higher the discrimination Δ, the higher the long-term inequality D of the job chances. This theorem does obviously not hold if for a long time *no jobs* become available or if *unemployment totally disappears:* In these two cases, either nobody or everyone gets a job. Consequently, these two situations will in the following *always be excluded.*

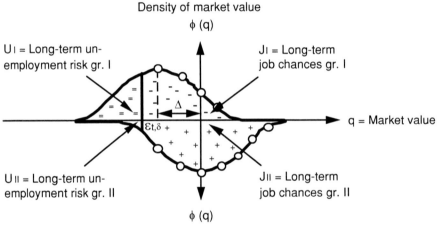

Figure 4. *The influence of the discrimination Δ of group I on the long-term job chances J_I and J_{II} of two cohorts which are both unemployed since time t*

In order to ensure that the reliability of the proposed labor queue model is not impaired by insufficient isomorphical relations to social reality, it has been tested with observational data. For this purpose we derived ex-post forecasts of the long-term unemployment of *immigrants* in Switzerland and compared these forecasts with real data supplied by the Swiss central statistical offices. Details of the method of forecasting, the estimation of the unknown discrimination parameter Δ, and the fit between the observational data and the corresponding forecasts are given in figure 5. Although the Pearson correlation beween the observed and the predicted unemployment figures is only 0.65, the predicted time series reproduces the real data pattern in terms of maxima, minima, and growth rates remarkably well. We thus can assume, that our model sketches a reliable picture of the real dynamics of long-term unemployment in Switzerland.

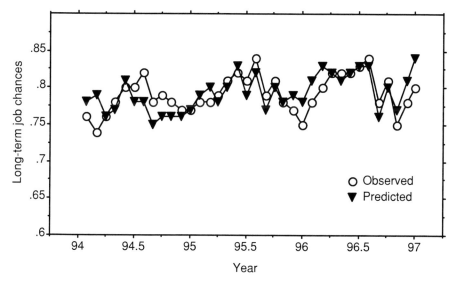

Figure 5. *Predicted and observed long-term job-chances of unemployed immigrants in Switzerland*

Goodness of fit:
r = 0.65   (p<0.001, N=36)

Raw data:
Nationally aggregated data about long-lerm unemployment of different social groups, published in [BUN 96].

Method of computation of predicted values:
Long-term_job_chances_of_immigrants =
$$1 - \Phi_{0,1}(\Phi_{0,1}{}^{-1}(\text{Long-term\_unemployment\_risks\_of\_nationals}) + \Delta) \qquad (3)$$
since, according to figure 4
$$U_I = \Phi_{-\Delta,1}(\Phi_{0,1}{}^{-1}(U_{II})) = \Phi_{0,1}(\Phi_{0,1}{}^{-1}(U_{II}) + \Delta) \qquad (4)$$
where:
$\Phi_{m,1}$ =   Cumulative normal distribution with mean value m and standard deviation 1.

Δ =   0.321 , estimated by OLS from the raw data on the grounds of equation (4).

3.2. Sample Problem 1: Exploring the Existence of Undesirable Consequences of a Social Policy

As any other product of human engineering, social policy and planning may have undesirable consequences which have not been anticipated when the policy was designed. Legal tax evasion by millionaries or cumulated welfare benefits exceeding comparable work incomes are just a few popular examples which illustrate this kind of problem.

In the following, it will be demonstrated how the proposed method of model exploration can be used in order to detect such deficiencies. For this purpose we will analyze the consequences of an *equal opportunity policy* which may possibly entail an unplanned and perhaps undesirable *inversion of the former inequality D*. Hence our analysis will concentrate on the following hypothesis:

There are situations in which an equal opportunity policy with discrimination $\Delta=0$ entails an inversion of the former inequality of long-term job chances D such that $D<0$.

According to the methodology developed in section 2, we next have to define a correspondence function which describes the degree of correspondence between the afore stated hypothesis and the output of the labor queue model with regard to the inequality of job chances. Due to our interest in *negative* inequality in favor of the formerly discriminated group I it imposes itself to define this correspondence function in the following way:

$$f(p_1, p_2, p_3, \ldots) = -D \tag{5}$$

where $p_1, p_2, p_3, \ldots$ are input parameters which describe the size of the different goups and cohorts and which are defined in the legend of table 1. Hence, the hypothesis in question is confirmed if we can identify a set of parameters $\pi_1, \pi_2, \pi_3, \ldots$ for which

$$f(\pi_1, \pi_2, \pi_3, \ldots) = -D \gg 0 \tag{6}$$

and consequently

$$D \ll 0 \tag{7}$$

The best way to find such a confirmation of our hypothesis is of course to *maximize* $f(p_1, p_2, p_3, \ldots)$ by varying the input $p_1, p_2, p_3, \ldots$ of the model. For this purpose 5 large samples of 100 to 500 constrained *random* vectors $(p_1, p_2, p_3, \ldots)$ were used as inputs of an SPSS computer program which simulated for each of the parameter vectors the dynamics of the discussed queues by means of a set of difference equations. The program calculated for each of these vectors $(p_1, p_2, p_3, \ldots)$ the *asymptotic value* of the inequality D such that the aformentioned 5 samples could be searched for the *maximum value of -D*. For each of the 5 samples this maximum is presented in table 1 which also contains further details of the definitions of these samples.

As table 1 shows, the attempt to find an example of a situation for which equal opportunity entails an inversion of the job chances has clearly failed: Even in the best case, -D never becomes really *greater than zero*. However, this result could also be a research artifact due to the limitations of the described search process: The *limited sample size* and the *constraints of the parameters* (see legend of table 1) may have prevented us from finding a higher maximum of -D. Both possibilities exist, they are, however, rather unlikely: Since an increase of the *size* of the sample of input vectors from 100 to 500 has not improved the maximum value of the correspondence function f (see table 1), it is not very likely that samples with more than 500 input vectors would reveal substantially better values of f. Similarly, the *maxima* and *minima* of the parameters p_1, p_2, p_3, . . . have been very generously defined and exceed the respective layoff- and appointment-figures of Switzerland in 1995 by at least 100%.

Table 1. *The maximum values of the negative inequality of job chances -D for five subsequent random samples of model input*

Sample S	Definition of sample S of input scenarios	Size of S	Max. -D in sample S
# 1	100 random vectors (p_1, p_2, p_3, ...)	100	0.000
# 2	100 random vectors (p_1, p_2, p_3, ...) $\cup$ #1	200	0.000
# 3	100 random vectors (p_1, p_2, p_3, ...) $\cup$ #2	300	0.000
# 4	100 random vectors (p_1, p_2, p_3, ...) $\cup$ #3	400	0.000
# 5	100 random vectors (p_1, p_2, p_3, ...) $\cup$ #4	500	0.000

General definitions:
Start of the simulations at t=0 months.
End of the simulations at t=18 months.
D = J_{II} - J_I = Inequality of long-term job chances (see figure 4).
Δ = 0.00 (equal opportunity situation).
d = Legal maximum of the duration of unemployment benefits = 18 months.
$\cup$: Union of samples.

Definition of the components of the random vectors:
p_1 = Qualification limit $\varepsilon_{t,d}$ of cohorts which lost job at time t<0; -2 • p_1 • 2.
p_2 = Size of the cohorts of group I, which lost job at time t<0; 100 • p_2 • 20000.
p_3 = Size of the cohorts of group II, which lost job at time t<0; 100 • p_3 • 20000.
p_4 = Size of the cohorts of group I, which lost job at time t•0; 100 • p_4 • 20000.
p_5 = Size of the cohorts of group II, which lost job at time t•0; 100 • p_5 • 20000.
p_6 = Number of job opportunities at time t•0; 100 • p_6 • 40000.
All parameters p_1 . . . p_6 are statistically independent and have uniform distributions.

Missing values:
On the average 38.4% of the cases of a sample have been omitted in order to prevent trivial falsification of the hypothesis in situations where the cut-off point θ_t was outside the range [-5,+5] such that unemployment nearly disappeared or hardly any job opportunities became available (see 3.1).

To sum up, our analysis shows that equal opportunity will not invert the inequality of long-term job chances of the two groups. The fact that this result can also be deduced from figure 4 in a purely analytical way corroborates the strength of the proposed method of computer based inferencing.

3.3. Sample Problem 2: Proving the Universal Validity of a Monotonic Relation Between two Policy Variables.

One of the most prominent type of hypothesis in social science literature is the monotonic relation between two variables x and y which typically reads as:

The higher the variable x, the higher (lower) the variable y.

Although this type of hypothesis is often analytically deduced from general theories or inductively derived from observational data, it can obviously also be obtained by generalizing the results of unsystematic simulation experiments.

In the following, we will check whether our method of simulation assisted inferencing is able to test an example of such a hypothesis which in section 3.1 has *analytically* been deduced from the model and which thus should be a rather universally valid theorem. It refers to the relation between labor market discrimination and the long-term job chances and states as follows:

The higher the discrimination Δ of a group I as compared to a complementary group II, the higher the inequality D between the long-term job chances of the two groups.

In empirical social research this type of hypothesis would be tested by calculating the correlation between the discrimination Δ and the inequality of chances D. Similarly, for the artifical data of the labor queue model it is proposed to use a correlation coefficient in order to check the correspondence between the hypothesis and the model output. For the monotonic relation of the afore stated hypothesis the use of a *Spearman* rank-correlation [HIC 86: 268 ff.] would be an optimal choice. However, for reasons of computational simplicity, the *Pearson* correlation coefficient [HIC 86: 293 ff.] has been chosen in order to define the aforementioned correspondence function in the following way:

$$f(p_1, p_2, p_3, \ldots) = \text{corr}_{\text{Pearson}}(\Delta, D) \qquad (8)$$

where $p_1, p_2, p_3, \ldots$ are input parameters of the model describing the size of the different groups and cohorts. Due to the structure of the hypothesis explicitly claiming *universal validity* we have attempted to *falsify* this hypothesis by finding a set of parameters $\pi_1, \pi_2, \pi_3, \ldots$ for which the correspondence function $f(\pi_1, \pi_2, \pi_3, \ldots)$ is *minimized*. This task has been completed by generating several uniformly distributed *random samples* of 25 to 500 parameter vectors $(p_1, p_2, p_3, \ldots)$ which were used as inputs of an SPSS-based computer simulation model that was very similar to the one discussed in section 3.2. Since the model returned for each parameter vector $(p_1, p_2, p_3, \ldots)$ the asymptotic inequality of job chances D, it allowed to calculate for a given parameter vector the approximate correspondence $\text{corr}_{\text{Pearson}}(\Delta, D)$ between Δ and D. This way it became possible to identify those parameter values $\pi_1, \pi_2, \pi_3, \ldots$ which entail for a given sample the *worst case* correspondence $f(\pi_1, \pi_2, \pi_3, \ldots)$. For each of the 10 samples this minimum correlation as well as the more detailed definitions of these samples are given in table 2.

Table 2. *The worst case correlations between the discrimination Δ and the inequality of job chances D in 10 subsequent samples of model output*

Sample S	Definition of sample S of input scenarios		Size of S	Worst corr in sample S
# 1	25	random vectors (p_1, p_2, p_3, ...)	25	0.960
# 2	25	random vectors (p_1, p_2, p_3, ...) ∪ #1	50	0.954
# 3	25	random vectors (p_1, p_2, p_3, ...) ∪ #2	75	0.891
# 4	25	random vectors (p_1, p_2, p_3, ...) ∪ #3	100	0.891
# 5	25	random vectors (p_1, p_2, p_3, ...) ∪ #4	125	0.891
# 6	25	random vectors (p_1, p_2, p_3, ...) ∪ #5	150	0.794
# 7	50	random vectors (p_1, p_2, p_3, ...) ∪ #6	200	0.794
# 8	100	random vectors (p_1, p_2, p_3, ...) ∪ #7	300	0.794
# 9	100	random vectors (p_1, p_2, p_3, ...) ∪ #8	400	0.794
# 10	100	random vectors (p_1, p_2, p_3, ...) ∪ #9	500	0.794

General definitions:
Start of the simulations at t=0 months.
End of the simulations at t=18 months.
$\text{corr}_{\text{Pearson}}(\Delta, D)$ is calculated on the basis of the 10 values $\Delta = 0.25, 0.50, \ldots, 2.50$
    and the corresponding values of D.
∪:   Union of samples.
d = Legal maximum of the duration of unemployment benefits = 18 months.

Definition of the components of the random vectors:
See legend of table 1.

Missing values:
On the average 53.0% of the cases of a sample have been omitted in order to prevent trivial falsification of the hypothesis in situations where the cut-off point θ_t was outside the range [-5,+5] such that unemployment nearly disappeared or hardly any jobs became available (see 3.1).

An analysis of table 2 shows that our attempt to falsify the aforementioned hypothesis has clearly failed: In despite of all our efforts, the correlation $\text{corr}_{\text{Pearson}}(\Delta, D)$ has never fallen below 0.794 and consequently can be considered as statistically different from 0 at the 1% level of significance [VAN 69: p. 358]. Even if it were calculated not only with 10 but a much greater number of different values of Δ [VAN 69: p. 358] or by using the correlation definition of Spearman [HIC 86: 268 ff.] instead of Pearson [HIC 86: 293 ff.] it would of course also be highly significant. Besides, it seems to be rather unlikely that the described search process has missed a sample which contains a much lower correlation $\text{corr}_{\text{Pearson}}(\Delta, D)$ than the worst case shown in table 2: The relation between the size of a sample and the minimum correlation seems to converge to values somewhere around 0.79 . In sum, our method of model exploration seems to yield the result which we already know from analytical reasoning: The higher the discrimination Δ, the higher the long-term inequality D. This means for the practical purposes of social policy making that a decrease of labor market discrimination by equal opportunity measures should *always* reduce the inequality of long-term job chances, independently of the economic conditions under which the policy is implemented.

4. Summary: The Challenge of Optimization

One of the most important features of the proposed methodology of model exploration is certainly the optimization of the correspondence function f. Unfortunately, the optimization of f is not only the most important but also the most critical element of the whole exploration procedure: *Algorithmic optimization* which starts with a first estimate of the parameter values and then searches along the steepest gradients of the correspondence function often fails for one or several of the following reasons:

a) In many cases the *computation time* exceeds on a microcomputer several hours and is thus beyond reasonable limits.

b) Gradient methods often stop near a *local* instead of a *global* optimum of the correspondence function.

c) The optimization algorithm can be misled by the *numerical inaccuracy* of the calculated values of the correspondence function.

As an alternative to the *algorithmic optimization technique* this paper proposes the use of *random search procedures*. Their basic ideas as well as the practical examples presented in this paper suggest that they are with regard to the problems (b) and (c) superior to the aforementioned gradient based optimization algorithms. However, also random search is still a computationally intensive method that can occupy a standard PC for several hours in order to explore a medium sized model. In the actual situation it is probably the best to rely on future technical progress of hardware architecture. It is likely that the increase of computation power of PCs will soon allow to explore also more complicated models by means of the optimization technique which has been proposed in this paper.

5. References

[ADB 74] ADBY, P. R., DEMPSTER, M. A. H., *Introduction to Optimization Methods,* Chapman and Hall, 1974.

[BER 90] BERK, R., ROSSI, P. H., *Thinking about Program Evaluation,* Sage Publications, 1990.

[BUN 96] BUNDESAMT FUER INDUSTRIE, GEWERBE UND ARBEIT, *Arbeitslosigkeit in der Schweiz,* vols 1995 and 1996, Bern, 1996 and 1997.

[GLA 67] GLASER, B. G., STRAUSS, A. L., *The Discovery of Grounded Theory: Strategies for Qualitative Research,* Chicago, 1967.

[HAN 88] HANNEMAN, R. A., *Computer-Assisted Theory Building,* Sage Publications, 1988.

[HAN 95a] HANNEMAN, R. A., "Simulation Modeling and Theoretical Analysis in Sociology", *Sociological Perspectives,* vol. 38, p. 457 ff., 1995.

[HAN 95b] HANNEMAN, R. A., "Discovering Theory Dynamics by Computer Simulation: Experiments on State Legitimacy and Imperialist Capitalism", *Sociological Methodology,* vol. 25, p. 1 ff., 1995.

[HAR 96] HARDING, A. (ed.), *Microsimulation and Public Policy,* Elsevier, 1996.

[HIC 86] HICKEY, A. A., *An Introduction to Statistical Techniques for Social Research,* McGraw-Hill Publishing Company, 1986.

[MIC 97] MICHEL, J., *Crisis of the Welfare States: Bibliography on Reforming Social Security Systems,* Institut fuer Weltwirtschaft (Kiel), 1997.

[MUE 96] MUELLER, G., "Exploring and Testing Theories: On the Role of Parameter Optimization in Social Science Computer Simulation", in: K. G. Troitzsch et al. (eds), *Social Science Microsimulation,* Springer, 1996, p. 66 ff.

[MUE 00] MUELLER, G., "Computer-Assisted Inferencing: On the Use of Computer Simulation for Theory Construction", in: N. Gilbert et al. (eds), *Tools for Modeling, Parameter Optimization, and Sensitivity Analysis,* Physica Verlag, 2000.

[NOR 95] NORUSIS, M. J., *SPSS Advanced Statistics User's Guide,* SPSS Inc., 1995.

[POP 59] POPPER, K. R., *The Logic of Scientific Discovery,* Hutchinson Publishers, 1959.

[ORC 86] ORCUTT, G., MERZ, J., QUINKE, H., *Microanalytic Simulation Models to Support Social and Financial Policy,* North-Holland, 1986.

[RES 90] RESKIN, B. F., ROOS, P. A., *Job Queues, Gender Queues: Explaining Women's Inroads into Male Occupations,* Temple University Press, 1990.

[SAM 87] SAMUELSON, P. A., NORDHAUS, W. D., *Economics,* McGraw-Hill, 1987.

[SPS 92] SPSS INC., *SPSS Statistical Algorithms,* SPSS Inc., 1992.

[STR 87] STRAUSS, A. L., *Qualitative Analysis for Social Scientists,* Cambridge University Press, 1987.

[THU 69] THUROW, L. C., *Poverty and Discrimination,* Brookings Institution, 1969.

[THU 75] THUROW, L. C., *Generating Inequality,* Basic Books Inc., 1975.

[VAN 69] VAN DER WAERDEN, B. L., *Mathematical Statistics.* Springer, 1969.

[WEI 72] WEISS, C. H., *Evaluation Research: Methods for Assessing Program Effectiveness,* Prentice-Hall Inc., 1972.

6. Notes

[1] This research has been supported by a generous research fellowship of the Institute of Social Research of the University of Surrey (UK).

[2] See e.g. the algorithm of the SPSS module CNLR for constrained nonlinear regression which has proved to be very useful for the purposes discussed here [NOR 95: p. 209 ff.; SPS 92: p. 34 ff.]. For a more general discussion of constrained optimization see [ADB 74: chapter 5].

APPLICATIONS TO MANAGEMENT

Business Applications of Social Agent-Based Simulation

Eric Bonabeau

Eurobios
68 bis Boulevard Péreire
75017 Paris
France

eric.bonabeau@eurobios.com
http://www.eurobios.com

ABSTRACT: *Agent-based simulation is a powerful simulation modeling technique that has seen a number of applications in the last five years, including applications to real-world business problems. In this chapter I introduce agent-based simulation and review three applications to business problems: a theme park simulation, a stock market simulation, and a bankwide simulation.*

RÉSUMÉ: *La simulation par agents est une puissante technique de simulation qui a vu ces dernières années de nombreuses applications à des problèmes réels du monde industriel ou économique. Dans ce chapitre, j'introduis les concepts fondamentaux de la simulation par agents, et j'en passe en revue trois applications récentes : la simulation d'un parc d'attractions, la simulation d'un marché d'actions (le Nasdaq), et la simulation d'une banque.*

KEY WORDS: *simulation, agents, agent-based simulation, business applications*

MOTS-CLÉS: *simulation, agents, simulation par agents, applications pratiques*

1. Introduction

In agent-based modeling, systems are modeled as collections of autonomous decision-making entities, called agents. Each agent individually assesses its situation and makes decisions based upon a set of rules. Agents may execute various behaviors appropriate for the system they represent – for example, producing, consuming, or selling. Repetitive, competitive interactions between agents are a feature of agent-based modeling, which relies on the power of computers to explore dynamics out of the reach of pure mathematical methods [EPS 96, AXE 97].

Agent-based modeling results in a realistic simulation of a system because it emulates the manner in which the world really operates. At the simplest level, an agent-based model consists of a system of agents and the relationships between them. Even a simple agent-based model can exhibit complex behavior patterns [EPS 96] and provide valuable information about the dynamics of the real-world system that it emulates.

In addition, agents may be capable of evolving, allowing unanticipated behaviors to emerge. Sophisticated agent-based modeling sometimes incorporates neural networks and genetic algorithms to allow realistic learning and adaptation. Such models can be used in decision-making, as well as to develop flexible, adaptive strategies in dynamic business environments.

Simulation has been used in management science for many years [PID 98]. So it comes as no surprise that agent-based simulation techniques have begun to be applied to business problems, including management and organizational issues [PRI 98]. In addition to the intrinsic advantages of simulating a system through its agents – the agent-based description is often the most natural one –, this approach to simulation allows better control of the model's underlying assumptions and facilitates the process of populating and quantifying the model. Agent-based simulation modeling makes it easier to validate and calibrate the model through expert judgement because the agent-based description the model is using is often the most appropriate way of describing what is actually happening in the real world, and the experts can easily "connect" to the model. Finally, the agent-based description is inherently scalable, that is, more agents can be added to the model, and/or more complex agents. For example, one may start with a simple agent-based model, with purely stimulus-response agents, and later include such features as learning and adaptation.

Although it is out of the scope of the present chapter to precisely define and classify the various approaches to agent-based simulation modeling, I would like to illustrate its underlying principles using a totally non-social example: the sand pile. Imagine you're at the beach and you're dropping grains of sand to build a sand pile. Most of the time the addition of one grain will perhaps trigger the displacement of one or two other grains of sand. If you use the past to predict the future, you're not in good shape because here you would predict small events in the future based on the small events you have observed in the past. Yet a catastrophic event, an avalanche that sweeps the sand pile can occur. That's a rare event. It cannot be predicted by looking at the past –unless you look really, really, really far into the past when such an event may have occurred. In order to be able to predict such events, you have to build a model of the sand pile. It's the sand pile's internal dynamics that creates the potential for rare but extremely large events. So now we know we need to simulate the sand pile's physical processes. Where does the need for agent-based simulation come from? The description of the physical processes has to be "mesoscopic". It is not microscopic, that is, it does not include details about the molecules of sand; and it is not a large-scale description, where one would describe the sand pile as a whole – such a description would not permit to capture the causes of the sand pile's avalanches. It has to be just at the right level of description: the grain of sand. The model can be: when the addition of a grain of sand creates a local slope that is too steep, the grain and its neighbors topple, potentially triggering the toppling of other grains, and so forth. In this very simple model, the grains of sand are the active elements of the sand pile: they are the actors, those who actually do something (although most of the time they may stand idle). In simulation modeling we would call them "agents": grains of sand are not particularly smart agents but they are the relevant constituent units to describe the system's dynamics. There may be other ways of modeling the sand pile, but most would fail to capture the underlying causes of avalanches or at the very least would fail to be intuitive. In business, models have to be intuitive and easily understood by the practitioners, otherwise no one will use the model. By finding the agents in a system and modeling their activities, one can express very complicated dynamics with just a few simple words.

2. Theme park modeling

2.1. *Problem and agent-based approach*

One of the simplest examples of agent-based simulation of a "social" system in business is the work of Axtell and Epstein in theme park modeling.

A theme park resort had a dilemma; they were thinking about how to improve adaptability in labor scheduling, but knew that this depended on knowing more about the optimal balance of capacity and demand. Rob Axtell and Josh Epstein of the Brookings Institution, developed ResortScape, an agent-based model of the park that provides an integrated picture of the environment and all of the interacting elements that come into play in such a resort.

This kind of model is the basis for a revolutionary way to balance supply and demand in an ever-changing marketplace. It promises new insights on what affects optimal flow and satisfaction and provides a fast, *in silico* way for managers to identify, adjust, and watch the impact of any number of management levers such as:

- When or if to turn off a particular rides
- How to distribute rides per capita throughout the park space
- What is the tolerance level for wait times
- When to extend operating hours

In the simulation, agents represent a realistic and changeable mix of both supply (attractions, shops, food concessions) and demand (visitors with different preferences) elements of a day at the park. Leveraging existing resources and data – such as customer surveys, segmentation studies, queue timers, people counters, attendance estimates, and capacity figures – the model generates information about guest flow. Users can design and run an infinite number of scenarios to study the dynamics of the park space (interaction among agents and environment, ride utilization, traffic flow and mobility, visitor preferences and behavior), test the effectiveness of various management decisions, and track visitor satisfaction throughout the day.

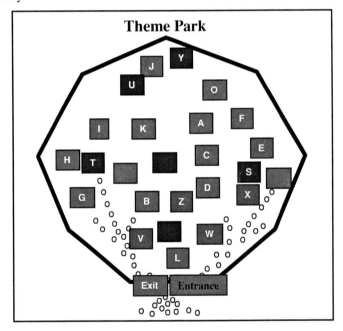

Figure 1. *Schematic representation of the theme park agent-based simulation model. Circles represent customers, squares represent attractions, restaurants, etc.*

2.2. Why use agent-based simulation?

It makes a lot of sense to use agent-based simulation in this context because the mapping between the agents' preferences and behaviors on the one hand, and the park's performance (in terms of average waiting times, number of attractions visited, total distance walked, etc) on the other hand is too complex to be dealt with using mathematical techniques and purely statistical analysis of the data. Why is mapping too complex? Because the time a given customer has to wait at a given attraction depends on what other customers are doing, how they respond to different park conditions, what their wish list is, etc. The flows of customers in the park, and the money they spend, is an "emergent" property of interactions among customers and between customers and the spatial layout of the park. Therefore simulating the park's operations with a given layout seems to be the only solution. Agent-based simulation is the most natural and easiest way of describing the system, because the actors of this system are customers (and attractions) with a behavior of their own. As the avalanche in the sand pile was a result of interacting grains of sand, waiting times in a theme park result from the interactions of many behavioral units, the customers. Finally, the data available to the modeler is naturally structured for agent-based simulation: what the modeler has is a description of the desires and behavior of a number of customers.

3. The Nasdaq stock market simulation

3.1. *Problem and agent-based approach*

The NASDAQ Stock Market considers changes in trading policies very carefully: NASDAQ stands to lose a great deal if a new rule provokes a negative network-wide response from investors, market makers, and issuers. What kinds of rules does NASDAQ consider? First, they need to know what regulations to put in place in order to avoid accusations of foul play, like collusion among dealers, or abuses of their electronic trading system by small investors called "SOES (Small Order Execution System) bandits." They would also like to be able to predict the impact of potential changes in SEC rules. In all cases, they want to know which rules are most resistant to abuses and least likely to affect market liquidity and volatility adversely.

In the past, NASDAQ executives have analyzed the financial marketplace through economic studies, financial models, and feedback from market participants. The Market Quality Committee establishes regulations largely as a result of input from economists, lawyers, lobbyists and policy makers. Recently, the NASDAQ Stock Market collaborated with Santa Fe-based Bios Group to develop a complexity-based approach to the analysis (Vince Darley, Sasha Outkin, personal communication): an agent-based model that simulates the impact of regulatory changes on the financial market under varying conditions. The new model allows regulators to test and predict the effects of different strategies, observe the behavior of agents in response to changes, and monitor developments, providing advance warning of unintended consequences of newly implemented regulations – in faster than real-time and without risking early tests in the real marketplace.

The model has already produced some highly suggestive and unexpected results. Specifically, the simulation suggests a reduction in the market's tick size (e.g. from $1/16 to a penny) can reduce the market's ability to perform price discovery. This effect is especially strong when parasitic strategies such as "SOES bandits" are present in the market. Parasitic strategies unwillingly aid price discovery if the tick-size is large. These findings and others are helping direct NASDAQ toward a more robust and flexible market system.

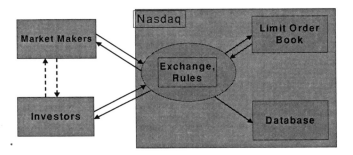

Figure 2. *Schematic representation of the stock market agent-based simulation model.*

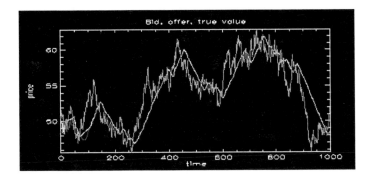

Figure 3. *Top figure: bid, offer and true prices of a given stock for a $0.01 tick size in the presence of parasites. Bottom figure: same for a $1/16th. It is apparent that the difference between the stock's true price and the bid and offer prices is larger when tick size is smaller*

In the user-guided simulation, Market Maker and investor agents (institutional investors, pension funds, day traders, casual investors) buy and sell shares using various strategies. The agents' access to price and volume information approximates that in the real-world market, and their behaviors range from very simple to complicated learning and evolutionary strategies. Neural networks, reinforcement learning, and genetic algorithms are used to generate strategies for agents. This creative element is important because NASDAQ regulators are especially interested in strategies that have not yet been discovered by players in the real market, again to their goal of designing a regulatory structure with as few loopholes as possible, in order to prevent abuses by devious players.

3.2. Why use agent-based simulation?

Here again, the power and scope of agent-based simulation is obvious. The interactions between investors, market makers and the operating rules of the NASDAQ stock market make the entire system's dynamics quite hard to understand. Predicting how it would change under a new set of operating regulations cannot be based on intuition or on classical modeling techniques because they are not suited to describe the complexities of the behavior of the stock market agents. For example, the mapping between tick size and spread can only be understood by taking into account details of the investors' and market makers' behavior to model the process of price discovery.

4. Bank simulation for operational risk management

4.1. Problem and agent-based approach

Banks and financial institutions face a number of risks, which can be subdivided into several major categories:
- Market risk is the risk to a financial institution's condition resulting from adverse movements in market rates or prices, such as interest rates, foreign exchange rates, equity prices.
- Credit risk arises from the potential that a borrower or counterparty will fail to perform an obligation.
- Operational risk arises from the potential that inadequate information systems, operational problems, breaches in internal controls, fraud, or unforeseen catastrophes will result in unexpected losses.

Market and credit risks are most familiar to financial institutions. While their definitions are fairly well agreed upon, operational risk is not as clearly defined. Many banks have defined operational risk as any risk not categorized as market or credit risk and some have defined it as the risk of loss arising from various types of human or technical error. According to the Basle Committee on Banking, operational risk involves breakdowns in internal controls and corporate governance that can lead to financial losses through error, fraud or failure to perform in a timely manner or cause the interests of the bank to be compromised in some other way, for example, by its dealers, lending officers or other staff exceeding their authority or conducting business in an unethical or risky manner.

Operational risk is increasingly viewed as the most important risk that banks face. Awareness of operational risk among bank boards and senior management is increasing.   Examples of large operational losses include Daiwa, Sumitomo, Barings, Salomon, Kidder Peabody, Orange County, Jardine Fleming and more recently NatWest Markets, the Common Fund or Yamaichi. Most banks have developed efficient and sometimes sophisticated ways of dealing with market risk and to large extent with credit risk, they are still in the early stages of developing operational risk measurement and monitoring. Conceptual issues and data needs have to be addressed to create a framework. Unlike market and perhaps credit risk, operational risk factors are largely internal to the bank and a clear mathematical or statistical link between individual risk factors and the size and frequency of operational loss does not exist. Experience with large losses is infrequent and many banks lack a time series of historical data on their own operational losses and their causes. Uncertainty about which factors are important arises from the absence of a direct relationship between the risk factors usually identified (measured through internal audit ratings, internal control self-assessment based on such indicators as volume, turnover, error rates and income volatility) and the size and frequency of loss events. This contrasts with market risk, where changes in prices have an easily computed impact on the value of the bank's trading portfolio, and perhaps to credit risk, where changes in the borrower's credit quality are often associated with changes in the interest rate spread of the borrower's obligations over a risk-free rate.

Given all the characteristics of operational risk, there are a number of immediate problems:
-    It is difficult to quantify.
-    There is currently no satisfactory framework or widely accepted methodology, neither from product vendors, nor from regulatory or advisory bodies. Banks develop their own custom framework, which makes comparisons difficult.
-    There is no commercially available adequate tool.
-    There are no adequate insurance policies to cover operational risk.
-    Operational historical data is so scarce that it is not possible to allocate capital reliably and efficiently, and it is not possible to obtain good VAR (Value-At-Risk) and RAROC (Risk-Adjusted Return on Capital) estimates. Capital allocation is important because it gives managers an incentive to keep operational risk under control.

Yet, there is an increasing pressure on financial institutions to quantify operational risk in a way that convinces both investors (efficient allocation of capital) and regulatory entities (risk under 'control'). More precisely, a financial institution must be able to quantify operational risk within a reliable framework to be able to keep risk under control, optimize economic capital allocation, and determine its insurance needs.

Given the characteristics of operational risk and the shortcomings of existing approaches to quantifying it, it appears that bottom-up enterprise-wide simulation is a promising approach [to low frequency, high impact operational risk], especially if it is combined with top-down analysis. What is needed is a framework that includes the possibility of nonlinear effects due to interactions among apparently [more or less] independent units and sub-units and cascading events. The framework should be able to operate with scarce data.

Hence the idea to simulate operations from the bottom up to generate a large, artificial data set that includes large events. The artificially generated data can then be used to apply classical capital allocation techniques. Eurobios and Ernst & Young have applied agent-based simulation techniques to measuring and managing operational risk in a bank's asset management business unit. A simulation model of the business unit's activities was designed, starting with business process modeling and workflow identification. Using the business process model and the workflows the bank's "agents" were then identified, their activities modeled as well as their interactions with other agents and the risk factors that could impact their activities. The activities had to be modeled in enough detail to capture the "physics" of the bank, not too much detail to make the tool tractable in the end. Then the risk factors had to be connected to the bank's P&L through potentially complex pathways in the bank. Then the bank's environment has to modeled – the markets, investors, etc – and how the bank is embedded into its environment. Finally, by simulating the model, it is possible to generate artificial earnings distributions, used to estimate potential losses and their likelihood. For example one can compute "Earnings-at-Risk", that is the minimum earnings (or the maximum losses) which could be observed in one year at the bank with a 95% level of confidence.

4.2. Why use agent-based simulation?

When you decide to model a bank using agent-based simulation you're not just making an arbitrary modeling decision. You are modeling the bank in a way that is natural to the practitioners, because you're modeling the activities of the bank by looking at what every actor does –human or else. Here are some examples of agents:

Event	Agent	Model
Fraud	Human	Probability of occurrence, honesty parameter
Human transaction error	Human	Probability of occurrence experience and fatigue
Information system error	Computer	Probability of occurrence,

		complexity parameter
Bad decision	Human	Probability of occurrence experience and mood
Market variations	Environment	Stochastic equations
Natural disaster	Environment	Probability of occurrence, magnitude and impact

Figure 4. *Examples of agents and their models in the bank simulation.*

If you were modeling the bank's processes instead, it would be more difficult for people to understand the model because one person's activities span many processes. That has important consequences when it comes to populating, validating and calibrating the model. If people "connect" to the simulation model, in the sense that they recognize and understand what the model is doing, they can improve it, more easily quantify what needs to be quantified, etc. Because they have a deep understanding of the risk drivers related to their own activity, it is easier to incorporate the relevant risk drivers into the model. Once they have their activities and the corresponding risk drivers in the model, they can suggest control and mitigation procedures and test them using the simulation tool.

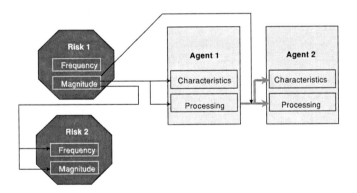

Figure 5. *"Real" agents have to define and quantify risk factors that are local to their activities, including interactions with other agents.*

In summary, there are a number of reasons to use agent-based modeling techniques:

Natural description
- Description of functions implemented by concrete entities.
- "Local" description of risk factors.
- Quantification is facilitated.
- Clear parallel with procedures manual.
- Qualitative as well as quantitative validation is easier.

Scalability
- A "classical" model quickly becomes intractable as its size increases.
- The level of complexity of the agents can be tuned.
- The number and type of characteristics of each agent can be tuned.
- The number of agents can be tuned.
- Agents can be aggregated or disaggregated.

Ownership
- Users can more easily connect to the tool.
- This feeling of "ownership" is most important when it comes to improving the model, validating and calibrating it and performing self-assessment.

5. Conclusion

As has become clear with the examples described throughout this chapter, agent-based simulation is a powerful technique when the active components of a system, the agents, interact with one another to produce complex, emergent patterns of behavior. That is, when the mapping between the agents' specifications (the behavior of individual agents) and the resulting system-level behavior is too nonlinear and high-dimensional, a direct statistical/mathematical analysis of the agents' specifications does not help. All the systems described in the chapter – theme park, stock market, bank – share this feature: only agent-based simulation can help harness the complexity of such systems. Most real-world systems share this feature; the number of real-world applications of agent-based simulation is therefore likely to increase dramatically in the coming years.

Acknowledgements

I would like to thank Rob Axtell and Josh Epstein of the Brookings Institution, and Sasha Outkin and Vince Darley of Bios Group, for giving me information about their respective works on theme park simulation and the Nasdaq simulation. Finally, many thanks to my Eurobios team for help with the bank simulation example.

Bibliography

[AXE 97] AXELROD R. M., *The complexity of cooperation: agent-based models of competition and collaboration*, Princeton, Princeton University Press, 1997.

[EPS 96] EPSTEIN J. M., AXTELL R. L., *Growing artificial societies: social science from the bottom up*, Cambridge, MIT Press, 1996.

[PID 98] PIDD M., *Computer simulation in management science*, New York, John Wiley & Sons, 1998.

[PRI 98] PRIETULA M., GASSER L., CARLEY K. (EDS), Simulating organizations: computational models of institutions and groups, Cambridge, MIT Press, 1998.

Cet ouvrage a été reproduit
et achevé d'imprimer sur les presses
d'Eurocopie (Buc) en Septembre 2000

Dépôt légal : Septembre 2000